THE ORIGINS AND DEVELOPMENT OF THE ANDEAN STATE

THE ORIGINS AND DEVELOPMENT OF THE ANDEAN STATE

EDITED BY

JONATHAN HAAS
School of American Research, Santa Fe, New Mexico

SHELIA POZORSKI
Pan American University, Edinburg, Texas

THOMAS POZORSKI
Pan American University, Edinburg, Texas

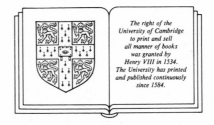

The right of the
University of Cambridge
to print and sell
all manner of books
was granted by
Henry VIII in 1534.
The University has printed
and published continuously
since 1584.

CAMBRIDGE UNIVERSITY PRESS

CAMBRIDGE

NEW YORK   NEW ROCHELLE   MELBOURNE   SYDNEY

To Richard P. Schaedel
for leading the way in the study of the Andean state

Published by the Press Syndicate of the University of Cambridge
The Pitt Building, Trumpington Street, Cambridge CB2 1RP
32 East 57th Street, New York, NY 10022, USA
10 Stamford Road, Oakleigh, Melbourne 3166, Australia

©Cambridge University Press 1987

First published 1987

Printed in Great Britain at the University Press, Cambridge

British Library cataloguing in publication data

The origins and development of the Andean State.
– (New directions in archaeology)
1. Andes – Civilization
I. Haas, Jonathan   II. Pozorski, Thomas
III. Pozorski, Sheila   IV. Series
305'.098   F2212

Library of Congress cataloguing in publication data

The origins and development of the Andean State.
(New directions in archaeology)
Bibliography.
Includes index.
1. Indians of South America – Peru – Antiquities.
2. Indians of South America – Peru – Politics and government.
3. Indians of South America – Andes Region – Antiquities.
4. Indians of South America – Andes Region – Politics and government.
5. Peru – Antiquities. 6. Andes Region – Antiquities.
I. Haas, Jonathan, 1949–   . II. Pozorski, Shelia Griffis.
III. Pozorski, Thomas George.   IV. Series.
F3429.075 1987.   985'.01   86-19332

ISBN 0 521 33102 1

CE

CONTENTS

CONTRIBUTORS

Jonathan Haas, School of American Research, Santa Fe, New Mexico

Shelia Pozorski, Pan American University, Edinburg, Texas

Thomas Pozorski, Pan American University, Edinburg, Texas

Robert Feldman, Field Museum of Natural History, Chicago, Illinois

John Topic, Trent University, Peterborough, Ontario

Theresa Topic, Trent University, Peterborough, Ontario

David J. Wilson, Southern Methodist University, Dallas, Texas

Richard Daggett, University of Massachusetts, Amherst, Massachusetts

William Isbell, State University of New York at Binghamton, Binghamton, New York

Katharina Schreiber, University of California at Santa Barbara, Santa Barbara, California

Alexandra M. Ulana Klymyshyn, Central Michigan University, Mount Pleasant, Michigan

Carol Mackey, California State University at Northridge, Northridge, California

Izumí Shimada, Harvard University, Cambridge, Massachusetts

Charles Hastings, University of Michigan, Ann Arbor, Michigan

Betty Meggers, Smithsonian Institution, Washington, D.C.

Malcolm Webb, University of New Orleans, New Orleans, Louisiana

INTRODUCTION

Jonathan Haas

The origins of states around the world have been the subject of intellectual inquiry since before the time of Christ. Plato pondered the question of why states first developed in the history of humankind, as did Aristotle and other early philosophers. With the discovery of the New World and the intellectual fervor of the Enlightenment, social scientists began to look more systematically at the emergence of states and formal government. It was soon recognized that the very first states in different parts of the world appeared back in the prehistoric past, and what started out as a philosophical inquiry into the nature of government became an archaeological inquiry into the rise of the world's first civilizations. Although the old philosophical debates continue about the role of government in society, archaeologists have turned more to the empirical study of the origins and development of government and the state. In doing so, particularly in the past two decades, they have generated a number of competing and complementary models of state formation and evolution.

The Andean region of South America offers an optimal laboratory for studying the origins and development of state-level societies. With a series of coastal valleys strung out along the Pacific Ocean and the fertile intermontane valleys nestled in between the steep sloping sides of the Andes, the physical setting of the region provided an ample cauldron of the rich growth and efflorescence of prehistoric polities. The papers in this volume take advantage of this social and environmental laboratory to examine the emergence of the first formal political systems in the beginning of the second millennium B.C. and follow the political development of Andean societies up through the formation and collapse of empires immediately preceding the arrival of the Spanish in the early 16th century A.D. They also encompass the great natural diversity of the Andes by looking at groups living along the coast, in the highland valleys of the north and south, and back in the *montaña* on the eastern slopes of the mountains.

As the papers in this volume reflect the temporal and spatial depth of state evolution in the Andes, they also reflect the broad range of theoretical perspectives on the origins and development of state-level societies. In representing this range of perspectives, it is inevitable that the authors do not all agree with one another. There is disagreement not only over how and why the state developed in the Andes, but also over when the state first appeared and even what a 'state' should look like in the archaeological record. Rather than painting a picture of academic confusion, however, the papers taken together represent a balanced, long-term view of Andean state evolution. While differences arise at the level of interpretation, there is broad agreement on the history and evolutionary progression of political society in the Andean region.

The notion of the state

The 'state' is a concept like 'culture' and 'tribe' that has been defined in many ways by many scholars. Generally, there are three different ways to look at the notion of 'state.'

1. The state can be seen as *the actual institutions of government* which maintain social order in complex stratified societies. It is the system of government, and as such stands apart and distinct from the society as a whole. This is the most common conception of state in political science (as in 'the separation of Church and State'), though it is not used often in archaeology and is not the direct subject of any of the papers in this volume.

2. In another view, the state is seen as identifying *a particular*, *bounded social entity*, as in the State of Illinois, or the Inca state. In this case, the notion is used to define a specific polity in time and space. Such state polities will experience their own individual evolutionary sequence, and have their own moment of origin, growth and decline. Individual chapters within this volume discuss the evolution of specific states, such as the state centered in the Casma Valley in the 2nd millennium B.C. (see S. Pozorski), or the Wari state in the Ayacucho Valley (see Schreiber).

3. The 'state' can also be taken to be *a general form of social and political organization* within a broad scheme of cultural evolution. This is the sense in which the term is used here as a focal point for the volume as a whole. In discussing the 'origins and development of the Andean state,' we are not referring to a single monolithic entity that began at 1800 B.C. in one of the coastal valleys and eventually grew into the Inca empire. Rather, we are referring to a particular type of political structure, the state, which arose in different parts of the Andean region at various times, and evolved along discrete historical tracts in those areas. At the same time, there was always significant interaction between the diverse state-level societies evolving in the Andes, and the area must be looked at as a regional system of complex political development.

Beyond looking at the state as a form of political organization, it remains necessary to address the problem of definition. What is a state: What are the definitive characteristics of this particular type of polity? These are questions that cannot be easily answered to everyone's satisfaction, since definitions, sometimes contradictory, abound in the literature. Clearly the authors in this volume are not all using the same definition of 'state.' In my discussion of power and early state development, for example, I see the state as a type of society in which rulers have control over production or procurement of basic resources and as a result exercise coercive power over their respective populations. Isbell, on the other hand, maintains that 'the definitive characteristic of the state is a specialized hierarchical administration that processes information, makes decisions, and enforces compliance' (Isbell, this volume: 83). Thus, while I emphasize the nature of the power relationship between rulers and their populations, Isbell emphasizes the formal and specialized nature of governmental institutions. Such differences affect not only the focus of a

scholar's research, they also have an impact on conclusions about state evolution. If one definition is used in an analysis of state origins on the north coast in the 2nd millennium B.C. and another is used in the analysis of state origins in the central highlands in the 6th century A.D., are the researchers in the two areas really talking about the same thing? Probably not. Is one definition and the accompanying analysis 'right' and the other 'wrong'? Probably not. Will the conclusions reached by the researchers working in the two areas necessarily be contradictory? Again, probably not. The polities themselves remain the same, regardless of the terms that are applied to them, and the validity of the scientific inquiry into the nature of those polities need not be affected by the definition of analytical terms. ('A rose by any other name smells as sweet.') However, conflicting definitions can lead to confusing and unproductive debates over the 'origins' of the *first* state in a particular world area. As with the concept of 'culture,' it is probably not possible to generate a meaningful definition of the concept 'state' which will be universally accepted by all archaeologists, anthropologists, political scientists, and so on. In place of such a universal definition, we must recognise that there are alternative working definitions of the concept which are applied by different scholars to help them in their efforts to understand the evolution and organization of prehistoric polities.

Origins and evolution

In looking at the evolution of the state, it is clear that there are two components to the evolutionary process: the emergence or origins of the first state-level polities in an area, and the subsequent development of those polities over time. Clearly these two components are not totally independent of one another as the causal variables leading to the emergence of a state in one area are likely to influence the long-term evolution of that state and its successors. However, in looking at origins versus development, attention is focused on different aspects of the evolutionary process.

Scholars dealing with state origins are generally trying to explain how and why the state form of organization first arose in a particular area or cross-culturally in different areas. An attempt is made to define the natural and social conditions which are both necessary and sufficient for the emergence of the state. Demography, the environment and local subsistence strategies are the most common variables seen as playing a causal role in state origins. Sometimes these variables are seen as operating alone, but more frequently they are seen as acting together in a complex pattern of long-term change and evolutionary transformation. Within this volume, the chapters by Feldman, Haas, S. Pozorski, Wilson and Daggett all deal with one or more aspects of state origins. Both Feldman and Haas look at that critical moment when the relatively simple societies that characterized the Andean region for thousands of years were undergoing a dramatic transformation to much more complex and centralized polities on the road to statehood. (When they actually arrived at statehood is a definitional question as discussed above.) Feldman analyzes the rise of 'chiefdoms' as manifested at sites such as Aspero on the central coast. At these sites, moderate sized artificial mounds appear for the first time in the Andes in the Cotton Preceramic Period. Furthermore this first appearance of political complexity and centralization on the coast takes place in the virtual absence of any large-scale agriculture. Haas goes one step beyond the chiefdoms described by Feldman and argues that the construction of significantly larger monumental architecture in the Initial Period marks the appearance of the first state-level polities in the Andean region. His argument is based on the premise that construction of such monumental architecture requires the exercise of a much higher order of coercive power than is found in chiefdom-level societies and therefore signals a new and different form of power relationship between the rulers and their subordinate populations.

S. Pozorski, Wilson and Daggett investigate the specific causal variables that gave rise to fully developed state polities, in particular coastal valley systems. Interestingly, all three examine the role of warfare in the origin of local states, though they each argue that warfare acted in very different ways in effecting state emergence. S. Pozorski sees the initial stages of state development in the Casma Valley as developing essentially in the absence of conflict or warfare. The warfare, she argues, comes later and transforms the indigenous Casma political system. Daggett, on the other hand, argues a classic warfare/conquest model of state formation. Following Carneiro (1970), Daggett argues that *within* valley warfare ultimately led to internal consolidation and the formation of the state in the Nepeña Valley. In contrast, Wilson argues that in the Santa Valley, just to the north of Nepeña, warfare arose not between valley residents, but between the residents of Santa and adjacent areas. Intravalley cooperation and alliance, in response to aggression from the outside, then led to the emergence of an indigenous state-level polity in the Santa Valley.

In addition to these papers dealing explicitly with state origins in the Andes, two papers in the volume deal with subsidiary issues. T. and S. Pozorski focus on the 'Early Horizon' and attempt to clarify the place of the 'Chavin phenomenon' in the Andean prehistoric sequence. A Chavin polity, with its center at the site of Chavin de Huantar, has often been considered to be the first state or 'mother civilization' of the Andean region – somewhat analogous to the Olmec in Mesoamerica. The Pozorskis, however, argue from new evidence that chronologically Chavin de Huantar appears very late in the Early Horizon, well after the appearance and widespread distribution of Chavin art and architecture in other parts of the Andes. They ultimately offer a complete revision of the sequence of political development in the northern Andes for the entire period from the Cotton Preceramic through the Early Horizon.

As a counterpoint to the other articles in the volume, Hastings, working in the central and eastern highlands of Peru, addresses the question of why the state does *not* emerge in certain areas prehistorically. Given the omnipresence of the state in the Andes, a negative case of 'non-emergence,' as Hastings calls it, provides a valuable perspective on the various theories of state origins. He outlines a complex interrelationship between local-level political authority and relative access to nonlocal resources to explain the absence of state development in this region.

Those scholars dealing with state developments rather than origins are not directly concerned with the *appearance* of the state so much as with what happens in the state system *after* it appears – how, for example, states are administratively organized, how production and distribution of goods are managed within these large polities, how states expand to become 'empires,' and what in turn brings about the collapse of empires. In the present volume, these questions are addressed with regard to the Moche, the Wari and the Chimu, all enormous regional states or empires. Shimada examines the internal development and expansion of the Moche and Sicán states on the north coast in terms of the 'vertical' relationships between the coastal valleys and the Andean highlands, and the 'horizontal' relationships between the valleys along the north coast. He outlines a complex evolution of a north coast–highland economic system with the extension of economic ties from the coast to the highlands, and the military expansion state's boundaries up and down the coast. Isbell and Schreiber in turn look at the formation, internal organization and imperial expansion of the Wari state in the central highlands. Isbell draws an extensive and systematic view of Wari political development and attempts to explain that development in terms of pressing environmental and economic variables. Schreiber takes off from Isbell's analysis and looks at why Wari expanded so rapidly after the initial stages of development and became one of the largest empires seen in the Andean region. She ultimately concludes that Wari was indeed a military empire based on expansion through conquest and forced incorporation of conquered areas under Wari hegemony.

Several of the authors deal with the late Chimu Empire, which arose on the north coast some centuries after the decline of the Moche polity and lasted until conquered by the Inca in the 15th century A.D. Klymyshyn addresses the question of how the Chimu administered their vast realm from the capital city of Chan Chan. She finds that the nature of administration changed as the Chimu expanded their empire and that the changes were reflected in the layout and contents of the monumental compounds at Chan Chan. T. Pozorski in turn looks at how the Chimu extended their irrigation systems, initially to provide more resources to support their imperial expansion and later as a political means of maintaining the position of the Chimu rulers. Interestingly, he finds that irrigation and the empire do not expand in coordination with one another; rather, irrigation responds more to the individual dictates of the rulers than to the dictates of demography and subsistence needs. Mackey concludes the Chimu discussion with her analysis of imperial administration of the Chimu hinterlands – those areas outside the heartland of the north coast which were incorporated by conquest into the empire during the second phase of expansion. Using data from the secondary administrative center of Manchan in the Casma Valley, she effectively documents the nature of the political and economic relationships between the central government at Chan Chan and the provincial centers in other parts of the empire.

The articles by S. Pozorski and Mackey, both focused on the Casma Valley, take the study of Andean state evolution from its inception in the second millennium B.C. to its imperial expansion in the years just prior to the intrusion of the Spanish in the 1500s. In the intervening centuries, the Andean region witnessed an incredible array of state-level societies with an equal diversity of culture, art, organization and religion. At the same time, there are broad similarities in Andean states which distinguish them from those polities evolving in the other world centers of civilization. We are only beginning to understand how and why the state evolved in this land of desert valleys and rugged mountains. New and continuing research up and down the coast as well as in various parts of the highlands promises to modify and magnify the current state of knowledge of the origins and development of the Andean state.

Chronology

Shelia Pozorski and Thomas Pozorski

Background: c.1900–1950

The history of scientific archaeology in Peru is the history of horizon styles, each characterized by a wide dissemination of related traits during a relatively brief time. It began with the work of Max Uhle near the turn of the century. As a result of prior work in Germany (Uhle and Stubel 1892, cited in Rowe 1954:2) which defined the Tiwanaku style and established its temporal priority relative to Inca, Uhle was uniquely able to assess the stratigraphic sequence of ceramics at Pachacamac (Uhle 1903a) and other collections from sites along much of the Peruvian coast. Without specifically defining the concept of horizon styles, Uhle established a pan-Peruvian six-phase sequence and cross dated local sequences on the basis of the pervasiveness of the Tiwanaku and Inca styles (Uhle 1903b, cited in Rowe 1963:45).

This initial relative ordering has withstood the test of time, and Uhle's scheme became widely accepted after 1920 as a result of published studies of his collections by Kroeber, Strong, and Gayton (Kroeber and Strong 1924a, 1924b; Kroeber 1925a, 1925b, 1926; Strong 1925; Gayton 1927; Gayton and Kroeber 1927). Significantly, as a result of this effort, Kroeber both defined the concept of horizon style (Kroeber 1944:108) and devised a system of four true periods which attempted to distinguish between style and time (Kroeber and Strong 1924:53; Kroeber 1925a:229–231). In final form the periods in this widely used scheme were called Early Period, Middle Period or Tiwanaku-Epigonal Horizon, Late Period, and Inca Period or Horizon (O'Neale and Kroeber 1930:24; Kroeber 1930:108–114).

Uhle's sequence was subsequently expanded through the efforts of Tello, who defined the Chavin phenomenon (Tello 1929, 1943) and promoted its acceptance as an earlier third horizon style. Finally, fieldwork during the 1940s sponsored by the Institute for Andean Research led to the discovery of both pre-Chavin pottery and the first Peruvian preceramic sites known (Bird 1948a, 1948b; Strong and Evans 1952), thereby extending the Andean sequence even earlier. Because the earlier portion of the Andean cultural sequence had been so amplified, Kroeber abandoned his period-based chronological scheme in 1943 because of a terminology problem which Strong aptly diagnosed as a 'rising waist line rapidly approaching the neck' (Strong 1948:96).

The Viru Valley Project, sponsored by the Institute for Andean Research in 1946, had tremendous impact, with ramifications beyond the limits of the Andean area. This systematic holistic study of an entire valley was methodologically innovative, especially Willey's (1953) settlement pattern study. Its effect on the Andean chronological scheme was also profound. A cultural sequence from preceramic to colonial times was *stratigraphically* established (Strong 1948; Ford 1949; Collier 1955). This consisted of a series of closely correlated chronological schemes formulated by different project members (Bennett 1948). These sequences were promoted by project members and their students and ultimately became the basis for syntheses of the entire Andean area (Bushnell 1963; Bennett and Bird 1964; Mason 1969). Although these chronologies were developmental and composed of stages defined on the basis of cultural content, most clearly retained divisions which could be easily recognized as the three horizons.

The Rowe–Lanning chronological framework

The single most systematic effort to refine Andean chronology since the Viru Valley Project was by John Rowe. Since a version of Rowe's chronological framework is followed in this volume, it is discussed in considerable detail. As early as 1956 he proposed the Horizon/Period sequence which is currently widely used (Rowe 1960), and his ideas were crystallized in an article published in 1962 (Rowe 1962a). Arguing against stage-based sequences because of their associated developmental preconceptions and their inadequacy in assessing trait origins and diffusion, Rowe proposed a sequence of six periods which were strictly units of time. Adapting concepts from Kroeber's abandoned sequences, he designated these periods Initial Period, Early Horizon, Early Intermediate Period, Middle Horizon, Late Intermediate Period, and Late Horizon. Critical to Rowe's effort to avoid basing his chronological divisions on cultural content, and thereby keep them distinct from stages, was his idea of linking the system of periods to a well-known local ceramic sequence within a single valley. The Ica Valley of the south coast was selected as the locus of this master sequence because the local chronology was among the most precisely defined at that time.

The advent of radiocarbon dating in the 1950s and its immediate application in Peru has obscured the original theoretical emphasis of Rowe's sequence formulation. Conceived as a *relative* dating system and as a means of bypassing the inaccuracies of early radiocarbon dating, which Rowe clearly did not initially trust (Rowe 1967a), the system of periods defined with references to a master sequence was designed to put relative dating strictly on the basis of contemporaneity. Therefore, the periods of the Ica sequence were defined on the basis of major events which could most easily be correlated with other local Andean sequences. A further indication of Rowe's emphasis on relative chronology is reflected in the division of the Ica periods into as many as ten or more units on the basis of ceramic style changes (Menzel 1977:88–89). These divisions are far finer than the precision of available absolute dating methods. Although Rowe recognized absolute data as the more obvious means of establishing contemporaneity between cultural units, he still placed greater emphasis on the value of repeatedly associated trade pieces and evidence of influence between two local styles.

Understanding the assumptions underlying the Rowe sequence helps both to place his chronological scheme in historical perspective and to understand its subsequent use. Most significantly, the acceptance of radiocarbon dates has

largely converted the Period/Horizon chronological framework into an absolute system. Lanning (1967) modified the Period/Horizon scheme to the extent that it has been referred to as the Rowe–Lanning sequence (see Willey 1971:83). Lanning adjusted the absolute dates correlated with each period on the basis of additional available radiocarbon dates and detailed the sequence of preceramic periods. *Peru before the Incas*, Lanning's widely consulted publication, was instrumental in promoting acceptance of the Period/Horizon framework.

The period-based Rowe–Lanning chronology has been widely accepted and followed, especially in attempts at general syntheses (Willey 1971; Bankes 1977; Moseley and Day 1982; Ravines 1982). Other general texts retain chronologies based on developmental stages (see Lumbreras 1974a; Kauffmann 1980), but no comprehensive attempt has been made to justify this approach. Reports on more localized sequences have employed the Rowe–Lanning system in different ways which generally reflect both physical proximity to the south coast master sequence and availability of radiocarbon dates. Studies conducted in the south highlands or south coast are most likely to contain chronologies closely correlated with the Ica sequence on the subperiod level (see, for example, Isbell 1977 and this volume; Paul 1982). In zones further from the south coast, but which generally lack carbon 14 dates, the sequence is followed at the period level, and date ranges quoted are taken from Rowe and Menzel's (1967:ii) or Lanning's (1967:25) chronological charts (see, for example, Proulx 1973; Donnan and Mackey 1978; Moseley 1983). Where radiocarbon dates are available, the period names are retained, but the date ranges are corrected to reflect local absolute dates (see, for example, Donnan 1982; Patterson *et al*. 1982). Finally, other scholars have proceeded independently of the Rowe–Lanning sequence to establish distinct local period-based schemes using abundant carbon 14 dates (see, for example, Shimada 1982 and this volume; MacNeish *et al*. 1981).

The latter two options provide indications of growing dissatisfaction with the Rowe–Lanning framework (see also Pozorski and Pozorski, this volume). The 'correcting' of absolute dates for a given major period contradicts the basic tenets of the master sequence correlation. Strict adherence to the system would require adjustment of each local chronological terminology to indicate that a single cultural phase spanned two or more of the major periods or horizons. Abandonment of the Rowe–Lanning sequence by some archaeologists is an even stronger indication that the periods as presently defined and correlated with the Ica sequence are no longer appropriate for describing newly emerging local sequences, especially in areas physically remote from Ica. Significantly, these discrepancies can be attributed to the increasing availability of radiocarbon dates.

However, in the absence of abundant absolute dates, the Rowe–Lanning relative dating scheme is still viable and generally accurate because of the horizon styles. The early definition by Uhle of two of these styles and the proposal of a

Chart 1. *Chronology of Andean area and relative placement of chapters presented in this volume*

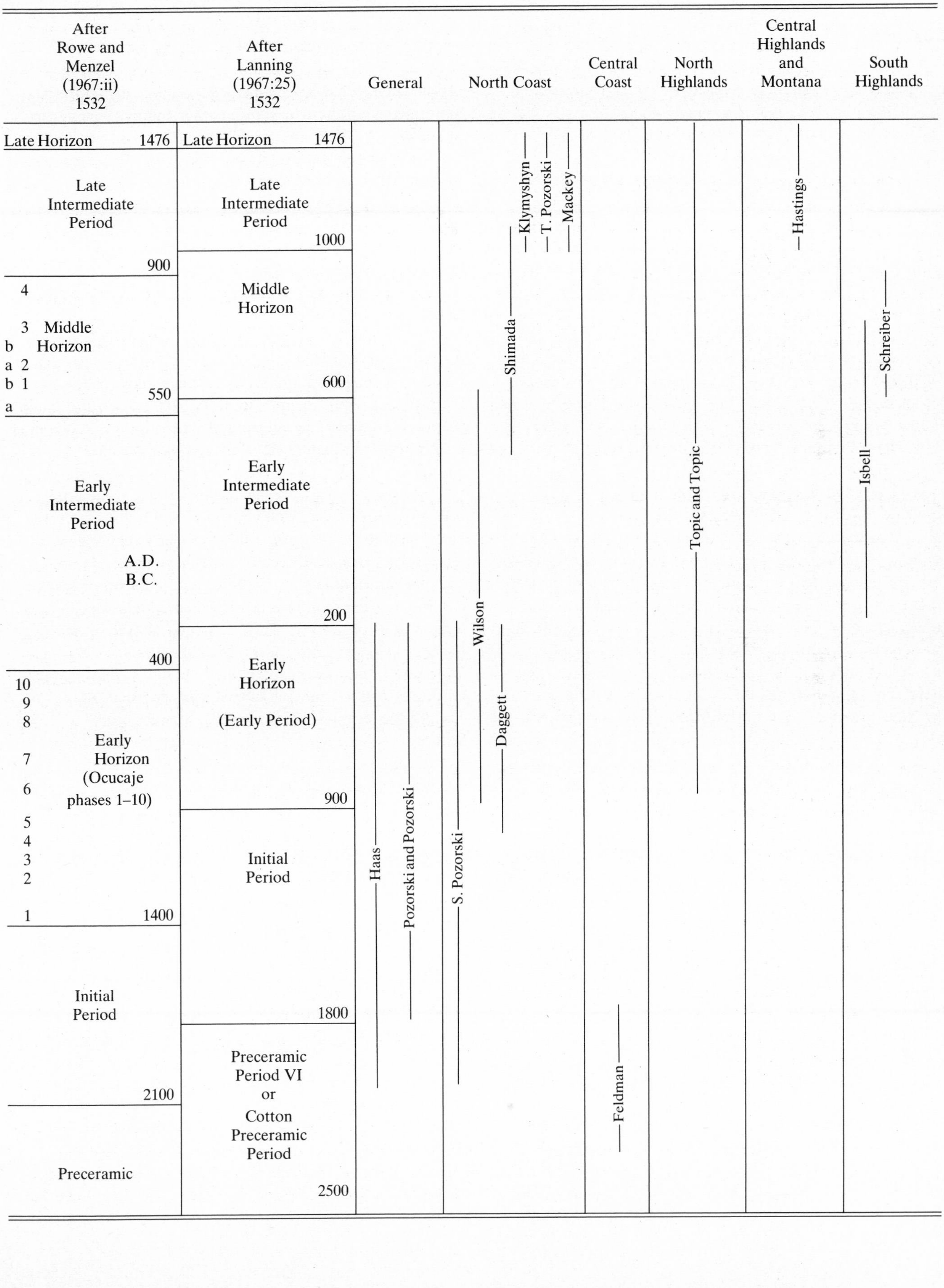

After Rowe and Menzel (1967:ii) 1532	After Lanning (1967:25) 1532	General	North Coast	Central Coast	North Highlands	Central Highlands and Montana	South Highlands
Late Horizon 1476	Late Horizon 1476		Klymyshyn — T. Pozorski — Mackey			Hastings	
Late Intermediate Period	Late Intermediate Period 1000						
900	Middle Horizon		Shimada				Schreiber
4							
3 Middle Horizon							
b a 2							
b 1	600						
a 550							
Early Intermediate Period	Early Intermediate Period					Topic and Topic	Isbell
A.D. B.C.			Wilson				
	200						
400	Early Horizon (Early Period)						
10 9 8			Daggett				
7 Early Horizon (Ocucaje phases 1–10)	900	Pozorski and Pozorski	S. Pozorski				
6 5 4 3 2	Initial Period	Haas					
1 1400							
Initial Period	1800						
2100	Preceramic Period VI or Cotton Preceramic Period			Feldman			
Preceramic	2500						

third within twenty years enable Peruvianists to place relatively most cultures *as they were discovered*, thereby avoiding the methodologically hindering effects of inaccurately ordered or extremely narrowly defined local sequences. These three 'horizons' have been characterized as both stages and periods, but the distinction has only recently become significant as absolute dates and a greatly increased data base are facilitating the internal refinement of these relatively gross divisions.

Application of the Rowe–Lanning framework to this volume

The Rowe–Lanning chronological framework is followed in this volume because it still best generally characterizes Andean development despite inherent problems (Chart 1). The first period relevant to this volume on state evolution, the Cotton Preceramic Period (2500–1800 B.C.), was the time during which complex polities first developed in Peru. This early development is particularly evident in remains found along the central and north central parts of the coast (see chapters by Feldman and S. Pozorski). The importance of the Initial Period (1800–900 B.C.), which follows the Cotton Preceramic Period, has been downplayed in the past, but increasing amounts of evidence point strongly to the existence of Initial Period states in at least some areas of Peru (see chapters by Haas and S. Pozorski).

The Early Horizon (900–200 B.C.) has been characterized as a time that witnessed the spread of the Chavin art style, purportedly a reflection of a unifying religious cult. However, as is evident in a number of papers in this volume (see chapters by Topic and Topic, Wilson, and Daggett), there was a considerable amount of warfare present, especially in the north highlands and on the north coast, that influenced the development of early states. In fact, there may have been so much discord during the Early Horizon that this time period should not be viewed as a time of relative unification of culture – i.e., a horizon – but rather as a time of cultural diversity – a period (see chapter by T. and S. Pozorski).

The Early Intermediate Period (200 B.C.–A.D. 600) was again a time of regional cultural diversity. Major cultures such as the Moche on the north coast, Nazca on the south coast, Cajamarca in the north highlands, and Recuay in the north central highlands flourished along with still lesser known cultures. Some of these cultures, such as Moche, exhibited state organization (see chapter by Wilson), apparently on a wider, more regional basis than known earlier cultures (chapter by Shimada).

The subsequent Middle Horizon (A.D. 600–1000) was dominated by the Wari state, which spread from the Ayacucho Basin of the southern highlands over much of Peru (chapter by Isbell). Again, however, as in the case of the Early Horizon, recent evidence indicates that the Wari state was not as widespread as previously believed (see chapter by Schreiber) and that non-Wari states controlled large areas of Peru (see chapter by Shimada).

The Late Intermediate Period (A.D. 1000–1476) was a time of regional diversity, but also a time of highly developed state, even empire, organization, as represented by the north-coast Chimu (chapters by Klymyshyn, T. Pozorski and Mackey). However, not all cultures during even this late time period attained a state level of organization (chapter by Hastings).

Altogether, the contents of this volume exemplify the necessity of employing a chronological and historical scheme based on true periods rather than 'developmental' stages. Only a framework unencumbered by developmental overtones can accommodate such diverse processes as Initial Period state origins and truncation in valleys such as Casma, which ceased to be centers of power by the Early Intermediate Period (chapter by S. Pozorski) or the Middle Horizon expansionist Wari polity which emerged quite late in the Ayacucho area (chapters by Isbell and Schreiber). The accompanying charts attempt to place the respective chapters and historical sequences in relative chronological relationship to one another; unfortunately, the persistent problems with the Andean chronological sequence remain to be resolved.

Chapter 1

Architectural evidence for the development of nonegalitarian social systems in coastal Peru

Robert A. Feldman

Introduction

The coast of Peru, which witnessed the ultimate rise of such major polities as the Nazca, Moche and Chimu, also witnessed the emergence of the first complex political systems in the Andean region. Beginning during the Cotton Preceramic Period (*c.* 2500 to 1800 B.C.), what appear to be centralized polities developed in a number of valleys along the north and central coasts. While archaeologists have been aware of large preceramic sites along the coast for some time, an understanding of their nature and complexity has been slow in coming. It is mainly within the last two decades that research on the organization of preceramic political systems has intensified. The site of Aspero, located near the ocean on the northern margin of the Supe Valley, in particular has been the focus of research directed at elucidating the nature of one of the first nonegalitarian social systems to arise in the Andean region.

The site of Aspero is one of the largest known settlements in Peru prior to the Initial Period. It combines extensive midden deposits extending over some 12 hectares with a variety of large constructions, including ceremonial mounds, plazas, and terraces (Moseley and Willey 1973; Feldman 1977, 1978, 1980, 1985). Excavations at Aspero by the author in 1973 and 1974 revealed a complicated pattern of rebuilt rooms and floors within the mounds. Carbon samples collected from within this architecture dated the latter phases of

contruction to between 4360±175 B.P. or 2410±175 B.C. and 3950±150 B.P. or 2000±150 B.C. (all dates are uncorrected), well within the range of dates from other Cotton Preceramic Period sites on the Peruvian coast.

It is not the purpose of this paper to debate the nature of preceramic subsistence. It is clear from recent studies, however, that the maritime versus agricultural dichotomy exemplified by Moseley (1975a) and Wilson (1981) is untenable. Analyses of midden remains, coprolites, and bone chemistry (such as orally presented by Weir and Benfer and by Pozorski and Pozorski at the Society for American Archaeology meetings in 1985) show that the coastal inhabitants were eating a mixed diet including wild and cultivated plants (such as legumes and *achira*), in addition to the main staples of marine fish, mammals, and invertebrates. Further, as the excellent summary paper by Burger (1985) points out, there was considerable interchange between the coast and the highlands prior to the second millennium B.C.

This paper will concentrate on a presentation and interpretation of architectural and artifactual data from Aspero. Details and overall patterns will be examined for what they can tell us about the nature of the labor mobilization and social organization behind their construction. Comparisons will then be made between the known coastal and highland preceramic architectural complexes. It will be argued that the architectural and settlement evidence from the highlands suggests a simpler,

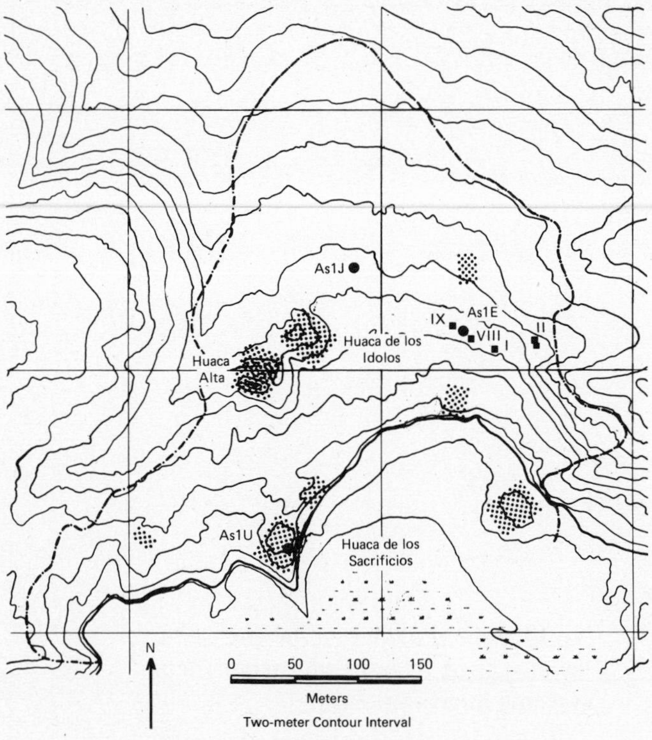

Fig. 1. Map of Aspero showing extent of midden (broken line) and main artificial mounds (dotted areas)

less stratified social organization there than on the coast, and that even with the contacts between the two areas, the locus of population concentration and political development was also in the coastal, predominantly marine oriented, communities.

Architectural evidence

Whatever the nature of the subsistence system at Aspero and other late preceramic settlements of the central Peruvian coast (cf. Moseley 1968, 1975a; Pickersgill 1969; Feldman 1977; Moseley and Feldman n.d.; and Osborne 1977a, 1977b; Raymond 1981; Wilson 1981), it is clear that the 150,000–200,000 cubic meters of cultural deposit at Aspero are indicative of a large, stable resident population. The most prominent features of this extensive midden are its irregular, pitted surface and a number of large artificial mounds. Fully one-third of the site is occupied by some type of construction, including domestic structures, small stone-lined pits, broad low terraces, plazas, and monumental mounds.

The most substantial constructions are the mounds (Figure 1). There are at least seven recognizable mounds and an additional six mound-like structures. The mounds are formed of interconnected rooms that were eventually filled in, either partially or completely, to form a raised platform for a new phase of wall and floor construction.

Major excavations were undertaken in two of the mounds, Huaca de los Idolos and Huaca de los Sacrificios, and a profile exposed by looters through a third, Huaca Alta, was cleaned and recorded. These excavations revealed that the

Table 1. *Radiocarbon dates*

Lab no.	Field no.	Age, B.P.	Corrected age
Site As8			
GX–3863	As8A–14 = 25	6085 ± 180*	6914 ± 190; 4964 B.C.
Huaca de los Sacrificios			
UCR–242	AsIU–5 = 26	3950 ± 150	4483 ± 217; 2533 B.C.
UCR–243	AsIU–5 = 62	4060 ± 150	4624 ± 217; 2674 B.C.
UCR–244	AsIU–8 = 5	4150 ± 150	4740 ± 217; 2790 B.C.
GX–3862	AsIU–8 = 5	4260 ± 150	4880 ± 225; 2930 B.C.
Average of UCR–244 and GX–3862			
		4205 ± 106	4807 ± 156; 2857 B.C.
Huaca de los Idolos			
GX–3861	AsIM–10 = 263	3970 ± 145	4508 ± 210; 2558 B.C.
GX–3860	AsIM–10 = 200	4360 ± 175*	5005 ± 211; 3055 B.C.
GX–3859	AsIM–10 = 198	4900 ± 160†	5658 ± 220; 3702 B.C.

* δC^{13} corrected.
† Rejected as too old.
Dates are based on a half-life of 5570 years.
Corrected using tables in Damon, Ferguson, Long, and Wallick (*American Antiquity*, 39(2):350–366).
All samples collected by Robert A. Feldman.

mounds are composed of successive phases of stone-walled rooms and are not simply earthen platforms supporting surficial summit structures as had been previously suggested (Moseley and Willey 1973). The larger walls, typically the outer terrace faces, are built of large angular blocks of basaltic rock set in ample amounts of mud or mud-and-grass mortar with the result being a smoothly aligned outer face. Smaller, typically internal, walls are built of oblong boulders about 30–50 cm long, which are set perpendicular to the wall in mud plaster. Both types of walls have plastered faces, which occasionally are painted red or yellow.

In Huaca de los Idolos, individual rooms within the excavated levels vary considerably in size, with the largest being 11 m × 16 m (Figure 2). This room, or more likely open court, is the main entry area of the complex, reached by a stairway leading to a two-meter wide doorway at the top of the mound's highest or eastern face. From this first room, passages lead back to smaller rooms at the rear and sides. The central room of the rear group, measuring 5.1 m × 4.4 m, is divided in half by a low wall, with a clapboard-like frieze on its eastern side. This wall is broken in the middle by a narrow doorway in the shape of a double-topped T. The walls of this room, as well as those of the rooms to the north and east, contain niches.

The central rooms of Huaca de los Idolos quickly underwent a series of refloorings and rebuildings that ultimately buried the level associated with the friezed wall under five floors. In the later phases, the fill placed on the old floors was clean quarried rock held in loose mesh bags made of cane, sedge, or cattail stems, a construction technique referred to as

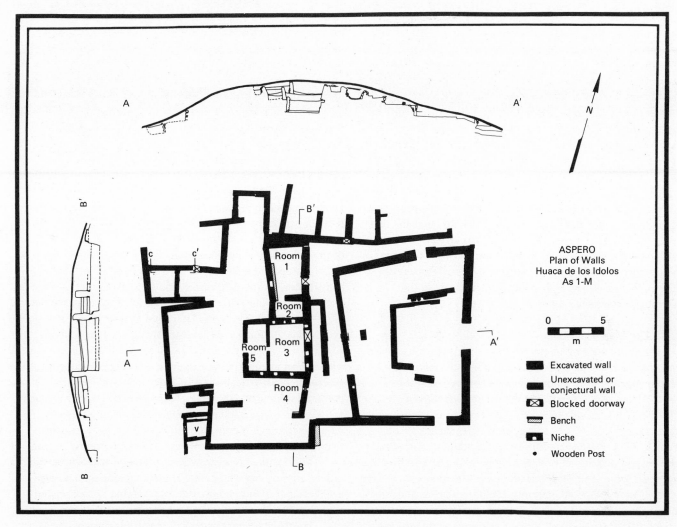

Fig. 2. Plan and profiles of architecture in the upper levels of Huaca de los Idolos

'cane bagging' or *shicra* (Huapaya 1977–78). These rebuildings do not appear to have been motivated by disrepair of the old level. As will be discussed below, the rebuildings suggest conspicuous displays of authority designed to assert and validate the power of the central corporate body.

The radiocarbon dates shown in Table 1 come from the upper quarter to third of the two largest mounds and represent the later end of mound construction at Aspero. The earliest constructions probably began 200 to 400 years earlier, or around 4500 to 4700 B.P. or 2550 to 2750 B.C. (uncorrected radiocarbon years).

Interpretation of the architecture

A number of features of the mounds indicate that they were not domestic structures, nor were they the products of individual or unorganized group labor; rather, they were built using *corporate labor*. Corporate labor (Moseley 1975a; Feldman 1980) is group labor that draws its work force from separate households, either from within a single community or from separate communities. The laborers work together in a

collective, integrated manner for a specific purpose, which is defined and sanctioned by an authoritative body that coordinates the project and to which the will of the individual laborer is subservient while the laborer is participating in the project. Corporate labor is an organizational concept that implies the existence of an authority with the rights and ability to mobilize people and direct their actions.

Several important features are noticeable in the architecture of Huaca de los Idolos. First, the architectural ornamentation and cached artifacts are concentrated in the central rooms, indicating a higher status for these rooms. Second, a pattern of graded access is reflected at least partially in doorway width: the largest doorway is from the outside to the large eastern court; smaller doorways lead to the central rooms; and the smallest doorway controls passage from Room 3 to Room 5 (Figure 2).

The patterns of ornamentation and increasingly restricted access suggest levels of ceremonial space open to selectively more and more restricted groups of people. This pattern is one that can be seen at slightly later ceremonial centers, such as Huaca de los Reyes in the Moche Valley, with its three plazas arranged in increasing elevation, decreasing size, and decreasing access (T. Pozorski 1976, 1980, 1982b).

In terms of physical access, the most restricted space in the excavated portion of Huaca de los Idolos is Room 5. The greatest concentration of ornamentation is in Rooms 3 and 5, though mainly in Room 3. The friezed wall physically divides these two rooms, but since it is only 1.25 m high, it does not block the view from one room to the other. It is decorated on the side facing Room 3, the one that would be seen by people able to enter from the eastern court. The 40 cm-wide doorway into Room 5 through the friezed wall is only wide enough to allow one person to pass through at a time, so it appears that, of the select group of people who were able to enter the 'inner sanctum' of Huaca de los Idolos, most had to be content to remain on the 'outside' of the friezed wall, as mere observers of the ever more select few who were able to pass through the doorway, enter Room 5, and actively participate in the ceremonies conducted there.

The Aspero chiefdom

The presence of an elite group, or a group with special functions and privileges, is one indication that Aspero is a central component in a nonegalitarian society. As will be shown, the Aspero society was what may be labeled a 'chiefdom,' a social evolutionary stage defined most explicitly by Service (1971, 1975; see also Fried 1967; Sahlins 1958; Adams 1975). Principal features of a chiefdom include social ranking and population centers from which leaders coordinate religious, social, and economic activities. Chiefdoms are usually larger in size and population than egalitarian bands and tribes, though they are smaller, less stratified, and less centrally organized than true states. While I recognize that there are pitfalls in assigning a discontinuous typological label to a very complex spectrum of social forms, the term 'chiefdom' does serve to distinguish certain types of societies from others. It also provides a convenient term for further discussions and comparisons.

Because of some similarities in degree of social ranking, size, and technology, the ethnographically described chiefdoms of Polynesia make useful analogies. Archaeologically, one of the principal features of the Polynesian chiefdoms analyzed by Sahlins (1958) is the pooling of labor for corporate construction projects. The structures at Aspero could possibly be interpreted as the products of an *ad hoc* organization, but their size, detail, and continuity of formal concept through time show the hand of organized control; we can clearly see evidence of corporate labor.

In another part of the world, Renfrew (1974) infers a chiefdom-level organization from third-millennium Maltese 'temples.' Although Renfrew himself notes that the only physical evidence for this designation is the structures themselves, they 'clearly required for their construction (a) the mobilization of large labor forces, and (b) the exercise of architectural and artistic skill' (Renfrew 1974:77). He

acknowledges that egalitarian societies can build large structures through accretional growth, but points out the 'purposive nature' of the temples, a 'central unifying concept' that signals the hand of a corporate body (Renfrew 1974:77). A number of specific features at Aspero show the purposive and unifying hand of corporate control.

The first is simply the size of the constructions. Although no domestic structures that could serve as direct comparisons were excavated at Aspero, habitations at other contemporary sites are much smaller, both in room size and overall size (Engel 1963; Wendt 1964; S. Pozorski and T. Pozorski 1979a). Huaca de los Idolos has a base of about 30 m × 50 m, and Huaca de los Sacrificios is of similar size. Some rooms within these structures are over 10 m square; walls are built of stone and are up to 1 m thick and at least 2.5 m in height; and some of the individual stones are almost 1 cu m in volume.

The second is the use of *shicra* or bagged fill. This construction technique is also found at El Paraíso (Engel 1967) and the Supe Valley preceramic site of Piedra Parada (Feldman 1980; Williams 1985). It was later used at such ceremonial sites as Las Haldas (Fung 1969; Matsuzawa 1978), Huaricanga (Ishida *et al.* 1960) and Huaca San José, a 100 m square mound with a 50 m circular plaza located in the Pativilca Valley (Feldman 1980; Williams 1985). *Shicra* is not a feature of domestic structures, where fill accumulates principally through natural action and midden accumulation; rather, it signals intentional, organized abandonment of a structure prior to rebuilding it in a more prominent, elevated position.

Third is the presence of special architectural decoration: niches, friezes, and wall paint. These are features that once again are not found in domestic contexts, but are associated with ceremonial structures and corporate constructions.

Fourth is the general lack of domestic refuse on the floors and within the fill of the structures. The few artifacts found occurred most often in the context of caches placed on the fill prior to the laying of a floor.

The above features, singly and in combination, point out the corporate nature of the Aspero mounds, and direct attention beyond the structures to the social system behind them. Renfrew recognizes two extremes on the continuum of chiefdoms: (1) the 'group-oriented' chiefdom, where there is little evidence of accumulation of personal wealth, but clear indications of communal or corporate activities; and (2) the 'individualizing' chiefdom, where evidence of marked differences in personal possessions and symbols of prestige is found, greatly outweighing community expressions of authority. Malta is given as an example of the former while the pre-Mycenean Aegean is cited for the latter (Renfrew 1974:74; cf. Haas 1982:11–13).

In placing Aspero in particular, and the Peruvian late preceramic in general, on Renfrew's scale, there is a predominance of community works over personal wealth, although status differences have been documented. Moseley (1975a:76) has noted a bimodal distribution of grave textiles in the burials Engels (1963) found at Asia, and has interpreted these differences as evidence of a social hierarchy. A richly adorned infant burial on Huaca de los Sacrificios (Feldman 1980:114) might indicate the presence of hereditary status differences, although overall, the evidence for major social differentiation is not strong.

The presence of luxury trade items, such as beads and *Spondylus* sp. shell, at Aspero (Feldman 1980:157) indicates differential access to wealth and goods, another characteristic of ranked societies (Fried 1967). Members of the elite group have the means to acquire special goods that serve to signal and enhance their rank. The demand they create for prestige goods encourages specialized craft production and trade in luxury goods. Conversely, the ownership of special or exotic goods can provide distinctions between emerging classes. Demand can create a supply *and* supply can create a demand.

Renfrew (1974) notes the probable interrelationship between the expansion of metallurgy and the rise of the Aegean chiefdoms. He calls this interaction the 'multiplier effect' (Renfrew 1972:37), whereby changes in different parts of a society reinforce and amplify each other. Demand created by changes in social structure can influence craft specialization and trade, *and* the development of new crafts can create a demand leading to social distinctions. The social differentiation, demand for luxury goods, and craft specialization and trade seen at Aspero can be seen as reflections of this process.

The pattern of restricted access seen in Huaca de los Idolos can be interpreted as further evidence of differential access to and control of ceremonial/religious activity by a small group of people. To date, the evidence indicates that during the late Cotton Preceramic Period on the coast, status differences related to ceremonial or religious activities were probably not sharply defined, though they certainly were by the Early Horizon (900 to 200 B.C.). Also, the available data indicate that the social differentiation found among the polities along the coast was much more highly developed than anything found among contemporary highland groups.

The coast and the highlands

More information is becoming available about early occupations in the highlands of Peru. The work at Kotosh (Ishida *et al.* 1960), La Galgada (Bueno and Grieder 1979; Grieder and Bueno 1981, 1985) and Huaricoto (Burger and Burger 1980, 1985) provides evidence of a widespread and elaborate highland ceremonial tradition existing in the late third millennium.

Several common features are readily apparent in these highland sites which Burger and Burger (1980) have called the 'Kotosh Religious Tradition.' In these sites, there are fire pits or central hearths, often with ventilator shafts running beneath the floor. The floor is often depressed in the center, forming a low bench against the walls. Since the rooms usually are squarish, with a single doorway centered in one wall, these benches result in a depressed, T-shaped floor area. Where the walls have been preserved to a sufficient height, ornamental niches, dados, and, at Kotosh, friezes have been observed.

Wall corners, especially exterior ones, are often rounded.

The highland temple structures are usually free-standing buildings of one room, or at most agglutinations of a few similar rooms that are not interconnected, but rather independently communicate with the outside. This arrangement is one of the most readily apparent differences between the highland and coastal structures. On the coast, the temples, exemplified by Huaca de los Idolos at Aspero and the more completely excavated and restored structure at El Paraiso (Engel 1967), are square-cornered, multi-room buildings with one or more outside entrances and a complex pattern of internal access from room to room. It is necessary to pass through some rooms to get to others, often in a graded hierarchy of decreasing size and ease of entrance.

A number of features are shared between the highland and coastal structures, including wall niches, colored plaster, and internal ceremonial hearths, although they are less common and of a slightly different form on the coast. There are also similarities in the artifacts found in the two zones. Some, such as bone needles with a notch in the end by the eye, reported from Kotosh and Aspero, are probably of limited significance, while others, such as bi-convex red stone beads, known from Aspero and Bandurria on the coast and Huaricoto in the highlands, indicate trade contacts between sites. The presence of coastal fish and shellfish remains at highland sites (Richard Burger, personal communication) and highland tubers at coastal sites (Martins 1976; Moseley 1985) indicates a probable network of interchange. It is doubtful that this interchange served exclusively to supply subsistence needs for proteins or carbohydrates. Rather, it seems more likely that the highlanders were receiving essential nutrients such as salt and iodine (Burger 1985; Sandweiss, personal communication).

Whatever the reasons for the movement of coastal products to the highlands and *vice versa*, there is mounting evidence that these contacts were extensive (Burger 1985). Thus, it is interesting to analyze the differences in the coastal and highland ceremonial architecture in terms of what it can tell us about differences in social structure. The single room highland temple, repeated a number of times at a site with little differentiation, shows less elaboration than the coastal structures. This difference can be interpreted as indicating less social differentiation in the highland than coastal groups. It could also reflect a smaller, less stable occupation. Indeed, Burger and Burger (1985) interpret the many structures at Huaricoto as indicating repeated temporary occupations. In social terms, the hierarchies of space and access in the coastal temples could indicate a more powerful and/or privileged elite; on the other hand, it could indicate wider public participation in some aspects of ritual beyond a possibly common rite held in the 'inner sanctum.'

While we have little indication of the rituals performed in the coastal structures, there is evidence for one highland rite. Pepper (*Capsicum* sp.) seeds were found in fire-pit ash at La Galgada (C. E. Smith, personal communication). Burning peppers would vaporize and fill the enclosed room with the chemicals responsible for pepper's distinctive taste, producing a strong burning sensation in the eyes, nose, and mouth of anyone exposed to the fumes. The highland temple thus may have functioned as a 'sweat house' (and one certainly conducive to 'seeing god'). In this respect, the sub-floor ventilator to the fire-pit makes good sense, as it allows air to reach the fire without diluting the potency of the pepper fumes accumulating within the room.

A highland site such as Huaricoto could thus be seen as a ritual center to which groups of people would go on occasion for rites of purification or penance. The temples would not need or necessarily have a large population resident near them. Indeed, such population concentrations seem unlikely at La Galgada, located as it is in a narrow dry gorge, up away from the resources of the coast, yet not high enough toward the rainfall zone to have supported much agriculture, even with irrigation.

In contrast, a coastal site such as Aspero shows evidence of an extensive and intensive resident occupation, and is well situated to take advantage of both marine and riverine resources. Later sites such as Piedra Parada and El Paraíso still maintain maritime access, but have shifted farther inland, presumably to take advantage of agricultural lands made available through the initiation of irrigation by the early part of the second millennium B.C. The large resident population at the coastal sites helps explain the more 'public-oriented' configuration of their temple structures, especially those with large frontal plazas. From this it is inferred that there was a division between the open, 'public' rituals and those performed within the inner rooms of the temples, and that this difference in ritual was reflected in parallel social differences.

Data from coastal sites such as Aspero clearly document the presence of chiefdoms with intrasocietal ranking and evidence of labor mobilization for monumental construction. In the highlands, a less complex social development is suggested by the smaller, simpler and more scattered temple complexes. This organizational and demographic 'head start' experienced by the coastal preceramic societies then provided a foundation for the rapid development of coastal political systems seen in the succeeding Initial Period and Early Horizon (see chapters by S. Pozorski and T. Pozorski and S. Pozorski, this volume).

Chapter 2

Theocracy vs. militarism: the significance of the Casma Valley in understanding early state formation

Shelia Pozorski

Introduction

In the early stages of state development along the coast of Peru, there was considerable variation in the nature of the different state polities. In some of the first states, such as those seen in the Santa and Nepeña Valleys (see chapters by Wilson and Daggett, this volume), warfare seems to have been a central variable in the emergence of the first statelike polities. These warfare-related states were characterized by predominantly secular and militaristic forms of government. In other areas, however, the first states appear to have arisen without significant warfare. In these cases, the emergent governments had a much more sacred or theocratic nature. Examples of these early theocratic states were established in the lower Casma Valley by about 1500 B.C., early in the Initial Period (1800 to 900 B.C.).

These early states in Casma drew and elaborated upon features of the antecedent Cotton Preceramic (2500 to 1800 B.C.) adaptation to the coastal zone. The apogee of Initial Period state development on the north Andean coast was marked by the consolidation of the Casma Valley and the construction of the largest mound known in the New World for that time period. Shortly after 1000 B.C., it appears that an invasion from outside the valley replaced this theocratic form of government with one that was significantly more secular and militaristic. This radical change is reflected in all levels of the archaeological record. For state development, it is especially

significant because it introduced the concepts of secularism and militarism to an area of emergent, theocratically oriented coastal states. The importance of this time of early development and sudden change is readily apparent in later Andean states such as Moche and Chimu where theocratic and secular elements are successfully blended with intense militarism.

Cotton Preceramic

To understand the formation of early Andean states, it is essential to review evidence from late Cotton Preceramic coastal sites. These sites share key features such as sedentism, subsistence inventory, and organizational principles with succeeding incipient states. Two substantial Cotton Preceramic sites, Huaynuná and preceramic Las Haldas, lie within the Casma Valley zone, and both were sampled through excavation.

Casma Valley Cotton Preceramic sites

Huaynuná. The Cotton Preceramic site of Huaynuná was first recorded by Collier (1962:411) and subsequently tested by Engel (1957a:56; 1957b:74–75). It lies north of Casma (Figure 1) in a protected area near the south end of Huaynuná Bay, a sandy arc bordered by rocky arms of the Andean foothills. The site is distinguishable on the surface as a concentration of dark ash with marine shells. Testing in two low mounds revealed a

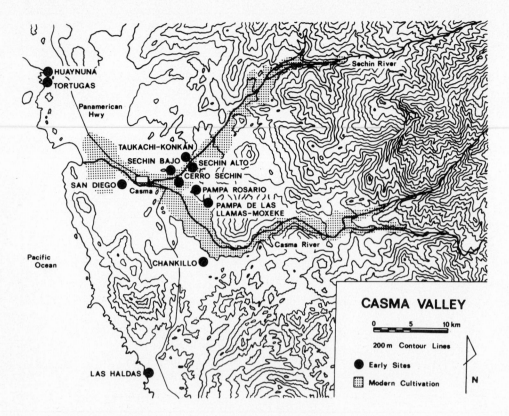

Fig. 1. Map showing location of early sites in the Casma Valley zone

stone masonry room and a small tiered platform, and comparable architecture probably underlies additional low rises at the site. In intervening areas, midden is up to 190 cm deep and contains a variety of both floral and faunal remains. These include rock and sand-dwelling shellfish and fish which were complemented by a plant inventory that included cotton, gourd, pepper, squash, *lúcuma*, potatoes and other tubers (Ugent *et al.* 1981, 1982). Twined cotton textiles, looped netting and a shell fishhook are the main artifacts recovered from the Huaynuná midden. Radiocarbon dates from Huaynuná range from 2250 ± 80 B.C. to 1775 ± 75 B.C. (Table 1).

Preceramic Las Haldas. The site of Las Haldas is also on the coast, about 20 km south of the Casma Valley (Figure 1). The Cotton Preceramic component is overlain by extensive ceramic period refuse and architecture which currently form the visible portion of the site. Preceramic deposits were found by previous excavators at four locations up to 200 m apart (Engel 1970:32, 42; Fung 1969; Grieder 1975). Architecture was encountered in only one excavation (Engel 1970:32, 42), but midden was consistently 2 m or more in depth at other locations. These data suggest that the buried preceramic occupation at Las Haldas is of a size and complexity comparable to Huaynuná. Like Huaynuná, the preceramic Las Haldas midden yielded large quantities of marine shellfish and fish. Plant preservation was poor; only small amounts of cotton, gourd, guava and common bean were collected. Poorly

preserved twined cotton textiles were the only artifacts recovered from the preceramic Las Haldas excavations. Engel (1966:82) has published a radiocarbon date of 1850 B.C. for preceramic Las Haldas, and recent dates range from 2010 ± 80 B.C. to 1795 ± 60 B.C. (Table 1).

Cotton Preceramic contributions to Initial Period development

The late Cotton Preceramic has recently received considerable attention in the controversy over the maritime foundation hypothesis set forth by Moseley (1975a, 1975b). Moseley proposed that the rich Peruvian biomass fostered the development of a lifestyle and aspects of social organization which 'preadapted' Cotton Preceramic peoples to assume increasingly complex ways of life. Opponents to this idea have argued that marine resources alone could not have supported such early advances (Osborn 1977b; Raymond 1981; Wilson 1981). It is likely that a resolution to this debate lies somewhere in between the two poles. Archaeological data from the Moche Valley and the Chillon area do indicate that marine resources were exploited by the *earliest* coastal inhabitants to the virtual exclusion of plant cultigens except cotton and gourd (Moseley 1968, 1975a; S. Pozorski 1976; Quilter and Stocker 1983). Initial efforts at flood plain cultivation were undoubtedly motivated by the need for these industrial cultigens which were essential to a marine economy. Significantly, in these early coastal states, there is no evidence of the social complexity which marks later Cotton Preceramic sites. It was only after

Table 1. *Radiocarbon dates from sites in the Casma Valley, Peru*[1]

Radiocarbon years		Calendar age	Location
4200±80	(UGA–4522	2250±80 B.C.	Huaynuma
4040±65	(UGA–4520	2090±65 B.C.	Huaynuma
3725±75	(UGA–4521	1775±75 B.C.	Huaynuma
3960±80	(UGA–4531)	2010±80 B.C.	Precer. Las Haldas
3800±80	(Engel 1966:82)	1850±80 B.C.	Precer. Las Haldas
3785±60	(UGA–4529	1835±60 B.C.	Precer. Las Haldas
3745±60	(UGA–4530)	1795±60 B.C.	Precer. Las Haldas
4655±95	(UGA–4510)	2705±95 B.C.	Pampa Llamas–Moxeke
3735±75	(UGA–4505)	1785±75 B.C.	Pampa Llamas–Moxeke
3490±75	(UGA–4506)	1540±75 B.C.	Pampa Llamas–Moxeke
3425±75	(UGA–4508)	1475±75 B.C.	Pampa Llamas–Moxeke
3390±150	(UGA–4507)	1440±150 B.C.	Pampa Llamas–Moxeke
3220±85	(UGA–4509)	1370–85 B.C.	Pampa Llamas–Moxeke
3175±90	(UGA–4511)	1225±90 B.C.	Pampa Llamas–Moxeke
3165±75	(UGA–4503)	1215±75 B.C.	Pampa Llamas–Moxeke
3070±85	(UGA–4504)	1120±85 B.C.	Pampa Llamas–Moxeke
4540±200	(UGA–4524)	2590±200 B.C.	Tortugas
4065±65	(UGA–4523)	2115±65 B.C.	Tortugas
3750±65	(UGA–4525)	1800±65 B.C.	Tortugas
3600±95	(Matsuzawa 1978:666)	1650±95 B.C.	Initial Period Las Haldas
3595±75	(UGA–4534)	1645±75 B.C.	Initial Period Las Haldas
3460±75	(UGA–4532)	1510±75 B.C.	Initial Period Las Haldas
3430±80	(Grieder 1975:99)	1480±80 B.C.	Initial Period Las Haldas
3150±90	(Matsuzawa 1978:666)	1200±90 B.C.	Initial Period Las Haldas
3140±75	(UGA–4533)	1190±75 B.C.	Initial Period Las Haldas
3140±80	(Grieder 1975:100)	1190±80 B.C.	Initial Period Las Haldas
2590±80	(Matsuzawa 1978:666)	640±80 B.C.	Initial Period Las Haldas
3400±100	(Berger *et al.* 1965:347)	1450±100 B.C.	Sechin Alto
2990±75	(UGA–4526)	1040±75 B.C.	Early Horizon Las Haldas
2195±60	(UGA–4527)	965±60 B.C.	Early Horizon Las Haldas
2845±80	(UGA–4528)	895±80 B.C.	Early Horizon Las Haldas
2830±70	(Grieder 1975:100)	880±70 B.C.	Early Horizon Las Haldas
2730±70	(Grieder 1975:109)	780±70 B.C.	Early Horizon Las Haldas
2680±150	(Matsuzawa 1968:666)	730±150 B.C.	Early Horizon Las Haldas
2360±95	(Matsuzawa 1968:666)	410±95 B.C.	Early Horizon Las Haldas
2760±75	(UGA–4535)	810±75 B.C.	Pampa Rosario
2535±75	(UGA–4537)	585±75 B.C.	Pampa Rosario
2400±70	(UGA–4536)	450±70 B.C.	Pampa Rosario
2510±115	(UGA–4514)	560±115 B.C.	San Diego
2490±60	(UGA–4512)	540±60 B.C.	San Diego
2455±70	(UGA–4517)	505±70 B.C.	San Diego
2305±55	(UGA–4513)	355±55 B.C.	San Diego
2245±60	(UGA–4516)	295±60 B.C.	San Diego
2940±120	(Radiocarbon Dates Association, Inc. n.d.)	990±120 B.C.	Cerro Sechin
2720±60	(Radiocarbon Dates Association, Inc. n.d.)	770±60 B.C.	Cerro Sechin
2292±80	(Olson and Broecker 1959:22)	342±80 B.C.	Chankillo
2070±100	(Radiocarbon Dates Association, Inc. n.d.)	120±100 B.C.	Chankillo

[1]All dates are uncorrected based upon the Libby half-life (5570±30 years).

food plants were introduced and gained importance in the diet that we see the sites increasing in size and internal complexity. Experimentation with irrigation agriculture probably also dates to this time (Patterson 1971a). However, marine resources were still perceived by the sites' inhabitants as more important, and this choice is reflected in the coastal location of the sites.

Despite the controversy over the late Cotton Preceramic subsistence base, the existence of complex preceramic antecedents to Andean state development is not disputed. Initial sedentism is directly attributable to the availability of marine resources which lured early transhumant groups to settle on the coast. Other key features of Cotton Preceramic life which carry over into Initial Period development include an increasingly varied subsistence base with both marine and plant resources and nonegalitarian forms of social organization. Evidence of nonresidential tiered platform mounds at sites such as Huaynuná suggests the existence of leaders who were probably in charge of simple chiefdoms (see Feldman, this volume). Such leaders were clearly able to promote nonresidential construction at these sites. The variety of plant remains suggests both advanced horticultural knowledge and early efforts at irrigation agriculture, and it is likely that the leaders' influence extended into this realm as well. The ability to organize a population for construction and possibly agricultural endeavors was an especially important preceramic

preadaptation that became more developed during the Initial Period.

Early Initial Period

The Initial Period in Casma was marked by the introduction of ceramics and woven textiles as well as a change in settlement pattern which saw the establishment of large inland sites with coastal satellites or colonies. Although these features differentiate Initial Period Casma from preceding periods, the Cotton Preceramic legacy cannot be ignored.

Casma Valley early Initial Period sites
Pampa de las Llamas–Moxeke. The inland site of Pampa de las Llamas–Moxeke is located within a large flat *quebrada* on the Casma branch of the valley about 18 km from the Pacific Ocean (Figure 1). This mound complex, including Pampa de las Llamas and Moxeke, was originally recognized and described as a single site (Tello 1956:44–46). Subsequent authors have either separated the complex into two or more sites or dealt only with the Moxeke component (Collier 1962:412; Kauffmann 1980:275–278; Lumbreras 1974a:68; Roe 1974:33–34; Thompson 1962a:294–297; Willey 1971:123). However, proximity, architectural similarities, alignment, and artifactual evidence argue for the treatment of the complex as a single site.

Dominating the 2 km sq area of the site (Figure 2) are

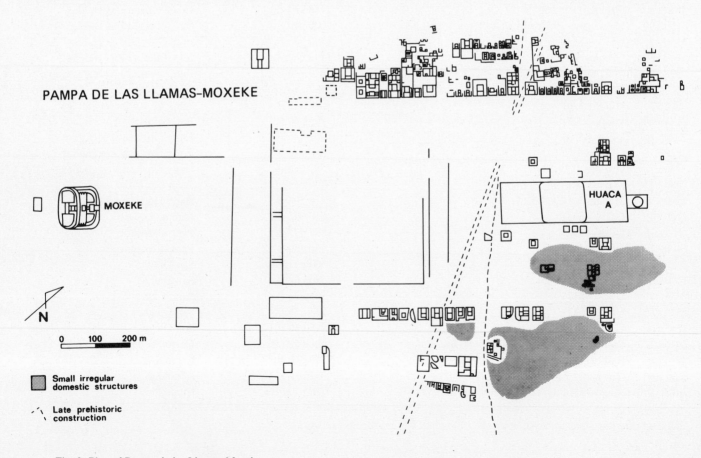

PAMPA DE LAS LLAMAS-MOXEKE

MOXEKE

HUACA A

N

0   100   200 m

▨ Small irregular
  domestic structures

⌇ Late prehistoric
  construction

Fig. 2. Plan of Pampa de las Llamas–Moxeke

two large mounds: Moxeke, which measures 160 m by 170 m by about 30 m high, and Huaca A, which is about 140 m square and 9 m high. The front of the northeast face of Moxeke is the locus of the large anthropomorphic friezes described by Tello (1956:54–66). Unlike Huaca A, which is primarily stone, much conical adobe masonry was used in Moxeke, especially in association with the friezes. The two mounds are aligned along a central axis, and Huaca A is unique in having plazas at each end. One series of plazas connects it to Moxeke whereas another rectangular plaza and a raised platform with a sunken circular court are present on the northeast end. The remaining architecture at the site consists of (1) over 50 small mounds or high-walled enclosures ranging from 10 to over 50 m on a side and 2 to 4 m high and (2) several hundred small single and multi-room domestic structures. Most of the small mounds are arranged in two long rows along the eastern and western edges of the site which parallel the central axis of the site. The domestic structures are concentrated in zones east of Huaca A and along the western site edge, just outside the western row of small mounds. Midden up to 1.5 m deep is associated with these structures.

Artifacts and subsistence remains were abundantly represented at Pampa de las Llamas–Moxeke. The ceramic inventory includes principally neckless ollas plus occasional bowls, jars and bottles as well as figurine fragments and spindle whorls. Ceramic decoration is largely restricted to a single row of deep punctuations along the angled shoulder of neckless ollas, but rare examples of small punctuations, zoned punctuations, incision, incised appliqué bumps, and plain and incised raised bands also occur. Interiors are well smoothed. Second only to ceramics in importance at Pampa de las Llamas–Moxeke are polished, flat-bottomed stone bowls or mortars. Rim fragments indicate diameters between 15 and 27 cm, a height of over 10 cm, and a bottom thickness of 2 to 7 cm. Most were discovered within a restricted area in the western sector of the site. Other artifacts include fragments of both twined and woven cotton textiles, projectile points and shell paint palettes coated with red pigment.

Most animal protein from Pampa de las Llamas–Moxeke came from marine resources including shellfish and fish; however, the remains of two land animals, deer and possibly fox, were also recovered. All of the plant species found at preceramic sites were recovered, along with additional tuber species (Ugent *et al*, 1981, 1982) and the important food plants peanuts and lima and common beans. Avocado and *cansaboca*, two free fruits, were also present by early Initial Period times.

A total of nine carbon 14 assays were run on charcoal from Pampa de las Llamas–Moxeke. Except for an excluded aberrant date of 2705 ± 95 B.C., all lie between 1120 ± 85 B.C. and 1785 ± 75 B.C. (Table 1).

Tortugas. The early Initial Period site of Tortugas is situated on the north side of Tortugas Bay, 11 km north of the Casma Valley (Figure 1). Due to modern development of the beach resort town of Tortugas, only about 1 ha of undisturbed midden remains of a site that was probably once at least 3 ha in area. Buried domestic structures of low stone walls are visible at several points where modern development has cut into midden, and testing along a rocky spur revealed part of a small nondomestic platform. Surrounding dark ashy midden reaches a depth of 140 cm.

The artifactual and subsistence inventories of Pampa de las Llamas–Moxeke are duplicated almost exactly at Tortugas where the same ceramics, a stone bowl fragment, and both twined and woven cotton textiles are present. Radiocarbon dates from Tortugas are problematic (Table 1). The latest date, 1800 ± 65 B.C., barely lies within the standard deviation of the earliest Pampa de las Llamas–Moxeke date, and the remaining dates of 2115 ± 65 B.C. and 2590 ± 200 B.C. are clearly too early because they predate local preceramic sites. In view of the similarities between Pampa de las Llamas–Moxeke and Tortugas, the carbon 14 dates from Pampa de las Llamas–Moxeke provide a range for the dating of Tortugas. However, the use of the much smaller coastal site may not have spanned the entire Pampa de las Llamas–Moxeke occupation. Instead, the site may have been abandoned early, as was the case for contemporaneous sites in the Moche Valley (S. Pozorski and T. Pozorski 1979b).

Early Initial Period Las Haldas. Directly overlying the weathered surface of the Cotton Preceramic refuse are the remains of a long Initial Period phase of construction and midden deposition. The currently visible temple is built upon this earlier deposit, and most of the outlying midden which surrounds the temple forms part of this 40 ha area of pretemple occupation. Pits by previous excavators (Matsuzawa 1978) encountered stone walls of domestic architecture associated with the dense midden which reaches a depth of several meters. The artifact inventory at Las Haldas is dominated by ceramics, but also includes woven textiles, looped and knotted netting, a bird bone tube, a grinding stone, and a reworked stone bowl fragment. The ceramics occur as neckless ollas, jars, bowls, and bottles with exterior decoration commonly in the form of incision, punctuation, and zoned punctuation as well as with more rare examples of interior decoration of textile and net impressions. Grieder (1975:104–105) additionally reports the use of exterior red and black paint. Marine resources exploited include shellfish, fish, and sea mammals from the local interspersed sandy and rocky habitats. Virtually all of the cultivated plants identified at Pampa de las Llamas–Moxeke and Tortugas were also recovered from early Initial Period deposits at Las Haldas. Published carbon 14 dates of 1650 ± 95 B.C., 1200 ± 90 B.C., 640 ± 80 B.C. (Matsuzawa 1978: 666), 1190 ± 80 B.C., and 1480 ± 80 B.C. (Grieder 1975:100, 106, 108–109) compared well with examples from recent excavations which range from 1645 ± 75 B.C. to 1190 ± 75 B.C. (Table 1).

Early Initial Period developments within the Casma Valley
The paired sites of Pampa de las Llamas–Moxeke and Tortugas, which are linked together by an exchange system

involving artifacts and subsistence items, typify early Initial Period development in the Casma Valley. Most significant are the size, complexity and inland location of the former site. The inland location of Pampa de las Llamas–Moxeke is the physical manifestation of a change in subsistence priorities whereby proximity to arable land has taken precedence over proximity to traditionally more heavily exploited marine resources. This change is the culmination of a long period of Cotton Preceramic efforts toward irrigation agriculture and a concomitant increase in emphasis on cultivated plants. New staple species of beans and peanuts were added to the diet and plant food production increased. Yet contact with the coast was still maintained by the establishment of the coastal colony or satellite of Tortugas which enjoyed a symbiotic relationship with Pampa de las Llamas–Moxeke, supplying marine resources in return for plant cultigens.

By the early Initial Period, organizational principles and evidence of intersite and intrasite hierarchies had become developed to the point where Pampa de las Llamas–Moxeke can be argued to be the center of a simple theocratic state. The planned layout of larger structures at the site in combination with the number and agglutinated configuration of the smallest houses indicate that the site is an urban settlement of about 3000 people. The linear site arrangement with large mounds along a central axis reveals that construction proceeded according to a predesigned plan. Clear differences between the two main mounds, the smaller mounds, and the agglutinated domestic architectural units indicate the possibility of three separate status distinctions within the site and polity. The existence of the coastal site of Tortugas also provides evidence of an intersite hierarchy. Localized stone bowl distribution within Pampa de las Llamas–Moxeke suggests an area of craft specialization. Finally, the two large mounds which dominate the site, the friezes which adorn Moxeke, and the orientation of the small mounds toward the central axis indicate that rule of the Pampa de las Llamas–Moxeke polity was dominated by religion.

Radiocarbon dates argue for the contemporaneity of

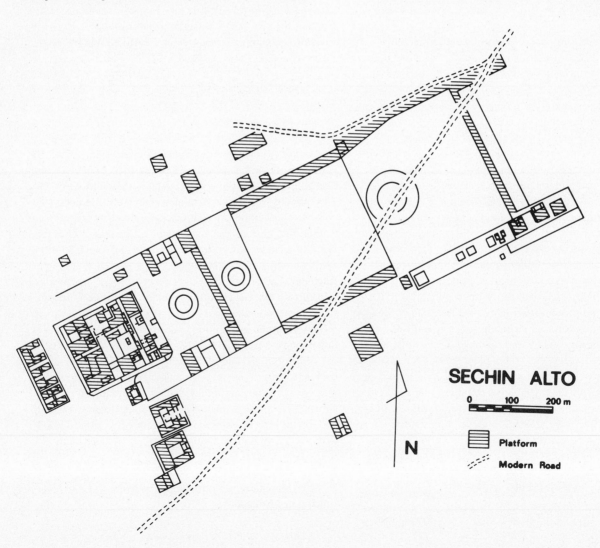

SECHIN ALTO

0   100   200 m

▦ Platform

- - - Modern Road

N

Fig. 3. Plan of Sechin Alto

pretemple Initial Period Las Haldas and the inland settlement of Pampa de las Llamas–Moxeke. However, since the artifact inventories, especially ceramics and textiles, are markedly dissimilar, it appears that pretemple Las Haldas was not closely affiliated with the Pampa de las Llamas–Moxeke polity. More likely, it was linked with Sechin Alto, an inland mound center which exhibited strong ties with the Las Haldas temple later in the Initial Period. Ceramic collections at the Field Museum of Natural History from Collier and Thompson's excavations at Sechin Alto (Carlevato 1979:166–168) contain examples from mound fill that are quite similar to the Las Haldas sample, along with a single sherd of Pampa de las Llamas–Moxeke type ceramics. Furthermore, looting has exposed a conical adobe core with frieze remnants which provides evidence of a Moxeke-like construction phase at Sechin Alto. These data in combination with a carbon 14 date of 1450 ± 100 B.C. (Berger *et al.* 1965:347) from mound fill at Sechin Alto indicate that an early phase of the site coexisted with the Pampa de las Llamas–Moxeke polity and pretemple Las Haldas.

The picture that emerges from these data is a pair of contemporary early Initial Period polities existing side by side in the two branches of the Casma River Valley. Based on evidence from Pampa de las Llamas–Moxeke, which was relatively unaltered in later times, an Initial Period pattern emerges whereby an inland mound center is associated with a much smaller coastal community. This symbiotic relationship is well documented for Pampa de las Llamas–Moxeke and Tortugas and strongly suggested for Las Haldas and Sechin Alto. Archaeological evidence from Pampa de las Llamas–Moxeke argues for a simple theocratically oriented state-level of organizational complexity, and both the size of the pretemple Las Haldas settlement and the probability of early monumental construction phases at Sechin Alto indicate that a polity of comparable magnitude existed in the Sechin branch as well.

Late Initial Period

During a relatively brief time span toward the end of the Initial Period, the polity centered at Sechin Alto in the Sechin branch of the Casma River Valley underwent a dramatic florescence. At this time, the largest Initial Period temple mound known for the Andean area was constructed along with subsidiary mound-oriented communities which are significant sites in their own right. The late Initial Period in Casma saw the construction of the final temple form at Las Haldas and Sechin Alto and the creation of the new sites of Sechin Bajo and Taukachi-Konkán.

Casma Valley late Initial Period sites

Sechin Alto. Clearly, by virtue of the magnitude of its late Initial Period construction, the mound complex of Sechin Alto was the central site in a state-level polity. The site lies within the limits of modern cultivation, yet remains visible after about 2500 years of local agriculture and still covers almost 2 sq. km (Figures 1 and 3). The central mound measures 250 m by 300 m

LAS HALDAS

0   50   100 m

▤ Platform

N

Fig. 4. Plan of Las Haldas

by 35 m high and numerous smaller mounds are clearly visible. In front of the main mound are a series of rectangular plazas, at least two of which contain circular forecourts. The plaza/forecourt association plus the alignment of subsidiary mounds parallel to the central site axis is reminiscent of Pampa de las Llamas–Moxeke. It is likely that a comparable urban support population is buried beneath the centuries of agricultural silt, and traces of Initial Period houses along the valley margins south of the site support this interpretation.

Late Initial Period Las Haldas. Simultaneously with the final construction of Sechin Alto, the currently visible Las Haldas temple was constructed (Figure 4). Taking advantage of the low hill, the builders created a linear arrangement of a main mound and series of plazas with a sunken circular forecourt that duplicates the Sechin Alto pattern. More complete excavation data for Las Haldas (Fung 1969; Grieder 1975; Ishida *et al.* 1960:194–197, 444–447; Matsuzawa 1978) reveal the existence of two construction phases for the main temple, with the east side temple and possible other associated mound structures created during the earlier phase. The total time of construction, however, was brief, for there is no noticeable accumulation of midden clearly associated with temple use. This corroborates Grieder's (1975:102–103) observation that the final temple construction was left unfinished.

Taukachi-Konkán. The site of Taukachi-Konkán lies slightly northwest of Sechin Alto on a plain at the edge of the Sechin River Valley (Figure 1). Though these were initially treated as two sites (Thompson 1961:211–217), investigators currently recognize connections across the pampa (Fung and Williams 1977:116–118), and all have compared its form with Sechin Alto (Fung and Williams 1977:116; Thompson 1961:217). Lying outside of cultivation, Taukachi-Konkán furnishes evidence of features not preserved at the larger site. Like Sechin Alto, Taukachi-Konkán consists of a central mound with associated plazas and sunken circles extending off the front in a linear orientation equal to Sechin Alto (Figure 5). Structures paralleling the main axis are present; and examples at the northeast end of the site are elaborate and have associated plazas and/or sunken circles. Like the Las Haldas temple, there is evidence at Taukachi-Konkán that construction was not completed before abandonment. At both ends of the

site are mounded areas of earth which are integral to the site layout, but which lack the stone facing characteristic of finished structures at the site. Areas of domestic architecture and midden which accompany extended site use are also absent. Taukachi-Konkán has been assigned a late Initial Period date solely on the basis of architectural similarities to Sechin Alto, Las Haldas and other early mound sites. Neither the efforts of earlier investigators nor our survey yielded associated early sherds, but there is general agreement on the early date (Fung and Williams 1977:116; Tello 1956:75; Thompson 1961:217). This paucity of both ceramic evidence and the remains of domestic occupation is a further indication that the site was rapidly constructed and probably never truly inhabited.

Sechin Bajo. The mound-dominated site of Sechin Bajo lies north of the Sechin River in the plain immediately west of the clearing occupied by Taukachi-Konkán (Figure 1). The main structure measures 150 m by 110 m by 16 m high. It is symmetrical along a central axis with an orientation that coincides with Sechin Alto and Taukachi-Konkán (Figure 6). Though obscured by later occupation of the area and cultivation, two sunken circles and pair of wings bordering a rectangular plaza are visible on air photographs. Like

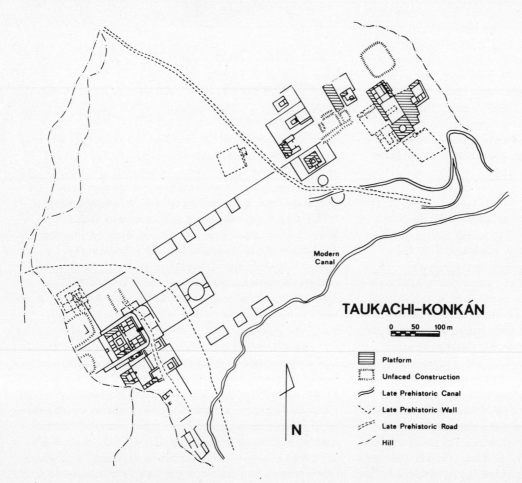

TAUKACHI-KONKÁN

0   50   100 m

▦ Platform

▨ Unfaced Construction

∿ Late Prehistoric Canal

⌐ Late Prehistoric Wall

= Late Prehistoric Road

— Hill

N

Fig. 5. Plan of Taukachi-Konkán

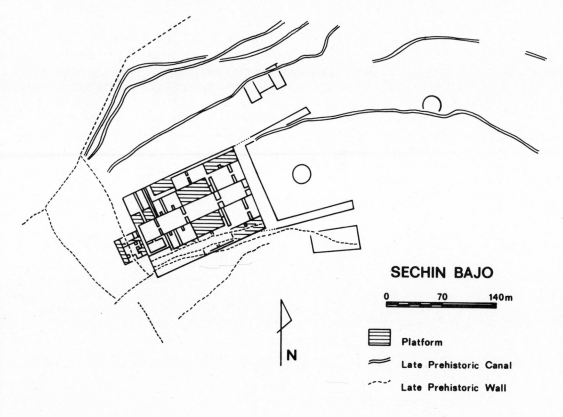

SECHIN BAJO

| 0   70   140 m |

⊞ **Platform**

〰 **Late Prehistoric Canal**

- - - **Late Prehistoric Wall**

Fig. 6. Plan of Sechin Bajo

Taukachi-Konkán, major portions of the Sechin Bajo main mound are unfaced and thus probably unfinished, suggesting that construction at Sechin Bajo was also never completed. The absence of parallel small mound structures and domestic occupation indicates that construction at Sechin Bajo had progressed little beyond the establishment of the main mound when the site was abandoned. Also like Taukachi-Konkán, the dating of Sechin Bajo is based on architectural similarities with other early sites because Sechin Bajo lacks associated early ceramics (Thompson 1961:224). These factors argue that construction efforts at Sechin Bajo were brief and that no substantial residential population had become associated.

Late Initial Period development within the Casma Valley

Late Initial Period development within the Casma is clearly an outgrowth of immediately preceding conditions within the valley. However, by late Initial Period times, the Casma Valley no longer contained two nearly equal coexisting polities. Instead, the polity centered at Sechin Alto had bounded ahead. Ties to the early Initial Period are readily evident: (1) coastal–inland symbiosis continued; (2) large central mounds dominated each site; and (3) central mounds were associated with rectangular plazas and sunken circular courts in a linear arrangement that was paralleled by lateral site structures. Thus, the late Initial Period Sechin Alto polity can

be characterized as a more complex theocratic state than the early Initial Period polities of both Sechin Alto and Pampa de las Llamas–Moxeke.

Temple mound construction on the north Peruvian coast was at its apogee during late Initial Period Casma Valley development. The Sechin Alto main mound, the size of 15 football fields in area, provides physical evidence of massive corporate labor recruitment. Successively smaller associated mounds argue for an intrasite status hierarchy with at least three to four levels including the main mound and the domestic occupation. Clearly, Sechin Alto is closely related to Taukachi-Konkán and Sechin Bajo; the three sites share a common orientation and configuration (Fung and Williams 1977:111–156). It is possible that all three are part of a single large settlement now interrupted by modern cultivation, but each is treated here as a separate site. The construction of these two mound centers plus the Las Haldas temple in late Initial Period times provides evidence of an intersite hierarchy of at least three levels. Finally, the unfinished construction and lack of occupation residues at the sites of Las Haldas, Taukachi-Konkán and Sechin Bajo argue that the late Initial Period florescence was brief and abruptly truncated, causing the abandonment of the site. No radiocarbon dates are available for this brief period, but dates from other Casma Valley sites which bracket the occupation suggest that it occurred about 1000 B.C.

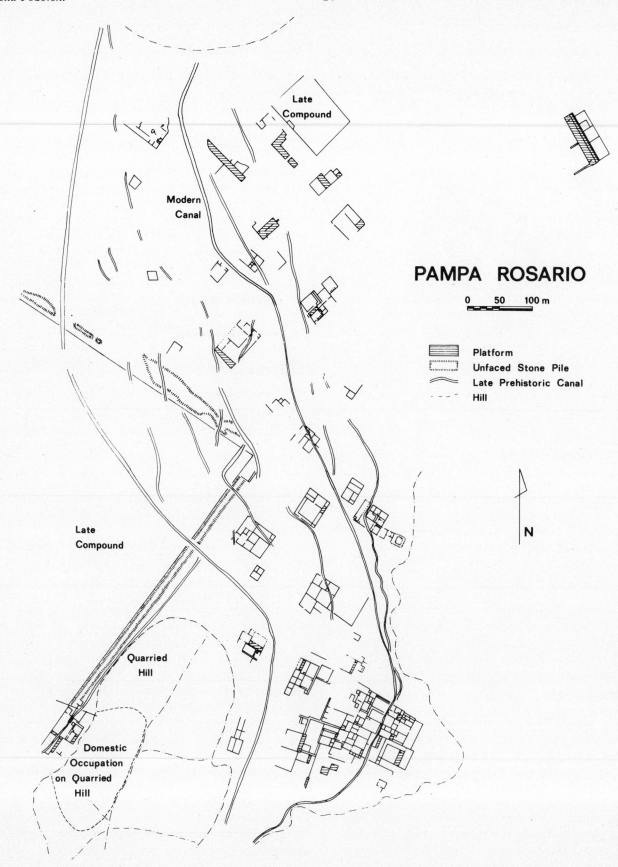

Fig. 7. Plan of Pampa Rosario

Early Horizon

Shortly after 1000 B.C., at a time which roughly corresponds to the beginning of the Early Horizon (900 to 200 B.C.), the Casma Valley saw the influx of a secular, militaristic, state-level society which effectively truncated existing Casma Valley Initial Period development. Sudden changes are observable in ceramics, the subsistence inventory, and architectural configuration – largely as a result of the introduction of new ideas. The suddenness of the change suggests invasion and conquest – a phenomenon commemorated at the site of Cerro Sechin. Initially, the existing sites of Sechin Alto, Pampa de las Llamas–Moxeke and Las Haldas were reoccupied, but the new sites of Pampa Rosario and San Diego were soon built.

Casma Valley Early Horizon sites
Reoccupation of Sechin Alto and Pampa de las Llamas–Moxeke. The surface of the main mound of Sechin Alto is a confusion of small rooms which bear no relationship to the central axis of the site (Figure 3). This area yielded a ceramic collection which correlates with ceramics from single component Early Horizon Casma Valley sites. A similar intrusive phenomenon can be observed on the Moxeke mound of Pampa de las Llamas–Moxeke, although alteration of the mound surface was not so severe.

Reoccupation of Las Haldas. Las Haldas provides the clearest evidence of post-temple reoccupation during the Early Horizon. Without regard to the site's prior function as a temple, the new inhabitants robbed building stones from the extant structures to construct small agglutinated shelters. These rested upon plaza surfaces in areas where the main mound's bulk afforded protection from the coastal breezes. Midden associated with the desecration overlies staircases and other architectural features of the temple. Excavations in this midden revealed that sea urchin test fragments, chiton plates, and charred marine algae are dominant within the refuse whereas ceramics and cultivated plants are relatively rare. However, the first evidence of maize within the Casma Valley come from this cut. Published radiocarbon dates for this terminal occupation of Las Haldas are 880 ± 70 B.C., 780 ± 70 B.C. (Grieder 1975: 100, 109), 730 ± 150 B.C., and 410 ± 95 B.C. (Matsuzawa 1978:666), but the unusually late date has been questioned (Matsuzawa 1978:667). Recent assays for the same deposit range from 1040 ± 75 B.C. to 895 ± 80 B.C. (Table 1).

Pampa Rosario. The site of Pampa Rosario lies on a flat plain between the two branches of the Casma River some 16 km inland (Figure 1). Despite destruction by prehistoric and modern constructions, about 40 hectares of the site are preserved. It consists of over 20 structures interspersed with areas of midden up to 2 m or more deep (Figure 7). The predominant architectural pattern consists of narrow platforms reached by paired ramps and associated with small courtyards and additional contiguous rooms. Entrances are often baffled.

The structures appear to be largely domestic in function, but differences in size and elaboration suggest status differences between members of the site population. Only one small freestanding mound is present at Pampa Rosario near the northeast edge of the site.

The artifacts and subsistence remains at Pampa Rosario provide a clearer picture of the Casma Valley Early Horizon occupation than do potentially mixed samples from reoccupied sites. At this time a ceramic assemblage appears with vessel forms including neckless ollas, narrow-neck and flaring-rim jars, bowls, grater bowls, bottles, and jars with thick stirrup spouts. Panpipes, figurines, spindle whorls and reworked pottery discs also characterize the assemblage. Decorative techniques include circle and dot designs, exterior textile and net impressions, zoned white paint, zoned and unzoned punctuations, appliqué nobs and modeling. Interiors of constructed vessels were very roughly finished when the clay was nearly dry – resulting in irregular holes and cracks. This assemblage shares many characteristics with the Patazca style and associated pottery types described by Collier (1962:412). Other artifacts which are typical of the period include ground slate points and woven cotton textiles with blue and white geometric designs.

Several major species make their first appearance in Casma in the course of the Early Horizon. Camelids (probably llama) and guinea pigs are introduced, and the new cultigen, maize, occurs in large quantities. Shellfish and fish are still important in the diet, and most Initial Period cultigens continue in use. Except for manioc, tubers are very rare and *lúcuma* is virtually absent. Radiocarbon dates for Pampa Rosario are 810 ± 75 B.C., 585 ± 75 B.C. and 450 ± 70 B.C. (Table 1).

San Diego. Located in the Lower Casma Valley, San Diego is some 5.5 km from the Pacific Ocean (Figure 1). The site is virtually unaffected by later occupation and covers an area of 50 hectares (Figure 8). Architectural patterns duplicate the low mound courtyard structures of Pampa Rosario, but none of the San Diego complexes attains the size of the largest Pampa Rosario structures. The artifact inventories and subsistence remains are also the same at both sites except that the inhabitants of San Diego exploited mainly marine species for animal protein. Radiocarbon dates from San Diego range from 295 ± 60 B.C. to 560 ± 115 B.C. (Table 1) and further confirm the contemporaneity of the two sites while indicating that the initial occupation of Pampa Rosario may have occurred slightly earlier than that of San Diego.

Cerro Sechin. Cerro Sechin, the most famous Casma Valley site, lies between the two Casma Valley river branches and about 13 km from the ocean (Figure 1). The main structure, which is about 51 m square and about four m high, is ornamented by carved stone monoliths which adorn all four sides. Excavations beginning as early as 1937 cleared the main structure, an earlier conical adobe core structure, and outlying constructions (Bueno and Samaniego 1969; Collier 1962;

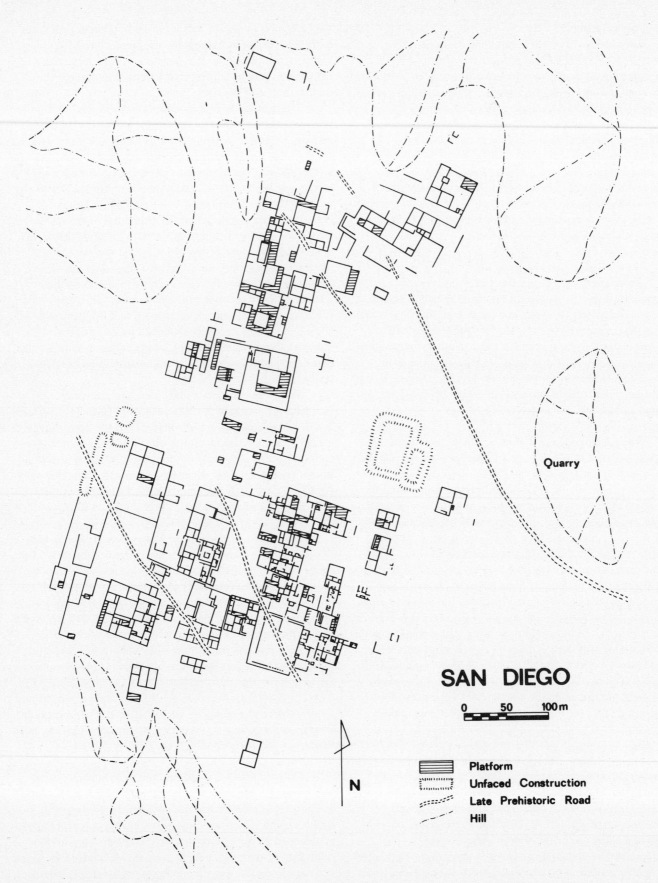

SAN DIEGO

0   50   100 m

N

▤ Platform

▦ Unfaced Construction

Late Prehistoric Road

Hill

Quarry

Fig. 8. Plan of San Diego

Samaniego 1973; Tello 1943: 1956). Despite these efforts, the chronological position of Cerro Sechin has not been firmly established. Ceramic collections from the site are generally without precise provenience, but early Casma Valley assemblages ranging from the early Initial Period through the Early Horizon are represented. Carbon 14 dates of 990 ± 120 B.C. and 770 ± 60 B.C. (Radiocarbon Dates Association, Inc. n.d.a) further confirm the Early Horizon occupation of the site. The clearly visible multiple construction phases confirm a long history for the site.

Early Horizon developments within the Casma Valley

Coincident with the beginning of the Early Horizon, the Casma Valley saw drastic changes in architecture, site layout, artifacts and subsistence that are best exploited as the results of the influx of a new group with a distinct set of values. Radiocarbon dates for post-temple Las Haldas indicate that this cultural intrusion involved reoccupation of major extant sites. Such a pattern may represent an effort to suppress firmly the Initial Period polity by desecrating its temples. The sites of Pampa Rosario and San Diego were soon established, and data from these centers provide the most comprehensive view of the conquering polity.

Early Horizon architectural configurations are completely different from those found in the Initial Period. Gone are the large mound-dominated sites oriented along a central axis. These theocratic complexes were replaced by room and platform complexes of a more secular nature with much less coincident orientations. Yet important architectural 'innovations' such as ramps and baffled entries were introduced. New artifact classes are also present, including ceramic forms such as panpipes, modes of ceramic decoration and distinct forms of stone and textile art. Maize was introduced and rapidly became a major staple, probably correlated with *chicha* production, as manifested in the manufacture of large ollas. Other cultigens declined in importance. The first evidence of domestic camelids and guinea pigs comes from these Early Horizon sites.

Despite the evidence from Pampa Rosario and San Diego, the question still remains as to whether the 'invasion through conquest' hypothesis best explains the Casma Valley data. Additional lines of evidence support this interpretation, however. First, key portions of the late Initial Period sites of Las Haldas, Taukachi-Konkán and Sechin Bajo were incomplete, indicating that building was abruptly interrupted before construction had been implemented as planned. This, in combination with the immediate desecration of the Las Haldas, Sechin Alto and Pampa de las Llamas–Moxeke mounds, suggests a scenario of sudden conquest and concomitant occupation of major centers of long tradition.

Cerro Sechin provides a second line of archaeological evidence favoring invasion. The monoliths of Cerro Sechin are most commonly interpreted as the commemoration of a battle (Alarco 1975:5; Bueno and Samaniego 1969:33; Jimenez 1969:39; Samaniego 1973:70–71). In his review of coastal

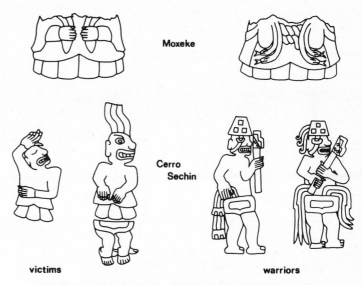

Fig. 9. Comparison of adobe friezes of Moxeke with the carved monoliths of Cerro Sechin. Note that the 'victims' at Cerro Sechin are dressed similarly to the Moxeke figures.

'Chavin' art, Roe (1974:34–36) describes similarities between the Moxeke friezes and the Cerro Sechin monoliths and places Moxeke earlier than Cerro Sechin on the basis of iconographic arguments. Since it is likely that the early central Cerro Sechin conical adobe temple with friezes was contemporaneous with Moxeke and the Sechin Alto adobe core, the outer temple of monoliths at Cerro Sechin would appear to postdate both Moxeke and Sechin Alto. Most important for this study are Roe's observations that the pleated kilt is common to figures at both sites (Figure 9), *and* the kilt appears *only* on defeated prisoner figures at Cerro Sechin (Roe 1974:34). With additional artifactual and radiocarbon dating evidence, it is possible to take these observations a step further and begin to interpret the Cerro Sechin monoliths. Pampa de las Llamas–Moxeke dates quite early in the Casma Valley sequence, and the continuity in dress (not just the pleated kilt, but also the scalloped tunic) between the friezes and the later Cerro Sechin prisoner figures supports the idea that the local Casma Valley population is being conquered by warriors from outside the zone. Cerro Sechin vividly depicts the nature of the conquerors' warfare, and such vicious practices as decapitation and mutilation would have been an effective tactic in bringing about the defeat of the nonmilitaristic Casma polity.

Finally, two major forts in the Casma Valley were established toward the end of the Early Horizon: the hilltop fort on Cerro Sechin and Chankillo. The latter exhibits architectural similarities with Pampa Rosario and San Diego in the form of a platform/room complex in the center, and radiocarbon dates of 342 ± 80 B.C. (Olson and Broecker 1959:22) and 120 ± 100 B.C. (Radiocarbon Dates Association, Inc., n.d.b) for the site reaffirm this chronological placement. Both fortifications are placed in the 'Late Formative' (late Early Horizon) by Thompson (1961:84–85, 87) who considers the local appearance of hilltop fortifications at that time as a complete innovation. Thus, in view of the different types of evidence, the changes in the Casma Valley during the Early Horizon are best explained by the arrival of a secular and militaristic group which conquered Casma, occupied the major sites, built their own settlements, commemorated their victory, and ultimately established fortifications.

Evidence of comparable development in other north-coast valleys

Though incomplete, archaeological data indicate that developments in the Casma Valley were generally paralleled in other Peruvian valleys of the north and central coast through the early part of the Initial Period. Subsequent events in Casma, however, exemplified by the polity centered at Sechin Alto, were of far greater magnitude than comparable developments elsewhere. Also, the most conclusive data for the ensuing Early Horizon invasion come from the Casma Valley. Nevertheless, evidence of its effects are much more far-reaching, and the degree of influence of the newly arrived ideas can be correlated with later state development on the north coast.

Cotton Preceramic Period

A large number of Cotton Preceramic sites comparable to the Casma Valley examples of Huaynuná and preceramic Las Haldas are known to exist along the Peruvian coast from Chicama to Omas (Engel 1957b; Moseley 1975a). These late preceramic sites are generally considered to be contemporary. Several examples such as Aspero (Feldman 1980; Moseley and Willey 1973), Rio Seco (Wendt 1964), and El Paraíso (Engel 1967) exhibit much greater architectural complexity than the Casma Valley examples, and their potential for contributing to subsequent Initial Period development is readily evident. Another important feature of Cotton Preceramic sites which only becomes apparent when one moves beyond the Casma Valley sample is the large number of characteristics shared by these coastal communities (Engel 1957b; Lanning 1967:60–61; S. Pozorski and T. Pozorski 1979a). These include common construction materials and techniques, similar technologies featuring such things as twined textiles, netting, and fishhooks, and generally coincident faunal and floral inventories which emphasize industrial plants. Moseley (1972:51–52) describes regular spacing between the large preceramic sites of the Ancon–Chillon region and argues for the control of local resources by each settlement. Such an interpretation, which may also apply to widely spaced large sites further north, indicates that adjacent settlements were well aware of each other. Shared traits, especially technological innovations which seem to have spread 'instantaneously,' argue strongly for developed communication networks between sites. This feature of the rapid flow of technologically useful ideas became increasingly important in later periods and ranks among the most important legacies of the Cotton Preceramic (see chapter by T. Pozorski and S. Pozorski, this volume).

Initial Period

Many features documented for the Initial Period in Casma are paralleled by developments in other valleys. The most important of these is the change in settlement pattern characterized by the establishment of major inland sites which are far larger and more complex than preceding coastal settlements. The sequence was first documented from the Ancon–Chillon region by Patterson and Moseley (1968; Moseley 1974) who also proposed that canal irrigation was the mitigating factor. A similar sequence of events occurred in the Moche Valley (S. Pozorski 1976; S. Pozorski and T. Pozorski 1979b; T. Pozorski 1976), where results are especially comparable to the Casma Valley situation because of the economic symbiosis between Caballo Muerto and Gramalote. Inland early mound sites are known from virtually all north and central coast valleys and, although precise data are not available, their existence suggests that the change to an emphasis on irrigation agriculture was rapid and widespread (S. Pozorski and T. Pozorski 1979b).

Other technological innovations, most notably ceramics and woven textiles, also spread rapidly along the coast. However, data from sites such as Pampa de las Llamas–Moxeke and Gramalote where twined textiles were slow to disappear (Conklin 1974; S. Pozorski and T. Pozorski 1979b), provide evidence that some major innovations were adopted at slightly different rates. Early inland sites also share important architectural patterns of site alignment along a central axis and the presence and form of major mounds. Yet despite the shared traits which make it possible to classify a site, a mound, a ceramic, or other features as 'early,' sufficient differences exist between Initial Period settlements in different valleys to indicate that similarities can be attributed to intervalley communication and not direct domination of one valley over many.

A crucial difference between Casma and the other coastal valleys becomes physically apparent near the end of the Initial Period. At this time the polity centered at Sechin Alto experienced a growth spurt not equalled on the Peruvian coast. Increasingly larger mounds may have been constructed in other valleys, but none approached Sechin Alto in size. The size of the labor force employed to construct simultaneously Las Haldas, Taukachi-Konkán, Sechin Bajo and the terminal phase of Sechin Alto argues for centralized control with allegiances strong enough to mobilize a labor force from outside the Casma Valley. Unfortunately, archaeological data are not available to test whether this intervalley linkage is reflected in architecture, ceramics, or other artifacts. Because of its size and complexity, the polity entered at Sechin Alto drew the focus of the Early Horizon intrusion into the coast, whereas other valleys, with smaller polities, were less directly affected.

Early Horizon and the early part of the Early Intermediate Period

Although Cotton Preceramic and especially early Initial Period developments along much of the north and north central

Peruvian coast generally paralleled the situation in Casma, an examination of data on Early Horizon and early Early Intermediate Period (200 B.C. to 0 B.C./A.D.) developments indicates major regional differences. Two groupings of valleys can be distinguished on the basis of the success of the invading polity in its conquest.

In the immediate vicinity of Casma, data from the valleys of Huarmey and Nepeña indicate that both were dominated and occupied by the polity which invaded Casma. Information from Huarmey is sketchy, but Thompson (1966) reports similar ceramics and site types, especially hilltop fortifications. The Early Horizon time period is much better known in Nepeña, where Daggett (1982a) has reported hilltop platform mound sites on ridges extending from above Jimbe down to about 200 m above sea level. Most were habitation sites, but examples with either a 'ceremonial' or defensive function are more common downvalley. Also downvalley, only 10 km from the coast, is the sprawling valley floor settlement of Caylán, which shares significant architectural features with Pampa Rosario and San Diego (Kosok 1965: Figures 20, 21:208–209; Proulx 1968:71–72). Also, the Nepeña hilltop sites and Caylán have artifact assemblages virtually identical to collections from the Early Horizon Casma Valley sites (see chapter by Daggett, this volume). Despite incomplete data from the Huarmey and upper Casma Valleys, similarities in artifacts, settlement pattern, and site types argue for the unification of at least the Nepeña, Casma and Huarmey Valleys under the militaristic group which probably first penetrated to the coast via Casma at the beginning of the Early Horizon.

Major changes also occurred in the Santa, Viru and Moche Valleys north of Casma, and these changes are both a response to and a result of occurrences further south. A time lag between developments in Casma and the northern valleys indicates that influences were moving gradually north. Settlement pattern studies in Santa (Wilson 1985) and Viru (Willey 1953) document a clustering of settlements in the upper reaches of both valleys during the late Early Horizon and early Early Intermediate Period (Willey 1953:61–101; Wilson 1985). Agglutinated habitation settlements and hilltop fortifications first appear at this time, and most forts are in the upper reaches on the south sides of both valleys. Additionally, Viru and possibly Santa contain valley floor mound sites dating to this time period. In Moche, Early Horizon settlement patterns are essentially unchanged, but by early Early Intermediate Period times, the Moche Valley contained a substantial upvalley occupation including at least two valley floor mound sites and the very large lower valley agglutinated settlement of Cerro Arena (Brennan 1978, 1982; Mujica 1975). T. Topic and J. Topic (1982) found no true forts in the Moche Valley at this time, but they describe an early Early Intermediate Period occupation at both the base and top of a steep hill and suggest that the defensible location was important despite the absence of defensive architecture (T. Topic and J. Topic 1982:3–4). Finally, isolated artifactual evidence from north of Casma – such as panpipes in Santa (Wilson 1985), ground slate blades at Cerro Arena (Brennan 1978:669–672; Mujica 1975:312–325), and a few ceramic types at late Early Horizon Caballo Muerto mounds (T. Pozorski 1976) – documents communication and selective adoption of traits, but not intervalley control of the type described from Nepeña to Huarmey.

Conclusions

Data from Early Horizon and early Early Intermediate Period sites in valleys from Huarmey to Moche indicate that: (1) Casma, the most highly developed of the coastal Initial Period polities, was conquered and along with Nepeña and Huarmey came under the control of a highland-based secular state. (2) In the Nepeña–Casma–Huarmey zone of direct control, strong local theocratic traditions were devastated and new settlement patterns and lifestyles were imposed. (3) The valleys north of Casma were not dominated by the polity which took over the Casma area. (4) The forts in the upper reaches and on the southern borders of the Santa and Viru Valleys were a successful defense against this conquest. (5) Despite the apparent conflict, numerous innovations which appeared in the north parallel changes brought about by the invasion of Casma. (6) However, further north, where influence was less, survival of earlier local traditions was more evident.

To summarize the north and north central coast Early Horizon and early Early Intermediate Period situation, there are two parallel, but interacting developments. The Nepeña–Casma–Huarmey area saw the settling in and development on the coast of an arm of a polity that was probably highland in origin. Clues are scanty, but evidence of similar ceramics and artifacts from the upper reaches of Nepeña (Richard Daggett, personal communication) and in the few inland Casma Valley sites known (Fung and Williams 1977; Tello 1956) plus Sechin-like stone carvings from the Callejón de Huaylas (Thompson 1962b) argue for a sierra source. The clustering of forts in the upper Santa and Viru Valleys supports this interpretation. Valleys immediately north of Casma apparently successfully resisted the intrusion by constructing fortifications, a new site type probably inspired by the invading polity. As far north as the Moche Valley, the virtual absence of contemporary fortifications suggests that no real threat was felt so far from the penetration to the coast in Casma.

In the absence of external control, local traditions continued to develop. Early Horizon and early Early Intermediate Period mound sites and continuous ceramic sequences are evidence of this. However, influence from the south filtered through, resulting in occasional new artifact types and especially the secular agglutinated settlement type whereby a population concentration exists without benefit of a central mound. The best example of this is Cerro Arena in the Moche Valley, which has been cited as the precursor to the later north coast Moche and Chimu states (Brennan 1980). Data from Casma and the intervening valleys north to Moche indicate a possible reason for the rise of successive states in the Moche Valley. At that locus, a *blending* of older local (coastal) theocratic principles and new ideas of militarism and secularism was possible because the influx of these new ideas was not so directly felt or devastating as in valleys such as Casma further south.

Overall, the Casma Valley data illustrate the very early emergence of centralized preceramic chiefdom societies along the Pacific coast. These chiefdoms were dependent upon the exploitation of marine resources augmented by limited cultivation of cotton and supplementary foodstuffs. Following this initial emergence of relatively complex, nonegalitarian societies, evolution in the Casma Valley proceeded rapidly. In the Initial Period, there was a movement inland which was concomitant with an irrigation-based agricultural subsistence strategy and the evolution of much more complex, theocratically oriented state type societies. This emergent state organization then effloresced into a major consolidated polity, which was unequaled anywhere in Peru at this time period. This consolidated state, centered at Sechin Alto, commanded the allegiance of adjacent valleys and still maintained its theocratic orientation. How this multi-valley state would have subsequently evolved is unfortunately unknown, since it was conquered by a foreign power and replaced by a much more secular, militaristic form of government.

When compared with developments in other parts of Peru, the Casma Valley sequence demonstrates that there was considerable local variability in the evolution of states in the Andean region. Thus, while warfare and militarism appear to have played causal roles in the emergence of some states along the coast (see chapters by Wilson and Daggett, this volume), these variables played highly secondary roles in the long-term development of the state in Casma. In place of warfare, irrigation and religion appear to have played interacting roles in bringing about the origin of the state in Casma.

Chapter 3

The exercise of power in early Andean state development

Jonathan Haas

Introduction

Unlike a majority of South American archaeologists, I believe that the state form of organization first arises in the Andean region no later than the end of the Initial Period or very beginning of the Early Horizon (Haas 1982). Its appearance is marked by a number of sites along the Peruvian coast which are characterized by truly monumental architecture. Specific sites that to me serve as early state markers include: La Florida in the Rimac Valley, Caballo Muerto in the Moche Valley, Sechin Alto in the Casma Valley (see chapter by S. Pozorski, this volume), and possibly Garagay in the Chillon Valley. I do not believe that these are the *only* manifestations of early states on the coast, but they are the sites best described in the literature. All of these sites contain elaborate ceremonial complexes and architecture of a significantly greater magnitude than anything that came before (Pozorski 1980; Matsuzawa 1978; Burger 1981; Moseley 1975a). Why then do I make this seemingly simplistic equation between monumental architecture and the state, when everyone else seems to be out looking for site size hierarchies, information exchange systems and patterns of consolidation through conquest?

Basically, it is because I think that the appearance of monumental architecture on the coast also marks the appearance of a new kind of power relationship between coastal rulers and their subordinate populations. I agree with Feldman (this volume) that the mounds at Aspero, for example, which range up to 6000 cu m in volume, mark the centralized authority structure of a chiefdom. But there are serious problems with the notion that only 200 years later, this same organizational structure was capable of engineering the construction of Huaca La Florida, with a volume of over 400 000 cu m (Kosok 1965; Lanning 1967; Lumbreras 1974a). While a number of scholars have argued that chiefdoms are capable of carrying out labor projects of equal or greater magnitude to the La Florida construction (e.g., Price 1977; Sanders and Price 1968; Renfrew 1973a), I have yet to find a single ethnographic or ethnohistoric case cited of such monumental construction taking place within the context of a bona fide chiefdom. There are numerous cases of Aspero-sized labor projects in chiefdoms, but nothing much larger. There are, of course, numerous ethnographic cases of truly monumental construction, but they are *invariably* in the context of a *state* form of organization. From Washington's monument to the Pyramids of Giza, from the Great Wall of China to Winchester Cathedral, monumental architecture occurs in state societies. Although it is certainly theoretically possible that there are cases of chiefdoms carrying out monumental labor projects, they have never been cited by those who argue that such projects are within the capability of a chiefdom. (In his discussion, Webb (this volume) brings up several cases of monumental construction in supposed *prehistoric* chiefdoms;

however, the inference that these were indeed chiefdoms rather than states requires a leap of faith.) Given the myriad cases of monumental construction in states and the dearth of such cases in chiefdoms, therefore, it is not unreasonable to infer that when such construction is encountered in the archaeological record, we are much more likely to be dealing with a state than a chiefdom.

This inference need not be based on negative evidence alone, however, because if we ask why state leaders can get their people to build giant edifices while chieftains cannot, it becomes apparent that the reason lies in the nature of the leader/population power relationship in the two kinds of societies. Specifically, in states, leaders exercise far greater power and more coercive power than in chiefdoms. What then is the basis for the major increase in the power exercised by state leaders? The answer, I believe, is to be found in the process of state formation itself. In looking at all the different theories offered to explain state formation, including warfare, irrigation and exchange models, we find that in each case, emergent state rulers exercise control over either the production or procurement of certain basic resources for that society (Wittfogel 1957; Webb 1975; Webster 1975; Wright and Johnson 1975; Haas 1982). This type of control, a common characteristic in modern and historic states, is not a trait of chiefdoms. In the latter, the leaders may gain control over resources through redistribution, but they do not control directly or indirectly the actual production or procurement activities (see, for example, Ferdon 1981; Drucker 1965; Middleton 1965; Service 1971, 1975). Thus, from the very beginning, emergent state leaders have a new, qualitatively greater kind of economic power base not found in chiefdoms. Furthermore, this economic power base can be exploited to allow the state leaders to develop or enlarge both military and ideological power bases; thereby increasing the 'power gap' between states and chiefdoms. The early monumental architecture, seen on the coast of Peru as well as in many other parts of the world, is then a physical manifestation of an emergent state power structure.

If, for the sake of argument, we can accept the idea that power is the primary variable distinguishing states from chiefdoms, then looking at the nature of the power structure in different state societies provides a direct means of measuring and understanding patterns of similarities and differences in those societies. Considerable insight can be gained into parallels and divergences in the organization and appearance of various Andean states by looking at the kind of power being exercised by the rulers and at the derivation of that power. In particular, the 'precociousness' of state development on the coast and the long delay in state development in the highlands can be better understood when the sources, or 'bases,' of power available to rulers in the two different areas are examined.

In looking at power in virtually any prehistoric state, we see that there are three alternative bases of power that may be exploited by early state rulers. The first is the economic base, which is derived from control over production and/or procurement of resources. The second is an ideological base, which is derived from control over iconography, ceremonial activities and religious paraphernalia. The third is a physical base derived from control over a specialized military and/or police force. Thus within the early state the leaders may be expected to have played varying roles as managers, priests and generals. This is not to say, however, that in each and every state all three power bases *must* be manifested, nor *must* there be a specialized managerial class separate from a priesthood and separate from a military general staff. Rather, economics, religion and the military simply serve as avenues to power open to the early state rulers, and manager, priest and general are the possible power roles that may be found in some combination in the early states. For example, it should be possible to have a state in which combined manager/priests exercised economic and ideological power but not physical power over their population. At the same time, a more complex polity might have trade merchants, irrigation managers, priests, generals and a chief of police all constituting subcomponents of a royal ruler's power structure.

As I have discussed the different power bases and their archaeological manifestations at much greater length elsewhere (Hass 1982) I would like to turn to a brief comparative view of power relationships in early Andean states. I would also like to concentrate not so much on specific cultures, but on general cross-cultural patterns and on new kinds of problem areas that arise when power becomes a focus of research.

The first real manifestations of leader/follower power relationships in the Andean area come toward the end of the third millennium B.C. These are marked by the appearance of fairly large-scale public architecture at highland sites such as Kotosh and La Galgada and coastal sites such as Aspero and El Paraíso (Izumi 1971; Moseley 1975a; Grieder and Bueno 1981; Feldman 1977, this volume). As mentioned earlier, architecture such as this appears to fall within the realm of known chiefdoms, but it nevertheless does reflect the exercise of power by leaders over followers. People simply do not go out and merrily build platform mounds without being told to do so by some authority figure. As regards the power base of these early leaders, the public building sites, both in the highlands and on the coast, have a strong ceremonial orientation. Thus, if they served as ceremonial centers for a surrounding population, leaders at these sites would have had a potential ideological base for exercising power. But was ideological power, based on control over ceremonial activities, sufficient to gain the obedience of the population for mound building? On the basis of evidence from other sites in both areas as well as from other parts of the world, the answer to this question is probably 'no.'

Specifically, there are other contemporaneous highland and coastal sites, such as Huaricoto and the preceramic occupation at the Tank Site, which have been interpreted as ceremonial centers but lack public architecture of a magnitude equal to that found on the other sites (Burger and Burger 1980; Moseley 1975a). The implication to be drawn from this pattern is that the leaders at Aspero, Kotosh, etc. had some additional base of power which allowed them to extract greater amounts of labor out of their respective populations. In certain cases, the additional power appears to have been economic and was based on control over limited pieces of productive land and the resources that came off that land. Aspero and El Paraíso on the coast, for example, are adjacent to arable river floodplains, whereas the Tank Site is more than 15 km from such land. In the highlands, the situation is less clear. Although both Kotosh and La Galgada are adjacent to productive river land, Huaricoto is not significantly removed from such land. Thus in the highlands, control over productive land does not appear to have provided an exploitable economic power base for societal leaders. A more likely, though essentially untested possibility is that the leaders at the public architecture sites were somehow tied into a long-distance trade network. By then controlling the procurement of desirable resources these leaders would have had a supplementary economic power base.

Whether or not this specific hypothesis is correct, there is still a clear pattern emerging in the Andean region at the end of the Preceramic Period in which leaders are exercising a combination of ideological and some form of economic power over their populations. This pattern then sets the stage for the first appearance of the state in the Andean region. Significantly, the appearance comes on the coast but not in the highlands. Why? Basically, the conditions for the pristine or endogenous development of a state-level economic power base are present on the coast during the second millennium B.C., but are essentially absent in the highlands. The specific conditions present on the coast and lacking in the highlands are a critical demand for arable land and environmental circumstances ripe for the development of centralized irrigation.

On the coast during the Initial Period and beginning of the Early Horizon, a shift to increased plant domestication and the initiation of water control provided an avenue for the emergence of a new economic base for exerting power. At the monumental architecture sites such as La Florida, Caballo Muerto and Sechin Alto, there is a physical move inland, and direct or indirect evidence of a new dependence on domesticated plants grown by means of irrigation (Moseley 1975a; MacNeish *et al.* 1975; S. Pozorski and T. Pozorski 1979b). Given at least the potential if not the absolute necessity for centralized control over an irrigation system, it seems likely that the move inland provided existing leaders a means to gain control over the actual production of new critical domesticated resources. Thus, irrigation provides a new *source* of economic power which helps explain the dramatically increased *exercise* of power manifested in the monumental architecture at these sites.

Supplementing this emergent economic base, ideology continued to be exploited as an alternative base of power. In fact, the overt physical manifestations of religious themes indicate that exploitation of ideology has increased significantly during this period. At all of the monumental architecture sites, the monuments are closely associated with large ceremonial complexes and elaborate religious artwork. At Caballo Muerto,

for example, the large platform mound of Huaca de los Reyes is composed of an intricate ceremonial complex of rooms and plazas, with the latter being decorated with an impressive series of adobe friezes (T. Pozorski 1980). The magnitude and visibility of this kind of religious art far exceeds anything yet uncovered from preceramic sites.

It should be pointed out at this juncture that state polities with the combined economic/ideological power structure did not spring up simultaneously and homogenously all up and down the coast. Rather, similar irrigation-based states seem to have evolved in one or two valleys along the central coast and up on the north coast. Other valleys, such as Viru, appear to have lagged behind on the evolutionary ladder; while still others, such as possibly Nepeña (Daggett 1982b), may have taken a more militaristic route to statehood. However, I believe that once the very first states had arisen on the coast, *all* subsequent development must be looked at as secondary, and must be examined from a regional perspective which includes both highlands and coastal zones (see Price 1977).

If we take this regional perspective and at the same time look at power, available evidence seems to indicate that further stimulus and development of the state in the Andes involved direct interaction between coastal valleys and highland zones. This interaction could have taken two different forms: (a) through economic exchange, following a form of verticality model; or (b) through warfare. Arguments could be made, for example, following the various economic models (see, for example, Childe 1951; Rathje 1971, 1972; Wright and Johnson 1975) that highland areas ultimately became organized along state lines in order to import critical resources or to manage the specialized production of resources within their zones. While such an organizational change conceivably could arise endogenously, as has been argued for southwestern Iran (Johnson 1973; Wright and Johnson 1975), it seems highly unlikely that the highland Andean polities could have evolved without some form of economic interaction with existing states on the coast. This is particularly the case given that there was substantial economic exchange going on between the coast and the highlands long before even a hint of state development in either area (MacNeish *et al.* 1975).

Aside from economic exchange, another argument could be made to the effect that after the first states had arisen on the coast, warfare provided a secondary avenue for state development in both the highlands and on the coast. Following the warfare models of Malcolm Webb (1975) and David Webster (1975), societies in either area may have found themselves subject to localized resource shortages and/or to predation from the outside, and consolidated into a state form of organization in order effectively to compete militarily with their geographical neighbors. The pattern David Wilson (this volume) uncovered in the Santa Valley, for example, would appear to fit this scenario. Again, it is *possible* but not likely that such consolidation could occur within interaction with outside states. The emergence of a centralized state power structure in any area gives that particular polity a distinct organizational advantage in conducting both offensive and defensive operations against prestate opponents. Furthermore, faced with less well-organized neighbors, it is not unreasonable to hypothesize that the early state rulers would have exploited their advantages through either intensified raiding or conquest. Thus, the military superiority of the few early coastal states would have served as a direct impetus for the secondary development of state forms of organization in adjacent valleys and highland zones. Of course the extent of interaction between the earliest states and other societies must be determined empirically, but I believe it will be difficult if not impossible to explain Peruvian state development after 1000 B.C. fully without looking at it as secondary evolutionary development.

To turn now from the initial stages of state formation to subsequent stages of state development, power continues to provide a useful framework for understanding similarities and differences in the evolution of Andean states. In particular, the combined economic/ideological power base of the early rulers comes to be augmented by the addition of a physical base in almost all subsequent states. Whether or not warfare was a primary causal variable in the *origin* of Andean states, it unquestionably effected long-term state *development* by introducing a major new physical power base. Beginning in the Early Horizon and intensifying in the Early Intermediate, the appearance of specialized fortifications, weaponry and militaristic art indicates that armies were becoming commonplace in the Andes (see chapter by J. Topic and T. Topic, this volume). While such armed forces had an overt role in carrying out warfare with foreign enemies, they would nevertheless have provided a strong physical component to a state's ruling power structure. Scholars throughout western history have pointed out that soldiers trained to fight abroad can be used quite effectively to maintain control over a home population.

The addition of the physical base carries with it certain implications with regard to the manifestations of the other two bases. First, it establishes a 'triadic' power structure, which is organizationally more stable than the earlier 'dyadic' structure. Economic sanctions can now be backed up with both physical and supernatural or ideological sanctions, and religion and the military can be used to reinforce each other. Thus, the interaction of three different bases provides a much stronger foundation for enforcing the decisions and demands of the ruling elite. Second, with the addition of a physical base the importance of the ideological base diminishes. Basically, with an army around to back up a ruler's edicts, there will be less need to apply the ideological base positively by convincing the population of the 'rightness' of those edicts or negatively by threatening supernatural sanctions to gain compliance. Finally, an army, particularly a successful army, not only provides a physical power base, but also supplements the economic base by either bringing new land under control or by capturing new resources from outside systems. Particularly during times of expansionist warfare, then, the economic base of the victorious

state's power structure is greatly strengthened by the exploits of the army.

If we look at specific cases of Andean state development in terms of the manifestation of power, it is apparent that following the end of the Early Horizon there is a progressive trend toward secularization in all Andean states. While the Moche, for example, have sometimes been referred to as a 'theocratic' state, the level of religious fervor uncovered to date in the Moche area does not really compare with the omnipresence of religion in the preceding 'Chavinoid' polities. It is true that the Moche consumed enormous quantities of labor in the construction of monstrous platform mounds all up and down the north coast, and that these mounds have widely been interpreted as having primarily a ceremonial function. However, the presence of myriad platform mounds is not necessarily an accurate measure of the dominant role of religion in Moche society. Many theocratic or religiously oriented polities exhibit minimal external manifestations of their religion. Witness, for example, the Amish or the Puebloans of the American southwest. Conversely, many nontheocratic polities have overwhelming ceremonial or public architecture. Witness the mall in Washington, D.C. or Red Square in Moscow, for example. This architecture, just like that in the Moche area, is first and foremost a manifestation of the power and grandeur of the reigning government. Thus, just because there is abundant ceremonial architecture in the Moche area does not mean that this was a society dominated by religion. It simply means that the Moche rulers were able to get their populations to comply with remarkable labor demands. Furthermore, the fact that the largest of the Moche platform mounds, such at Huaca del Sol at Moche or Huaca Grande at Pampa Grande, lack the kind of religious decoration found at Caballo Muerto, for example, would point to a significant trend toward secularization between the Early Horizon and the Early Intermediate on the north coast. This trend can be at least partially explained by considering the fact that the Early Intermediate ushered in major warfare and the addition of the physical power base provided by the army. Thus, the increased power of the Moche is manifested in the construction of the platform mounds, while the decreased importance of the ideological base is manifested in the decline in public religious art.

In the highlands, the absence of centralized irrigation systems dampened the ability of highland leaders to gain a substantive economic base of power and thus dampened the rise of highland states until roughly the middle to end of the Early Horizon. At that time, the polity centered at Chavin de Huantar appears to have evolved into a state level of organization. The overwhelming theocratic orientation of Chavin de Huantar (Tello 1956; Lumbreras 1971; Rowe 1967b) points to the clear presence of a strong ideological power base. Again, however, this theocratic orientation does not necessarily mean that the polity centered at Chavin de Huantar was a strict 'theocracy.' Since earlier theocratically oriented polities in the highlands never evolved beyond a chiefdom stage, it is likely that the rulers at Chavin de Huantar augmented their ideological power with both economic and physical power bases. Unfortunately, the extremely limited data base from the Callejón de Huaylas area prevents an assessment of the nature of the economic base. The physical base can be inferred indirectly by the presence of Early Horizon fortifications in the highlands just to the north of the Callejón de Huaylas (see chapter by J. Topic and T. Topic, this volume), and the contemporaneous signs of warfare in the adjacent Casma Valley on the coast. While these manifestations of warfare and military do not relate directly to the Chavin de Huantar polity, it seems improbable that such a polity could have existed in peaceful harmony with aggressive neighbors on at least two sides.

Subsequent to the Early Horizon, state development in the highlands resembled the coast in being increasingly secular, and having less and less of a theocratic orientation. The rise of the imperialistic polity centered at Wari in the Ayacucho Basin in the Early Intermediate Period marks the culmination of this long-term process of secularization (see chapter by Isbell, this volume). There is less emphasis on religion at Wari than at the capital of Moche and the rapid military expansion of the Wari state amply attests to the presence of a strong physical base of power available to the Wari rulers (see chapters by Schreiber and Isbell, this volume). The development of irrigation and Isbell's 'economic archipelagos' also provided the foundation for the rulers to exploit one or more economic power bases.

No one would argue that the entire Andean region underwent a uniform process of political evolution. Clearly there were significant differences from one valley to the next, from the north highlands to the south highlands and between the coast and the highlands. At the same time, there were broad similarities in the individual patterns of specific evolution found in different areas. All of the first states in the Andes, from La Florida to Sechin Alto to Chavin de Huantar, were marked by strong religious overtones. With the subsequent rise of warfare between valleys and between the coast and the highlands, and the intensification of irrigation and exchange networks, the physical power of the military and the economic power provided by resource control began to supersede the ideological power of religion. The expansion of coastal and highland states by military imperialism ultimately solidified (and reified) the central role of economic and military power in the governmental organization of all the Andean states.

Chapter 4

Chavin, the Early Horizon and the Initial Period

Thomas Pozorski and Shelia Pozorski

Introduction

In discussions of the origins of the state in the Andes, Chavin and the Early Horizon inevitably are mentioned. The Chavin phenomenon has been compared with the Olmec culture of Mesoamerica and is often depicted as the 'Mother Culture' of all Andean civilization. It has variously been interpreted as a culture, a religion, an art style, and an empire. However, only recently has enough information become available to allow a more realistic understanding of the Chavin phenomenon and the earlier stages of Andean state development.

Julio C. Tello recognized the Chavin phenomenon as an important force in the early development of Peruvian civilization more than fifty years ago (Tello 1929, 1930). He spent the greater part of his archaeological career promulgating the idea that the Chavin phenomenon constituted a third horizon marker, similar in extent and nature to the later horizons dominated by the Wari (Tiwanaku) and Inca cultures (Tello 1939, 1942, 1943, 1956, 1960). Other scholars (Bennett 1939) were slow to accept this idea, primarily because of the lack of excavated data to support his claims, but by the early 1940s, the Chavin phenomenon was becoming generally accepted as a third horizon marker or style (Larco 1941; Bennett 1943, 1944; Kroeber 1944; Willey 1945). In addition, concurrent work clearly established the existence of preceramic

(Willey 1946:232; Bird 1948a, 1948b) and early ceramic cultures (Strong and Evans 1952; Willey and Corbett 1954) without apparent connections to the Chavin phenomenon. The advent of radiocarbon dating in the early 1950s helped to confirm the early dating for all these cultures previously dated only by relative means.

Over the past thirty years, increasing amounts of research have been done on the late preceramic and early ceramic cultures of Peru. Using the chronological framework set up by Rowe (1960, 1962a) in the late 1950s and refined by Lanning (1967) in the late 1960s, most scholars have come to accept the existence of three chronological periods that span most of the last three millennia B.C.: the Cotton Preceramic, the Initial Period, and the Early Horizon. Existence of a preceramic period with cotton textiles as opposed to a preceramic period without textiles has been known since the 1940s (Bennet and Bird 1964:86–91; Mason 1969:31–37). The absence of pottery clearly differentiates the Cotton Preceramic period from subsequent ceramic periods, but there was also a certain degree of social complexity, reflected in monumental architecture and textiles, that laid the foundations for further societal developments in later periods (Lanning 1967:57–79; Moseley 1975a). In his most definitive statement on Peruvian chronology, Rowe (1962a:49), on the basis of the ceramic sequence established in the Ica Valley, designated the Initial

Period as the time of the introduction of pottery into Ica. According to Rowe (1960:628, 1962a:49), the beginning of the Early Horizon is marked by the first appearance of Chavin influence in Ica, is characterized by the Chavin art style, and lasts until polychrome slip painting replaces resin painting in that valley.

With the acceptance of the Rowe chronological sequence, or even while using different terminology involving stages of development rather than absolute time periods, most authors have settled upon the following scenario for the two ceramic periods (Bushnell 1963:41–69; Bennett and Bird 1964:86–102; Mason 1969:38–72; Busto 1970:17–33; Keatinge 1981:173–177). The Initial Period is marked by the introduction of pottery and a few new cultigens which distinguish this period from the preceding Cotton Preceramic Period. Subsistence patterns for both are often viewed as being very similar. On the coast, shellfish gathering, fishing, and agriculture practiced in narrow river floodplains of coastal valleys provided sustenance for coastal inhabitants for several hundred years. A gradual increase in the use of agricultural products, possibly accompanied by incipient use of irrigation, is generally acknowledged, but without producing any radical changes in other cultural aspects. In the highlands, agriculture in combination with camelid and guinea pig domestication is presumed to have provided for basic subsistence needs. In general, settlements were small and scattered, population density fairly low but increasing, and monumental architecture small-scale and mostly comparable to Cotton Preceramic examples. A few large coastal mounds such as La Florida and Las Haldas are usually recognized (Lanning 1967:90–95; Willey 1971:109–111; Lumbreras 1974a:52), but generally these are viewed as anomalies in an otherwise generally undistinguished period of time.

All this changes upon discussion of the Early Horizon. The Chavin phenomenon, seen to dominate this time period, is viewed as an art style representing the rapid nonmilitaristic spread of a religious cult over much of Peru (Lanning 1967:102; Willey 1971:130; Lumbreras 1974a:67–71). The cohesive nature of this cult is said to have stimulated the rapid rise of civilization and state formation, represented by large U-shaped monumental structures on the coast and in the highlands, often decorated with large figures rendered in the Chavin art style; elaborate pottery; fancy decorated textiles; and other decorative portable artifacts and paraphernalia. The spread of the Chavin phenomenon is sometimes linked with the spread of maize (Bushnell 1963:54–55; Bennett and Bird 1964:94; Bird and Bird 1980:325), which is said to have been the basic staple for most of the advanced cultures of Peru, and indeed, for most of the New World.

Absolute dates given for the Initial Period and Early Horizon vary from author to author, but two chronological schemes are most often consulted. Rowe and Menzel (1967:vi–vii) date the Initial Period between 2100 and 1400 B.C. and the Early Horizon between 1400 and 400 B.C. The

second, and more often cited dates, are those of Lanning (1967:25), which have been repeated by others (Willey 1971:84–85): Initial Period 1800 to 900 B.C. and Early Horizon 900 to 200 B.C.

Despite numerous articles and publications to the contrary (Burger 1981; Bawden and Conrad 1982:26–27; Ravines 1982:136), the above reconstruction of early Peruvian cultural development is still frequently put forth whenever a general summary of Peruvian prehistory is written (Alarco 1971:135–264; Kauffmann 1980:155–287; Busto n.d.:76–105). Increasing importance is being given the Cotton Preceramic Period for its contributions to later developments (see chapter by Feldman, this volume; Moseley 1975a; 1983), but in comparisons of the Initial Period and Early Horizon, the Initial Period always comes out a poor second. The remainder of this chapter is devoted to a re-examination and reinterpretation of the current evidence available for the Initial Period and Early Horizon.

The Initial Period and Early Horizon reconsidered

Close examination of the published data upon which descriptions of the Initial Period and Early Horizon are based reveals a number of anomalies – patterns and relationships that do not coincide with the common cultural reconstruction for the Initial Period and Early Horizon. This transcends all aspects of early Andean culture; especially relevant examples are discussed in the following section. These include ceramics, absolute chronology, iconography and architecture.

Ceramic evidence

Ceramic decorative motifs often proclaimed to be markers of the Chavin horizon, such as the circle and dot (Fung 1969:138; Patterson 1971b:33; Proulx 1973:23–25; Burger 1978), plain or dentate rocker-stamping (Collier 1955:210; Flores 1960:343; Matos 1968:229), feline motifs (Shady 1976:588), pattern burnishing (Rowe 1960:628; Daggett 1983), and combing (Rosas 1976:568, 572), have been found in pre-Chavin contexts in various parts of Peru (Izumi and Sono 1963:140, 153; Rosas and Shady 1970:9; Izumi 1971:59, 67, 69; Lathrap 1971:75; Patterson 1971b:32; Izumi and Terada 1972:186–189; Rosas 1976:568; Burger 1978:99–102; Kano 1979:28–38; T. Pozorski 1983:25–28). Such a lack of clear consensus on the differentiation between Initial Period and Early Horizon ceramic decoration has not helped clarify the nature of either period and has often confused matters.

The concept of horizon

Also crucial is the lack of agreement on the duration of the Early Horizon. By definition, a horizon is a relatively short-lived yet widespread phenomenon (Willey 1951:11; Willey and Phillips 1958:29–34). The most conservative estimate (Lanning 1974:76) sees the Early Horizon as lasting for at least 400 years. More liberal estimates for the duration of the Early Horizon often range up to 1000 years (Engel 1966:41;

Rowe 1967a:21, 26; Sawyer 1968:18–19; Mason 1969:43; Lumbreras 1970:41; Willey 1971:84–85; Proulx 1976:6; Moseley 1978a:495), a span which is as long as or longer than the preceding Initial Period or indeed *any* post-preceramic period in Peruvian prehistory. Thus, even using the shortest of these time estimates, the Early Horizon cannot be considered a 'short-lived phenomenon.'

Radiocarbon evidence

A more positive approach to the Initial Period–Early Horizon question results from an examination of radiocarbon dates for the two time periods. A review of the published literature reveals two significant patterns. First, it is evident that the earliest ceramic sites on the coast date substantially earlier than examples from the highlands (Burger 1981:596–599; T. Pozorski 1983:28–31). Highland sites attributed to the Initial Period because they represent the first appearance of pottery have dates ranging from 1850 to 460 B.C., with most dates clustering around 1000 B.C. (Izumi and Sono 1963:154–156; Izumi 1971:59–62; Rosas 1976:568; Burger 1981:596). Early Horizon highland sites have dates ranging from 1420 to 200 B.C. with most dates clustering around 500 B.C. (Izumi and Sono 1963:154–156; Izumi and Terada 1972:310; Burger 1981:596–599).

Of particular interest is the site of Chavin de Huantar, which is almost always seen as a major center of the Chavin art style or religious cult, if not the ultimate center of Chavin origins (Mason 1969:44; Lumbreras 1974a:67; Roe 1974; Kauffmann 1980:107–164). A recent article by Burger (1981) has been most revealing. Isolated early dates ranging from 1420 to 940 B.C. have been reported for Chavin de Huantar (Lumbreras 1970:133; Amat 1976:544). Burger (1981:596), however, feels that these dates are incorrect because the samples were contaminated by groundwater carbonates. More secure dating obtained by Burger (1979:154; 1981:594–596) at the site correlates well with a majority of the dates obtained by Lumbreras (1972:78). Burger (1981:596) dates the Initial Period Urabarriu occupation from 850 to 460 B.C. and the two Early Horizon phases, Chakinani and Janabarriu, as 460 to 390 B.C. and 390 to 200 B.C. respectively. The last phase, Janabarriu, is the one to which Burger (1978:396; 1981:600) ascribes the spread of Chavin influence over a pan-Andean area.

By contrast, dates from coastal sites show a distinctly different pattern. Dates for sites attributed to the Early Horizon on the coast range from 1090 to 342 B.C., with the majority of dates in the 800 to 700 B.C. range (Bird 1951:40; Collier 1955:25, 1962:413; Ishida *et al.* 1960:518; Kigoshi *et al.* 1961:92; Rowe 1967a:27–30; Fung 1969:180–186; Grieder 1975:100, 109; Matsuzawa 1978:666). The more abundant dates from sites labeled as Initial Period range from 1940 to 570 B.C., with most falling within the 1600 to 1100 B.C. time span (Bird 1951:40; Collier 1955:25; Berger *et al.* 1965:347; Rowe 1967a:26–30; Matos 1968:230; Patterson 1968:423; Fung 1969:180–186; Grieder 1975:99–100; S. Pozorski and T. Pozorski 1979b:418, 420; Burger 1981:594; Ravines

1982:158–165, 174–175; Shimada 1982:200). It is particularly significant that the dated sites containing monumental frieze decoration (Caballo Muerto, Garagay, and Pampa de las Llamas–Moxeke) all date before 1100 B.C. (Ravines 1982a:164–165; S. Pozorski 1983, this volume; T. Pozorski 1975: 247–248, 1976:112–113, 1980:108, 1982a:529, 1982b:248, 1983:6).

Hence, two patterns emerge from a consideration of the absolute dates available for early ceramic sites in the Andean area. As a whole, the dates from coastal sites are substantially older than dates from highland sites when coastal and sierra sites presumed contemporary on the basis of shared ceramic traits are compared. There is strong evidence to indicate that on the coast, what is defined as the Initial Period or pre-Chavin pottery tradition, dominated by the neckless olla, goes back to at least 1800 B.C. and lasts for 700 years or more. In contrast, highland ceramic components containing decorative and form attributes similar to the coast and assigned to the Initial Period, at sites like Kotosh, Chavin de Huantar, and Shillacoto, date closer to 1000 B.C., or, as at Chavin de Huantar, 200 to 500 years later (Burger 1981:596–599). To be sure, there are sites in the highlands with Initial Period pottery components – Waira-jirca pottery from Kotosh (Izumi and Terada 1972:186–189) and early pottery from Huaricoto (Burger and Burger 1980:31) and Pacopampa (Rosas 1976:568) – that are comparable only in date to early Initial Period sites on the coast. Ceramics from these early highland sites are distinct from the coastal ceramics and bear evidence of ties with regions east of the Andes.

The same distinction between coast and highlands can be made for so-called Chavin-related sites attributed to the Early Horizon. Coastal sites with Early Horizon components such as Huaca Prieta and Las Haldas date closer to 1000 B.C. whereas sierra examples date nearer to 500 B.C. Clearly, highland sites attributed to the Initial Period and the Early Horizon date much later than coastal ones which have similar ceramic traits and are considered to belong to these two time periods.

Examination of the Rowe Chavin art style seriation

Students of the development of early civilization may be surprised by the preceding analysis of the Initial Period and Early Horizon. A critic might point out that the famous coastal sites of Punkurí, Cerro Blanco, Moxeke, Garagay, and Caballo Muerto all have or had friezes with 'classic Chavin' designs which can be readily fitted into the later phases of the Rowe Chavin seriation (Rowe 1967b:76; Roe 1974:37–38; 1978:7–8). One begins to wonder, however, about the validity of that seriation upon examination of the associated ceramic, artifactual, and especially radiocarbon evidence. Specifically, because almost all the available radiocarbon assays for coastal sites containing friezed decorations (Caballo Muerto, Pampa de las Llamas–Moxeke, and Garagay) predate 1100 B.C. and date some 500 to 1000 years before the 'type site' of Chavin de Huantar, it is time to re-examine the basic evidence used in the original formulation of the Chavin seriation.

In 1962, John Rowe (1962b:5–6; 1967b:73–74) offered a seriation of the Chavin art style based on the master ceramic sequence of the Ica Valley on the south coast (Menzel *et al.* 1964) and on his own observations of the architecture and carved sculpture at the type site of Chavin de Huantar. Absolute dates were later assigned to the sequence (Rowe and Menzel 1967:vi–viii), indicating that the Chavin style and the mechanisms that spread the style originated somewhere north of Ica in the late Initial Period. The arrival of the Chavin style in the Ica Valley signalled the start of the Early Horizon.

There are four phases in the Rowe Chavin seriation, AB, C, D, and EF; the phases with two letters being a provision for potential future subdivision (Rowe 1967b:76). Rowe and Menzel (1967:vi–vii) indicate that Phase AB began in the Ancash area north of the Ica Valley about 1500 B.C. and arrived in Ica about 1400 B.C. The succeeding phases are spaced out over the next several hundred years.

At a later date, Peter Roe (1974; 1978) extended Rowe's Chavin seriation to include most objects and monuments in Peru believed to be of the Chavin style. His extension of the original Rowe seriation, however, is biased because (1) he assumes that all Chavin-related elements emanated from Chavin de Huantar, and (2) he uncritically follows the original seriation, which was meant as a preliminary suggestive guide (Rowe 1967b:76), without accounting for associated noniconographic evidence.

Reassessment of the evidence upon which the original seriation is based reveals a surprisingly meager data base. At Chavin de Huantar, there are several dozen pieces of monumental carved sculpture, but fewer than ten of these are used in the formulation of the seriation (Rowe 1967b:76). Of the pieces considered, only four are believed by Rowe to be in their original positions – the Lanzón or Great Image, considered the main representation of Phase AB, and the three pieces forming the Black and White Portal unit and believed representative of Phase D. Principal pieces exemplifying the other two phases – the Tello Obelisk for Phase C and the Raimondi Stela for Phase EF – were not found *in situ* at Chavin de Huantar and are fitted into the sequence only by similiary arguments.

The beginning and end points, always crucial to any seriation, were established on the basis of an architectural sequence of construction at the site. The Phase AB Lanzón is built into a gallery within what Rowe designated as the Old Temple, a U-shaped structure covering the northern half of the site. The Black and White Portal adorns the face of what has come to be called the New Temple, a second U-shaped temple, the main body of which is made up of purported southern additions on to the south wing of the U-shaped Old Temple (Rowe 1962b:9, Figure 8; 1967b:Figure 2). More detailed and subtle changes within the proposed seriation are based on a ten-phase ceramic sequence for the Ica Valley on the south coast (Menzel *et al.* 1964).

Both at Chavin de Huantar and in Ica, however, there is evidence that refutes the proposed Chavin seriation. At Chavin, some pieces of sculpture used in the original seriation are situated or were found in positions that do not correspond to the proposed architectural sequence. In particular, an *in situ* cornice stone on the southwest corner of the New Temple is attributed to Phase AB, whereas, according to the position of the Black and White Portal, the New Temple should not be decorated by sculpture dating any earlier than Phase D. Similarly, a cornice stone fragment dated to Phase D was found near the northeast corner of the south wing of the Old Temple where only sculpture belonging to Phases AB or C should be found. Rowe (1967b:75) noted these discrepancies in his original formulation, explaining that older sculptures were reused in later construction phases at the site. His basis for such an explanation is a stylistic argument: early sculptures should not be found in late contexts and *vice versa*. This reasoning is circular, though, and cannot be used as an independent check on the validity of his sequence formulation.

The architectural history of Chavin de Huantar is little known. Most authors follow Rowe's suggested sequence with the New Temple postdating the Old Temple (Willey 1971:117–121; Lumbreras 1974a:59–60; Kauffmann 1980:203–209). This architectural sequence, however, is based almost exclusively on an examination made more than twenty years ago of the exterior stone facing of the site as well as the interior construction of some of the galleries. Though no one since that time has reported in detail on the architecture of Chavin de Huantar as a whole, enough subsequent work has been done to make possible additional observations pertinent to the present discussion.

During the authors' visits to the site, the stone masonry of both the New and Old Temples was examined, and two important discoveries were made. First, the stone facing for the New and Old Temples is very similar, both in patterning and finish (Figure 1a–f). On the face of the New Temple, three types of stonework are present in horizontal bands that span the width of the temple face: (1) very large roughly hewn stones which constitute the base of the New Temple; (2) a band of smaller, roughly hewn stones immediately above and similar to the larger ones; and (3) finely finished stonework, similar in size to the smaller roughly hewn stones and which constitute approximately the upper one-third of the New Temple facing (Figure 1a–e). Although almost half of the width of the New Temple is supposedly made up of the south wing of the Old Temple (Rowe 1962b:9, Figure 8; 1967b:Figure 2; Willey 1971:118), there is no indication of architectural disjunction. Instead, the face of the New Temple shows continuous similar stonework across its entire width. Though not exposed to the level where the basal stonework type would be apparent, the north wing of the Old Temple shows evidence of the two upper bands of stonework types seen in the facing of the New Temple (Figure 1f).

The second on-site discovery at Chavin de Huantar concerns the stonework of the panels that line both the rectangular New Temple plaza and the circular Old Temple plaza. The stone panels used in both are almost identical in

Fig. 1a-f. a-e: series of photographs showing the east façade of the New Temple of Chavin de Huantar, from south to north. Note the three distinctive types of stonework present in horizontal bands: large, roughly hewn stones topped by smaller roughly hewn stones capped by finely finished stonework. f: View of the south face of the north wing of the Old Temple showing two types of stonework – small, roughly hewn stones topped by finely finished stones – the same upper two types of stonework present across the entire façade of the New Temple

terms of size, shape, and material. The main difference is that many examples in the Old Temple plaza are decorated with profile feline carvings (Lumbreras 1977:20–28). Finally, the positioning of now-visible staircases near the northwest corner of the New Temple plaza suggests an integrated functional connection of that plaza with the Old Temple. The concurrent use of both temples is compatible with evidence of similar principal and auxiliary temple associations observed at various coastal sites (T. Pozorski 1976:287). Though chronologically earlier, Huaca de los Reyes in the Moche Valley is especially analogous because its lateral temples are also adorned with profile felines (T. Pozorski 1976:74–76).

To summarize, close inspection of the visible architectural remains at Chavin de Huantar suggests that the two temples were constructed and functioned simultaneously. In terms of this scenario, the architectural basis for the direction of the Rowe seriation is greatly weakened.

Examination of the independent ceramic evidence from Ica is also revealing. Most of the ten proposed Ocucaje phases of Ica are based on a seriation of unassociated pottery vessels. Chavin influence is said to be reflected in Ocucaje phases 1 through 8 and especially strong in phases 4 and 5 (Menzel *et al.* 1964:257). The only stratigraphic evidence to support the seriation comes from the site of Cerrillos, where phase 3 pottery underlies refuse containing mixed pottery from phases 5, 7, 8, and 9 (Menzel *et al.* 1964:20–21, 103–104). Some phases are represented by very small pottery samples. Phases 1 and 2 are defined on the basis of a total of only 12 vessels; phase 3, 38 vessels; phase 4, 12 vessels; phase 5, 18 vessels; and phase 6, 38 vessels. Phases 1 and 2 are correlated with Chavin Phase AB, phase 3 with Chavin Phase C, phase 4 with Chavin Phase D, phase 5 partially with Chavin Phases D and EF, and phases 6 through 8 with Chavin Phase EF (Menzel *et al.* 1964:258).

Both Roe (1974:31; 1978:12–13) and Burger (1978:389–91) have reinterpreted the entire Ica sequence as dating no earlier than Chavin Phase D, and such a reinterpretation seriously undermines the basis of the total Rowe seriation because of its dependence on the Ica sequence (Paulsen 1977:737). Radiocarbon dates from Ica also argue for the compaction of and late chronological positioning of the Ica sequence. Overlapping dates from Cerrillos for Ocucaje phase 3 (459 B.C. ± 214) and phase 9 (451 B.C. ± 110) (Rowe 1967a:28–30) are within the range of Burger's (1981:595–596) dates for the Janabarriu phase at Chavin de Huantar, which he correlates with Chavin Phase D (Burger 1978:389–391). The data from Chavin de Huantar and Ica may suggest a possible relationship between the two, but it is clear that both postdate and could not have contributed to the earlier Initial Period developments on the north and central coasts.

The stylistic variety of sculpture present at Chavin de Huantar remains to be explained. Various lines of evidence suggest that all are contemporaneous despite attributed stylistic differences. Excavation data from the coastal site of Huaca de los Reyes at Caballo Muerto (T. Pozorski 1975:246–247, 1976:185–187, 1980:108, 1982a:527–528, 1982b:248) show that a wide variety of sculpture was used contemporaneously and that variation need not always reflect chronological differences. It is highly likely that prehistoric peoples were capable of a wider variety of artistic expression and that more variation was acceptable than many scholars are willing to concede. This indeed may have been the case at Chavin de Huantar.

To summarize, it is clear that the often-cited expressions of the Chavin phenomenon at coastal sites with decorated friezes have nothing to do with Chavin de Huantar and the Chavin style seriation. If anything, the coastal iconography of the human figure (Huaca de los Reyes, Moxeke, Cerro Sechin and Garagay), the feline (Huaca de los Reyes and Punkurí) and the Ofrendas monster (Garagay) reflects coastal iconographic influence at Chavin de Huantar which was introduced along with coastal architecture (U-shaped mounds and sunken circular forecourts) and coastal ceramic traits (stirrup spout bottles) (Burger 1981:599–600; T. Pozorski 1983:36–37).

A revision of the Cotton Preceramic through Early Horizon sequence

Previous sections of this paper have pointed out the late date of Chavin de Huantar relative to much earlier major coastal sites. Many of these coastal sites, such as Moxeke, Cerro Blanco, and Caballo Muerto, were once believed to be influenced by and contemporary with or later than Chavin de Huantar (Willey 1971:123–126; Lumbreras 1974a:167–171). New data, in the form of excavation results and carbon 14 dates, have essentially reversed this traditional sequence, which was based almost entirely on seriational arguments. This dramatic restructuring calls into question the very existence of an 'Early Horizon,' as well as the early conceptualizations of the Initial Period and Cotton Preceramic. It also makes necessary a revision of the early portion of the Andean chronological sequence.

Since the sequence proposed by Rowe (1960) has been followed throughout most of this volume, at this point we are proposing only to modify his sequence by downgrading the Early Horizon to simply the Early Period and by modifying the chronologies of early temporal divisions on the basis of new absolute dates. The justification for this new approach will become clear as the Cotton Preceramic, Initial Period, and Early Period are discussed in turn.

Cotton Preceramic Period

Popular conceptualization of the Cotton Preceramic inhabitants of coastal Peru has come a long way since Bird's (1948a, 1948b) initial description of their incipient agricultural lifeways. This is best seen in Willey's assessment of the Cotton Preceramic site of Aspero in 1941 and 1942 and thirty years later (Willey and Corbett 1954; Moseley and Willey 1973). More recently, and in this volume, much has been made of the complexities of Cotton Preceramic lifeways and how large coastal communities were preadapted forerunners of subsequent Andean states (Feldman 1977, 1980; Moseley 1975, 1978).

The Cotton Preceramic legacy has many facets. At many sites from Alto Salaverry (S. Pozorski and T. Pozorski 1979a) and Salinas de Chao (Alva 1978) on the north coast to El Paraíso (Engel 1966) on the central coast, there is clear evidence of societal development beyond the egalitarian level. This is reflected mainly in temple mounds or other examples of nondomestic architecture, but is also manifest in lapidary and textile art. Equally important is the striking similarity between the more than two dozen major known Cotton Preceramic sites stretched all along the coast. Shared traits range from more predictably similar technologies for maritime exploitation to parallels in architectural forms and textile manufacture. These similarities led Engel (1963, 1966) to postulate a Cotton Preceramic 'horizon' along the coast, but the shared traits appear to be the result of extensive communication networks. They do *not* reflect the political or religious suprasocietal linkage that the concept 'horizon' suggests. Such similarities, however, are not limited to the coast. In the last fifteen years, excavations in the highlands at such sites as Kotosh, Huaricoto, and La Galgada have explored distinctive shared preceramic architectural forms which document the existence of a second

highly developed sierra communication network distinct from the coast (Burger and Burger 1980).

On the coast, this communication and interaction between preceramic sites appears to have given rise to unusually large evenly spaced communities (Moseley 1972) which may have had rights to specific zones of coastal and inland resources and/or to labor input. Throughout the Cotton Preceramic, there is evidence of increasing use of river valley land for cultivation as the floral inventories of early sites become both diverse and abundant (Pozorski and Pozorski 1979a). However, inland settlements at this time are small and rarely preserved archaeologically (Patterson 1971a, 1973). This early pattern of dominant coastal sites with control or influence over a specific zone of resources (Figure 2) provides evidence of increasing political complexity during the Cotton Preceramic.

Initial Period

Traditionally, the Initial Period has been viewed as a continuation of the Cotton Preceramic with the addition of ceramics, and, in some instances, maize (Lanning 1967:88). A corollary to this was the idea that all things monumental and

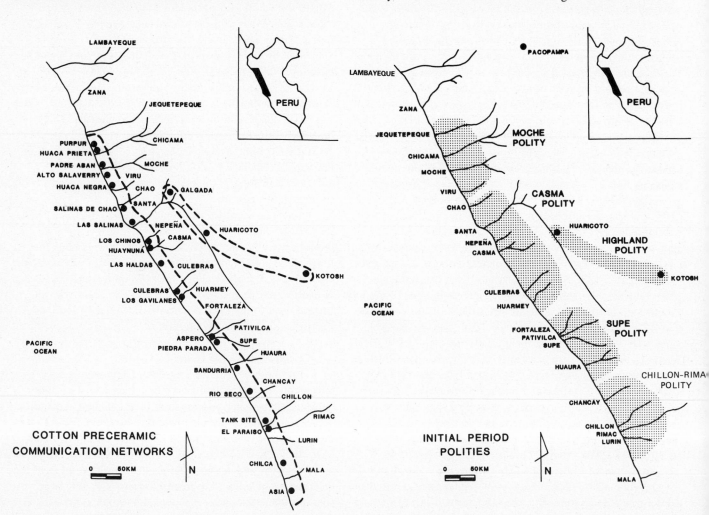

Fig. 2. Preceramic coastal and highland communication networks

Fig. 3. Initial Period coastal and highland polities

iconographically adorned were both attributable to the Early Horizon and causally linked to the Chavin phenomenon. In the same way that early conceptions of the Cotton Preceramic have been dispelled, recent data and especially carbon 14 dates have resulted in an appreciation of the complexities of Initial Period developments.

Initial Period developments on the north and central Peruvian coast have proved to be very advanced. They represent a quantum jump from their preceramic counterparts, but still have clear roots in the earlier period. The major differences are the advent of irrigation agriculture and the social cohesion reflected in the construction of truly monumental architecture, often adorned with adobe friezes. Although experimentation with irrigation agriculture probably began in the Cotton Preceramic as efforts to expand the land available through simple floodplain farming, it is not until the Initial Period that there is evidence of agricultural production on a large scale. This is reflected most markedly in the settlement pattern. For the first time, the largest sites are located well inland, near optimal locales for irrigation and canal intakes, instead of on the coast near the marine resources. Data from the Moche Valley document an increase in abundance and size of cultigens between the Cotton Preceramic and Initial Period, thereby providing additional evidence of the effects of irrigation agriculture (S. Pozorski 1976, 1983; S. Pozorski and T. Pozorski 1979a). New cultigens were added to the floral inventory during the Initial Period, but maize was not among the most important. It was not present in the Casma Valley Initial Period subsistence sample and was very rare in refuse at the Moche Valley site of Gramalote (S. Pozorski 1976, 1983).

The sites now believed to characterize the Initial Period occupation of Peruvian coastal valleys from Lambayeque to Rimac are inland mounds or clusters of mounds. They are generally U-shaped and often clearly oriented upvalley, perhaps in deference to the source of water for irrigation. All are corporate labor constructions which drew on a sizable local and perhaps regional population base for their construction and maintenance. Friezes which adorn temple mounds at Limoncarro in the Jequetepeque Valley (Jorge Zevallos and Oscar Lostenau, personal communication 1974), Huaca de los Reyes in the Moche Valley (T. Pozorski 1975, 1976, 1980), Punkurí and Cerro Blanco in the Nepeña Valley (Larco 1941; Tello 1943; Kauffmann 1980:272–273), Sechin Alto, the Cerro Sechin inner temple, and Moxeke in the Casma Valley (Tello 1943, 1956; Lumbreras 1974a:69–70; Kauffmann 1980:274–277), and Garagay in the Rimac Valley (Ravines and Isbell 1975) suggest that the motivation behind these monumental constructions and their associated irrigation networks was religious in nature. It may have been on the level of hero or ancestor worship (T. Pozorski 1980).

At one time, all the known friezes, which were then only in the Nepeña and Casma Valleys, were grouped together as part of the Chavin phenomenon (Tello 1943). Now the Casma, Moche and Rimac examples are known to be Initial Period in date, and a close examination of the friezes currently known

reveals both similarities and differences. The same is true for other unifying aspects. Initial Period coastal ceramics share important aspects, such as an emphasis on plastic decoration and the predominance of the neckless olla form which was probably modeled after gourd vessels. Initial Period coastal valley architecture has many common features such as mound form and the use of distinctive construction materials such as conical adobes and stones encased on loose cane bags. Even settlement pattern changes and the associated change to irrigation agriculture are evident in all the coastal valleys with known Initial Period sites.

Ironically, in view of the refined chronology, sites of the Initial Period emerge as more indicative of the existence of an 'Early Horizon' than do settlements of the subsequent period. However, the pan-regional political cohesiveness indicated by the horizon concept is still lacking. The many unifying aspects of the Initial Period are attributable to the communication network that has its roots in the Preceramic. However, by Initial Period times, there is clear evidence of the emergence of regional polities.

The rise of regional polities

Probably because of factors which differed from region to region, small polities in some areas continued to grow and develop and become regional polities whereas others maintained their *status quo* and became subservient to the nearest developing polity. Concentrations of or exceptionally large early inland mounds are interpreted as the centers of enlarging polities, and such evidence suggests that major early political entities formed in the valleys of Moche, Casma, Supe, and Chillon–Rimac on the coast and possibly at centers in the highlands. In addition to concentrations or elaborations of mounds, there are other features such as architecture, iconography, ceramics, and geographic boundaries which point to these areas as political centers. Architecture and ceramics in particular begin to have a more regional distribution at this time, which would presumably reflect either the emergence or stabilization of political boundaries (Figure 3).

Moche Valley polity

In the north, the Caballo Muerto complex of eight mounds in the Moche Valley is seen as the center of a polity which probably dominated valleys as far north as Jequetepeque and at least as far south as Viru. With respect to architecture, the sequentially constructed U-shaped mounds with wings conform to local tenets of form that can also be seen in more remote constructions in other dependent valleys. Although the sunken circular court is present in both the Moche and Chao Valleys in the Cotton Preceramic, this architectural detail was apparently not incorporated as an important feature of the Initial Period polity architecture. The power of the Moche polity may be correlated with local iconography as reflected in aspects such as the Huaca de los Reyes friezes and the developing Cupisnique ceramic style.

Casma Valley polity

The largest center known is in the Casma Valley, where a state-level polity had its capital at the immense, 1.5 km long mound complex of Sechin Alto. Sechin Alto was associated with the other substantial Casma sites of Sechin Bajo and Taukachi-Konkán plus Las Haldas, the most elaborate Initial Period coastal construction known. Architectural form, especially the use of the sunken circular court, was highly standardized, and the distribution of such circles suggests that Casma was the center of that distribution and that influence from Casma may have extended as far north as Chao and as far south as Huarmey. The presence of three major mound sites with frieze decoration suggests that iconographic depictions were closely tied to influence of the polity. Our detailed reconstruction of Casma Valley prehistory places this emphasis on architectural iconographic decoration at a point in time which coincides with Huaca de los Reyes in the Caballo Muerto complex.

Supe Valley polity

The north boundary of the Supe-centered polity is difficult to define because the use of sunken circular courts was also an important aspect of this political unit. Additionally, the Huaura to Chancay area is not well known. Therefore, the Supe polity is postulated to have extended between the Fortaleza and Huaura Valleys mainly on the basis of large physical separations between river valleys at either end. Although the nature of this polity is the least well defined, the tremendous concentration of multiple-mound sites with circular courts within Supe and decreasing numbers within nearby valleys argue for a focus of power within the zone. The substantial Cotton Preceramic site of Aspero with its corporate labor constructions and the Cotton Preceramic mound of Piedra Parada which has a circular forecourt are both near the mouth of the Supe Valley. Taken together, they could have provided the labor pool, political organization and architectural details reflected in the early ceramic inland constructions within Supe.

Chillon–Rimac Polity

In the Chillon–Rimac region, the sheer size of mound sites such as La Florida and Garagay argues for their importance, and there is a significant local precedent for power concentration and labor mobilization in the Cotton Preceramic site of El Paraíso. Since deeply buried circular courts are known from Garagay, it is possible that this architectural feature was also important in Chillon and Rimac and that other buried examples may be discovered. The U-shaped mound form is certainly a significant element of local polity architecture. The Garagay murals are an important feature of the regional polity because, like Moche and Casma, they may be symbolically correlated with the Chillon–Rimac power base.

Highlands

In the central highlands, Initial Period occupations at Huaricoto and Kotosh are clearly outgrowths of earlier preceramic settlements at the same loci. The distinctive shared sierra ceramic styles show a tropical forest influence. The highland architectural style centers around the small rectanguloid sunken room with rounded corners, niches, and usually a subfloor ventilation shaft. These continuities and similarities suggest the presence of a highland polity which is distinct from contemporary coastal developments.

Early Period

The time period which immediately follows the Initial Period and which dates between 900 and 200 B.C. cannot be characterized as a horizon. In fact, in many respects, it is the most fragmented of the three early periods considered in this paper. Although regional polities are still present, and some traits, such as an emphasis on plastic decoration in ceramics, persist, the communication network documented by Cotton Preceramic and Initial Period uniformities has clearly been disrupted. Rather than drastically restructure the chronological sequence as outlined by Rowe (1960), we have chosen simply to drop 'Horizon' from Rowe's name for this period, thereby distinguishing it simply as the Early Period.

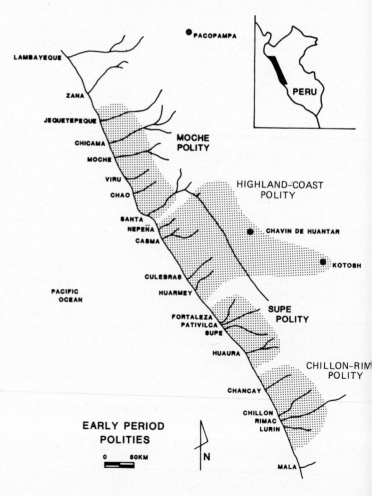

Fig. 4. Early Period coastal and highland polities

Now that it is evident that early coastal mounds once believed to be Early Horizon in date are really much earlier and belong to the Initial Period, we are left with a void where once we had the Early Horizon. Looking more closely at areas where dates and excavation data are available, we see changes and deviations from the Initial Period configuration for regional polities (Figure 4).

North central highland to coastal polity

The peculiar designation for this polity derives from the fact that most of what we know of this political unit comes from the Casma Valley, which was invaded by a sierra group about 1000–900 B.C., at the end of the Initial Period. As discussed elsewhere (S. Pozorski, this volume), a militaristic group from the highlands introduced radically different architecture, ceramics, and food plants and animals into Casma, and simultaneously truncated local development. Hilltop fortifications sprang up in response as far north as the Viru Valley; and the configuration of these fortified sites suggests that the invaders came from a zone inland and north of Casma and slightly south of Viru and Santa. Ceramic traits and other artifacts such as ground slate blades were widely disseminated outside the physical limits of the polity. These document communication with polities as far north as the Moche Valley and as far south as Kotosh, but in such remote areas, they are always in association with a strong local style. Perhaps these ideas spread along old established Initial Period communication routes. Although too limited in extent to define a horizon, this militaristic group was especially important because it incorporated a segment of both the coast and the highlands into a single polity. This was repeated by the Wari/Tiwanaku and Inca states of the Middle Horizon and Late Horizon, and always the movement was from the highlands to the coast.

Chavin de Huantar

There may have been a politically unified group centered at or in the vicinity of Chavin de Huantar, but it certainly had nowhere near the power often attributed to it. The site of Pallka in the upper Casma Valley shares many architectural and ceramic similarities with Chavin de Huantar, and the two sites may have been in contact via a natural topographic corridor which leads into the Callejón de Huaylas from the Pallka zone of the Casma drainage. When we examine the two sites in light of their chronological position, the Chavin de Huantar polity takes on the role of amalgamator of anachronisms rather than disseminator of ideas. For example, the U-shaped mound and the circular forecourt were no longer in use in coastal valleys such as Casma by the time they were instituted at Chavin de Huantar. The two sites share ceramic traits with the polity which devastated Casma, but, again, Chavin de Huantar and Pallka appear to have been the recipients, not the originators of the new style.

Moche Valley polity

In contrast to the drastic changes which occurred on the north central coast during the Early Period, development in the Moche Valley was much less affected. At Caballo Muerto, mounds continued to be constructed and other mound sites such as Puente Serrano and Menocucho were established further upvalley, possibly as a response to unrest in the sierra. Along the southern limits of the Early Period Moche Valley polity and further south in the Santa Valley, which had been aligned with Casma, forts were constructed on the southern valley margins. This suggests a unified effort by the northern polity, which had increased in extent, to resist the group that conquered Casma; and archaeological evidence suggests they were successful in keeping out the militaristic polity.

In the absence of archaeological data on polities such as Supe and Chillon–Rimac, at present we are assuming that they developed essentially unchanged through the Early Period. We feel this assumption is justified because neither early fortified hilltop sites nor early nonmound sites are described for these zones (Kosok 1965; Feldman 1980).

By the Early Intermediate Period, regional groupings had crystallized into major polities such as Moche, Sicán, Recuay, and Nazca, to name the best known. Painting is the dominant form of ceramic decoration, and rectangular adobes are used with stone to construct both mounds and large expanses of secular architecture. Although Early Intermediate Period polities owe much to their Early Period legacy, the many differences and innovations mark the beginning of yet another chronological period.

Conclusions

A critical examination of the Early Horizon and Initial Period in ancient Peru has shown that the Chavin phenomenon can no longer be viewed as a 'Mother Culture' from which sprang all succeeding Andean civilizations. Instead, the foundations of Andean civilization and state development lie in the Cotton Preceramic Period when two separate networks of chiefdom level polities developed – along the coast and in the highlands. True early state formation occurred during the Initial Period along the north and central coast, where there arose a series of interacting polities centered in the Moche, Casma, Supe, and Chillon–Rimac Valleys. There is evidence of polity development in the highlands at the same time, but the polities seem less complex and show little evidence of contact with the coast. As in the Cotton Preceramic Period, there were two separate communication networks present, one on the coast and another in the highlands, along which spread certain ideas related to technology, ideology, ceramic production, and architectural layout.

In contrast, the Early Horizon, heretofore almost always considered a time of unification and coalescence of early Peruvian culture by means of the Chavin phenomenon, can now be viewed as a time of disruption of the older communication networks and established state-level polities. On the north coast, the Casma polity was decimated by a foreign militaristic group from the highlands which united a portion of the highlands and the coast for the first time in Peruvian prehistory. The Chavin phenomenon, centered at

Chavin de Huantar, appeared late in the Early Horizon and covered only a limited area in north central Peru. More importantly, the Chavin de Huantar polity was the recipient of a variety of influences from other regions to the east and west rather than a disseminator of ideas. In fact, the disruptive nature of and the length of the Early Horizon indicate that this time period should be called the Early Period rather than the Early Horizon.

Chapter 5

The archaeological investigation of Andean militarism: some cautionary observations

John Topic and Theresa Topic

Introduction

Andeanists have, from the early stirrings of the discipline more than a century ago, shown a strong interest in questions involving prehistoric warfare and militarism. We are fortunate to be able to draw on several lines of evidence: iconographic representations of warfare and its effects; well-preserved remains of fortifications; and eye-witness accounts of native weapons, tactics, and strategies recorded by Spanish conquerors in the 16th century. While much of the early work on prehistoric warfare in the Andes is essentially descriptive, there has been a significant change in warfare studies in the last decade. Not only has there been a marked increase in the number of studies directed at questions of warfare, but much of this work and the resulting discussions center on explanation of observed patterns. The current tendency is to seek reasons for warfare in the natural and social environments of societies and not in some vague Toynbee-esque cyclicity to which civilization might be prone.

Warfare has also become respectable among theorists of state origins, most of whom view conflict as one of the factors promoting emergence of complex society, and some of whom, most notably Carneiro (1970, 1978, 1981), see conflict as the most important variable. Carneiro's scenario of resource concentration producing conflict is compelling (Carneiro 1970:736–737), although his models of environmental and social

circumscription are so simplified that it is difficult to apply them in a straightforward way to the areas and problems we will be discussing here. As discussed at length in the chapters by Wilson and Daggett, there is a raging debate over a causal role of warfare in the emergence of states. Empirical battles are also being waged over whether similar circumstances, namely circumscription, population growth, and restricted resource availability, lead to internal cooperation and unification or internal conflict and conquest. For the moment, the various debates over the role of warfare in the emergence of Andean states will be postponed. Instead, more mundane, though nevertheless critical issues, will be discussed.

The first section is concerned with methodological problems in the study of prehistoric conflict. Results of a four-season field survey in northern Peru directed specifically at fortifications and defensive constructions make it possible to offer new empirical insight into prehistoric warfare in the Andes. This survey sampled diverse zones from the coast to the continental divide (J. Topic and T. Topic 1982). More recently, a study of the Huamachuco area began, which is producing interesting comparative material (J. Topic and T. Topic 1982). The second section of this paper will present an overview of the historic development of fortifications and fortification strategies through time in the parts of northern Peru included in our surveys.

Methodological problems

As prehistoric warfare receives more attention and becomes a more important research topic, it is necessary to give careful consideration to the basic question of what constitutes evidence of conflict in the prehistoric record. Discussions of militarism and related issues by Andeanists have not always been characterized by especially high levels of precision. Both recent and older publications often dismiss as 'non-military' constructions which are quite clearly fortifications, while some archaeologists are willing to class as 'defensive' or 'fortified' settlements and buildings which may have served quite different functions.

A starting-point for defining reliable indicators of militarism must be a consideration of the kinds of tactics used by prehistoric Andean armies, and of the sorts of evidence we can expect to find preserved. Weapons used in the central Andes were not very elaborate. Close-range fighting relied heavily on clubs and similar 'bashing' implements. Reliance on cutting or thrusting weapons probably was low and more typical of specialized warriors than of part-time militia who provided the numbers so important in the rather simple tactics of later prehistory. The most effective long-range weapon appears to have been the sling. Expertise in its use was probably common among the male population from an early age in most parts of Peru, and certainly the ammunition was abundant.

It is most likely that many battles were fought in the open, and not from fortified positions. Scenes on Moche pottery corroborate ethnohistoric sources (summarized in Bram 1941 and Rowe 1946) which state that open field fighting was common. The chances of recognizing such a battlefield are very slim. The most reliable indicator of conflict, or at least the potential for conflict, is military architecture – structures built specifically for defensive and/or offensive purposes.

There is a longstanding misconception (e.g. Squier 1877; Sanders 1973) that a high wall implies a defensive function. Certainly a high wall serves as a barrier, but true defensibility requires the presence of a parapet. Elite compounds defined by high walls are a common feature of many important sites in the central Andes, and archaeologists have been uncritical in imputing military functions to barriers which are clearly social. An elite compound wall lacking a parapet is not defensible. In fact, an unparapeted compound wall can confer an advantage on attackers rather than defenders. While defenders must hurl projectiles (for example slingstones) blindly over high walls at attackers whose numbers and positions cannot be gauged, attackers need only hurl inflammable devices at rooftops inside the compound. While it is entirely possible that high walled compounds, elite or otherwise, functioned as fortifications in prehistory, they could not have done so effectively. In such cases, defenders, like the Spanish in the siege of Cuzco in 1535, would have found themselves trapped in structures never intended for defense.

Attributes of defensive structures

The archaeological record offers many examples of structures built specifically for defense. The least ambiguous cases share four attributes: (1) parapeted walls, (2) slingstones, (3) moats outside the walls, and (4) defensible location with restricted access.

Very often on the north coast parapeted walls consist of a wall 50–100 cm thick against which a bench 150–200 cm wide has been built. At times, however, parapeted walls are formed by building three to five contiguous walls in which the outer wall forms the breastwork. Thus, exceptionally thick walls (i.e. 2.5 m thick or more) should be examined for potential defensibility. Since the breastwork is at the top of the wall and is often not particularly massive, excavation may be necessary to confirm the presence of a parapeted wall. In the handful of cases in which the breastwork appears to be completely preserved, it is only about 80 cm high; this height is consistent with the use of slings as a principal weapon. In the north sierra, the bench and wall type of parapet exists but is rare. The most common pattern is a terrace on which the retaining wall projects above the terrace level and is double faced. Defenders enjoy the advantage of greater height, depending on the differential in surface levels on top of and below the terrace, and the protection of the breastwork. Similar parapeted terraces exist on the coast, where they are often associated with slingstone piles.

Slingstones comprise the second major class of evidence for fortification. Slingstones are common on the north coast, but none have yet been found in the sierra. On the coast, the slingstones are generally river-rolled cobbles selected for a spherical shape, roughly 10 cm in diameter. Since they do not occur naturally on the hillsides on which most fortifications are built, they must have been brought from nearby *quebradas* and are conspicuously out of place on the surface on which they are found. Slingstones found on top of the benches of parapeted walls are usually placed in piles. The spacing of the piles at intervals of 2–3 m is consistent with the presumed spacing of defenders using slings. If the defenders were closer together they would have insufficient room to work their slings.

Defensive dry moats are prominent features of fortifications on the coast, in the mid-valleys, and in the sierra. In the area of the fortification survey, they are most common in the mid-valley area, quite common in the sierra, and least common on the coast. On the coast they may be a chronological marker, occurring during the latter part of the Early Intermediate Period through the Middle Horizon. Moats vary greatly in length, width, and depth. Invariably, however, they protect access across the least inclined slope(s) in the area of the fortification. Thus, the moat at a coastal site like Galindo in the Moche Valley parallels the wall and provides a break in the gently sloping topography of an alluvial fan. In the deeply cut topography of the middle valleys and in the sierra, shorter moats, often composed of a set of 2–4 parallel trenches, impede access along the spines of ridges. In these inland areas the temporal distribution of moats may be continuous from the late Early Horizon on.

A final attribute of fortified sites is their situation in

naturally defensible locations. Generally, these locations are on steep ridges, isolated hilltops, or the slopes of hills.

Problems with the identification of defensive attributes

These attributes are useful in inferring the defensive nature of sites, but there are many ambiguous cases. The least diagnostic of the attributes is defensible location. The present survey has encountered cases (e.g. Cruz Blanca Divide, 12 km upstream from Galindo) of ceremonial platform and plaza complexes located high on ridges 200 m above the irrigated land. In other cases, platform and plaza complexes are located on low hills, but are also surrounded by large unparapeted walls. The Castillo de Tomoval in the Viru Valley is a platform complex on a hill in what may be considered a strategic location. It is surrounded by walls which may at times be parapeted, but the evidence is ambiguous. Defensible, or even strategic, location by itself is poor evidence for warfare. A site should exhibit other attributes of defense before it is classed as a fortification.

The presence of a dry moat is better, although not incontrovertible, evidence for warfare. Pacatnamú, the ceremonial center in the Jequetepeque Valley with occupation probably spanning late Early Intermediate Period through Late Intermediate Period, has a large thick wall paralleled by a dry moat at its southeast edge. The wall is high enough (3 m) to be an effective barrier and thick enough (*c.* 4 m) to have supported a parapet, though none is preserved. The upper portion of the wall is built of silt, sand, and rock fill which had been obtained from the digging of the moat. It is difficult to tell in this case whether the moat and wall form a defensive barrier, or whether the moat is simply a borrow pit and the wall is a social or ceremonial barrier.

Both Pacatnamú and the nearby site of Charcape illustrate problems in identifying slingstones. Like Pacatnamú, Charcape has a large wall which is in part paralleled by a moat. Along portions of this wall are piles of angular stones unsorted by size, derived from local outcrops. The top of the wall at Pacatnamú also has quantities of rounded stones of various sizes which come from the alluvial sediments underlying the site. Because of the combination of attributes (i.e. walls, moats, piles of stones) at these sites, it is possible that they are, in fact, fortified sites. If so, the unsorted nature of the stones suggests that in this part of the Jequetepeque Valley, stones were hurled by hand rather than with slings. It is also possible that we are only encountering a coincidence of individual attributes which leads to a false appearance of fortification.

Parapets, when they are preserved, are usually unambiguous. Some problems do occur, especially in sierra sites, in interpreting poorly preserved terrace and wall-type parapets. This problem is compounded by the lack of reported slingstones on sierra sites thus far.

While these four attributes have been most useful in this study, they are not the only kinds of evidence of militarism which could conceivably occur. Andean iconography and ethnohistory depict warriors with clubs, swords, darts, arrows, special axes or knives for taking heads, helmets, shields, etc. Evidence for these items, however, is simply not found in significant quantities or reliable contexts at the sites studied. Architectural evidence of fortification figures less prominently in both iconography and ethnohistory, but salient angles, bastions, and gate closures are known from those sources.

Some of the evidence for warfare can be expected to be poorly preserved at different sites, but it should be remembered that entire sites have been lost. Examples of washouts and landslides leave no illusions of total preservation. Moreover, many sites have been reoccupied several times, making it extremely difficult to date specific fortifications without excavation.

Studies of fortifications and warfare are hampered, then, at times by poor preservation, lack of adequate information on weaponry, tactics, and strategy, and a variety of ambiguities in specific situations. In many cases it is simply impossible to be sure whether a given site was fortified or not. Quisque in the Nepeña Valley and Chankillo on the southern edge of Casma are two classic examples of fortifications which are ambiguous. In the case of Quisque, it is impossible to be certain of specific details since the site is unfinished; in its present state, the height of the breastwork would hinder slingers and the upslope side of the fortress, which in most coastal fortifications is heavily fortified, has not even been enclosed. Chankillo has massively thick walls, certainly wide enough to walk on. Stairways provide access to the tops of walls, and gates are baffled and offset. However, the closures for the gates, consisting of stone pins set in small wall niches, are located in every case on the exterior faces of the walls.

These are ambiguous cases, and the reason for the ambiguity is clear. Many other cases are relatively straightforward, but have been incorrectly interpreted for years simply because archaeologists have not been rigorous in their thinking about fortifications.

A case in point is the 'great wall' at Galindo, a Moche V site in the Moche Valley. The wall is cited by both Haas (1981) and Bawden (1977, 1982a) as evidence of internal stress and class conflict at the site. The wall is explained as a social barrier, separating lower-class residents from upper-class areas of the site. But the wall is one of the clearest examples of purposive fortification construction that we have encountered on the north coast. The wall underwent at least three modifications as a result of washouts. The final modifications of the wall incorporate a parapet, running the full 1+ km length of the wall. Slingstones are distributed evenly along the wall at a rate of approximately 150 per running meter. Outside the wall is a dry moat with causeways offset in relation to the infrequent gates in the wall. These are all quite clear defensive fortification features, and they reflect a threat external to the site rather than intrasite conflict since elite architecture is on the outside of the wall and storage, as well as lower-class residences, on the inside. While a scenario can be devised in which lower-class residents erect temporary barricades from which to fight their oppressors, this massive wall, with specialized features and evidence of multiple stages of construction and modification, can in no way be designated a 'temporary barricade.' Clearly, it defines a section of the site that was to serve as 'place of refuge' for all residents of the community in time of need.

A contrasting example is provided by Marcahuamachuco, which has often been considered the epitome of a fortified city. Parts of the site are described as 'round forts,' the 'castillo,' and the 'double defensive wall' (McCown 1945). In fact, the 'double defensive wall' consists of discrete multi-storied buildings (probably residences) placed along the edges of one section of the site. The distribution is discontinuous, with many long gaps and frequent points of access from below. In only a few places is the site bounded by a single wall, and nowhere is the wall parapeted or of an appropriate height from which to fight. The round 'forts' of Cerro las Monjas are misnamed, probably having been intended as residential buildings. They lack the defining features of fortifications. If they were ever used defensively, it was probably in a relatively unsophisticated way such as by throwing rocks from the roof. It is only in the attribute of 'defensible location' that Marcahuamachuco can be grouped with true fortified sites; but the many points of access and the lack of concern with blocking access from below suggest that the locale was chosen less for its defensive potential than for symbolic reasons; the plateau dominates the countryside and the site is visible for at least 15 km in all directions. On the basis of comparison of these single sites, one would have to conclude that Galindo was subject to a much greater threat of conflict than Marcahuamachuco.

Despite all of these cautions and ambiguities, the study of fortifications is by no means impossible, especially when numerous examples can be compared in the field. Such a study is not only a necessary prelude to the evaluation of theoretical models of warfare, but also provides a fascinating perspective on the cultural history of a region.

Fortification patterns

During the past several years, the authors have conducted surveys in contiguous areas of the coast, the western sierra slopes, and in the Huamachuco area. Much of this survey work was specifically oriented toward the study of fortifications within a broadly regional perspective encompassing a cross-section of ecological and cultural zones. The data from these surveys are not yet completely analyzed, but enough is known to outline the following sequence of fortification patterns (Carmichael 1980; Coupland 1979; DeHetre 1979; Haley 1979; Mackenzie 1980, 1985; Melly 1983; J. Topic and T. Topic 1983a, 1985).

Preceramic Period

Although early phases are poorly represented by fortification, one site is potentially very important. This site is located on an old uplifted bay in the Salinas de Santa. The site, a small village dating to about 3000 B.C., predates the Cotton Preceramic (Moseley, personal communication). There are no major walls, but discrete piles of slingstones bound the village on two sides. These piles are arranged in two rows, one on each side of the site, commencing at the old beach and extending inland for 75 to 100 m. The average spacing of the piles is consistent with the spacing required between individual slingers. There are a few ceramics in the vicinity of the site (probably Middle Horizon and Late Intermediate Period), but the association of the slingstone piles and the preceramic village, though based on surface evidence, appears to be good.

The major problem with the Salinas de Santa site is that it stands alone. There are no contemporary fortifications or manifestations of conflict to which the site can be compared. In fact, we have no other well-dated fortifications north of Santa until the beginning of the Early Intermediate Period, when they become quite common.

Early Intermediate Period (early)

On the coast during the early part of the Early Intermediate Period, both poor preservation and the tendency for many sites to be multi-component make it difficult to discuss discrete attributes. Sites such as Cerro Bitín in the Viru Valley document the use of terrace and wall type parapets and slingstones. While Cerro Bitín served as a place of refuge and lacked a large permanent population, many other Puerto Moorin and Salinar sites were probably fortified villages. These villages are concentrated in the narrow valley sector (about 200–800 m above sea level). It is not entirely clear against whom the fortifications were built (see chapter by S. Pozorski, this volume), but Layzon ceramics from Cajamarca found at Piedra Molina in the Chicama Valley and at Cerro Pongo (V–212) in Viru indicate wide-ranging interaction.

Only a handful of the fortifications in the sierra portion of the survey zone can be dated to the early part of the Early Intermediate Period. On the western slopes, these include the castle-like Mis Pasday and the 'great wall' Muro de Sango, both near the Hacienda Motil in the province of Otuzco. In addition, parts of the site complex of Los Mellizos, located on the divide between the Moche, La Cuesta, and Chicama Rivers, date to this phase. All of these fortifications are located near the upper limit of agriculture between 3400 and 3900 m. Muro de Sango in fact demarcates the modern limit of agriculture in that area. This site is equipped with fortified hilltop watch-stations while the other sites have both parapeted walls (wall and terrace type) and dry moats. Fortifications in these areas may reflect increasing pressure on herding land and local conflict.

Cerro Campana East, near Huamachuco, dates to the late Early Horizon with some possible continuity into the Early Intermediate Period. This village site is not heavily fortified and is probably located on a road at an important natural crossroads. However, the site is placed on a defensible ridge, incorporates a possible watch-station, and is partially enclosed by a defensible wall and terrace.

Early Intermediate Period (middle and late)

During the later Early Intermediate Period we see considerable continuity on the coast, but marked change in the

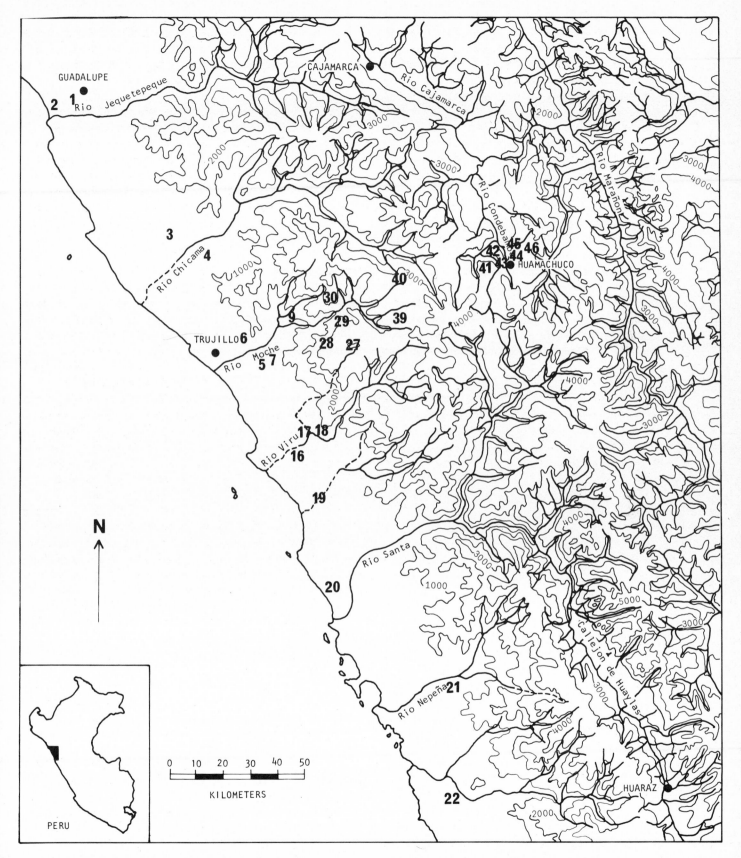

Fig. 1. Sites surveyed during fortification study: 1. Charcape; 2. Pacatnamú; 3. Cerro Facalá; 4. Piedra Molina; 5. Cerro Orejas; 6. Galindo; 7. Cerro Blanco del León; 9. Cruz Blanca; 16. Cerro Bitin; 17. Tomoval; 18. Cerro Pongo; 19. Cerro Coronado; 20. Salinas de Santa; 21. Quisque; 22. Chankillo; 27. Cerro Quinga; 28. Chamana; 29. Cuidista; 30. Carpaico; 39. Cerro Campana Chica; 40. Ochoconday; 41. Cerro Grande; 42. Marcahuamachuco; 43. Cerro Amaru; 44. Cerro Tuscan; 45. Viracochapampa; 46. Cerro Campana East

sierra. In the Viru Valley many sites with Puerto Moorin components continued to be occupied during the Early Intermediate Period. While this continuity makes it difficult to sort out the defensive attributes associated with each phase, it seems likely that slingstones, parapeted walls, and dry moats all occur. Fortifications, including fortified villages, fortified administrative/elite centers, and fortresses, are still concentrated in the middle valley rather than in the lower valley. The situation in the Moche Valley is quite similar, where it is likely that Gallinazo-style ceramics continued in use during Moche Phases I and II in the middle valley. In both valleys, foreign trade sherds are often found on Gallinazo phase sites, though they rarely filter down into the lower valleys. These trade wares come from Cajamarca, the Callejón de Huaylas, and the nearby Otuzco area (Czwarno 1983).

Although many fortified sites continue in use during Moche III and IV, only one fortified site is known to have been built during this period in the area surveyed. This site, Huacamochal, is located on a high ridge in the middle Moche Valley and was probably the major settlement in the area at this time. The site is enclosed by a combination of canal, low wall, and partial dry moat; no slingstones are present and the level of preparedness is not impressive. Foreign trade sherds cannot be securely associated with the Moche III–IV occupations of any of the sites we surveyed.

In the province of Otuzco during the Early Intermediate Period there is change as well as continuity. The Motil area continues to be an important focus of occupation. The Muro de Sango continues in use during much of the Early Intermediate Period and serves as an outer defense for the site of Ayangay. Ayangay is a major site with public architecture incorporating carved stone heads in the walls and both elite and non-elite domestic architecture (Zaki 1978). Other sites in the area include towns such as Sango, Gemelos, and Cerro Caupar.

Changes in the Otuzco area include the relatively rapid expansion of settlement on the Carabamba Plateau and the beginnings of development in the Mache area, which links the Carabamba Plateau to the Motil area (Figure 2). The Carabamba Plateau, located between the upper Viru (Huacapongo) and the Moche Rivers, is ideally situated for interaction with the coast. Interaction is indicated by the distribution of a white and orange on red ceramic style (the

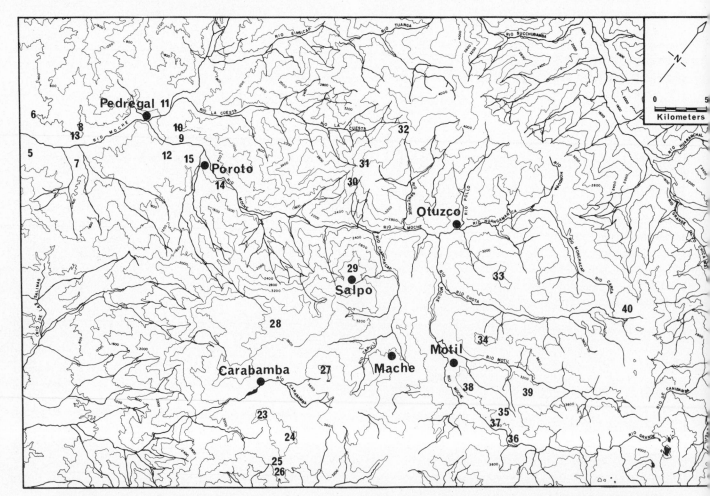

Fig. 2. Sites surveyed during fortification study: 5. Cerro Orejas; 6. Galindo; 7. Cerro Blanco del León; 8. Santa Rosa Baja; 9. Cruz Blanca; 10. Cruz Blanca Divide 3; 11. Cumbray; 12. La Botija; 13. Puente Serrano; 14. Siete Vueltas; 15. Huacamochal; 23. Cerro Suldha; 24. Paredones; 25. Churre; 26. Mollepuquio; 27. Cerro Quinga; 28. Chamana; 29. Cuidista; 30. Carpaico; 31. Rogoday; 32. Los Mellizos; 33. Mis Pasday. 34. Cerro Caupar; 35. Muro de Sango; 36. Sango; 37. Ayangay; 38. Gemelos; 39. Cerro Campana Chica; 40. Ochoconday

Castillo R/W/O of Bennett (1950) and Ford (1949)) which occurs frequently on the Carabamba Plateau as well as in middle valley coastal sites, but rarely in the lower valleys. The Carabamba Plateau probably also was a link in the interaction between the Callejón de Huaylas and Gallinazo phase sites on the coast. Two Carabamba area sites, Paredones and Cerro Sulcha, have sectors which may have served as *tambo*s. It is also likely that Ayangay was involved in this interaction.

Not all sites in these areas are clearly fortified. Most occupy defensible positions, and many are surrounded by walls and terraces which could be defended. Some incorporate a citadel within the town, others have outlying watch-stations. Some are clearly fortified towns or villages, while a few sites appear to be fortresses with only small populations.

Several sites (e.g. Churre, Cerro Mollepuquio, Cerro Sulcha, Gemelos, and Ayangay) have multi-storied architecture with specific attributes suggesting influence from the Huamachuco area. During the later part of the Early Intermediate Period Huamachuco probably maintained a route which passed through the Motil, Mache, and Carabamba area. A series of impressive sites extend in a linear pattern through the area, but only three (Ochoconday near Usquil, Cerro Campana Chica near Motil, and Cerro Quinga) have been studied. Ceramics at the first two sites clearly relate to the Huamachuco area. At the third site, which is unfinished, ceramics are rare. Curiously, these three sites are less similar architecturally to classic Huamachuco architecture than the other sites mentioned above. The degree of Huamachuco control over the province of Otuzco is still unclear.

The early part of the Early Intermediate Period in Huamachuco is still poorly understood. There are a few small fortified sites which probably date to the period. These are characterized by defensible location, parapeted walls, and, usually, dry moats. All appear to be small towns or villages. Current evidence indicates that classic Huamachuco architecture dates to the latter part of the Early Intermediate Period. As noted earlier, while Marcahuamachuco and other sites of the later Early Intermediate Period are often located on hilltops, there is no indication that this location was determined by defensive needs.

Middle Horizon

In contrast to the Early Intermediate Period, the Middle Horizon saw much change on the coast, but less in the highlands. Our best evidence from the coast comes from the Moche Valley; the situation is much less clear in the Chicama and Viru Valleys. Overall, the picture which emerges is one of collapse and fragmentation. Moche V ceramics were found only in the Moche Valley. Four sites (Cruz Blanca, Cumbray, La Botija, and Cerro Blanco del León) which were foci of coast–sierra interaction during the Gallinazo phases were reoccupied and refortified. Cruz Blanca was a major midvalley settlement, while the fortress of La Botija defended the southern approaches to the site. A fortress, Siete Vueltas, was constructed overlooking a valley neck just upriver from Cruz

Blanca, and Cumbray defended access down the Sinsicap River. In addition to Cruz Blanca, cities and towns such as Galindo and Puente Serrano were heavily fortified. It is possible that the middle valley was lost at the end of Moche V since a massive wall seems to cross the valley at Pedregal, somewhat downriver from Cruz Blanca. Evidence of Chimu expansion, which may have begun in the late Middle Horizon, indicates a reconquest of the area above Pedregal.

While much of the Middle Horizon in the province of Otuzco probably represents a continuation of existing patterns, at some point during the Middle Horizon there is a geographic shift in the emphasis of Huamachuco influence. Whereas the old pattern of interaction had focused on the area between the Moche and Viru Rivers, the new focus is on the divide between the Moche and Chicama Rivers. Evidence for this shift occurs in the form of ceramic distributions and settlement patterns. A brownware decorated style with punctuated fillets, called Huamachuco Impressed (Krzanowski 1977; McCown 1945), occurs throughout the Huamachuco and Otuzco areas but most commonly on the Moche–Chicama divide. This style continues into the Late Intermediate Period (J. Topic and T. Topic 1983b). Local sites along the divide are often associated with walled roads and are usually fortified or incorporate citadels.

In addition to maintaining links with the province of Otuzco, Huamachuco was certainly interacting with Wari during the Middle Horizon. The spatial and temporal focus for this interaction seems to be the site of Cerro Amaru during Middle Horizon 1b. At that time, ceramics and other materials indicate that Huamachuco was interacting with a number of areas including the south-central highlands, the central highlands and coast, and the north highlands (T. Topic and J. Topic 1984). Surprisingly, there appears to have been little effect on Marcahuamachuco during this period and this site experienced no break in occupation or orientation. Although construction began at Viracochapampa, a presumed Wari administrative center, the site was neither finished nor occupied (J. Topic and T. Topic 1983b). We have not been able to date securely any fortifications in Huamachuco to the Middle Horizon.

Late Intermediate Period

Ethnohistory (Rowe 1948; Kosok 1965) tells us that the early kings of Chimor had to reconquer and unite the Moche Valley, and the archaeological evidence supports this. Although most of the reconquest took place during the Late Intermediate Period, some fortifications probably date to the Middle Horizon. The earliest Chimu fortress may be at Cerro Orejas, only 17 km from the ocean and directly across the valley from Galindo. Cerro Orejas, however, is rather isolated, and the real reconquest seems to have taken place from Pedregal, about 25 km inland, through the district of Poroto, 36 km inland. Through this zone, the density of Chimu fortifications, fortresses, and fortified settlements is the highest documented anywhere, with the possible exception of the middle Viru Valley. Most of these fortifications were built and abandoned before the middle of the Late Intermediate Period. While there is some indication of a stage by stage advance up the Moche Valley, this pattern is not clearcut.

The Viru Valley also contains a dense pattern of fortifications in the middle valley, though these generally date somewhat later than examples in the Moche Valley. The lack of fortifications in the lower valley is surprising since the pattern of Chimu expansion is indicated in the lower portions of other coastal valleys. Other valleys were not surveyed intensively, but informal survey indicates that the Chao, the Jequetepeque, and probably the Chicama Valleys, had fortified sites of local affiliation during the Middle Horizon and early Late Intermediate Period, and were conquered by the Chimu during the first half of the Late Intermediate Period. In both the Chao and Chicama Valleys there are Chimu fortifications (Cerro Coronado and Cerro Facalá respectively) which were either incomplete or were never completely occupied, indicating ongoing expansion. In these valleys, there is the distinct possibility that these fortifications can be directly related to the first phase of Chimu expansion postulated by Klymyshyn, Mackey, and T. Pozorski (see chapters by Klymyshyn, Mackey, and T. Pozorski, this volume). In Viru, there is no evidence of local fortifications during the Middle Horizon in either the lower or middle valley.

Chimu expansion inland relates to events in the province of Otuzco. Chimu influence reached the highlands of the province during the early part of the Late Intermediate Period. At this time, the Chimu probably entered the Carabamba area through the site of Chamana. They maintained and fortified the route to 1200 m along a ridge which rises rapidly overlooking Poroto, 37 km inland. During the later Late Intermediate Period, the Chimu entered the highlands through two routes further inland. The Cuidista route (about 52 km from the ocean) leads past the modern town of Salpo and continues through Mache, bypassing the Carabamba Plateau. The second, more important route, passed through Carpaico and swung around to the west, north, and east of Otuzco to join with the late Huamachuco route. These latter two routes were maintained and fortified by Cuidista and Carpaico from about 2600 m. Although Chimu ceramics occur in low frequencies throughout the province of Otuzco, a Chimu site has never been found there; the inland boundary of the Chimu empire was probably located at about the 1200 m contour.

Information on the Late Intermediate Period in Huamachuco is far from complete. Marcahuamachuco continued to be occupied. A number of sites are located on high hills or ridges, but only one (Cerro Grande) appears fortified. Huamachuco-inspired architectural attributes at a number of sites in the Otuzco area, especially along the Carpaico route, suggest that Huamachuco was still interacting to the west.

Late Horizon

Late Horizon fortifications are scarce in all three regions. Most Chimu fortifications have little evidence of use in the late Late Intermediate Period. Some exceptions occur in the middle Viru, notably a parapeted wall about 1 km long. This wall, which is unfinished, dates to the end of the Late Intermediate Period or conceivably to the Late Horizon. In the Otuzco area, where agricultural terracing is not very common in earlier periods, a number of sites with extensive terracing occur. We studied only one such site, Rogoday, which dates to the Late Horizon and is associated with three small hilltop forts. Rogoday is located squarely on the Carpaico route which was used by both the Chimu and the Huamachuquinos. The other terraced sites are located on or near this route. In Huamachuco, architectural evidence indicates that the major Inca installation was located where the modern town of Huamachuco now stands. The fortress on Cerro Tuscán, overlooking the town, may then be a Late Horizon installation designed to protect the Inca settlement.

Conclusions

When Andeanists discourse upon the origins of complex society and/or the state, the range of time periods, cultures, and levels of development on which they focus is extraordinarily wide, ranging from at least the Preceramic (Moseley 1975a) to the Middle Horizon (Isbell and Schreiber 1978). In Carneiro's (1981) view, with which the authors agree, the most crucial changes in social organization predate state formation and encompass the emergence of chiefdoms, social ranking, and economic inequality. Carneiro's model, which derives class structure from warfare, predicts significant conflict at a much earlier date than many Andeanists would allow.

The evidence at Salinas de Santa in particular conforms to the expectations of Carneiro's model, and supports the presence of conflict over desired but concentrated resources as early as 3000 B.C. It is unfortunate that there is only a single case, and one that is so peripheral to the main line of preceramic development. If evidence for preceramic warfare were sought more diligently in other areas, it would probably be found. If occupants of the relatively thinly settled and underdeveloped north coast are in conflict with one another over access to favored resources, the conflict should be more pronounced further south along the more densely settled central coast. Similarly, on the central coast, methods of avoiding conflict (alliance, forfeiture of community autonomy, shared ideology and corporate projects) as well as means of settling conflict (law, militarism) should have developed more quickly.

The patterning of the earliest fortifications in the province of Otuzco suggests that resource concentration is again an important factor. The location of sites in a narrow band along the margins of the *jalca* grasslands indicates a mixed tuber agriculture and herding economy. Because of the high productivity of tuber agriculture, herding land, and hence animal protein would be the limited resource.

In both cases, then, a linear settlement pattern developed along the zone in which desired resources were concentrated. As the number of settlements in each line increased, population pressure built up and with it the potential for conflict. We do not share Carneiro's (1970:737, 1978:207, 1981:65) emphasis on the conquest and subjugation of populations at this stage, and feel that, much as in Amazonia, warfare probably functioned as a dispersal mechanism discouraging overexploitation. However, larger and more complex settlements would be at an advantage and these might develop through reduced fissioning (Carneiro 1981:64).

Neither on the coast nor in the highlands is the initial appearance of fortifications related to environmental or social circumscription. Functioning as a dispersal mechanism, warfare would gradually force groups into exploiting less desirable territories. In the highlands, lower-lying lands allowed for the expansion of agriculture and greatly increased population density at the cost of reduced availability of animal protein. On the coast, the cultivation of cotton and the manufacture of netting allowed for a more intensive exploitation of marine protein resources, while the gradual expansion of agriculture provided increasing numbers of calories. Warfare was involved in this transformation, but the level of warfare during the period was probably not intense.

On the coast, in fact, fortifications dating to the late Preceramic, Initial Period, and Early Horizon were not encountered in our survey. While this negative evidence should not be viewed as synonymous with a lack of warfare, it suggests that military expansion had not yet become an important factor. Instead, a combination of factors, of which warfare was one, led to increasing complexity during this time. When fortifications again become common at the beginning of the Early Intermediate Period, it is clear that a quantum leap in group complexity has already occurred.

The outstanding characteristic of fortifications in the Moche and Viru Valleys is long-term locational stability; the same hilltops were occupied repeatedly throughout the Early Intermediate Period, Middle Horizon and Late Intermediate Period. Fortifications here suggest an inland boundary which moved only about 10 km in either direction from a 600 m above sea level baseline during approximately 1700 years. Throughout the survey area, fortifications are often associated with road fragments and trade ceramics (J. Topic and T. Topic 1983a, 1985). Thus the evidence suggests that one of the major functions of warfare was to maintain territorial and cultural boundaries. The emphasis on boundary maintenance was perhaps strongest during the Early Intermediate Period when differences between a number of essentially similar cultures were symbolized not only by defended territorial boundaries but also by elaborate 'state' art styles. Fortifications served not only as defenses against military attack but also as control points regulating interaction between cultures (J. Topic and T. Topic 1983a).

Fortifications, as essentially defensive installations, are of limited use in assessing the role of warfare as a mechanism of political expansion (Carneiro 1978). The best case from our survey is that of Chimu expansion, which left a sequence of abandoned fortifications in its wake. Although less well documented, it is likely that the Huamachuco and Moche cultures expanded at least in part through military conquest. On the side, the fact that Moche V settlements in the Moche Valley were heavily fortified shows that warfare was an important mechanism in the collapse of the culture. We have no evidence of Wari fortifications and only a few Inca fortifications within the survey zone.

The reasons for territorial expansion are not an issue here, but it is interesting to review the data available for the later periods to elucidate the patterns present in the various cycles of expansion which can be documented or hypothesized. First, coastal polities do not attempt to conquer the sierra, although they defend their inland borders. Second, control of coast–sierra trade routes is a major determinant of the location of military installations. Third, militarily weaker polities such as those in the Otuzco area during the Late Intermediate Period were able to preserve independence of action by relying on the natural topography and by serving as middlemen for more powerful neighbors, and probably also by judicious selection of patrons and exploitations of weaknesses among neighboring polities.

This chapter began with some cautionary observations on the problems inherent in the study of prehistoric warfare; those cautions probably apply to the Andean area as a whole. The sequence of fortifications we presented in the second section, however, is a local sequence and there is no reason to expect it to be paralleled in other areas of the Andes. Finally, we have related the sequence of fortifications from our survey area to the theoretical views of Carneiro.

Chapter 6

Reconstructing patterns of early warfare in the lower Santa Valley: new data on the role of conflict in the origins of complex north-coast society

David J. Wilson

Introduction

Recent studies of the role of warfare in the origins and development of prehispanic central Andean state societies have relied on essentially three kinds of evidence. These include *ethnohistorical accounts* from the 16th- and 17th-century Spanish documentary sources of Inca and immediately pre-Inca warfare; *archaeological data* from studies of fortress structures, walls, and weapons of war placed as burial offerings dating as far back in time as the Early Horizon (*c*. 1000–350 B.C.); and *iconographic evidence* from pottery, textiles, and rock carvings depicting warriors, battle scenes, and the taking of prisoners dating to periods from the Early Horizon on to the end of the prehispanic sequence (e.g., see Bram 1941; Carneiro 1970; Gorenstein 1963; Proulx 1971; Rawls 1979). The ethnohistorical and archaeological data on the Inca constitute, of course, the most complete record available of the role of military activities and installations in a central Andean society, although the rich body of iconographic evidence on the pottery of the Moche state (*c*. A.D. 400–650) provides an exceptionally detailed picture of the importance of war and conquest at a much earlier time in the sequence (e.g., see Benson 1972; Donnan 1976; Kutscher 1954).

What has been lacking, however, in studies of prehispanic central Andean warfare has been a detailed regional study that focused systematically and comprehensively not only on the role of conflict in societal evolution (e.g., by

retrieving data on the nature, distribution, and dating of all fortress sites in a region), but also on how conflict relates to other potentially critical factors such as the establishment of irrigation agriculture, population growth, and overall patterns of settlement (e.g., by retrieving data on the size, density of occupational remains, and dating of all habitation and ceremonial–civic sites). Archaeological studies of a general regional scope had been carried out prior to 1979 in several north-coast valleys containing extensive defensive systems – including Nepeña (Proulx 1968, 1973), Viru (Willey 1953), and Moche (J. Topic and T. Topic 1978). But the lack of systematic regional coverage in these valleys, as well as incomplete retrieval of data on size and occupational density of habitation sites, made it difficult to reconstruct changing demographic patterns in relation to the number and distribution of fortress sites.

Yet, in spite of the absence of these and other data necessary for constructing a comprehensive picture of the evolutionary role of warfare in the prehispanic coastal setting, it is interesting to note that one of the leading theorists of state origins (Carneiro 1970) had proposed a detailed developmental sequence based on the Peruvian data and involving population growth and internecine, or within-region, warfare. According to Carneiro's scheme, the early prestate sequence following the establishment of agriculture in a typical coastal valley would have been characterized by continuing conflict and fighting

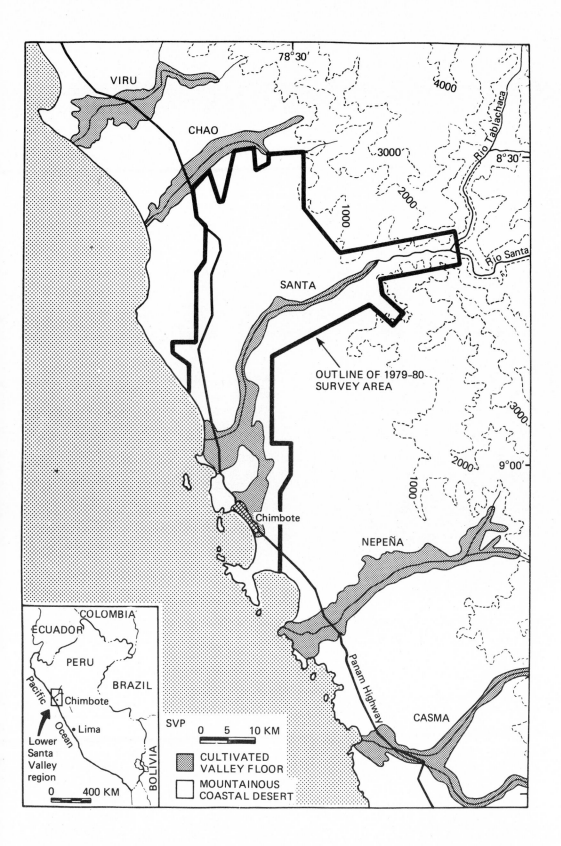

Fig. 1. Lower Santa Valley survey area and adjacent coastal valleys

Table 1. *Data on estimated population size, selected site types, and average location of habitation and defensive sites for the early agricultural periods in the lower Santa Valley sequence, pre-1800 B.C. to c. A.D. 650*

Period	Total population estimate	Total number of sites	Number of non-defensive habitation sites	Number of defensive sites	Average elevation of habitation and defensive sites above valley floor (in m)	Average distance of habitation and defensive sites away from floor (in m)
Guadalupito	22 020	205	79	—	15*	90*
Late Suchimancillo	29 765	153	91	32	80	270
Early Suchimancillo	20 110	130	72	40	110	250
Vinzos	7855	45	30	12	135†	680†
Cayhuamarca	5960	54	24	20	160‡	740‡

*Excludes sites located out on the valley floor itself.
†Includes only sites located in the immediate area of the main valley floor, and not those located in the desert out to the north.
‡Excludes SVP–CAY–54, a maritime site in the far southern part of the survey region.

among settlements over access to the increasingly limited supply of locally available irrigable land – at least given the assumptions that (1) local villages jealously guarded their autonomy, and (2) populations had quickly begun to press against the capacity of the land to sustain them. In the face of this pressure, demographically and militaristically superior villages at the level of incipient chiefdoms would have coerced weaker villages into becoming part of local polities of ever-increasing scope and complexity, eventually leading to the rise of stratified society at the regional level and, ultimately, to the formation of multivalley conquest states. Thus, as the coercive theory would have it, the state arose in a context characterized first (and most importantly) by within-valley conflict among neighboring groups of people – with warrior-chiefs forming the hierarchical apex of emerging polities – and only later by hostilities between different coastal valley regions.

Overview of the Santa Valley project

In 1979–80, with the help of a number of field assistants from Peru, Argentina, and the U.S. and grants from the National Science Foundation, the Wenner-Gren Foundation for Anthropological Research, and other sources, the author carried out a comprehensive survey of all extant prehispanic surface remains in the lower Santa Valley region (Figure 1). The Santa Valley is located near the southern end of the ten-valley 'core' area comprising the center of prehispanic north-coast cultural developments and state formation, from the Lambeyeque Valley in the north to the Casma Valley in the south. It is therefore situated strategically with respect to the principal developments leading to the rise of the Moche state. In this regard, it was hoped that outlining a detailed regional sequence of changing site types and patterns of settlement would provide a sensitive indicator of the main developmental processes characterizing Santa and adjacent valleys to the north and south.

During the course of the fieldwork, full-coverage survey was extended over an area of more than 750 km – including the desert margins and the valley floor comprising the entire 70 km-long coastal sector of the Santa River, as well as a 50 km-long stretch of Pacific coastline and the inland part of the intervalley desert between Santa and Chao Valleys. As in recent comprehensive studies in the Near East and Mesoamerica, large-scale matte-finish airphotos were used for field orientation and to mark down directly the size, extent, and dating of surface remains as the survey team proceeded systematically across the terrain. A consistent attempt was made throughout the fieldwork to estimate precisely both (1) the outline and size of each site encountered on the basis of the overall extent of structural remains and occupational debris; and (2) any period-to-period changes in the areal extent of occupation on multicomponent (i.e. multiperiod) sites, primarily on the basis of the variable extent of ceramic temporal diagnostics.

Given the limited amount of irrigable land in Santa (c. 11 300 ha), as well as the excellent preservation of habitation structures on the majority of sites dating as far back as the Cotton Preceramic (pre-1800 B.C.), an argument can be constructed that the lower Santa Valley survey data closely approximate a 100% sample of all prehispanic occupations that existed in the region (detailed support for this argument is outlined in Wilson 1985; note that the total number of occupations is 1246, compared to about 500 for the next complete survey in the Viru Valley). In addition, given the estimates of regional population based on the systematic assessment of structural densities on inhabited sites of all ten periods in the sequence, the Lower Santa research has resulted in the first empirically based demographic profile for a coastal Peruvian valley (note that estimates for the early periods are shown in Table 1; for the overall profile, see Wilson 1983, 1985).

Of particular relevance to the focus of this paper are the data gathered on the nature and chronology of early defensive

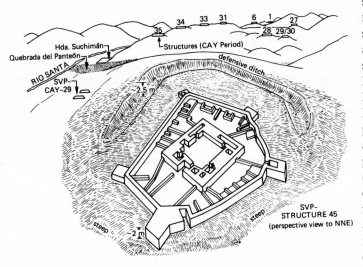

Fig. 2. Perspective view of Structure 45/SVP–CAY–28. with nearby Cayhuamarca Period sites shown in schematic background sketch

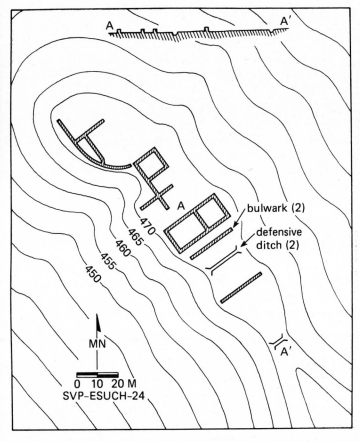

Fig. 3. Plan and profile views of SVP–ESUCH–24, a minor ridgetop fortress site dating to the Early Suchimancillo Period

sites in the main valley area. The results of the 1979–80 fieldwork indicate that fully 57 out of 62 discrete fortress structures in this area date to one or more of the four early agricultural periods preceding the rise of multivalley state society – including Cayhuamarca Period (Early Horizon or EH), Vinzos Period (Early Intermediate Period 1 or EIP 1), Early Suchimancillo Period (EIP 2), and Late Suchimancillo Period (EIP 3). In general, fortresses were found to be of two principal types: the first consists of larger structures designated as 'citadels' (e.g., Figure 2), which usually are found on higher peaks and ridges above and away from the valley floor (elevations above the floor range as high as 700 m, and distances range as far as 3.3 km away from it). Among the main features of citadels are massive enclosure walls measuring an average of 2 m wide and 2–4 m high, bastions, a limited number of entrances, simple ramparts and parapets, evidence of interior and/or exterior habitation generally numbering over an estimated 100 persons, and associated dry ditches and bulwark walls cutting across any relatively gentle access slopes running up to the site.

The second type of defensive site consists of 'minor fortresses' (Figure 3), which usually are found on narrow ridges immediately overlooking habitation sites located at the edge of the valley floor. Minor fortresses generally have fewer and smaller structures than citadels, as well as more limited evidence of habitation and associated defensive ditches and bulwarks protecting the main site area. Judging from associated ceramic diagnostics, minor fortresses are primarily characteristic of Early and Late Suchimancillo Periods (EIP 2 and EIP 3). Major citadel structures, on the other hand, are an important feature of the settlement systems of all four of the early agricultural periods. In general, as shown in Table 1, defensive sites of both types range in number between 12 in the Vinzos Period and 40 in the Early Suchimancillo Period (EIP 2). But, as indicated on the settlement pattern maps (Figures 4 and 5–8), fortress sites are distributed widely throughout most or all of the settlement systems of each of the four early periods. In sharp contrast, we found no obvious fortress sites at all dating to the Guadalupito Period (EIP 4) (Figure 9), the time of the Moche occupation of the valley. The data thus appear to point not only to the fundamental importance of warfare in the prestate periods, but also to a striking change in the overall nature of the regional subsistence-settlement system once Santa became a province of the Moche state.

Aspects of the socioenvironmental setting

Before I go on to present the archaeological data on patterns of early settlement, it will be useful briefly to outline selected aspects of the physical setting within which such critical processes as the development of agriculture, population growth, and ongoing warfare were occurring. As mentioned earlier, the coastal region of the Santa River extends for a distance of some 70 km, descending on a relatively gentle average gradient of 1.4% from the confluence of the Santa and Tablachaca Rivers to the ocean. Having cut steeply and

Chart 1. Prehispanic periods of the lower Santa Valley region and related sequences

Estimated absolute chronology	Santa Valley Period	Viru Valley Period	Central Andean Period
1532			
	Late Tambo Real	Estero	Late Horizon
1350			
	Early Tambo Real	La Plata	Late Intermediate
1150			
	Late Tanguche		
900		Tomoval	Middle Horizon
	Early Tanguche		
650			
	Guadalupito	Huanchaco	4
400			
	Late Suchimancillo	L	3
200		Gallinazo M	Early Intermediate
	Early Suchimancillo	E	2
A.D.			
B.C.		L	
	Vinzos	Puerto Moorin	1
		E	
350			
		L	
	Cayhuamarca	Guañape	
		M	Early Horizon
1000			
	(?)	E	Initial Period
1800			
	Las Salinas	Cerro Prieto	Preceramic

narrowly down through the main western cordillera in the preceding 85 km, the canyon of the Santa does not begin to open up appreciably until it reaches a point roughly halfway between the Santa–Tablachaca confluence and the ocean. This aspect of the setting is intimately related to the distribution of irrigable land along the lower 70 km of the river.

Thus, in the upper valley sector between the Santa–Tablachaca confluence and a point 30 km downvalley, only 470 ha of cultivable valley floor are available – representing a minuscule 4.1% of all land in the region that can be farmed using traditional contour canals. In the next 20 km that constitute the middle valley sector, the valley opens up to form a wider pocket containing an estimated 1430 ha of cultivable land – or 12.7% of the total. The remaining 9400 ha of the 11 300 ha estimated to have been suitable for prehispanic cultivation – or 82.3% of the total – are located in the wider lower valley sector, which covers the remaining 20 km of the coastal region and includes the mouths of both Santa Valley proper and Quebrada de Lacramarca (adjacent to the modern town of Chimbote, in Figure 1). However, in spite of the fact that most of the cultivable land in the region is situated in the lower valley, the earliest significant developments following the establishment of irrigation agriculture took place almost entirely in the upper and middle valley sectors. This seems likely to be due in part to the relative ease of irrigating fields with shorter canals in the context of low population numbers and a steeper river gradient, but the strong upvalley focus of early settlement may well be due in part to the relatively greater protection provided by the steep, rugged terrain of the upvalley sectors.

Another aspect of the setting that has importance for understanding patterns of early warfare is the nature of traditional canals in the valley. As the detailed maps of the Oficina Nacional de Evaluación de Recursos Naturales (ONERN 1972, 1973) make clear, traditional canal networks in Santa (and adjacent Viru and Nepeña) are positioned throughout most of the valley in intricate patterns that imply interdependency, if not outright cooperation, among farmers of various local areas. Thus, even though in Santa the upper and middle valley sectors form a single, interconnected network that stands essentially apart from the lower valley, the intakes for the main canals of this last sector are located in the lowermost part of the middle valley. Farmers of the lower valley are therefore dependent upon the good offices of those in the lower middle valley in ensuring the continued integrity of canal intakes so that water will reach the fields. As we shall see later, this aspect of the traditional agricultural adaptation has critical implications for understanding the nature of early warfare – in Santa as well as adjacent valleys – since by the time of Cayhuamarca Period (EH), irrigation agriculture probably had become the major source of subsistence.

A final important aspect of the physical environment is that while Santa and adjacent valleys are roughly comparable with respect to the total supply of land, the Santa is unique in being one of the few coastal rivers that extend deeply into the adjacent western *cordillera* of the Andes. Its giant catchment basin of 10 200 km provides over ten times the amount of water required to irrigate intensively the land associated with traditional canal networks. With a benign climate year-round and the possibility of obtaining as many as two or three crops throughout the year, prehispanic inhabitants of the region thus had the potential to produce relatively larger and more continuous annual harvests than other nearby valleys of comparable or larger size limited by a seasonal water supply.

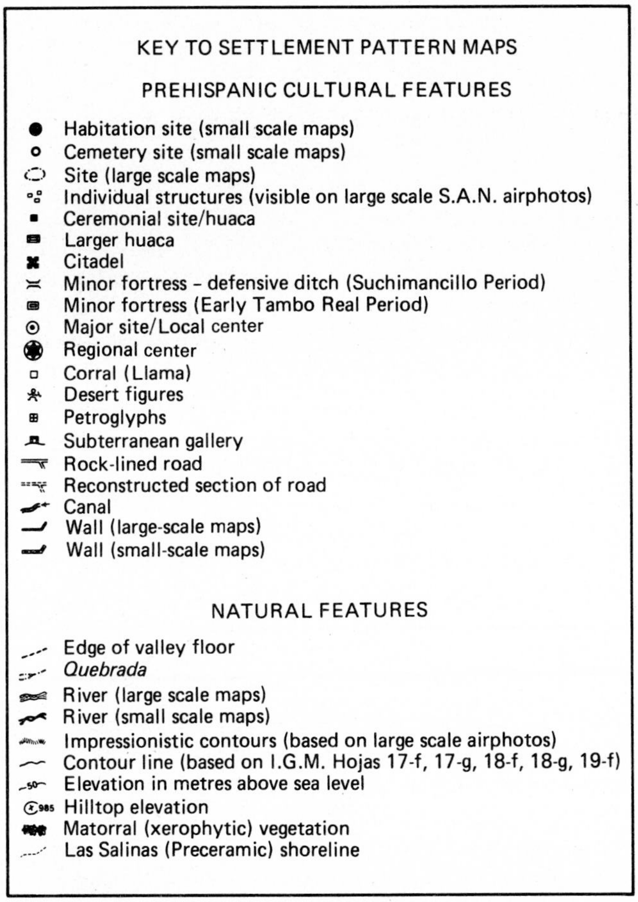
KEY TO SETTLEMENT PATTERN MAPS
PREHISPANIC CULTURAL FEATURES
Habitation site (small scale maps)
Cemetery site (small scale maps)
Site (large scale maps)
Individual structures (visible on large scale S.A.N. airphotos)
Ceremonial site/huaca
Larger huaca
Citadel
Minor fortress - defensive ditch (Suchimancillo Period)
Minor fortress (Early Tambo Real Period)
Major site/Local center
Regional center
Corral (Llama)
Desert figures
Petroglyphs
Subterranean gallery
Rock-lined road
Reconstructed section of road
Canal
Wall (large-scale maps)
Wall (small-scale maps)
NATURAL FEATURES
Edge of valley floor
Quebrada
River (large scale maps)
River (small scale maps)
Impressionistic contours (based on large scale airphotos)
Contour line (based on I.G.M. Hojas 17-f, 17-g, 18-f, 18-g, 19-f)
Elevation in metres above sea level
Hilltop elevation
Matorral (xerophytic) vegetation
Las Salinas (Preceramic) shoreline

Fig. 4. Key to settlement pattern maps in Figures 5–9

Indeed, the fundamental difference between Santa and valleys such as Viru, Nepeña, and Casma is that all of the latter are reliant upon second-class streams for subsistence (Kroeber 1930). That is, water is only available on a relatively limited and unpredictable seasonal basis lasting several months each year. As argued later, this has additional implications for the nature of warfare in the early periods.

Archaeological data and the analysis of the early periods

Cayhuamarca Period (Early Horizon)

Given the overall nature of the Cayhuamarca Period (EH) settlement pattern (Figure 5), two fundamental assertions can be made about the nature of the Early Horizon system in Santa Valley. In the first place, the physical evidence for warfare is present everywhere in the form of a series of 20 ridgetop and hilltop citadels that extend over a distance of 40 km, between sites in the uppermost part of the upper valley and those in the lower part of the middle valley. Second, it is highly probable not only that the subsistence system was based on intensive irrigation agriculture, but also that the nature of

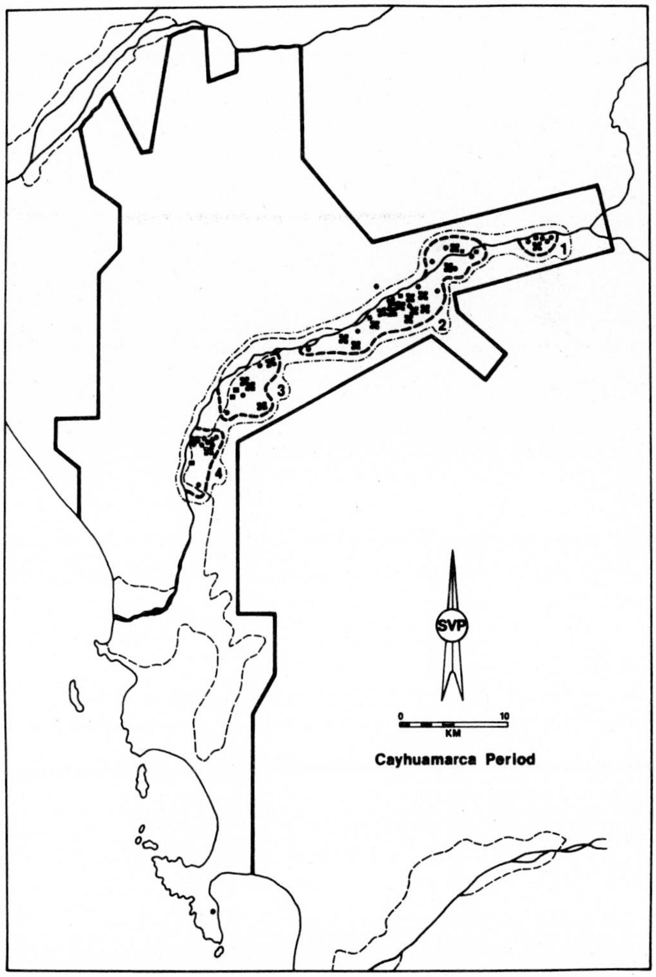
1
2
3
4
SVP
0
10
KM
Cayhuamarca Period

Fig. 5. Settlement pattern map of Cayhuamarca/Early Horizon Period (*c*. 1000–350 B.C.)

this system was such that it required a general context of peaceful intersite relations, if not cooperation, among most sites.

This latter assertion related to subsistence is based partly on (1) data including the presence of such cultigens as maize, beans, and squash from excavated Early Horizon contexts in other nearby valleys (see Bird 1948b; Pozorski 1979b; note that the earliest preserved surface cultigens found during our research date to Early Suchimancillo (EIP 2)); and partly on (2) the analysis of maize-based carrying capacity of the Cayhuamarca (EH) system. As argued elsewhere (Wilson 1983:257–263, 1985), the relatively large population of nearly 6000 persons probably could have sustained itself only on an intensive agricultural base. The analysis indicates that slightly over 1300 ha out of the 1900 ha associated with sites in the upper and middle valley would have been sufficient to support the estimated population – assuming that two fundamental conditions were met. The first is that it would have been necessary to practice double cropping on these 1300 ha. Second, since there was not enough land in the upper valley to support the nearly 4000 persons estimated to have inhabited Clusters 1 and 2 – even assuming a strategy based on triple cropping – people of this sector would have had to have access to land farther downvalley in the area of Clusters 3 and 4 (Table 2). However, assuming a general context of peaceful within-valley relations, there was more than enough land adjacent to sites in the entire subsistence-settlement system to support the general population. The analysis thus strongly suggests that such a context existed, and that the threat of warfare was from outside the lower Santa region.

Another feature of the Cayhuamarca (EH) settlement pattern that is of importance in throwing light on developments of later periods is the general location of the three major site types – ceremonial–civic sites, habitation sites, and citadels. As shown schematically in Figure 5, only the last two types are consistently located well out in the desert and at higher elevations. The choice of site locations obviously was constrained generally by the nature of the available terrain, but on the average Cayhuamarca (EH) habitation and citadel sites are still located higher above the valley floor and farther away from it than in any other following period (Table 1). In sharp contrast, ceremonial–civic sites are consistently located at low elevations down on or immediately adjacent to the cultivated valley floor (e.g., see SVP–CAY–29, in Figure 2). Moreover, these sites are spread more or less evenly in limited numbers throughout the four Cayhuamarca (EH) settlement clusters, which suggests that they served as foci of local supracommunity activities.

A final intriguing feature of the Cayhuamarca settlement pattern is the location of nearly all sites on the south desert margin of the valley. It is tempting to speculate that this implies a threat of raiding primarily from the north – with the massive flow of water in the Santa River itself acting as an effective first line of defense. Nevertheless, the analysis of interregional ceramic relationships argues against this: Of the 12 principal

Table 2. *Intra-cluster subsistence analysis for the early ceramic periods showing (a) maximum amount of irrigable land and (b) triple-crop human carrying capacity, compared to (c) estimated actual population size of cluster**

Period†		Clusters				
		1	2	3	4	5
LSUCH	(a)	381	1432	3603		
	(b)	2880	10 835	27 260	—	—
	(c)	18 835	7645	3285		
ESUCH	(a)	11	1890	2995		
	(b)	80	13 900	22 020	—	—
	(c)	1070	15 030	4010		
VIN	(a)	11	82	237	866	350
	(b)	75	570	1645	6110	2430
	(c)	1180	825	955	995	1310
CAY	(a)	11	368	380	275	
	(b)	75	2510	2590	1875	—
	(c)	950	3005	1040	950	

*(a) measured in hectares; (b) persons; (c) persons (Note: see Wilson 1983 for a detailed presentation of the analytical procedures used in preparing this table).
†LSUCH=Late Suchimancillo, ESUCH=Early Suchimancillo, VIN=Vinzos, CAY=Cayhuamarca.

diagnostic ceramic types of the Cayhuamarca Period (EH), fully 75% can be related on the basis of form, paste, and surface treatment to contemporaneous Guañape types in Viru Valley, while only 33% can be so related to types in Nepeña and Casma Valleys to the south (Wilson 1985). These data may therefore indicate greater socioeconomic ties with people to the north, and that the probable threat of attack was from the south. Indeed, of the two best-known valleys to the south and north of the survey region, Nepeña presents an Early Horizon settlement pattern that is more like that of the lower Santa area – with a diversity of occupations including habitation sites, fortresses, and ceremonial–civic sites located entirely in the upper and middle sectors (Proulx 1973, Figure 4, p. 17). The contemporaneous Early Horizon (Middle–Late Guañape) system of Viru Valley, on the other hand, is different from either Santa or Nepeña in two important ways – including the presence of sites scattered throughout all sectors of the valley, but especially concentrated in the lower valley, and the absence of fortified sites (Willey 1953).

Vinzos Period (Early Intermediate Period 1)

The settlement pattern of the Vinzos Period (EIP 1) (Figure 6) presents a number of continuities as well as several major breaks with the pattern of the preceding period. As a comparison of the settlement maps shows, perhaps the most striking similarity is that the overall location of settlements in the upper and middle valley sectors is essentially the same. And, as in the Cayhuamarca Period (EH), there is no occupation in the lower part of the main valley. On the other hand, as indicated in Figure 6, the principal difference between the two periods is the appearance of two major population concentrations out in the desert along the north side of the valley. One of these consists of a single site containing an estimated 2050 persons located inland from the ocean on the north side of the mouth of the valley. The other consists of eight sites containing an estimated total population of nearly 550 persons in Cluster 6, located in the upper reaches of a *quebrada* lying out to the north of the middle valley sector. For purposes of the present discussion, the most important features of these northern sites are their exposed position on gently sloping pampas and the absence of any associated defensive works.

In contrast, nearly all of the occupations of the upper and middle valley exhibit the same reasonably tight association between citadels and surrounding habitation sites that

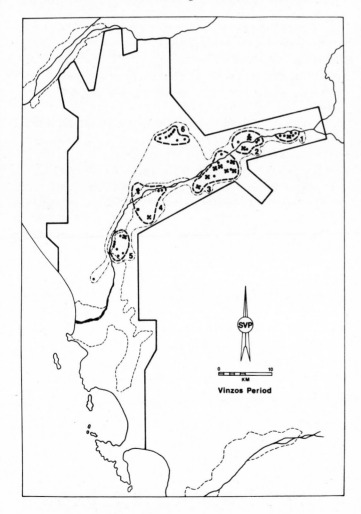

Fig. 6. Settlement pattern map of Vinzos/Early Intermediate Period 1 (*c.* 350 B.C. to B.C./A.D.)

characterized the Cayhuamarca system – with the principal exception of Vinzos Cluster 4, where major sites are spread out in a relatively sparse distribution and located on opposite sides of the river. Interestingly, although to judge from architectural features and associated ceramic diagnostics no new fortresses were built in the Vinzos Period (EIP 1), 12 of the 20 Cayhuamarca Period (EH) citadels in the upvalley sectors continued to be occupied in this period. While this number is thus only a little more than half that of the preceding period, citadels with associated Vinzos occupational debris are distributed throughout Clusters 1–5.

With an estimate of nearly 8000 persons in the Vinzos system, it may be pointed out by way of comparison with the Cayhuamarca Period (EH) that the analysis of maize-based carrying capacity suggests that double cropping some 1700 out of the 1900 ha in the upper and middle valley would have been sufficient to support the entire population. However, in some contrast to Cayhuamarca, the analysis of cluster-by-cluster carrying capacity indicates that while Vinzos (EIP 1) Clusters 1–3 most probably would have had to be part of the same socioeconomic network, Clusters 4 and 5 could have subsisted independently of the others (Table 2). Although it is therefore conceivable that the combined population of Clusters 4 and 5 (*c.* 2300 persons) could have been engaged in warfare with that of Clusters 1–3 (*c.* 2950 persons), there are at least two immediate reasons why such within-valley conflict is unlikely to have been occurring. First, the disproportionately large number of 10 citadels in Clusters 1–3 compared to only two in Clusters 4 and 5 would appear to argue strongly against balanced, between-cluster warfare – especially considering the numerical superiority of the population in the upper three clusters. Second, since there are no defensive works at nearby sites in the desert out to the north, it is unlikely that the overall Vinzos (EIP 1) system was characterized by internal strife.

Instead, as with the Cayhuamarca (EH) system, the threat of warfare probably continued to be from the south. Although it may be noted that this period marks the first appearance of fortified sites in Viru – including seven occupations located primarily on hills rising above the south desert margin of the valley – the analysis of ceramic relationships shows that 11 out of the 12 principal diagnostic ceramic types of Vinzos (EIP 1) Period – or 92% – can be related on the basis of form, paste, and surface treatment to the contemporaneous Huacapongo Polished Plain type of Viru Valley (cf. Wilson 1985). In contrast, almost no specific ceramic similarities exist between Santa and valleys to the south during the Vinzos Period (EIP 1) – with the possible exception of the minor continuance of the pattern burnished bowl type, which is essentially an Early Horizon diagnostic shared among Casma, Nepeña, Santa, and sites of the adjacent sierra (Wilson 1982:232).

Early Suchimancillo Period (Early Intermediate Period 2)
The settlement pattern of the Early Suchimancillo Period (EIP 2) (Figure 7) represents a continuation of trends begun in

the preceding Cayhuamarca and Vinzos Periods (EH and EIP 1) – including the continued rise of regional population, an increase in the number of sites and site types, and a greater number of fortresses, as well as the establishment of the first major occupation of the early agricultural period in the lower valley and on the north desert margin. With an estimated 20 110 persons now inhabiting the region, the margins on both sides of the upper and middle valley are occupied nearly continuously. Cluster 2 alone contains an estimated 15 000 persons, or 75% of the regional population – with roughly half of this number distributed along each side of the river. This filling-in of the upvalley sectors was accompanied by continuing use of some of the Cayhuamarca citadels, as well as by the construction of numerous citadels and minor defensive sites on both sides of the valley throughout most of the occupied area. The only exceptions to this general pattern are sites of the very small Cluster 1 group and sites on the northern side of Cluster 3. However, the former group seems well protected by its remote location in the narrow canyon of the upper valley, and the latter group represents a relatively very insignificant population estimate of 15 persons.

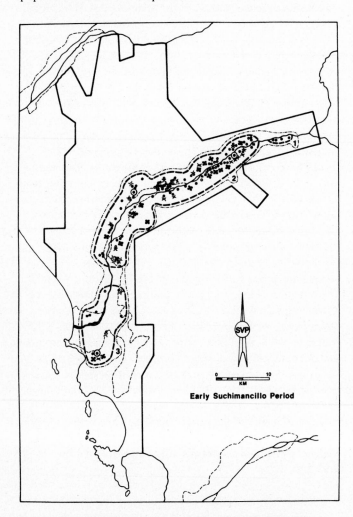

Fig. 7. Settlement pattern map of Early Suchimancillo/Early Intermediate Period 2 (*c.* B.C./A.D. to A.D. 200)

With regard to the nature of warfare, at least four features of the subsistence-settlement system of Early Suchimancillo Period (EIP 2) support the argument that it probably continued to be an inter-regional, rather than within-valley, phenomenon. First, the essentially continuous distribution of settlement on both sides of Cluster 2 argues against any pattern of local-level conflict on either side of the river in the upvalley sectors. Second, although it is conceivable that warfare was occurring between groups on opposite sides of the river (e.g., canal systems are entirely separate), our data showing the essential similarity of major types in the ceramic assemblages of both sides argue against this. Third, the overwhelming lack of demographic parity between the three clusters (see estimates in Table 2) argues against any possible conflict between clusters. Finally, the analysis of carrying capacity indicates that the combined population estimate of 16 100 persons in Clusters 1 and 2 was slightly larger than the maximum size that could be supported by the land available in the upper and middle valley – even assuming a continuous year-round strategy of triple cropping. This clearly implies that by this period people in the upvalley sectors were relying at least to some degree on land in the lower valley. Indeed, the appearance of sites in this last sector in and of itself supports the argument that the population estimates based on the sample of sites are reasonably accurate. In sum, Early Suchimancillo (EIP 2) appears to exhibit the continued growth of the within-valley cooperative network established in the preceding two periods.

With regard to interregional ceramic relationships, this period marks the beginning of what appear to have been strong ties of a possible socioeconomic nature between the Lower Santa region and the adjacent sierra – including the Pashash and Callejón de Huaylas areas. Some 10 out of the 20 principal ceramic diagnostics of Early Suchimancillo (EIP 2) are related on the basis of form, paste, and surface treatment to contemporaneous types in the sierra. In contrast, only 5 of the 20 types are related to Early Intermediate Period 2 (Early and Middle Gallinazo) types of the Viru Valley, which represents a sharp drop from the 92% of the preceding period. Whether or not this argues for the rise of conflict between Santa and valleys to the north is difficult to say, although it may be noted that fortress sites of the contemporaneous Early Intermediate Period in Viru are located on the south desert margin of the valley. In any case, the apparently complete lack of any similarity between the Early Suchimancillo (EIP 2) assemblages and those of valleys to the south suggests that the primary nature of relations with these valleys continued to be one of conflict.

Late Suchimancillo Period (Early Intermediate Period 3)
Just as the Cayhuamarca Period (EH) and the Vinzos Period (EIP 1) are essentially similar in terms of the general nature of the subsistence-settlement system, so too are the Early Suchimancillo Period (EIP 2) and the Late Suchimancillo Period (EIP 3) similar in a number of ways – including

relatively very large regional populations, a principal focus of settlement in the upper and middle valley, and an evenly distributed population on both the north and south desert margins. Nevertheless, this last period in the pre-Guadalupito Period (EIP 4) sequence clearly represents a time of relatively greater settlement and sociopolitical complexity than in the preceding period. Indeed, compared to any other earlier or later period in the entire sequence, Late Suchimancillo (EIP 3) represents the time of maximum development, focused specifically on the upper and middle valley. Thus, as shown in Figure 8, both sides of the valley are occupied nearly continuously from just above the Santa–Tablachaca confluence down to the lower part of the middle valley.

The total population estimate for the upvalley sectors is nearly 26 500 persons, or almost 90% of the entire regional population. The estimate for Cluster 1 alone is 18 835 persons, which represents some 16 000 more persons than could have been sustained even by intensive year-round triple cropping on the minuscule 381 ha of land associated with the cluster (see Table 2). Moreover, even assuming that all 1900 ha of irrigable land in the upper and middle valley were farmed using a

triple-cropping strategy, the excess population in Clusters 1 and 2 is *still* over 12 000 persons. On the other hand, with the continued expansion of the lower valley subsistence-settlement system and the relatively large extent of associated land in this sector, there were more than enough hectares of irrigable valley floor throughout the system to sustain the entire population – at least assuming a general context of peaceful within-valley relations. While the analysis therefore clearly supports the assertion that warfare continued to be interregional in nature, it is both interesting and enigmatic that the population of Clusters 1, 2, and 3 is distributed in nearly exact inverse proportion to the amount of associated irrigable land.

As shown in Table 1, a total of 32 defensive sites appears to have been occupied in Late Suchimancillo Period (EIP 3). Although the number of defensive structures therefore remains relatively high, the distribution of these sites is different from any other previous period. As shown in Figure 8, the distribution is more or less even throughout Clusters 2 and 3. In contrast, only sites in the lower third of Cluster 1 were found to have associated defensive works. It is probably no coincidence that this is precisely the point where the canyon of the Santa begins to open up appreciably beyond a narrow width of 200–300 m. The distribution of fortresses is thus confined entirely to the area where the relatively lower Andean foothills begin, and where the inhabitants of the valley may have been more vulnerable to attack by raiders crossing over these hills or entering the valley via the *quebrada* access routes.

Since in the upper two-thirds of the upper valley sector there are several routes into the Andean sierra via steep, narrow trails – and people in this sector therefore were potentially vulnerable to attack out of the sierra – the lack of fortresses here seems likely to be due more to peaceful and intensive socioeconomic relations with adjacent Andean groups than to the relative security provided by the uniformly steep canyon slopes bordering the river. This assertion is supported at least to some degree by the fact that nearly 30% (8/28) of the principal ceramic types of the period can be related to the Pashash and Callejón de Huaylas areas. Although the coast–sierra relationship thus seems at first glance to be less strong than in Early Suchimancillo (EIP 2) – with 50% of the assemblage related to types of the adjacent sierra – this is countered in large part by an increase in the total percentage of sierra-influenced and/or sierra-derived kaolin wares (lumped together as a single category in the ceramic analysis, primarily due to their great diversity). Thus, from 4.4% of the Early Suchimancillo assemblage, the percentage of kaolin ware in the Late Suchimancillo ceramic rises to 12.7%. In addition, 50% (14/28) of the ceramic types of this period can be related to contemporaneous Early Intermediate Period 3 (Late Gallinazo) types in Virú Valley. Since very few, if any, relationships can be demonstrated between Suchimancillo/Gallinazo wares and those in Nepeña and Casma, it is likely that the threat of raiding continued to be from the south.

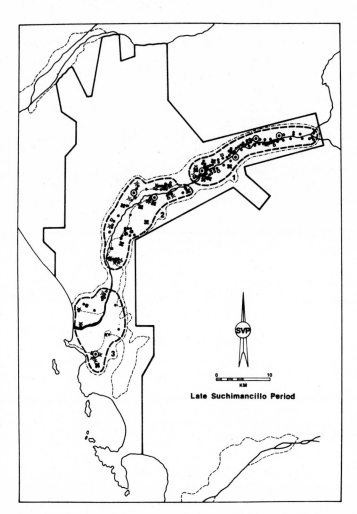

Fig. 8. Settlement pattern map of Late Suchimancillo/Early Intermediate Period 3 (*c.* A.D. 200–400)

Guadalupito Period (Early Intermediate Period 4)

The settlement pattern of the Guadalupito Period (EIP 4) (Figure 9) marks an abrupt shift in the lower Santa subsistence-settlement system. Indeed, in some respects the Guadalupito system is nearly the reverse of that of Late Suchimancillo, with settlements and population now distributed more or less in accordance with the relative amounts of irrigable land in each of the main valley sectors. And from a primary focus of settlement in the upper valley, the focus has now shifted primarily to the lower valley (population estimate here is 18 375 persons). In this regard, it is interesting to note that the opening up of Quebrada de Lacramarca (located, as mentioned earlier, to the south of the Santa Valley mouth) to settlement and agriculture is a unique phenomenon restricted to the Guadalupito Period (EIP 4) – i.e., there is no evidence of any use of this area in the earlier or later periods in the sequence.

Two other changes are apparent in the Guadalupito settlement pattern, both of which appear to be of substantial significance in understanding the nature of societal development and warfare. The first of these is a shift away from the characteristic pattern of preceding periods of locating all or many sites at some remove from the valley floor to one of locating sites either just above canals running along the edge of the valley floor or out on low dunes and hills rising above the floor. Thus, with the exception of a few adobe pyramidal mounds located on higher hills in the midst of the valley floor, virtually all sites are located in exposed, essentially non-defensible positions for the first time in the early agricultural sequence. This change is exemplified by the fact that on the average Guadalupito sites are located closer to the valley floor and at lower elevations than during any of the preceding early periods (Table 1). The second fundamental change consists of a universal absence of the kind of defensive structures that characterize all of the preceding four periods.

In spite of the clear evidence that the integration of north-coast valleys during this period was achieved by violence and conquest, we thus have the situation of a subsistence-settlement system that is characterized by the absence of physical evidence for warfare – at least with regard to patterns of site location and construction of defensive works. However, the most intriguing aspect of the rise of the multivalley Moche polity in valleys like Santa is that there is clear iconographic evidence in pottery and murals both for interregional warfare and for conquest. One of the best examples suggesting that warfare, leading to the rise of the first central Andean state, was interregional in nature comes in a scene from a pottery vessel of Trujillo (Moche Valley) provenience. As shown in Figure 10, the scene depicts a battle between warriors of two apparently distinct cultural backgrounds – probably representing Moche and some other coastal valley. The victorious warriors – shown on the left in each pair of combatants in the lower panel and on the right in the upper panel – presumably are members of the Moche army. That the other warriors are in fact losing the battle is amply evident from such features as clubs bashing faces, blood pouring from noses or face wounds, ropes around necks, and removal of clothes (this last feature apparently being the ultimate disgrace in north-coast society, judging from the way prisoners are depicted in Moche art; see Benson 1972:147; Donnan 1978:25). Another aspect of some interest in this scene is that the depiction of cactus plants suggests that the battle is being fought in the intervalley desert, or at least on the desert margin away from the valley floor. This suggests that warriors did not necessarily wait passively in fortresses when their valley was under siege, but rather went out actively to engage the attacking Moche army.

The battle scene from Moche Valley takes on particular significance when viewed in comparison to a scene from a pottery vessel of Chimbote (Santa Valley) provenience. As shown in Figure 11, the scene on this latter vessel depicts members of the victorious Moche army leading naked and bleeding prisoners out across the intervalley desert. If nothing else, the scenes on both of these vessels lend support to the assertion of interregional rivalries of some time depth, fierce battles in defense of regional autonomy, and the apparent

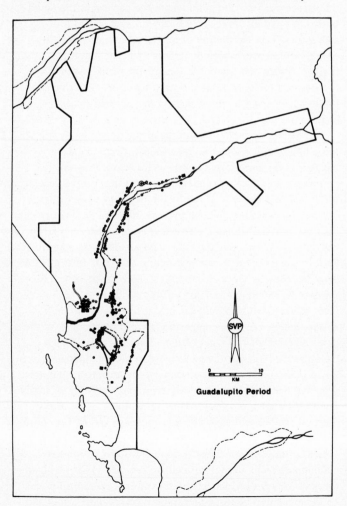

Fig. 9. Settlement pattern map of Guadalupito/Early Intermediate Period 4 (*c.* A.D. 400–650)

Fig. 10. Scene from a Moche pottery vessel of Trujillo provenience, showing a battle between warriors of the Moche army and those of another coastal region. Redrawn from Kutscher (1954:21)

Fig. 11. Scene from a pottery vessel of Chimbote provenience, showing warriors of the Moche army leading prisoners across the intervalley desert. Redrawn from Kutscher (1954:24)

defiance of prisoners even in defeat (e.g., see the prisoner in Figure 11, top left).

Additional evidence of militaristic iconography comes from our own research in Santa Valley, in the form of a mural found on the face of SVP–GUAD–93/El Castillo site, one of the major adobe pyramidal structures built during the Guadalupito Period (EIP 4) and located near the east desert margin in the narrow upvalley part of the lower valley sector. As shown in Figure 12, the mural consists of at least four club-and-shield motifs, and would have been highly visible to people living in nearby sites out to the north as well as to passersby down on the valley floor. Similar militaristic scenes showing warriors in hand-to-hand combat have been found at Pañamarca, the principal Moche Period pyramidal structure in Nepeña Valley (Bonavia 1974:60–63; Proulx 1968:78–80; Schaedel 1951b). Considering the apparent importance in formal Moche art of scenes in which warriors of the army are depicted as victorious over warriors of other regions, it seems likely that placing large murals filled with militaristic symbolism on the sides of structures already imbued with the power of the state was intended to reinforce obedience to it. In other words, murals such as those in Santa and Nepeña would have served as an effective warning of retribution to those who might attempt to subvert the dominion of the Moche state.

Summary and conclusions

As we have seen, ample physical evidence for warfare exists throughout most or all of the settlement systems of the Cayhuamarca Period (EH), Vinzos Period (EIP 1), Early Suchimancillo Period (EIP 2), and Late Suchimancillo Period (EIP 3). Thus, the lower Santa Valley data have provided support for the assertion that warfare was a continuously important factor in societal development during these periods, and in addition the essentially even distribution of defensive sites suggests that at each developmental stage warfare was affecting the system as a whole. In contrast, in the Guadalupito Period (EIPH) there is no evidence in the settlement pattern for warfare, although there is ample iconographic evidence that the rise of the Moche state occurred as the result of interregional warfare and conquest. As implied earlier, we thus have the remarkable paradox that the ultimate period of warfare in the early sequence – namely, that leading to the defeat of Santa Valley and a sweeping reorganization of cultural priorities – resulted in a settlement pattern that for the first time reflects a state of peace, not conflict. In other words, we see the probable imposition of what in essence is a *Pax Moche* on the provincial regions comprising the pristine multivalley state.

With regard to the nature of prestate conflict, at least two fundamental aspects of the socioenvironmental setting support

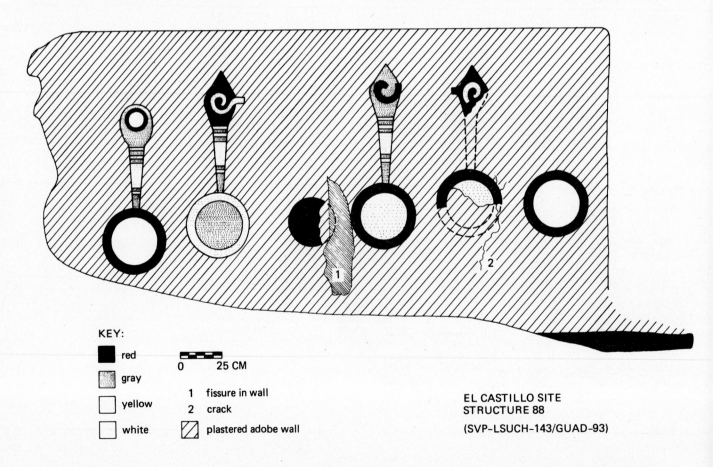

KEY:

■ red
▨ gray
□ yellow
□ white

0   25 CM

1 fissure in wall
2 crack
▨ plastered adobe wall

EL CASTILLO SITE
STRUCTURE 88
(SVP–LSUCH–143/GUAD–93)

Fig. 12. Elevation detail of polychrome club-and-shield mural, located on the lower north face of Structure 88 at SVP–GUAD–93/E1 Castillo site

the argument that warfare was interregional from the start of irrigation agriculture. First, the uneven distribution of population in relation to locally available irrigable land and the analysis of maize-based carrying capacity together indicate that essentially none of the clusters in the early agricultural system could have been engaged in within-valley, or internecine, conflict. A minor exception to this pattern has been pointed out for the Vinzos Period (EIPI), but in general there seems every reason to suppose that from the start of agriculture all or most settlements in the region were part of increasingly larger cooperative networks – both for the efficient practice of widespread cultivation of the valley floor and for defense against raids from outside the region. In this regard, it may be suggested that the dual requirements of subsistence and defense together brought about the pattern of widespread distribution of settlements along with the marked clustering that characterizes the Cayhuamarca and Vinzos Period systems.

As discussed in the section on aspects of the socioenvironmental setting, the second set of data supporting the assertion of interregional warfare comes from a consideration of the nature of traditional canal networks in the valley. The complex interconnectedness and vulnerability of the networks of Viru, Santa, and Nepeña imply that while between-cluster relations may have been neutral at best, there is simply no way early agriculturalists could have been engaged in continual internecine warfare and still have provided adequately for subsistence needs. In other words, warfare was not a process carried out among local, socioeconomically related neighbors in the same region, who had little to gain and much to lose by engaging in hostilities; rather, it occurred between less related *foreigners* located at much greater distances apart, and separated not only by wide stretches of desert but also by different socioeconomic problems (e.g., different environmental regimes).

Moroever, the analysis of the data strongly suggests that if from the start of agriculture, people in the Santa Valley were organized in supravillage cooperative networks for subsistence and defense, then people in valleys to the south also were organized in a similar manner. The strong differences in regimes of water flow in the rivers offer a possible reason for the raids carried out against Santa. If it is assumed that for whatever reasons the people in valleys to the south suffered food shortages brought about by the extended and unpredictable period of reduced water flow, then the attractiveness of a valley with a year-round supply of crops might explain the reason for the raiding. What the data thus imply is that while in Santa one finds no evidence of early population pressure in relation to such potential limiting factors as total supply of irrigable land and water, it may well be the case that such pressure was operative in valleys to the south.

In any case, since one sees interrelated and mutually reliant cooperative networks arising in this area of the north coast essentially in full-blown form by Early Horizon times, it seems clear that none of the valleys ever experienced a stage of within-valley warfare such as argued by the coercive theorists. Following arguments by Price (1971:28), it may also be

suggested that similar demographic pressures as well as subsistence needs may have provided the adaptive context for the origins and development of societal complexity in the Moche Valley – thereby giving rise first to a regional polity and later providing the principal reason for the formation of a conquest state that included the well-watered Santa Valley.

Can it therefore be argued that the results of the Santa research, in particular, have cross-cultural significance with regard to theories of state origins that go beyond the confines of knowledge of a single regional sequence? The answer must be in the affirmative, at least to the extent that the interrelated developmental processes giving rise to the multivalley Moche polity represent the best, if not the only, example we have from the central Andes of pristine state formation (cf. Haas, this volume, S. Pozorski, this volume). Nevertheless, at least two contributions of the coercive theory remain intact in light of the lower Santa research. The first is that the theory points usefully to the adaptive problems posed by the process of impaction, or population growth within a circumscribed setting. For example, in the prestate sequence of Santa, a narrow valley floor surrounded on three sides by vast areas of unusable desert provided a fundamental constraint in the context of continual raiding from outside the region and the concomitant need for a dispersed settlement pattern to farm the required areas of the main valley. Likewise, impaction is clearly a factor in nearby valleys to the north and south – given the dual factors of population and a limited, unpredictable seasonal water supply. The second contribution of the coercive theory is that it correctly points to the fundamental role of conflict in the rise of sociocultural complexity, at least on the north coast of Peru – in spite of the clear indication that its prediction of a long initial stage of internecine conflict is not supported by the research.

As argued earlier, several other factors appear to have played a fundamental role in early societal evolution on the coast as well – including population growth, the need to cultivate efficiently a narrow valley floor of variable width, the need to ensure local-level supravillage cooperation, and the rise of supravillage ceremonial–civic foci. In the most fundamental sense, then, what I am suggesting is that it is possible in the prehispanic north-coast data to find 'necessary and sufficient' causes for the rise of societal complexity in the synergistic combination of adaptive problems posed by the socioenvironmental setting. The data therefore support the approach taken by the multivariate theorists, in that neither warfare nor any other single factor can be viewed as having played the central role in the formation of early societal complexity on the coast of Peru. But there is only one way to test the efficacy of unicausal and multivariate theories: namely, through the construction of empirically based hypotheses and the use of systematic research methods aimed at understanding these processes in light of the archaeological record itself. Given increasing commitment to this approach, it is likely that the prehispanic coastal Peruvian data will prove to be of substantial importance in advancing our general knowledge of warfare and other factors related to the origins and development of complex society.

Chapter 7

Toward the development of the state on the north central coast of Peru

Richard Daggett

Introduction

In developing one of the most often cited theories of state formation, Robert Carneiro (1970) argued that the coastal valleys of Peru represented optimal circumscribed environments for the emergence of states. Basically, Carneiro argued that in circumscribed environments, such as the Peruvian coastal valleys, population growth will eventually lead to a shortage of resources, which will in turn bring about competition over resources between the various social units within that circumscribed zone. Over time, this competition intensifies into warfare which ultimately results in the subordination of weaker groups by stronger groups. The consolidation of the entire circumscribed zone under the hegemony of the military victor marks the emergence of the state in Carneiro's argument.

Like most major theories, Carneiro's circumscription/ warfare theory has received both widespread criticism (see Johnson 1973; Service 1975; Wright and Johnson 1975; Haas 1982) and acclaim (see Webb 1975; Webster 1975). However, it has not been subjected to rigorous empirical testing. Given that Carneiro cites the Peruvian coastal valleys as prime examples fulfilling the requirements of his model, it is appropriate to begin testing the model using Peruvian data.

The coastal valleys of Peru are circumscribed by the Andean mountains on the east, the Pacific Ocean on the west, and by barren deserts to the north and south. Furthermore,

population growth associated with the development of agriculture is clearly evident all up and down the coast. Equally evident at various stages in coastal prehistory is widespread warfare, militarism, and conquest. The question then arises when warfare first developed in any given region, and how the initiation of warfare was coordinated with the cultural and political development of the area. Using defensive architecture as a marker of warfare, it appears that some valleys such as Moche (J. Topic and T. Topic 1978) on the north coast (Figure 1) and Lurin (Earle 1972) on the central coast did not witness systematic warfare until the Early Intermediate Period. However, there is now a growing body of evidence indicating that armed conflict was taking place elsewhere during the preceding Early Horizon.

Recent investigations in the Casma Valley on the north coast have uncovered a dramatic shift from a coastal to a highland architectural tradition, accompanied by the introduction of hilltop redoubts, during the Early Horizon (S. Pozorski and T. Pozorski n.d.). In the Nepeña Valley immediately to the north distinctive Early Horizon artifacts dominate surface collections at a pair of upper valley parapeted stone fortresses, leading to the speculation that settlement of the valley at this time was by means of a highland invasion (Proulx and Daggett 1980). Similar parapeted fortresses, dating to the end of the Early Horizon, are now known to exist in large numbers in the upper part of the Santa Valley just north

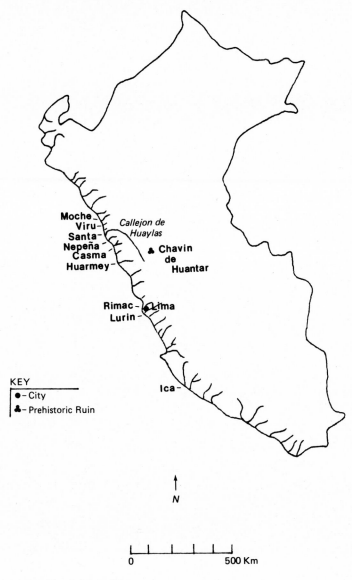

KEY
●—City
♣—Prehistoric Ruin

0   500 Km

Fig. 1. Map of Peru

In Nepeña, a trend toward more complex social organization is accompanied first by the introduction and later by the refinement of defensive architecture. Though Nepeña remains open to interaction with neighboring highland and coastal valleys, the existence of natural and social barriers makes it possible to understand changes taking place there as being essentially internal in nature. In this view, warfare remains central to the development of complex society though it is acknowledged that such a society will expand via established routes of communication and transportation (Webb 1975:191).

The Nepeña Valley

The Nepeña Valley is located approximately 400 km north of Lima, the modern-day capital of Peru (Figure 1). About 60 km in length, this valley is narrow relative to others and lacks a fan-shaped coastal plain (Kosok 1965:207). To the north and south it is bordered by the Santa and Casma Valleys while to the east, the Santa River has carved out an intermontane valley known as the Callejón de Huaylas. For the purpose of discussion the Nepeña Valley has been divided into lower, middle and upper parts (Proulx 1968:5). The lower valley (Figure 2) extends from the shore to just west of Caylán. The bottleneck above the community of San Jacinto marks the juncture of the middle and upper parts of the valley. The upper part extends above the town of Jimbe to about 1550 m in elevation (Daggett 1982a).

The upper part of the valley has a striking configuration which is reflected both in modern and historic patterns of settlement. The far upper valley is formed by the upper tributaries of the Nepeña River which are bordered by a number of ridges extending in fingerlike fashion down from the Andes. Jimbe, which is situated on the centermost ridge, is today the only major settlement in the far upper valley, though smaller communities and individual farmsteads dot the landscape. Below Jimbe the upper tributaries merge to form the Nepeña River, which results in a considerable narrowing of the valley floor.

The next major settlements in the upper valley are to be found below the Salitre area in an expanse of agricultural land known as the Moro Pocket (Kosok 1965:95). It is in the Moro Pocket that the last major tributary, the Vinchamarca River, merges with the Nepeña River. A study of aerial photographs led Kosok (1965:95) to conclude that the Moro Pocket was fully capable of supporting economic and political development independent of any other part of the valley. In the light of this, it is of interest to note that in the latter part of the 19th century the census for the Moro–Jimbe area showed it to be not only more populous than any other area in Nepeña but more so than any area in either the Santa or Casma Valleys (Raimondi 1873:115).

Early Horizon research in the Nepeña Valley

Much of the early work in the Nepeña Valley revealed artifactual, artistic, and settlement patterns which appeared to

of Nepeña (see chapter by Wilson, this volume). Further north in the Viru Valley, the end of the Early Horizon apparently witnessed the introduction of highland forms of construction, including hilltop redoubts (Willey 1953).

It must be cautioned at this juncture that the archaeological manifestations of warfare in these four valleys do not constitute firm evidence that all Peruvian warfare originated in this general area of the north and central coast. For the purpose of this discussion the significant fact is that the phenomenon of armed conflict seems to occur first during the Early Horizon. The discussion to follow will focus upon the patterns of Early Horizon settlement recently proposed for the Nepeña Valley (Daggett 1982a, 1982b). The pattern of warfare seen in Nepeña can then be contrasted with the patterns seen in Casma (see chapter by S. Pozorski, this volume) and Santa (see chapter by Wilson, this volume). Together, the three valleys provide a much more comprehensive picture of early Peruvian warfare.

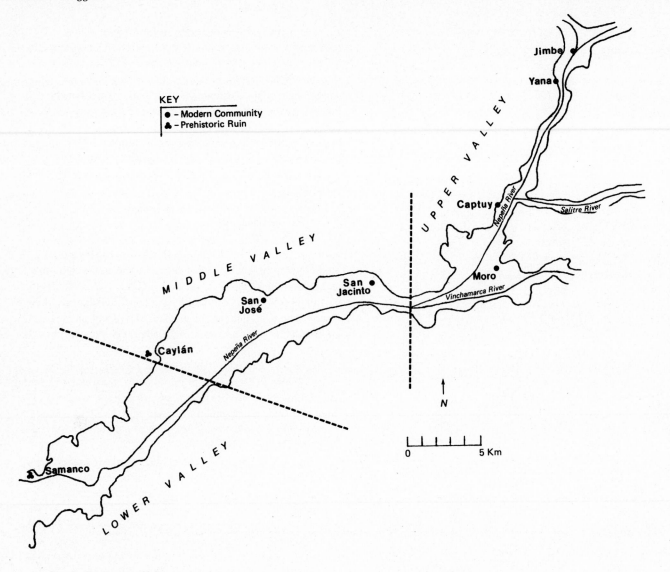

Fig. 2. The Nepeña Valley

indicate that there were ties between the valley and Chavin de Huantar, and that there may have been a highland invasion of the valley in the Early Horizon (Tello 1930; 1943; Proulx and Daggett 1980). At least one investigator (Larco 1938, 1941) viewed the Nepeña–Chavin de Huantar connection differently. To him, the sites of Punkurí and Cerro Blanco in the lower Nepeña Valley represented evidence of a coastal Chavin or Cupisnique culture that predated and later influenced the development of Chavin de Huantar. However, revised dating for Chavin de Huantar (Burger 1981) accompanied by new work in the Nepeña Valley has led to a significantly revised interpretation of the Early Horizon in Nepeña.

From July 1980 to July 1981, I conducted an intensive survey of Early Horizon settlements in the Nepeña Valley. In addition to revisiting some of the 220 sites recorded by Proulx (1968, 1973), I recorded a total of 143 sites, yielding 363 sites known in the Nepeña Valley. Though no excavations were carried out, a similiary seriation (arrangement of materials in a chronological order based on resemblance: see Rowe 1961:326)

of the considerable amount of surface material recovered during my survey has made it possible to offer a sequence of three phases of Early Horizon occupation for the Nepeña Valley. The proposed sequence includes a transitional phase between an early pattern marked by the association of stamped circle-and-dot ceramics with ridgetop platform mounds and a later pattern marked by the association of pattern burnished ceramics with megalithic ruins. These three phases will now be discussed in terms of diagnostic artifacts, site types, and settlement patterns.

Early Horizon Phase I

Artifacts. Early Horizon Phase I sites are defined by the presence of sherds decorated with linear and curvilinear incision, punctuation and/or stamped circles. Singly and in combination, a total of fifteen permutations is permitted by these four decorative elements. Two of them, linear and curvilinear incision, each with stamped circles, have not been found in surface collections. Of the remaining thirteen, only ten are well represented, with curvilinear designs and those which incorporate the stamped circle and punctuation clearly being favored. The most common forms of pottery are the neckless jar and a bowl with an inturned or convex rim. This unique treatment of the rim creates an exterior panel which is universally decorated at this time. Included in the other artifacts making up the Phase I assemblage are the flanged bowl, the grater bowl, the ceramic panpipe, perforated and unperforated ceramic discs, and ground stone blades.

Site type and settlement pattern. Nearly 100 of the 363 sites documented for Nepeña are now known to have experienced a Phase I occupation, and the vast majority of these Phase I sites are located in the upper valley (Figure 3). Typically, they consist of one or more stone faced ridgetop mounds constructed of earth and rubble and stepped at either end with platforms. The Jimbe area is characterized by isolated platform mounds; elsewhere in the upper valley and in part of the middle valley, combinations of platform mounds and

platforms, each supporting fieldstone structures, are to be found. The sites of Vinchamarca (PV31–344) and San Cristobal (PV31–347) in the upper and middle valley respectively are especially complex in this regard. Further upvalley the sites of Salitre Alto (PV31–303) in the Yana area and Huaca Grande (PV31–266) in the vicinity of Jimbe are considered to have been important given the presence at each of extraordinarily rich surface debris.

The only ceremonial site in the upper valley for this phase is located in the Moro Pocket. Just west of Vinchamarca at either end of a natural ridge is Virahuanca Alto (PV31–326), which features the largest platform mound (70 m by 20 m by 2 m) known for the valley (Figure 4). This ridge drops steeply at the rear to a narrow ridge extension, part of which was transformed into a plaza defined by lateral earthen mounds. The termination of the higher part of the ridge is all the more impressive when viewed from this plaza. There, a sheer face formed by a sheet of exposed bedrock suggests that it was the intent of Phase I architects to capture the full effects of this

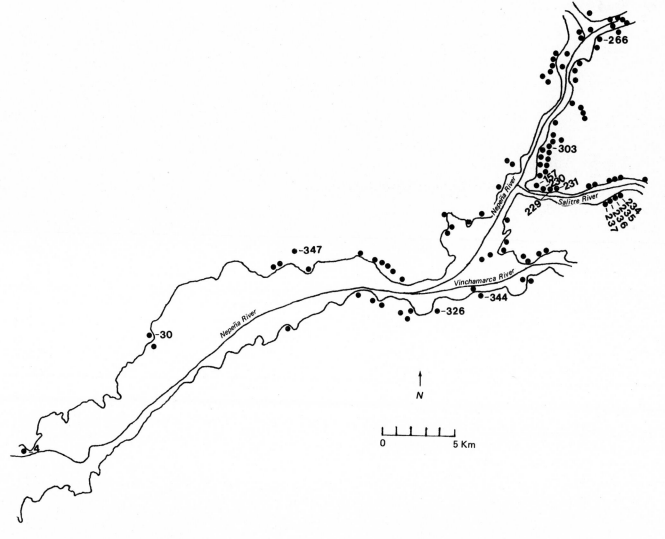

Fig. 3. Early Horizon Phase I sites

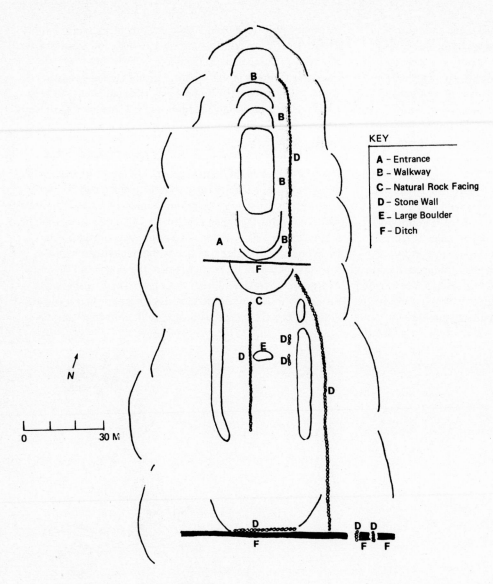

KEY

A – Entrance
B – Walkway
C – Natural Rock Facing
D – Stone Wall
E – Large Boulder
F – Ditch

N

0   30 M

Fig. 4. Virahuanca Alto – PV31–326

imposing natural feature. The central platform mound and the later mounds form a 'U,' a layout typical of Early Horizon ceremonial centers.

Finally, two other sites in the valley should be mentioned. Lower in the valley, ridgetop platform mound sites are not present, but there are some Early Horizon Phase I sites located along the valley bottom margins. The site of Caylán (PV31–30) is situated at the base of a mountain at the juncture of the middle and lower parts of the valley. It is 0.5 sq km in area, and it consists of two parts. The first is a hill that has been covered by earthen platforms and plastered stone walls. This hill overlooks the second part, which consists of a large valley floor complex of stone walled structures centered on a stone faced platform mound (see Kosok 1965:208–209, Figures 20–21; Proulx 1968:175, Plate 7c). Significantly, this mound is fronted by what may be a sunken rectangular plaza. While Caylán is the only Phase I site positively identified in the lower valley, at least one other may exist. Artifacts characteristic of Phase I

have been discovered at the complex valley floor site of PV31–4 situated at the base of Cerro Samanco.

Early Horizon Phase II

Artifacts. With the possible exception of the grater bowl and a cup form which is rare even for Phase I, all Phase I bowl, jar and bottle forms continue in use during Phase II, as do ceramic panpipes, perforated and unperforated ceramic discs, and ground stone blades. The convex or carinated bowl retains its popularity with some localized variation in different parts of the valley. Most diagnostic of Phase II, however, are carinated bowls bearing no decoration. The ubiquitous neckless jar reflects experimentation through the occasional addition of a strap handle or a pouring spout. New pottery forms in the Phase II occupation of the valley include the high necked jar and new decorative techniques including fabric impressions, bossing, and appliqué.

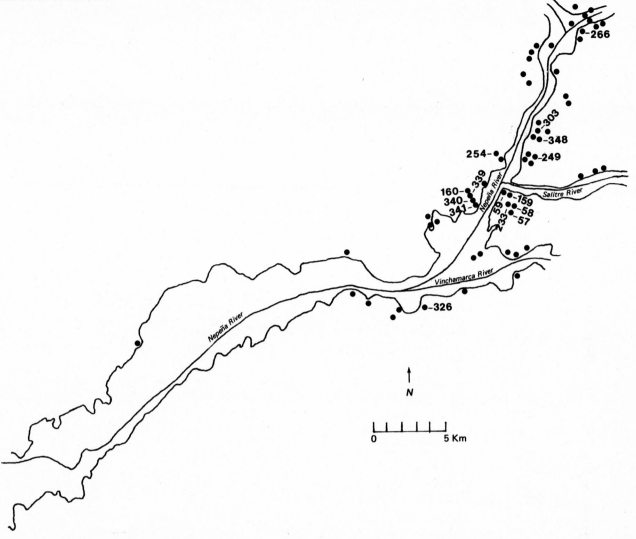

Fig. 5. Early Horizon Phase II sites

Site type and settlement pattern. Of a total of 59 Phase II sites, 42 have been found above the Moro Pocket whereas only 17 have been recorded for the valley below (Figure 5). For the valley as a whole, Phase II locational preference mirrors that of Phase I with ridgetop sites to be found on either side of the valley, throughout the upper valley and into the middle valley. The virtual absence of Phase II sites in the lower valley reflects sparse occupation of that zone similar to the scanty occupation of the lower valley documented for Phase I. The vast majority of sites at this time, however, are still located in the upper valley, and all but one of nine new sites are situated in the Salitre area.

During Phase II there was a notable reduction in the intensity of the occupation of Huaca Grande (PV31–266) and Salitre Alto (PV31–303) as measured by diagnostic surface artifacts. This is probably explicable in terms of changes taking place in the Salitre area. The abandonment of a group of sites on either side of the Salitre River (PV31–157, 229, 230, and 231; PV31–234, 235, 236, and 237) and the concomitant occupation of two new ridges separated by the Nepeña River highlight the changes occurring there. A triangular stone

fortress (PV31–160) crowns a high ridge overlooking the upper entrance to the Moro Pocket, and on the ridge below are two spatially distinct platform mounds (PV31–339 and 340), each of which is defended by a stone wall at the front and a ditch at the rear. The fourth new site on this ridge is a stone-lined cist (PV31–341) situated about a hundred meters below the closest mound.

The ridge upon which these new sites are located provides an unobstructed view of the valley down to the bottleneck at the lower end of the Moro Pocket and up to the Yana area. Visible, too, are a second group of new sites consisting of a network of platform mounds and platforms (PV31–57, 58, and 233), a stone walled compound (PV31–159), and a plateau site, Huancarpón (PV31–59), which was to become the most important ceremonial site in the upper valley.

Early Horizon Phase III

Artifacts. Phase III links with Phase II are demonstrable, but they are also tenuous in comparison with those which have already been discussed for Phases II and I. During Phase III, bowls and jars continue to be the most popular shape categories

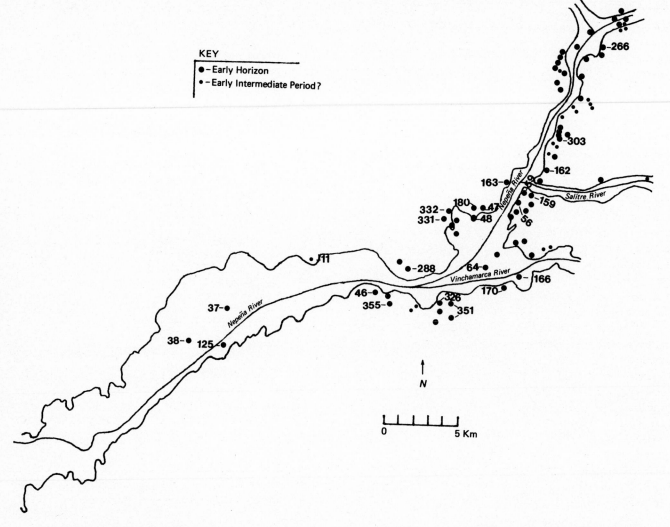

Fig. 6. Early Horizon Phase III sites

though most of the Phase II forms have been replaced by new ones. Bottles are no longer in use, necked jars are occasionally appended by strap handles and large underground storage jars are newly featured. The trend toward the manufacture of high necked jars, first noted for Phase II, continues at this time though neck heights are not as extreme as they were in Phase II.

The neckless jar retains its popularity. The carinated bowl, however, is replaced as the pre-eminent bowl form by a deeper one with a contoured base and side walls that flare slightly outward. This new bowl is characterized by decoration, over a red slipped finish, of pattern burnishing and/or geometric scratching. Cross-hatching is by far the most popular burnished design and it is occasionally accentuated by painting with graphite. Except for rare examples of body sherds decorated with appliqué fillet (probably from jars), the plastic decorative techniques favored during Phase II are at this time discontinued. Ceramic discs, ceramic panpipes, and ground stone blades are still being produced though in far fewer numbers, while ground stone donut-shaped digging stick weights or club heads are an innovation.

Site type and settlement pattern. In Phase III, settlement apparently occurred only in the middle and upper parts of the valley (Figure 6), with the vast majority of sites found in the upper valley. Eighty-three sites have Phase II artifacts. Forty sites dating to Phase II were abandoned in Phase III while 30 new sites were founded and occupied. Since pattern burnishing dates to the early part of the Early Intermediate Period as well as to the Early Horizon (Menzel *et al.* 1964), it is possible that the Phase III site count is slightly inflated. Sites conceivably dating only to the Early Intermediate Period are noted on Figure 6. Their inclusion in the site count, though, does not affect the general interpretation of settlement patterns for Phase III.

Megalithic architecture characterizes Phase III. Sites fall into one of three categories – aligned mounds, compounds or fortresses. Cists are found in distinctive ceremonial contexts.

Settlement in the Jimbe and Yana areas continues essentially as it was during Phase II while the Salitre area witnesses the culmination of settlement trends noted in Phase II. Even more of the sites initially occupied during Phase I are abandoned now than were abandoned during Phase II. This practice extends to defended sites and even includes the Phase II cluster at the upper entrance of the Moro Pocket. However, one should not be misled into thinking that there was a movement away from defensive architecture. On the contrary, there are a number of Phase III fortified sites which reflect an improvement in overall design.

Phase III sees the construction of a pair of parapeted stone fortresses on either side of the confluence of the Nepeña and Salitre Rivers. These fortresses (PV31–162 and 163 in Figure 6), like others now known in the upper Santa Valley (see chapter by Wilson, this volume), have walls constructed by alternating rows of large and small stones. Though these fortresses have surface artifacts from all three Early Horizon phases, it is believed that they date to Phase III because (1) pattern burnished pottery has been found isolated from Phase I and Phase II ceramics at similar fortresses in the Santa Valley (see chapter by Wilson, this volume) and (2) the defensive architecture at the two sites is much more complicated than the simple defensive techniques utilized in Phase II.

The most striking change manifested in the Salitre area is not the construction of these fortresses, however, but the addition of a huge compound to the cluster of sites surrounding Huancarpón (PV31–39). Nearly a kilometer in length and constructed in the large stone/small stone fashion, the megalithic compound of Kushipampa (PV31–56) is very impressive. Like the smaller compound of PV31–159, Kushipampa contrasts sharply with the alignment of platform mounds making up the principal part of the ceremonial site of Huancarpón. Settlement of the Salitre area during Phase II is clearly focused on these neighboring plateau sites. Their construction in addition to the network of nearby canals

evidences the marked local development of cooperative labor practices.

The recent discovery of a Phase III site in the Moro Pocket has led to an improved understanding of the relationship between sites such as Huancarpón and Kushipampa (Daggett 1982b). This site, Virahuanca Bajo (PV31–351), is located immediately upvalley from the ceremonial site of Virahuanca Alto (PV31–326). This new site consists of spatially distinct parts (Figure 7): two stone walled compounds (A and B); a stone faced platform; a platform mound containing six stone cists, enclosed by a low stone wall; five quadrangular structures; and three low earth platforms, one of which has three stone cists, enclosed by a trapezoidal compound. The site of Virahuanca Bajo as a whole is associated with a system of canals cut into encircling hills and low mountains.

The discovery of this site takes on major proportions because for the first time other sites previously thought to be distinct may now be understood to be components of a larger integrated settlement. In this manner the megalithic compound of Kushipampa (PV31–56) and the alignment of platform mounds at Huancarpón (PV31–59) may be seen as the principal components of an Early Horizon Phase III center. The discovery of both underground storage jars and cists at Huancarpón as well as typical Phase III ceramics does nothing to dispel this idea. In like manner the megalithic compound of Paredones (PV31–64) is associated with an alignment of low earthen platforms to the south. The platforms of the site of Anta (PV31–170) share with those at Virahuanca Bajo the features of an enclosing stone wall and surface cists. At both Paredones and Anta, characteristic late Early Horizon pottery has been found. Other sites with similar architectural alignments include Motocachy (PV31–48) and Santa Lucía (PV31–355).

As for the remainder of the Phase III sites in the Moro Pocket, they tie directly or indirectly into one of the four centers there. In this latter category are a number of fortified sites or sites suspected to be so. The megalithic ruin of Quisque (PV31–46) at midridge on the south side of the valley bottleneck is considered by most to be a fortress. Across the way on a peak of Cerro Pimpón is a platform mound site (PV31–288), defended below by a system of ditches and walls. In all likelihood the ditches and walls date to the Late Intermediate Period but, by the same token, there is no reason not to believe that the Phase III occupation of this site was defensive in nature as well.

These two sites would have controlled access to the Moro Pocket by way of the valley bottleneck while a series of five stone walls in association with other walls and a pair of ridgetop platform mounds (PV31–331 and 332) would have overseen entry via the more unconventional route through the Quebrada Solivin (Figure 8). Normally dry, this *quebrada* twice witnessed heavy water flow during the past decade, so the possibility exists of a natural impediment to traveling through it as well. Entry by way of the Salitre area was guarded by the

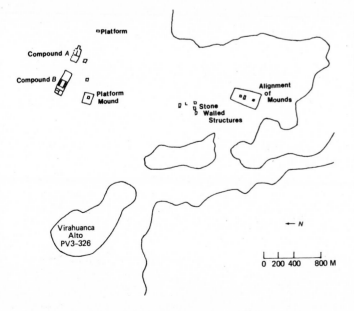

Fig. 7. Virahuanca Bajo – PV31–351

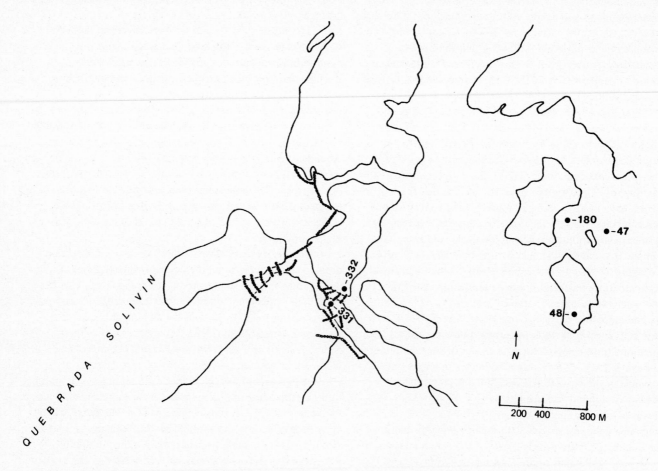

Fig. 8. Early Horizon Phase III sites and associated walls, northern side of Moro Pocket

above-mentioned pair of parapeted stone fortresses (PV31–162 and 163). The only other feasible point of entry into the Moro Pocket would have been from the south side, where a defended site (PV31–166) at the mouth of the Vinchamarca River may have been occupied during Phase III. In sum, the Moro Pocket and the Salitre area would have been defended by a ring of fortresses and stone walls; there is no evidence for defensive structures within this core area.

Lower in the valley, evidence for Phase III sites is scanty. Bowl fragments decorated both with circle stamping and pattern burnishing were found recently just below the ruins of the post-Early Horizon site of Punkurí Alto (PV31–11). Pañamarca has a well-cut stone wall structure which may be Early Horizon in date (Tello 1943:138). A 1967 collection from there contains a pattern burnished sherd (Donald Proulx, personal communication). This evidence from both sites suggests underlying early Early Horizon occupations.

Two other sites, PV31–37 and Huaca Partida, in the lower valley may have been occupied during Phase III. PV31–37, a large mound adjacent to Cerro Blanco, has well-cut stonework and has typical Phase III artifacts on its surface. The facing and overall construction of Huaca Partida (PV31–125)

are suggestive of Phase III architecture (Proulx 1973:152–153, Figure 34, 281, Plate 24A).

Discussion

Before commenting on the meaning of changes in settlement patterning noted as occurring in Nepeña during the Early Horizon, it is necessary to place the events there within the wider context of the preceding late Initial Period. Below it is concluded that the construction of impressive public monuments in the nearby Casma Valley during the Initial Period was facilitated by labor drawn from the Nepeña Valley. For the subsequent Early Horizon, it is concluded that Nepeña was essentially unoccupied at the start of the Early Horizon and that it was subsequently settled by highlanders. For a variety of reasons these settlers chose to inhabit ridges. It was not until Early Horizon Phase II that serious internal conflict arose. This conflict likely centered on the control of natural exchange routes to the highlands and its resolution appears to have been achieved by Phase III. At this later time a single polity was established in the upper valley represented archaeologically by a number of centers collectively defended by a system of fortresses and stone walls.

Recent evidence indicates that the late Initial Period was a time during which previously isolated regional interaction spheres became components of a larger interregional exchange network (Burger and Asaro 1977). At the same time the practice of agriculture was spreading into new areas (Parsons and Matos 1978).

During the past few years, it has become increasingly evident that the sunken circular court characterized late Initial Period ceremonial centers on the north, north central, and central parts of the coast. This feature may have originated on the northern part of the coast (Williams 1978–80). Sunken circular courts which may date to the late Initial Period (Shelia and Thomas Pozorski, personal communication) are present in the Santa Valley (Kosok 1965:192, Figure 15; see chapter by Wilson, this volume) to the north of Nepeña and are abundant at Initial Period sites in the Casma Valley (see chapter by S. Pozorski, this volume; S. Pozorski and T. Pozorski n.d.) to the south. Hence, it is logical to expect to find examples of sunken circular courts in the Nepeña Valley. However, not one has been found, nor has any other evidence for a late Initial Period occupation been documented in terms of architecture or pottery. This is probably best explained by the fact that only 25 km separate the Casma and Nepeña Valleys. A real possibility exists that the spectacular late Initial Period achievements in Casma (see chapter by S. Pozorski, this volume) were the result of the efforts of a labor force drawn both from Casma and Nepeña. Subsequent settlement of the Nepeña Valley during the Early Horizon took place in the absence of armed conflict.

The Phase I pattern now emerging in Nepeña of distinct lower and upper valley settlement types is corroborated by recent survey and excavation in the Casma Valley. There, large ground floor sites in the lower part of the valley have yielded artifacts typical of Phase I sites in Nepeña (see chapter by S. Pozorski, this volume). Subsistence remains from these Casma sites indicate that diet was dependent upon a combination of maritime and terrestrial resources and that, in the case of the latter, maize was for the first time present in substantial amounts (see chapter by S. Pozorski, this volume). While research has tended to concentrate in the lower part of this valley, examples of ridgetop platform mounds dating to this time period have been reported (Tello 1956).

A like pattern of upper valley ridgetop platform mounds and lower valley large ground floor sites, each marked by artifacts typical of Phase I sites in Nepeña, is known to exist in the Huarmey Valley – one valley removed and to the south of Casma (Tabio 1977:105–108). Noteworthy too is the fact that research in the Viru Valley has uncovered a pattern of fundamentally divergent subsistence activities for the Early Horizon (Lynch 1972:276). A generalized strategy in the lower valley encompassing hunting and fishing as well as limited animal husbandry and cultivation differs markedly from an upper valley strategy stessing full-time cultivation (Lynch 1972). Though ridgetop platform mound sites have been reported (Willey 1953), artifacts typical of Phase I in Nepeña have not;

this suggests that a different ceramic tradition existed in Viru and/or that this phenomenon occurred at a slightly later time. It would seem that the pattern of settlement as proposed for Phase I of the Early Horizon in Nepeña is not at odds with information recovered from other north-coast valleys.

There are several possible functions for the upper valley Early Horizon Phase I ridgetop settlements, including activities concerning ritual, defense, administration, and habitation. Of the four possible functional categories, though, it is believed that most, if not all, of these sites were mainly habitational. Other functions or activities can be discounted for a variety of reasons detailed below.

Ritual activity is the easiest to discount given the recent discovery of Virahuanca Alto (PV31–326). It seems reasonable to expect that if one or more of the remaining ridgetop sites had been designed specifically for the purpose of coordinating ritual activities then the layout of such sites should be large and U-shaped like Virahuanca Alto or other ceremonial sites on the north coast. The absence of any other such site in the valley at this time argues persuasively that Virahuanca Alto was unique as a ceremonial center. This is not to say that rituals could not have been performed elsewhere, only that there were no other public places designed specifically for the enactment of ritual group behavior.

In terms of defense, it may be argued that a setting off the valley floor in itself provides a natural protection against human predation. By the same token, however, protection is afforded as well against animal predators, flash floods, mud and rock slides, insects and even the heat of the midday sun. To emphasize the threat of human predation is to ignore the greater threat of natural disaster and the mundane discomforts normally associated with life on the valley floor. In addition, insistence on the view that ridgetop settlement was by its nature defensive and, hence, socially fragmenting, serves to ignore an equally plausible explanation which emphasizes group affiliation. In the absence of ground cover, which today characterizes the upper Nepeña Valley, Early Horizon settlers, had they chosen to live off the valley floor, would have facilitated social cohesion through excellent site-to-site visibility. In addition the absence of architectural features specifically related to warfare (e.g. encircling walls or ditches or even radical inaccessibility) argues against the notion that Early Horizon Phase I ridgetop sites functioned specifically to thwart human aggression.

As for administration, the question naturally arises regarding who it was that was being administered and where those being administered lived. Though it might be postulated that residency was primarily on the valley floor, such a proposition is contrary to subsequent prehistoric and historic living practices where residence was and still is along the valley margins. Assuming that Phase I habitations were not located on the valley bottom where they would have been subjected to the vicissitudes of natural catastrophe, it is a reasonable expectation that evidence for habitation should be found on the elevated valley margins where preservation is greatly improved.

The total absence of evidence of this kind in the face of an intensive survey of the valley runs counter to expectations. In combination with the fact that ridgetop sites are now known to occur in large numbers throughout the upper valley, the above argument acts to cast serious doubt upon the idea that these ridgetop sites were administrative in function. Thus, it appears most likely that the ridgetop sites were mainly habitation sites.

The reluctance to accept the idea of ridgetop habitation is understandable, but cultural bias should not be allowed to impede gaining insight into prehistoric patterns of behavior. For example, in the present-day Jimbe area, movement across a vertical landscape is accomplished regardless of age, sex or health, and there is little reason to assume that such movement did not occur in prehistoric times. From this perspective it is clear that the vast majority of Phase I sites are within easy reach of anyone accustomed to climbing. Likewise, once on a ridge footpaths take one from site to site just as they surely did in times past. Given settlement of the upper valley by highlanders during the Early Horizon, tradition may help to explain this unorthodox and uniquely Andean habitation practice.

To return to a consideration of Early Horizon settlement patterning in Nepeña, it has been postulated that during Phase I habitation was primarily on the valley floor in the lower valley and primarily off the valley floor in the upper valley. The question, then, is: What was the nature and extent of interaction which took place among those choosing different lifestyles?

Intravalley exchange is to be expected given a distribution pattern which restricts natural resources to specific parts of the valley. From an ecological perspective, exchange is an adaptive response to an unstable environment (Daggett 1980). As an alternative to taking, exchange promotes the establishment of personal relationships which may be tapped in the event that the effects of natural disaster are unequally manifested within the sphere of interaction. A probable example of exchange between lower and upper valley residents is reflected by the presence of marine shellfish remains at upper valley sites. Likewise, behavior of this kind is an important stimulant to the maintenance of an effective marriage pool. It will be assumed herein that the direct and indirect benefits of exchange served residents of the various parts of the Nepeña Valley during Phase I of the Early Horizon.

Phase I settlement probably did not occur in a manner very different from that known to characterize the settlement of riverine areas in general. Hence, settlement likely began near the center of the valley (in this case the Moro Pocket) and, from there, expansion would have been symmetrical both upstream and downstream. During the expansionary stage there would have been a continuous process of daughter communities moving out from parent communities until some socially determined spacing was reached. The occupation of what have been identified as major Phase I sites would likely have occurred very early in the Early Horizon. Later they

would have been the focus of competition within the valley for increasingly limited resources.

For those living in the furthest reaches of the valley, far away from much of the valley population, an effective strategy would have been to establish relationships with sierra residents on either side of the Cordillera Negra separating Nepeña from the Callejón de Huaylas. Itinerant traders would be a natural consequence of the settlement of these contiguous highland and coastal areas, and such individuals would be expected to traverse the intermediary zone via *quebradas* formed by the upper tributaries of the Nepeña River. Circumstances such as these may help to explain the exceptional nature of the sites of Huaca Grande (PV31–266) and Salitre Alto (PV31–303) during Phase I.

Similar reasoning may help toward understanding the dense settlement of the Salitre area, a settlement certainly not conditioned by access to extensive tracts of land or soils of exceptional quality. Instead, the fact that the Salitre River has carved a natural route to the Callejón, historically the most active highway between these highland and coastal valleys (Raimondi 1873:111), is significant. Artifacts typical of Phase I in Nepeña are well known in the Callejón and other parts of the north-central highlands. The radical change in site type and associated artifacts at the beginning of the Early Horizon in the neighboring Casma Valley is argued to be the result of highland settlement there (see chapter by S. Pozorski, this volume; S. Pozorski and T. Pozorski n.d.). It is not unreasonable to expect, then, that the Salitre area would have been one of the first areas to have been settled in Nepeña. As a natural consequence, the strategic value of this locale in terms of monitoring travel along this highway would have been realized.

Early Horizon Phase I sites are characterized by a pan-valley decorative treatment of carinated bowls. At Phase II sites, carinated bowls are undecorated. Although the assumption of cultural affinity based upon artifact similarity is always risky (Wobst 1977), it seems an unlikely coincidence that division of the valley according to treatment of the carinated bowl should be precisely marked by the introduction of purely defensive architecture. With the possible exception of Virahuanca Alto (PV31–326), defense of platform mounds by one or more ditches is restricted to the Salitre area (PV31–249, 254, 339, 340, and 348), which leads to the conclusion that during Phase II the valley witnessed a sociopolitical schism.

The desire to monopolize intravalley and intervalley exchange may help to explain the early appearance of defensive construction, indicative of warfare, in the Salitre area. This would also account for the reduction in the importance of Huaca Grande (PV31–266) and Salitre Alto (PV31–303). The concentrated settlement of the Salitre area makes it clear that the route to the Callejón via the Salitre *quebrada* had assumed primacy at this time.

Public architecture is for the first time manifested above the Moro Pocket during Phase II. The compound of PV31–159 has an obvious economic function whereas Huancarpón (PV31–59) is known to have become the most important

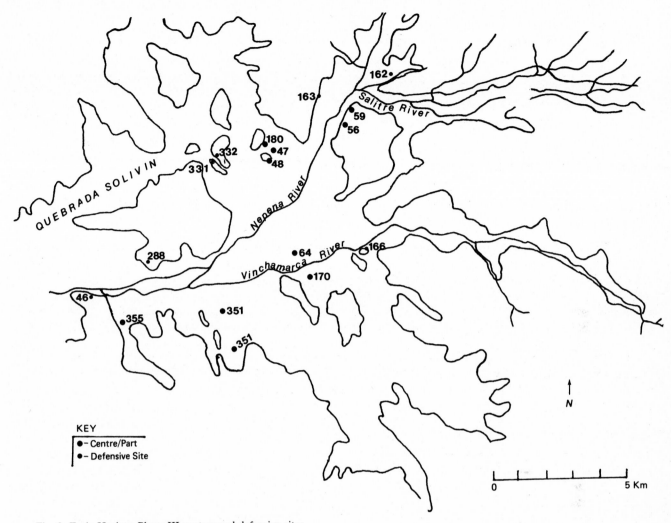

Fig. 9. Early Horizon Phase III centers and defensive sites

ceremonial center in the upper valley. The emergence of a ritual center in competition with Virahuanca Alto is not an unreasonable expectation given what has been discussed. Though the absence of decoration of the panel of carinated bowls is probably more an indication of access to ideas circulating outside Nepeña, it may also be seen as evidence for the fact that the upper valley was being socially divided at this time. Viewed as forming competing polities, those living in these distinct parts of the upper valley may be seen as controlling access to specific strategic resources.

Those living in the Moro Pocket would have enjoyed the benefits of a disproportionate share of cultivable soil. In addition, they would have been ideally situated to control exchange between those living in lower and upper parts of the valley. As for those living in the Salitre area, control of intervalley exchange via the Salitre *quebrada* is an obvious locational advantage. Less obvious is the fact that confinement to the Salitre area would tend to make its inhabitants more prone to social cohesion than those living elsewhere in the valley. In contrast, those residing in the Moro Pocket were naturally spaced quite far apart, which would have affected

their ability to respond, first, to trade restrictions imposed from the Salitre area and, later, to competition from the same area over land. The image of Virahuanca Alto as the place of final refuge before capitulation is suggested by the data, but cannot be demonstrated by it.

Settlement of the upper valley during Phase III seems tailored perfectly to an aftermath of intravalley strife of this kind (Figure 8). A defensive network which features large stone fortresses and which encloses a sociopolitical core made up of the Moro Pocket and the Salitre area is a predictable result of the aggressive reunification of the valley population in response to external threats. Increased social complexity is mirrored in public works while the separation of distinctly ceremonial and non-ceremonial structures is indicative of the fact that we are dealing with something very different from the theocratic societies characteristic of the Initial Period. Whether the compounds were designed for the purpose of manufacture, storage and/or elite residence is unknown, but it seems certain that exchange with highland groups prompted this construction phase in Nepeña.

An orientation toward the Callejón de Huaylas by way of

the Salitre *quebrada* is reflected in a Phase III pattern of settlement heavily biased towards the lower part of the upper valley. Of the five centers known to have existed in the core, the largest and most costly in terms of labor is that which includes the megalithic compound of Kushipampa (PV31–56). The four centers in the Moro Pocket are situated on the valley margin, a practice likely designed to make effective use of as much bottom land as possible for agriculture. The network of canals that apparently connects these centers reflects both a concern for maximizing agricultural land and an increased population. The valley above the Salitre area continues to look as though it were a cultural backwater, though it would have served as an outlet for demographic pressure building up within the core.

As for the middle and lower parts of the valley, evidence to date suggests a fairly unremarkable settlement there. Proximity to the ocean and heavy post-Early Horizon occupation, however, may serve to disguise the true nature and extent of Phase III occupation. An external threat most likely prompted the extraordinary efforts to defend the upper valley centers.

Conclusions

To conclude, changes in settlement patterning in the Nepeña Valley during the Early Horizon support the circumscription theory for the development of complex society. This is so in spite of the fact that outside influence has not been entirely eliminated from the Phase II of the Nepeña sequence. Though total isolation may be said to be a theoretical requirement, it is at the same time a practical impossibility. Mountains, deserts and oceans are natural barriers to human interaction, but it is artificial to see them as absolute barriers. To insist, for example, that *quebradas* which permitted settlement of the Nepeña Valley from without must have been sealed once the valley was settled is simply at odds with reality and, I believe, beyond the intent of the theoretician. Developments in the valley, then, should not be seen as occurring within a cultural vacuum. Rather, population growth and resultant intravalley competition for limited resources may be understood as having established social barriers to extravalley influences. It is recognized that regional exchange did play a role during Early Horizon times in the Nepeña area, but developments within the valley were mainly the result of conflicts on the intravalley level.

Chapter 8

State origins in the Ayacucho Valley, central highlands, Peru

William H. Isbell

Introduction

At the time of the Spanish conquest of Peru, the Inca polity was a complex and elaborate state, or empire. It possessed many administrative institutions of such sophistication that they could hardly have been invented by a newly emerging, pristine state. Consequently, when John Rowe (1946, 1948) demonstrated how recently the Incas had achieved hegemony in even the south-central highlands, he looked for an earlier state with a sufficiently elaborate government to have provided a model for the rapid Inca achievement. In the 1940s, Chan Chan and the Chimu state provided virtually the only example of a documented pre-Inca governmental system of sufficient complexity. Although some scholars continue to argue that many Inca administrative institutions were borrowed directly from the Chimu (cf. Moseley and Day 1982), this position becomes increasingly untenable as the antiquity of Andean government is pushed backward in time and the number of known pre-Inca states expands.

This paper discusses the rise of the Middle Horizon Wari state in the Ayacucho Valley of Peru's central highlands. While there is some controversy over when the state arose in this area (see MacNeish 1981), available data are consistent with the interpretation that state government and empire administration appeared almost simultaneously in the first epoch of the Middle Horizon (*c.* A.D. 600 to 700). This proposition may run counter to many theoretical expectations, but it does identify a distinct set of systemic conditions and influential events that I feel were critical for state evolution in Ayacucho and the central Andes.

Indicators of the state

Before turning to the conditions extant in Ayacucho at the beginning of the sixth century A.D., when state administration was about to emerge, it is necessary to discuss the state, and what archaeological evidence I believe is indicative of state government. Four principal features are proposed, along with several archaeological indicators of each.

First, the definitive characteristic of the state is a specialized hierarchical administration that processes information, makes decisions, and enforces compliance (Wright and Johnson 1975; Isbell and Schreiber 1978). Such an administrative structure should be manifested archaeologically in a number of different ways. (1) Such administration requires specialized personnel with appropriate facilities that include residences, offices, council chambers, and courts which are likely to be manifested in the archaeological record. (2) There should be some system for recording information, since state administration requires some means of processing substantial quantities of data. This recording system does not have to be a formal system of writing, however. (3) As settlement patterns also tend to reflect administrative structure (Johnson 1973; Wright and Johnson 1975), state administration should be revealed in a hierarchical regional structure of communities containing identifiable administrative and prestigious features.

Second, the state must collect revenue to support its officials and to conduct public works. In the Inca state there was no monetary system to facilitate tax payment, and citizens were not required to contribute food or goods produced with their own resources except for a few wild species that were collected or hunted. Consequently, tax payment was in labor, following traditional practices of reciprocal exchange of work among families. In fact, the payment of labor tax was conceptualized in terms of reciprocal exchange, and the Inca state maintained the appearance of reciprocity by conspicuous generosity to its citizens while they labored for the state (Rowe, 1946; Murra 1964, 1972, 1975; Godelier 1977). A citizen engaged in a state work project was housed, fed, clothed, and treated to festive drinking bouts. Morris (1967, 1972, 1974, 1978; Morris and Thompson 1970) has shown that this form of revenue collection required elaborate facilities distributed throughout the provinces of the Inca empire. Looking at such practices archaeologically, three different kinds of manifestations can be expected. (1) Abundant storage buildings were required at administrative centers. The stored goods were needed not only for the maintenance of full-time bureaucrats, but also for the tax payers who periodically worked at the capital, or were brought in for feasts and drinking bouts. (2) Workers brought to the administrative centers had to be housed while away from their homes, so barracks-like quarters would have been constructed. (3) Large kitchens were necessary to prepare large quantities of food and drink, and large plazas would be located in areas occupied by higher officials where the tax payers would have been assembled for feasts. At the secondary Inca capital of Huánuco Pampa, for example, these kitchens and courtyards are associated with great quantities of large brewing and cooking urns, and small serving vessels.

Third, states are divided into distinct social classes that possess differential access to the means of production, as well as to the products (Fried 1967). In the Inca state, three caste-like classes can be distinguished, each with significant internal differentiation. Incas by blood constituted the upper class eligible for high state office. The highest was that of king or *Sapa Inca*, and below the king was a host of lower officials and relatives. A second caste was composed of Incas by privilege, ethnic groups closely related to the Incas who occupied lesser bureaucratic posts. Finally, a third heterogeneous caste consisted of all non-Incas, including the kings and nobles of conquered ethnic groups (called *curaca*) as well as Inca commoners (Rowe 1946).

With rare exceptions, kings are as lavishly distinguished in death as they are in life (Huntington and Metcalf 1978). Consequently, their tombs are usually easy to recognize. Unfortunately, Spanish persecution of the worshipers of deceased Inca kings did not facilitate the collection of information about the resting places of these kings. The identification of non-Inca royal tombs at Sillustani (Julian 1978) and Chan Chan (T. Pozorski 1971; Conrad 1981, 1982) may

further facilitate the recognition of earlier royal tombs in the Andean archaeological record. (1) Archaeologically, a state's social class system should be recognizable by the presence of distinct royal tombs, elite burials and commoners' graves. (2) Comparable differences should be seen in residential structures, including royal palaces, elite houses, and commoner dwellings. (3) Differential distribution of wealth and luxury goods should be apparent, and greater quantities of sumptuary goods should be found with tombs and residences interpreted as elite or royal. (4) Settlements occupied by distinct social classes may be divided by natural features or by walls to isolate the sectors occupied by each class.

Fourth, successful governance by a state bureaucracy is dependent upon citizen acceptance of inequality and hierarchical authority. Communication of the necessary attitude is facilitated by symbols of state authority and prestige. Although the actual meanings of such symbols may be lost for ever, hierarchical relationships are often apparent in the composition of artistic themes as well as the size, quality, and distribution of the symbols. Among the physical symbols of Inca government, for example, were sun temples, ceremonial plazas, *ushnu* structures, *callanca* chambers, cut stone facades, *keros*, and perhaps even Cuzco-style pottery. (1) Archaeologically, state government may be detected by iconographic depictions of hierarchies or hierarchical relationships. (2) The distribution of prestigious symbols, and especially monuments, should reveal state administrative structure, with the greatest concentration in the single capital, lesser numbers in several provincial centers, fewer in numerous local centers, and so on down to the many residential communities lacking specialized administrative function, and probably also lacking symbols of the state.

Indicators of the state in Ayacucho

The absence of facilities necessary for a specialized administrative bureaucracy during the Early Intermediate Period is a significant variable in determining when the state first arose in the Ayacucho Basin. The absence of such facilities particularly should not be ignored in deference to theoretical assumptions that the emergence of state government must inevitably precede imperial conquest and expansion by various centuries. Many Early Intermediate Period settlements with Huarpa pottery are like Lagunillas (Lumbreras 1974a, 1981), where hillsides bear evidence of contour terracing and irrigation canals. Scattered about are sherd concentrations, sometimes associated with simple stone wall structures, circular, irregular or rectangular in plan, that were probably dwellings. Near Luricocha, another large Early Intermediate Period settlement, named Tantawasi (site 397), crowns a low hill. At the top of the hill, remains of small, rectangular stone-walled rooms are visible, and the foundation of a larger wall, perhaps placed for defensive or divisional purposes, is located along one edge of the hill. Similar remains are preserved at Trigopampa (site 138) and other sites, including the deepest portion of a stratigraphic excavation in a road-cut profile in the western portions of Wari

(Knobloch 1981). In no case, however, is there evidence to suggest the kind of specialization of function associated with state-level bureaucratic activities.

One Early Intermediate Period site, Ñawinpukyu (site 21), has been considered exceptional. Extensive remains of stone architecture are preserved on the top of this hill in the southern end of the Ayacucho Valley. Lumbreras (1974a:104–105; 1981:182–183) has suggested that the similarity between the masonry of the terrace walls and the other buildings implies centralized direction of work. He also feels that elite residences, storage structures, and ceremonial buildings can be recognized. However, this interpretation is based on a hypothetical reconstruction of building form, since the three test pits excavated at Ñawinpukyu were all outside the significant architectural zones. Furthermore, architecture is poorly preserved at the site, and no systematic surface collections can be cited in support of the functional interpretations. Menzel (1964) has also pointed out that later Wari period pottery is found at Ñawinpukyu only around these stone buildings, which brings the date of the buildings into question.

Finally there are two possibly Early Intermediate Period sites with remains of large rectangular enclosures similar to later buildings associated with administration. One section of Simpapata (site 135) has two or three such enclosures, but early Middle Horizon pottery dominates surface collections from this section of the site, while Early Intermediate Period Huarpa pottery is more common across a small ravine. Tablapampa (site 299) possesses a single large enclosure, but Huarpa, early Wari, and green glazed colonial wares have all been observed in its vicinity.

To summarize, there is no firm evidence for specialized facilities for bureaucrats or state activities in the Ayacucho area during the Early Intermediate Period. Future research may reveal dynamic evolutionary change within the Early Intermediate Period, with administrative institutions developing into a state system before the close of the period. Present data, however, tend to support the proposition that facilities associated with bureaucratic activities did not appear before the beginning of the Middle Horizon.

Another indicator of a specialized administrative hierarchy is hierarchical, regional structure in settlement pattern. Although MacNeish (1981) is the source for Early Intermediate Period settlement pattern data, his chronological assignments of settlements and his classification of settlement types are not completely satisfactory. For the Huarpa Phase, which MacNeish (1981:244–247) assigns to the first half of the Early Intermediate Period, there are seven 'towns,' eighteen 'villages,' and numerous 'hamlets' and camp sites in Ayacucho. No single settlement dominated the valley, or even a substantial portion of the valley, except perhaps Tantawasi (site 397), located in the north end of the valley 16 km from the nearest town to the south. However, the average distance from a town to its nearest neighboring town is only about 7 km, which makes it exceedingly unlikely that each was the capital of an

independent state. Indeed, three of the towns and five villages are located within a 6 km circle on the most productive stretch of bottom lands along the river. Such close proximity of comparably large centers is inconsistent with centralized political authority, and is difficult to explain by any means other than competition for prime resources. However, none of the settlements reveals efforts to fortify it, so this interpretation seems unlikely as well. The Huarpa Phase settlement pattern is considered in more detail below, but it is significant that Parsons *et al.* (1982) discovered a similar concentration of populations into large settlements very close to one another during the Late Preclassic phase in the Chalco–Xochimilco area of the Valley of Mexico shortly before Teotihuacan established control throughout the valley.

Ñawinpukyu's position in the Ayacucho Valley Huarpa Phase settlement system deserves special attention. It lies about 10 km south of the concentration of three towns and five villages, and 7 km north of the nearest town. Consequently, it seems relatively isolated from other towns as well as potential secondary capitals. This evaluation, however, depends on the classification of Conchopata (site 3), located 3 km to the north, and Acuchimay (site 2), located 2 km to the west, as only 'hamlet' and 'unoccupied,' respectively, during the Huarpa Phase. From personal reconnaissance, it appears entirely possible that both of these sites were as large as Ñawinpukyu by at least the end of Early Intermediate Period. If so, the situation around Ñawinpukyu may have been similar to the cluster of three towns and five villages 10 km to the north.

A third cluster of large settlements may have existed in the area that was to become Wari. Although the evidence is partially obscured by later occupational remains, there is reason to believe that three or four substantial Huarpa communities were located there, and future excavations may reveal more (cf. MacNeish 1981). Thus, on the basis of the few data currently available, the most salient feature of the Early Intermediate Period Ayacucho Valley settlement system appears to be the clustering of large settlements in three areas.

Overall, during the Early Intermediate Period, the lack of facilities for bureaucratic activities, the lack of any evidence for a system of recording information, and the lack of hierarchical, centralized regional settlement pattern all argue for the absence of state government in Ayacucho. Conversely, all of these are present in the Middle Horizon between A.D. 550 and 1000. During this time, Wari grew into a city with a central architectural core of about 400 hectares. At least some of the old ceremonial buildings were abandoned and walled compounds consisting of plazas, hallways and complexes of multistoried rooms were constructed during Epoch 1b (*c.* A.D. 650–750) of the Middle Horizon, and perhaps earlier.

Near the center of Wari one seemingly typical compound has been partially excavated. It was bordered on the east by a double walled alley. However, its main entrance probably opened to the south, where the architectural remains were destroyed by modern road construction. Several distinct building forms are present, but the most common is a courtyard surrounded on all sides by elongated multistoried rooms arranged in series. In the north center of the compound are four such units, all almost square, while two smaller, trapezoidal examples lie just to the south. At least some of the ground floors in the elongated structures were kitchens, as evidenced by hearths and domestic refuse. Other rooms had numerous hemispherical pits for caches of goods carefully hidden under the plaster floors, and in one or perhaps two cases raised platforms were located at one end of the room, or in one corner. The central court was open to the air except along its edges where raised benches about 1.5 m wide and 30 cm high were probably covered by long eaves projecting from the roofs of the elongated rooms.

None of the excavations in this compound has revealed agricultural tools or evidence of craft production. By contrast, Christine Brewster-Wray (1983) has shown that serving vessels occur in a frequency significantly higher than would be expected in normal domestic refuse. She has argued that this indicates conspicuous generosity associated with administrative activities. The discovery of Pachacamac style pottery in this compound may also relate its occupants to the central coast, and perhaps even the administration of affairs relevant to the central coast (Isbell 1982).

At Wari, architectural remains indicate facilities appropriate for bureaucratic functions, and the associated features and artifacts also support this interpretation. With regard to formal mechanisms for processing information, no recording devices have been recovered from Wari itself. However, William Conklin (1982) has recently demonstrated the existence of information recording devices very similar to the Inca *quipu* during the Middle Horizon. One set of examples comes from the Nazca region of the south coast, where they were discovered in a burial that also contained Wari style pottery of Middle Horizon Epoch 2.

During the Middle Horizon, settlement pattern in the Ayacucho Valley experienced a dramatic shift. Isbell and Schreiber (1978) have shown that settlements conform to three size modes, with Wari as the singular, main settlement many times larger than any other. Four approximately equivalent settlements were located around Wari, with smaller sites surrounding them, or in more distant strategic positions within the valley. What is more, several of these settlements have planned architectural compounds similar to those excavated at Wari and believed to be associated with administrative activities. MacNeish (1981:252) has also recognized the hierarchical structures of the Ayacucho's Middle Horizon settlement system, and classified Wari as the highest order settlement, a city.

The second principal feature of the state is collection of revenue to support its bureaucracy and undertake public works. At Huánuco Pampa, for example, Inca labor tax collection was associated with facilities for storing vast quantities of food and goods; with barracks-like residential quarters, and kitchens, utensils and courtyards for great feasts and drinking bouts (Morris 1976). By analogy with Inca storehouse form, state storage facilities have been claimed for the Chimu as well as

Middle Horizon north-coast cities of Pampa Grande (Day 1982a, 1982b; Anders 1975) and Galindo (Bawden 1982a). By the same analogy with Inca building form, large-scale Wari storage complexes exist at Azángaro in the Huanta portion of the Ayacucho Valley (Anders 1982, Isbell and Schreiber 1978) and at Pikillaqta in Cuzco (Sanders 1973). The developmental history of storage complexes at Wari itself is still undocumented and must await future excavation.

Barracks-like residential facilities are perhaps the dominant feature of Wari architecture. Large enclosures are divided into rectangular units that possess central courts surrounded by multistoried, elongated rooms. At Wari, one set of such units has been interpreted as apartment house residences for family units because of indoor kitchens and caches of goods. At Jincamocco, similar units were found to have a single large hearth in the courtyard and no caches of luxury goods (Schreiber 1978). This may reflect temporary residence by tax payers in barracks-like conditions. Similarly, Sanders (1973) felt that Pikillaqta provided barracks-like residential facilities, and Anders (1982) has argued that foreign labourers were quartered at Azángaro, only about 20 km from Wari. Comparable barracks-like residential facilities are unknown from the Early Intermediate Period of Ayacucho.

Great kitchens, plazas, brewing and cooking urns, and large numbers of serving vessels are the archaeological indicators of feasting and drinking bouts associated with Inca administration at Huánuco Pampa (Morris 1976). Richard Keatinge (1974) has found similar indices of administration at small, rural Chimu installations in the vicinity of Chan Chan; especially at Quebrada del Oso, where almost all the surface sherds come from bowls appropriate for serving food and drink. The antecedent for this practice of conspicuous feasting can be seen in Wari administrative installations. At the little site of Jargampata, near Wari, a planned rectangular enclosure was built at the beginning of Middle Horizon Epoch 2 (c. A.D. 700 to 800). Ceramic remains from activities associated with the enclosure average about 30% jars, 60% bowls, and 10% other forms, whereas relative frequencies of vessel shapes from trash not associated with use of the enclosure are about 45% jars, 45% bowls, and 10% other forms (Isbell 1977; Isbell and Schreiber 1978). Clearly, the enclosure was used for activities that involved a great number of serving vessels, and reasonably reflects the expected feasts and drinking bouts that would be sponsored by a state for its tax-paying citizens. These manifestations of feasts and drinking bouts, coupled with the large-scale and centralized storages and barracks-like residences, all document Inca-style revenue collection through labor tax during the Middle Horizon in Ayacucho, and none of these are indicated for the Early Intermediate Period occupation of Ayacucho.

Social classes, as evidenced by royal, elite, and commoner burials, were present in the Andean region at least by the Late Intermediate Period at Chan Chan, and subsequently in the *altiplano* and Cuzco areas. If we look specifically at the Ayacucho Basin, antecedents for these Late Intermediate Period burial patterns may be found in the badly looted tombs and graves at Wari and adjacent Middle Horizon settlements. These remains suggest that three modes of burial might be defined. The simplest, probably belonging to commoners, is flexed and seated burial in a circular pit which may or may not be lined, floored and capped with flat stone slabs. Offerings range from nothing imperishable to a few items of personal adornment such as shell or stone beads, or perhaps a pottery vessel or two. Examples of such burials have come from Jargampata (Isbell 1977), Conchopata (Lumbreras 1974a) and Wari.

Elite burials may be represented by recent finds at Wari as well as tombs reported by Lumbreras (1974a) from Tambobamba and Lirio Moqo. At Wari, carefully excavated cists a meter or more deep and about 80 cm in diameter have been found under the floors of two adjacent rooms. Some are excavated into bedrock while others are stone lined and plastered with a fine white covering. The lid is a single stone worked into a circular disk or square slab. One or two holes, that were probably sealed with pestle-like stone plugs, were cut through the lids. No intact examples have been found, but human bones, many pieces of very fine ceramics, many shell beads, and objects of gold, missed or ignored by the looters, have been found nearby.

Carefully cut and dressed stone chambers preserved at several places within Wari may represent the remains of looted royal burials. Cheqo Wasi, recently excavated by Mario Benavides (1975) had been thoroughly looted before investigation, but produced human remains as well as abundant luxury goods, including gold. Carefully constructed filled stone walls surrounded a series of megalithic, dressed stone containers. In at least two cases, five such containers are located within one circular or rectangular enclosure. In other examples, the dressed stone containers include several chambers, and three levels in a single example. Many of the containers have circular holes cut through their lids, and even semicircular grooves in the walls of the chambers.

Whether the Cheqo Wasi cut stone chambers might represent one or many royal tombs is unclear. Similar boxes have been exposed by looters about one-half kilometer to the west of Cheqo Wasi. What Bennett (1953) called Canterón A is a huge artificial hole with field stone and cut block masonry that has also been disastrously looted. Subterranean rooms with cut stone roofs are found at Monqa Chayua as well as two other places at Wari. If each of these represents the remains of a single royal tomb, that would account for at least six Wari kings. In fact, if the suggestion that Wari's stone chambers represent royal burials is correct, they become the earliest evidence for royal burials in the Central Andes.

Early Intermediate Period burial in Ayacucho is poorly known, but Lumbreras (1981:180) reports a fixed burial with two simple pottery vessels that may have been associated with a Huarpa Phase building. Another, more spectacular burial of late Early Intermediate Period date is reported from Conchopata (Lumbreras 1974a:112–114). Here, an extended burial with a copper pin and two fine pottery vessels was found in a shaft tomb cut into soft bedrock. This might be taken as evidence of status differentiation during the Early Intermediate Period, but even hints of commoner, elite and royal burials do not occur in Ayacucho until the Middle Horizon.

Royal, elite, and commoners' residences have not been identified specifically at Wari, where little of the site has been excavated, and the poor condition of the architecture makes it almost impossible to determine even general forms of buildings without excavations. There are huge compounds with walls several hundred meters long, modestly sized compounds such as that excavated at Moraduchayuq, and areas with refuse that lack stone architecture. The residential architecture at Moraduchayuq in Wari, at Conchopata (Lumbreras 1974a, 1981) at Jargampata (Isbell 1977) and at Tunasniyoq (Lumbreras 1974a, 1981) grades from better to poorer in that order. Differential access to labor, however, is manifested in the fact that Moraduchayuq was constructed in planned blocks of rooms with bonded walls while housing at Jargampata was built by the addition of one or two rooms at a time. Perhaps the strongest evidence for class differentiation comes from Azángaro, where Anders (1982) found a well-made residence she associates with the elite as well as small cubicles that may have been occupied by laborers.

Identifiable Early Intermediate Period residences are limited to single-room, stone-walled houses identified at Chupas and Lagunillas (Lumbreras 1974a, 1981). Although the rise of class differentiation between the Early Intermediate Period and Middle Horizon cannot be confirmed on the basis of housing, the available evidence is at least consistent with that hypothesis.

The distribution of luxury goods is also consistent with the hypothesis that class differences arose between the Early Intermediate Period and the Middle Horizon. While few items of great value have been reported from Early Intermediate Period Huarpa contexts, an impressive array of valuables has been found in Middle Horizon Ayacucho sites. Fancy pottery, *Spondylus* sp. shell ornaments, copper pins, shell beads, green stone objects, false turquoise pieces, lapis, gold, and even cowrie shells have been recovered in open sites; and where preservation of organic material occurs, textiles, carved wood, and other items are added to the list. No systematic studies are available, but more luxury items were found in the excavations of the dressed stone chambers at Cheqo Wasi than at Moraduchayuq. On the other hand, Moraduchayuq has much more of value than the residential areas of Conchopata. Finally, Jargampata and Tunasniyoq possess the fewest objects of value. Further studies will probably reveal even greater differences in wealth which should correspond with other variables such as quality of architecture, position of the settlement in the regional hierarchy, and probably a class hierarchy as well.

Division of sites by natural features is common in Ayacucho during both the Early Intermediate Period and the Middle Horizon. Simpapata, for example, is divided by a shallow ravine and the division may separate a section that possesses administrative architecture from another that does not. It may also be that the administrative buildings belong to the early Middle Horizon while most of the remaining occupation dates from the Early Intermediate Period. Other Huarpa Phase settlements that may have been divided in two by walls include Trigoloma and Tantawasi, although nothing in particular would suggest that these divisions isolate distinctive residential areas. The walls may even have been canals carrying water through a more or less central portion of the settlement. Lumbreras (1974a, 1981) also feels that Ñawinpukyu was divided into three sectors, representing socially significant areas but probably not classes or castes. If he is correct it still remains to be shown that the divisions date to the Early Intermediate Period.

By the time of the Middle Horizon, Wari was composed of walled compounds with restricted access. In fact, the city was so heavily divided by great compound walls that it is difficult to imagine how traffic flowed through it. Perhaps more significant than the compound wall as indicators of class differences are huge walls that isolate entire areas of the city. One such wall separates Wari Pampa, a flat area with little visible architecture, from the northern margin of the site, where the largest and best preserved compounds are located. This particular wall was 5 m thick – the thickest observed at Wari. At Azángaro, Anders (1982) has documented an obvious walled separation within the settlement that corresponds to apparent class lines.

In summary, burial patterns, residences, the distribution of luxury goods, and the deliberate divisions of settlements into isolated segments all support the interpretation that the Middle Horizon society in Ayacucho was divided into distinct social classes. While further confirmation requires a more complete archaeological data base, the contrasts between the Early Intermediate Period and the Middle Horizon demonstrate reorganization of society with greater status differentiation and concentration of new wealth in the hands of a portion of the populace.

The final characteristic of the state to be considered is the ideology of hierarchical authority, without which state control is impossible. Communication of this ideology has been achieved with symbols of various kinds. The American flag represents the union of the fifty states. The king of England possessed two bodies, the body politic and the body of flesh (Huntington and Metcalf 1978), and the Pharaoh of Egypt physically united the symbols of both upper and lower Egypt. Wari appears to have symbolized itself with a mythical being generally referred to as the 'front face' deity (Menzel 1964). This figure occurs throughout the area of Wari hegemony and was frequently reduced to a disembodied head. In its more complete representations, however, supreme importance of the deity was expressed by elevating it on a pyramidal platform, by setting two vertical staffs in its outstretched arms (probably representing the union of opposed halves, into which Andean wholes were virtually always divided), and by its elaborate headdress and clothing.

Hierarchy in the symbols adopted by Wari was made still more explicit. In the earliest iconography of the Middle

Horizon in Ayacucho, the front face deity with staffs was accompanied by a number of attendant beings, who were depicted in profile and generally with a single staff (Menzel 1964, 1977; Cook 1979). In turn, these figures appear in relation to nonmythical humans whose lower status was sometimes made explicit by representing them in smaller size, upside down, or with arms bound behind the back. Cook (1979) argues that the hierarchy of beings was simplified during Wari's subsequent expansive phase in order to emphasize the most important figure, the front face deity with staffs. In Epoch 2 of the Middle Horizon, Wari ceramic decorations emphasized the front face deity, whereas the art of the south coast emphasized the profile attendants (Menzel 1964). This suggests that the relationship between the south coast and Wari was equivalent to that of the profile attendants to the front face staff deity.

On the central coast, and into the central highlands around Huancayo, another figure predominates in the art of Middle Horizon Epoch 2. Menzel (1964, 1968) has called this profile creature the 'Pachacamac griffin,' arguing that its virtual absence at Wari implies the religious and political independence of the Pachacamac sphere of influence. However, in the Moraduchayuq compound of Wari, Christine Brewster-Wray and Michael Wray have discovered new evidence for the Pachacamac griffin. Possible antecedents of the Pachacamac griffin in early Middle Horizon artistic depictions in Ayacucho and its limited presence at Wari may indeed indicate that the Pachacamac polity was to Wari what the griffin was to the front face deity.

Monumental symbols of political authority have been very important in Andean prehistory. In the Moche area, for example, large platform mounds, ranging up to 3 000 000 cu m in size, were employed as clear symbols of authority both within the Moche Valley itself and in subordinate valleys to the north and south (Kosok 1965; Moseley 1975c; Haas 1982). Similarly, Tiwanaku seems to have constructed semisubterranean temples of platforms with sunken courts, smaller than those found at the capital, at its secondary and perhaps even tertiary centers. Inca monumental symbols of authority were more varied. Provincial administrative centers such as Raqchi, Vilcas Huamán and Huánuco Pampa were constructed throughout the highland portion of the empire, and sometimes on the coast. Sun temples were built on the coast, and sometimes in the highlands. No two of these are identical, or even have the same plan, in spite of many shared and highly diagnostic architectural features.

Wari's monumental symbols of political authority are most comparable to those of the Incas. Architectural complexes with similar, but never identical floor plans, and numerous diagnostic architectural features can be attributed to Wari on the basis of form and associated ceramics (Isbell and Schreiber 1978). Like the Inca installations, Wari centers probably had both administrative and ceremonial functions. The model for these complexes comes from Wari itself, where immense walled enclosures are typical of the better-preserved architectural remains. The excavated compound at Moraduchayuq, and similar complexes at Wari, employ rectangular or square courtyards surrounded by multistoried elongated rooms, which are the most common components in the provincial centers.

The greatest concentration of monumental, 'Wari-style' compounds is at Wari itself, where at least 200 ha of the architectural core was probably devoted to such structures. Two great enclosures of 30 to 70 ha are known outside Wari: Viracochapampa in the north highlands near Huamachuco, and Pikillaqta in the south highlands near Cuzco. Smaller enclosures are more numerous. In Ayacucho, two are located within 10 km of Wari: one tops Cerro Churu, to the south of Wari, and the second, Tawacocha, is about the same distance west of Wari. Other sites with similar compounds include: Azángaro, also within the Ayacucho Basin; Jargampata, in the next valley to the east; Jincamocco, about half way between Ayacucho and Nazca to the south; and about half way to Pachacamac to the north is Wari Willca. Other sites attributed to Wari on the basis of the architectural remains have been reported, including one at Yanahuanca near Cerro de Pasco, Wisajirca near La Union, Honco Pampa near Huarás, and Otuzco near Cajamarca. The lack of research at any of these sites, though, makes the identification questionable.

The abundant evidence for symbolic communication of state authority associated with Wari and the Middle Horizon contrasts sharply with the Early Intermediate Period in Ayacucho. Huarpa style ceramic decorations was almost never representational and nothing can be identified in the archaeological record that appears to be an iconographic system symbolic of power. Furthermore, the architectural forms of Early Intermediate Period Ayacucho also appear to lack symbols of power and authority, although Huarpa monuments are poorly known.

This review of the archaeological information from Ayacucho has revealed that facilities for bureaucrats, information recording devices, and a hierarchically structured settlement pattern all appear with the rise of Wari in the Middle Horizon. More or less simultaneously, large-scale storage complexes, barracks-like housing, and evidence for conspicuous generosity in the form of feasts and drinking bouts also appear. As all of these are intimately associated with the Inca state revenue collection system, a similar system of labor tax can be inferred for Wari. Some degree of status differentiation is seen in the Early Intermediate Period archaeological record, but class differences are not present until the Middle Horizon. At that time, variation in mortuary practices, residential facilities, the distribution of luxury goods, and the deliberate division of settlements into sectors are all consistent with the hypothesis that class or caste differences existed. Finally, Wari and the Middle Horizon abound with symbols of hierarchical authority, all of which are lacking in the Early Intermediate Period.

Explanation of Wari state government

The archaeological record strongly supports the interpretation that state government in the central highlands arose at the beginning of the Middle Horizon. Furthermore, Wari ceramics of Middle Horizon Epoch 1b have been found at Pikillaqta and near Viracochapampa, implying that imperial administration followed almost immediately. What caused this rapid transformational change in Ayacucho?

During the Early Horizon (see chapter by T. and S. Pozorski, this volume), Ayacucho appears to have been organized into small polities centralized around modest ceremonial centers. The Early Intermediate Period, however, does not seem to have continued the same pattern of integration, since platform mounds decreased in importance relative to the labor available to construct them. Although population estimates for the valley are impossible until a more careful site survey is completed and a more precise chronology worked out, the large number of Huarpa Period settlements implies a dense population (cf. MacNeish 1981).

The construction of agricultural terraces reclaimed a great deal of marginal hillside land for intensive cultivation during the Early Intermediate Period. Careful studies of these facilities should be carried out, but it seems likely that some terraces were dry farmed, so their cultivation would have been a high-risk activity. Lumbreras (1974a) has argued that other sections of terraces were irrigated by complex canal systems skillfully designed to catch and redistribute rain water. These also would have been high-risk fields, since rains in Ayacucho may come too late or end too early to insure a satisfactory crop. Regardless of how efficient the redistribution of rain waters was, nothing could have been done to alter the timing of water availability. Finally, permanent water sources were tapped for irrigation as well.

Early Intermediate Period hydraulic systems that drew water from permanent sources were probably small and numerous. The valley floor is narrow, steep, and irregular, so that large-scale water management systems would have been impossible. Cultivation of higher slopes depends on water from tiny streams and small springs, so that the canals of even a single modern community often draw upon several distinct sources.

The Wari area may have been an exception to the generalization that hydraulic systems of the region were small and independent. Today, a single water management system is shared by the community of Quinoa, above Wari, as well as the community of Pacaicasa and Hacienda Haullapampa below Wari. If, as suggested above, several Huarpa communities occupied the Wari area during the Early Intermediate Period, they probably also shared a single irrigation system for the local area, although much of the agricultural land was probably dry farmed or cultivated with networks of rain catchment canals.

The largest cluster of towns and villages during the Early Intermediate Period of Ayacucho, located in the center of the valley, could not have shared a single hydraulic system. Two of the towns and two villages are located on the left bank of the Pongora River, a third village is on the right bank of the Tomarenga River, and the remaining two villages and town are on the right bank of the Pongora River. In fact, if this latter town cultivated land on its side of the river and shared the hydraulic system used by other communities on that side of the river, it would, in fact, have been participating in the Wari-area system.

The cluster of villages in the south end of the valley probably also had two or three different water sources. However, it is possible that Ñawinpukyu, Acuchimay, and even Conchopata all participated in the management of water from a single, high elevation source that currently supplies drinking water to modern Ayacucho.

Another aspect of the Ayacucho economic system may have called for cooperation and even management among diverse groups. Murra (1972) has argued that the traditional Andean economic system involved exploitation of an archipelago of zones, each one different from the others because of its elevation, climate and resources. Consequently, the lands exploited by an ethnic group were not contiguous, but spread through a wide range of microenvironments. This kind of system could exist only if hostilities could be controlled among the different groups with temporary or permanent colonies located at considerable distances from their home communities, since the architectural facilities, produce, and caravans required to transport the produce could not be effectively defended at these distant colonies.

Evidence for vertical archipelago economics can be seen in the central Andean region just about at the time of the initial Wari expansion. At the end of the Early Intermediate Period and beginning of the Middle Horizon, intense Wari influence appeared in the Nazca Valley. The impact is so obvious that several settlements, including Huaca del Loro, Tres Palos II and perhaps Pacheco, can best be interpreted as Wari colonies. Each of these sites possesses a circular building in highland style, which, in the case of Huaca del Loro, has been interpreted as a temple (Strong 1957). As was the case among the concentrations of Huarpa settlements in Ayacucho, there was no attempt to fortify these communities on the south coast.

Late in the Early Intermediate Period, the population of Ayacucho had probably grown well beyond any previous maximum. Irrigation systems and far-flung economic archipelagos were being initiated, though it would appear that the management was not centralized or hierarchical since a dominant capital is not apparent in the archaeological record of this time period.

By the end of the Early Intermediate Period, new pressures were being exerted on the system. The climate began to deteriorate and desiccation set in (Isbell 1978). High-risk agriculture, both dry farming and cultivation with rainfall catchment canals, would have failed more and more frequently. Greater emphasis and dependence would have been placed on cultivation based on irrigation from permanent water sources, and on the exploitation of distant ecozones. Even if the latter were also becoming less dependable, they would not have shared exactly the same bad years with the Ayacucho Valley. Finally, in times of decreasing productivity, conflict would have increased, threatening the old, nonhierarchical system of management with disastrous collapse. This combination of factors would have constituted a strong, selective pressure favoring the concentration of authority and power in the hands of a centralized, hierarchical government capable of making decisions based on carefully collected and processed information.

The Wari communities may have had some advantages of experience and been exposed to stronger selective pressures for centralization and hierarchical organization, because of their single, coordinated irrigation system. Selective pressures, however, do not necessarily create adaptive responses. Since the residents of Ayacucho had direct contact with one south highlands group and either direct or indirect contact with a second, exposure to different forms of organization may have stimulated experimentation with novel solutions.

Early in Middle Horizon Epoch 1a a new iconography appeared at Conchopata in southern Ayacucho. The new iconography, probably introduced by people from the *montaña* east of Lake Titicaca, consisted of the front face deity with staffs as well as a host of attendant beings. The religious ideology behind this iconography was probably based on a high god with ultimate authority and power who stood at the apex of a hierarchical pantheon, free of attachments to ancestors of a specific group. Consequently, the new religion presented a model for hierarchical authority that could unify unrelated ethnic groups.

At about the same time, Wari borrowed a new form of ceremonial structure from Tiwanaku. Hierarchical ritual organization was already characteristic of Tiwanaku. Local copies of its temples were probably the facilities employed to disseminate the new ideology of a high god or hierarchical centralized authority, and to consolidate authority and power at Wari itself.

During Middle Horizon Epoch 1a, a semisubterranean temple similar to the example at Tiwanaku was built in the Moraduchayuq sector of Wari; however, it was used for only a brief time. In Epoch 1b of the Middle Horizon, the temple was leveled and the Moraduchayuq compound constructed according to a plan characteristic of buildings associated with bureaucratic administration. Wari grew rapidly at this time, reorganizing the Ayacucho Valley settlement system and establishing provincial capitals far beyond Ayacucho.

Apparently, Wari did more than simply borrow iconography ideology, hierarchical organization and religious facilities from different foreign sources. It actually combined these foreign elements with its old management skills, which had been developed to manage the reciprocity-based irrigation and vertical archipelago systems. Wari thus invented a hierarchical centralized system that employed a fictitious, reciprocal relationship between the citizen and state to extract revenue in the form of labor. Facilities and bureaucracy were created to carry out the state's obligations, giving birth to class structure, the state and the administrative pattern for empire. At a time when selective pressures for efficient hierarchical government were very strong, Wari spread its dominion rapidly to embrace much of the central Andes.

Chapter 9

From state to empire: the expansion of Wari outside the Ayacucho Basin

Katharina J. Schreiber

The problem

The Middle Horizon period of Andean prehistory (*c.* A.D. 600 to 1000) witnessed the evolution of a complex political organization centered around the city of Wari in the Ayacucho Basin of the central highlands. Although there is little doubt that Wari politically dominated this heartland, there is much dispute over the extent and nature of Wari influence outside this zone. This paper is an attempt to clarify this situation and offer some understanding of the evolutionary processes which account for the apparent occurrence of Wari cultural traits outside the Ayacucho Basin.

This, of course, requires some understanding of the development of the Wari state in Ayacucho, from the later phases of the Early Intermediate Period (*c.* A.D. 400 to 600) through Middle Horizon Epoch 1a (*c.* A.D. 600 to 700). Ideally, this involves documenting population growth and changes in settlement patterns reflecting the growth of an urban system in Ayacucho, as well as understanding the apparent interaction between Wari and Nazca (Menzel 1964) and between Wari and Tiwanaku (Cook 1979). While Isbell has touched on some aspects of the problem elsewhere in this volume, I would like to separate the issues of Wari inside the Ayacucho Basin versus Wari outside the Ayacucho Basin, and address three major problems.

First, do manifestations of Wari exist outside the Ayacucho Basin, and if so, where and in what contexts do these occur? Some researchers argue that Wari traits are limited to the Wari heartland; others see some limited distribution outside Ayacucho; while still others see Wari traits as pervasive throughout the entire Andean region north of Lake Titicaca. Second, if Wari manifestations exist outside the Ayacucho Basin, what mechanism best accounts for these and their distribution? Some would argue that the apparent presence of Wari traits outside Ayacucho was the result of simple reciprocal trade (Shady and Ruiz 1979), while at the other extreme some argue that these traits were spread as the result of the expansion of an all-powerful military empire. Third, given the mechanism which best accounts for these manifestations, what can be said about the evolutionary processes involved in the development of this complex political system?

My specific temporal concern is the period beginning with Middle Horizon Epoch 1b (*c.* A.D. 700). By this time state-level organizations had probably evolved in a number of areas in the Andean region, including those centered in Moche on the north coast (Moseley 1978a; T. Topic 1982), Tiwanaku in the far south highlands (Browman 1982), and Cahuachi in the Nasca drainage on the south coast (Schreiber n.d.). The central coast and the Callejón de Huaylas may also have been characterized by complex political organization. Therefore, the theoretical problem in the Middle Horizon is not to document the development of the 'pristine' state, but rather to understand why manifestations of one particular state came to have an apparently widespread distribution throughout portions of the Andean region while other states did not. The question to ask seems to be not, 'Was Wari a state?,' but rather, 'What was Wari doing outside the Ayacucho Basin, and why?' (cf. Isbell and Schreiber 1978).

Wari manifestations and related events of the Middle Horizon

Ceramics

Wari styles and iconography, closely related provincial styles, and local copies of these have been found in various contexts throughout the central Andes north of the zone of Tiwanaku domination. Their apparent absence in the south has been widely interpreted as reflecting a border beween Wari and Tiwanaku (Menzel 1964). The presence of pure and derived Wari styles elsewhere is explained as the result of any one of many processes. Relatively 'pure' Wari styles occur in the highlands from Cuzco to Cajamarca, and on the south and central coast. The situation in the far north highlands and on the north coast is less clear; few pure Wari style ceramics are found, although some examples which may be derived or copied from Wari styles do seem to occur.

Architecture

A second manifestation of Wari outside the Ayacucho Basin is the occurrence of a number of rectangular structures, ranging in size from 25 to 800 m on a side, and built in a distinctive and unique architectural style. Clear examples of these structures occur in the highlands from Cuzco and Cajamarca, and possibly on the south and central coast as well (Schreiber 1978). These sites (Figure 1) have been interpreted as storage facilities, *tambo* (way stations), fortresses, and/or administrative centers. The similarity in style and elements of layout of all of these sites suggests that their construction was directly supervised by architectural specialists from Wari. Regardless of their function or the mechanism through which they came to be distributed, the existence of these sites in various areas implies some direct input from Wari in those areas. Furthermore, the distribution on these sites is probably the best delimiter of the zone of direct Wari 'influence.'

Road system

The association of these architectural facilities with particular long-distance roads, many later coopted by the Incas as part of their system of 'royal highways,' implies the existence of a formal system of roads in the Middle Horizon (Lumbreras 1974a, Schreiber 1978). The association of Wari sites with the roads would indicate that Wari may have been responsible for formalizing and maintaining a system of long-distance roads. The labor input necessary in the construction and maintenance of these roads suggests that they were not merely local trails.

Exchange

Recognition of long-distance trade is certainly not new for the Middle Horizon, but it is worth pointing out that some of this trade in exotics seems clearly associated with Wari. Wari participation in some sort of long-distance trade network is indicated by the presence of various exotic goods at pure Wari sites, including gold, bronze, *Spondylus* sp, turquoise, etc. (Schreiber 1978). In some cases, notably that of turquoise, raw materials were apparently brought to Wari itself, where the finished products were manufactured. Obsidian was also widely traded since preceramic times, as has been well documented by Burger and Asaro (1977). They point out that obsidian from the major Quispisisa source reached its widest distribution during the Middle Horizon and attribute this to some sort of Wari control.

Settlement patterns

In much of the Andean region, especially in the highlands, many local settlement patterns seem to undergo major shifts in the Middle Horizon (Browman 1976; Schreiber 1982). Various explanations of this change include: environmental change, population growth, the introduction of maize cultivation, and even direct interference by Wari itself. I do not suggest here that these changes are a direct manifestation of Wari outside Ayacucho, but rather that any significant cultural developments during the Middle Horizon may be relevant to the understanding of the Wari situation.

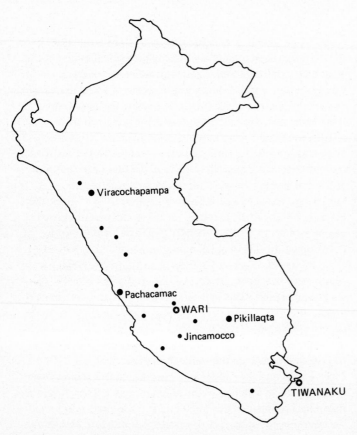

Fig. 1. Distribution of sites with Wari architecture

Other political developments

Among other events of the Middle Horizon, some mention should be made of other major political changes during this period. First, we see the fragmentation and apparent relocation of central authority in the Moche state from the site of Moche to the site of Pampa Grande further north in the Lambayeque Valley (Day 1972b; T. Topic 1982). Second, we see the growth of several new polities including Cajamarca, Sicán (Shimada 1982), and Pachacamac (Menzel 1977). And third, the Nazca culture underwent a degree of fragmentations and the loss of Cahuachi as the center of authority.

Mechanisms

A number of mechanisms have been suggested in the literature that purport to explain the spread of Wari traits outside Ayacucho. In this section I discuss three possible mechanisms and briefly evaluate each of these in terms of the Wari manifestations and events of the Middle Horizon discussed above.

Religion

Religion has been suggested by some as the mechanism by which Wari traits came to be distributed throughout much of the Andean region (Menzel 1964). That is, the Wari 'expansion' was an active proselytizing effort to spread a particular set of religious beliefs. Certainly the spread of Wari iconography, including specific mythical beings, as well as the presence of the offering tradition in Epoch 1, could argue in favor of this interpretation (cf. Cook 1979). However, if religion were the only factor involved, one probably would not expect the presence of the large secular architectural facilities and an associated road system. I suggest that if religion were a factor in the spread of Wari traits outside Ayacucho it was more likely a corollary of some other mechanism, rather than a primary mechanism in its own right.

Commerce

It has been suggested that Wari was one of several urban systems during the Middle Horizon and that extensive trade between these commercial centers accounts for the distribution of Wari traits outside Ayacucho (Shady and Ruiz 1979). The distribution of ceramics, specifically when found in these other urban centers, would support this notion. On the other hand, how would one account for the apparent lack of commerce between these centers and Tiwanaku in the south? Again, the presence of major architectural facilities does not entirely support the notion that Wari extended outward for trade reasons alone. If such were the case, one would not expect the major investment of the labor and resources manifested in these structures. More importantly, the fact that all of these facilities were apparently built by just one of the proposed 'commercial centers' argues against this notion.

The existence of a road system would be consistent with extensive trade between commercial centers; however, the investment of labor and resources necessary for its construction and maintenance again could be expected to be beyond the means of an individual center. Likewise, the shift in settlement patterns seen in many areas is not entirely consistent with the idea that Wari was one of several co-equal commercial centers, unless a change in subsistence strategies reflects an increased emphasis on particular products to be exchanged in these networks. Furthermore, the growth of new political centers and the eclipse of others outside the Ayacucho Basin could be attributed to their position and success in the proposed kind of major trading network.

As a whole, the participation of Wari in long-distance trade is consistent with the idea that it was a major commercial center, though other kinds of data do not completely confirm this as the sole cause of Wari expansion and influence outside the Ayacucho Basin. Nevertheless, whatever the mechanism that accounts for Wari traits outside Ayacucho, commerce clearly plays a part.

Political expansion/conquest

A third mechanism that has been suggested to account for the distribution of Wari traits is that of political domination. In other words, it has been suggested that Wari may be viewed as a political empire which came to dominate large portions of the Andean region (Menzel 1968, Isbell 1978). The distribution of ceramics outside Ayacucho is consistent with this possibility, although ceramics might also be found outside the boundaries of actual political control.

This notion is consistent with the distribution of architectural facilities, especially if these are interpreted as primarily administrative facilities, which may have functioned additionally as *tambo*, storehouses, and defensive sites. Certainly the maintenance of an administrative hierarchy would require the construction of intrusive administrative facilities, particularly where local levels of administration were insufficiently complex to fulfill imperial needs.

A system of well-defined and maintained roads is to be expected in this situation in order to facilitate communication within the domain, to facilitate movement of military forces through the domain, and to control the movement of people within the domain. The existence of long-distance trade is also consistent with political domination, though it cannot be taken as strong supporting evidence of the general hypothesis.

Changes in settlement patterns and subsistence, if the result of environmental change or major population growth, may simply represent local responses to the same factors which led to the rise of Wari in the first place. However, in the case with which I am most familiar, a strong argument can be made that major changes in the settlement/subsistence system were a direct result of Wari domination (Schreiber 1982).

Finally, the political changes of the Middle Horizon are not inconsistent with the notion of Wari domination, especially the growth of new polities, such as Cajamarca and Sicán, around the apparent periphery of the Wari domain. Indeed, the decentralization of political authority in Nasca during the

Middle Horizon might be interpreted as the result of the imposition of political control from Wari; and the apparent fact that Nazca collapsed along with Wari at the end of Middle Horizon Epoch 2b is also consistent with this view.

To summarize, religion alone cannot account for the existence of Wari traits outside Ayacucho. Although the commercial center/trade network possibility is very attractive, two points argue fairly strongly against this notion: (1) the presence of major architectural facilities, and especially the immense cost of establishing such facilities, and (2) the apparent one-sided nature of this commercial network. I would suggest, then, that on the basis of our present state of

knowledge and interpretation, the strongest argument can be made in favor of political domination as the mechanism which best accounts for the presence of Wari manifestations outside the Ayacucho Basin. The three possible mechanisms are certainly not mutually exclusive, and religious and commercial concerns probably played some part in the overall process.

CARAHUARAZO VALLEY Lucanas, Ayacucho, Peru

CARAHUARAZO VALLEY Lucanas, Ayacucho, Peru

Scale: Kilometers   Contour interval 100 m
0 1 2 3 4 5

▲ Village   • Hamlet

Fig. 2. Carahuarazo Valley settlement pattern during the Early Jincamocco Phase

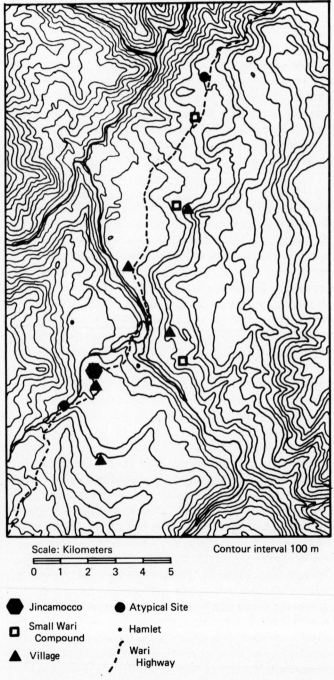

Scale: Kilometers   Contour interval 100 m
0 1 2 3 4 5

⬡ Jincamocco   ● Atypical Site
◻ Small Wari   • Hamlet
   Compound
▲ Village   ┇ Wari
                   Highway

Fig. 3. Carahuarazo Valley settlement pattern during the Late Jincamocco Phase

A case in the Carahuarazo Valley

One brief example may serve to emphasize some of these points. The Carahuarazo Valley is located in the south highlands just over the continental divide from the Nazca drainage, about four days' travel (by foot) from Cahuachi, and about six from Wari. Although located in the modern department of Ayacucho, the valley lies a considerable distance from the Ayacucho Basin and did not participate in any direct way in the development of the Wari state before Middle Horizon Epoch 1b.

When the Wari presence was first felt, there were seven small villages and seventeen seasonally occupied hamlets in the valley (Figure 2). During the period of Wari domination a number of major changes occurred in the valley (Figure 3). (1) The highest villages, those located at the juncture of the herding and tuber growing zones, were abandoned and new villages were established at the juncture of the tuber and grain growing zones. (2) The site of Jincamocco, a medium-sized Wari enclosure, was built in Epoch 1b. During its occupation it grew to some 27 ha in extent through the addition of more structures around the outside of the original enclosure. (This is the only case with which I am familiar of a Wari enclosure which did not stand isolated from other structures.) (3) At least three more small Wari enclosures were built, two adjacent to grain zones, the third along the road to Wari. (4) Two major stepped and paved roads were built out of the valley to the north and south, and a bridge was probably constructed over the rivers. (5) Much of the valley was terraced at this time, and irrigation systems were probably developed concurrently. This fact, along with the downward shift in settlement location, suggests the introduction of, or the intensification of, maize cultivation.

The construction of all of these features must have been extremely demanding in terms of labor and resources as well as administrative time. The sheer volume of construction suggests that it was not all done at local initiative or expense, accomplished by participation in a commercial network. More likely, it was organized and 'financed' by Wari, and was a direct result of political domination and reorganization of the local system by Wari. And what did Wari get in return? The valley was probably a good stopping-off point on the journey between Wari and Nazca, and may have served as an important node in the communication network. It is possible that Wari was exploiting a small obsidian source in the valley. However, the analysis done by Burger and Asaro (1977) shows that although obsidian from this source was predominant on sites within the valley at all time periods, it has not been found at Wari, and its distribution during the Middle Horizon does not imply Wari control. Finally, the construction of terraces and the downward shift in settlement locations might suggest that increased quantities of maize were grown, and may have served as tribute payments to Wari.

The evolution of empire

If we accept political domination as the mechanism which best accounts for the distribution of Wari traits outside the Ayacucho Basin, what can we say about the evolution of such an expanding state? For ease of discussion, I divide this evolution into three successive stages.

Initial impetus to expansion

After the evolution of state-level administration and, usually, urban society, there are a number of cases in history or prehistory in which a political organization rapidly and suddenly expanded the boundaries of its control. In these cases the area that came to be controlled was vastly larger than the initial heartland. Furthermore, such 'imperial' states may be contrasted with other states that only gradually expand their borders and do so to a much lesser degree.

What causes a state to expand suddenly in this fashion? A number of suggestions have been offered, including: proselytizing religion (Menzel 1964), control of trade, environmental or population stress leading to a need to control new resource zones (Paulsen 1976; Isbell 1978), and the dictates of certain laws of heredity (Conrad 1981). In the case of Wari, I suspect the answer to this question can only come from an increased knowledge of the processes inherent in the evolution of Wari as a state in Ayacucho (cf. Isbell 1980). Certainly the Wari expansion had the effect of spreading its religion, controlling at least some long-distance trade, and controlling new resource zones. Whatever the initial impetus, Wari suddenly and rapidly expanded outside of Ayacucho beginning in Middle Horizon Epoch 1b.

Expansion and consolidation

The second stage in the evolution of empires involves two interrelated processes: expansion and consolidation. The directions in which an empire expanded, the order in which it expanded, and especially the order in which areas were consolidated under imperial rule sometimes can be reconstructed more or less directly from the archaeological remains. The process of expansion generally involves some combination of diplomacy and militarism. As new regions are included in this expansion, the process of consolidation begins, and involves the establishment of economic and political ties between the imperial capital and the newly incorporated region. The actual manifestation of this process is the result of the interplay between a number of complex factors including general relations between the two groups, location of the new region within the empire, the administrative requirements of the empire, and the level of complexity of the local political system. In the case of Wari the processes of expansion and consolidation are manifested most clearly in presence of major facilities in some areas, as well as the sequence of their construction.

I do not mean to imply that reconstruction of imperial expansion is a simple process. In fact, political conquest empires are notoriously difficult to see archaeologically, even when one has prior knowledge of their existence. It is precisely this difficulty that suggests that, at least in the Andean region, we may be dealing with two rather different forms of expanding states. At the risk of oversimplifying a complex situation on the north coast, in the cases of Moche and Chimu, we see examples of expanding states which might be termed to be characterized by *intensive* forms of control. That is, these states expanded rapidly to the north and south, controlling each successive valley in turn, and imposed major visible administrative structures in each (see chapter by Mackey, this volume).

On the other hand, Wari, as well as the Inca empire and possibly Tiwanaku, might be said to exhibit more *extensive* forms of control. Political control seems to be extended over a much larger area by these polities; yet within the total area visible manifestations of imperial control tend to be unequally distributed. That is, control is apparent in border areas, areas with significant resources, hostile areas, and areas lacking sufficient levels of complexity for imperial needs. Other areas seem to be totally devoid of any overt manifestations of imperial control, quite unlike the much more pervasive manifestations of the north-coast polities. In the highland cases, those areas which appear to lack any sort of imperial control may indeed lack such control; they also may represent areas within the domain that were passed over because they were not needed by or threatening to the empire; or they may have been ruled through diplomatic alliances with local leaders. This latter

situation is extremely problematic in that I can see no immediate means of evaluating it archaeologically.

Given that sites with visible remains of Wari control have a rather spotty distribution throughout the domain, it seems most feasible to suggest that the overall extent and distribution of sites with Wari architecture and the associated road system gives us the best approximation of the boundaries of the Wari Empire (Figure 4). In other words, I would argue that the Wari political domain, by the end of Epoch 2b, included all of the highlands from Pikillaqta, south of Cuzco, to Yanabamba, just south of Cajamarca, as well as the south and central coast. The order of expansion, judging from the ceramics associated with the Wari sites throughout the empire, proceeded first to the southeast toward Nazca and north to Huamachuco or even Cajamarca. Only later were major portions of the central highlands north of Ayacucho incorporated into the empire, and expansion proceeded to the southeast nearly to the Titicaca Basin.

Collapse

The third and final stage in the evolution of empires is, of course, their ultimate collapse. It is a curious aspect of most empires, at least those of the extensive type, that once they cease to expand they do not seem able to maintain themselves. This certainly seems true of Wari. Furthermore, once this point had been reached, the economic and political organization of Wari had changed to such a degree (it was so geared to an expansionist economy, if you will) that not only did the empire collapse, but the Wari state within the Ayacucho Basin also collapsed, and Wari was abandoned. In addition, those polities which were closely tied to Wari, particularly Nazca and to a lesser degree Pachacamac, also collapsed. On the other hand, states on its periphery, such as Tiwanaku, Cajamarca and Sicán, continued to exist, and eventually another complex state/empire arose on the north coast.

Many reasons have been proposed to account for the collapse of complex civilizations in different parts of the world. As in the case of understanding the first stage of empire evolution, the initial impetus to expansion, the real reasons for collapse may be extremely complex, and difficult to see in the archaeological record. As a first step, however, I would suggest not asking why empires such as Wari collapsed, but rather, why did such polities stop expanding? In the case of Wari, the answer to the latter question probably lies in the existence of other complex political organizations to both the north and south of the Wari domain, which it could not or would not subsume. I suggest that Wari itself regarded these areas as outside its domain, and built its two largest facilities near these border zones: Viracochapampa, just short of the Cajamarca polity to the north, and Pikillaqta, just short of the Tiwanaku domain to the south. The recognition by Wari of these as the limits of its domain and the failure to continue expanding beyond these limits may have preordained the collapse of the Wari empire.

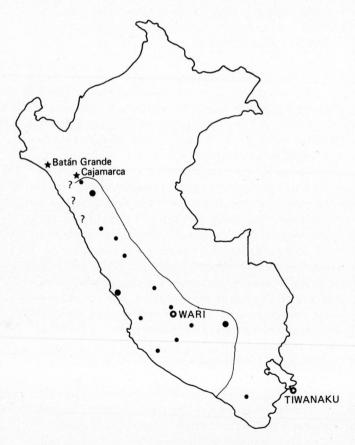

Fig. 4. Probable boundaries of the Wari Empire

Chapter 10

The development of Chimu administration in Chan Chan

Alexandra M. Ulana Klymyshyn

Introduction

State societies can be distinguished from less complex societies in part by the nature of the institutions through which decisions are made and implemented. Specifically, a hierarchical network of administrators provides the information on which decisions are based and then implements these decisions. Such networks of specialized administrators are not found in less complex societies, including chiefdoms (e.g., Flannery 1972; Wright 1977).

The development of administrative networks in evolving state societies can be attributed to several related factors, including: an increase in the size of the territory and population controlled by individual polities; increased specialization of production; an intensification of local and/or long-distance exchange networks; and large-scale public construction projects. Each of these factors leads both to an increase in the number of persons involved in the making and implementing of decisions and to an increase in the diversity of their tasks. The relationship between these factors and the development of administrative networks can be summarized as follows.

(1) An increase in the size of the territory and population leads to a greater number of units or groups to be administered. Diversity also exists in the type and size of administrative networks in different regions, depending on local variations in population density and organization (Carneiro 1967; Flannery 1972; Mair 1977: Chs 4 and 6; Johnson 1978).

(2) Increased specialization of production, especially in cases involving full-time craft specialists organized in workshops, results in the creation of a larger number of more discrete and interdependent groups within the general population. Further, since these groups are less self-sufficient, a more complex system of distributing both raw materials and finished products is required. Different groups of specialists might also require different types of administrative networks.

(3) The intensification of exchange networks relates closely to increased specialization of production, in that the intensification of exchange networks potentially results from increased specialization. Both the increase in specialization and the intensification of exchange networks increase administrative tasks, such as supervision, record-keeping, processing of information, standardization of weights and measures, and the storage and movement of goods (cf. Polanyi 1957; Rathje 1971; Johnson 1973; Sabloff and Lamberg-Karlovsky 1975; Wright and Johnson 1975; Wright 1978).

(4) The relationship between administration and large-scale public construction has been recognized since Wittfogel's (1955, 1957) discussion of the role of large-scale irrigation systems in the development of the state. Briefly, the argument states that the planning, construction, subsequent maintenance, regulation and defense of these irrigation systems are more efficient if carried out by a central organization including specialized administrators (see Sanders *et al.* 1979 for

a recent discussion). A similar argument can be made for other large-scale constructions, such as pyramids and monumental platform mounds. In these cases, however, there may be no need for subsequent regulation (cf. Moseley 1975a; Haas 1982).

In addition to differences in the size and responsibilities of the administrative network, states differ from chiefdoms in the organization and recruitment of administrative personnel. (1) In chiefdoms, the persons responsible for making and implementing decisions are usually relatives of the chief. In states, because of the greater number of personnel, and because state control encompasses several unrelated groups, administrative personnel are no longer recruited primarily on the basis of kinship or some other personal relationship with the rulers. (2) Because the administrative tasks of state societies are more diverse and numerous than those of chiefdoms, administrators in state societies are more highly specialized. (3) There are fewer historical levels in the administrative networks of chiefdoms than in those of states. With more units or groups to be administered, rulers create middle or intervening levels of administrators to improve efficiency and effectiveness. The middle-level administrators are responsible for providing information to upper-level administrators and for implementing decisions that come down from those upper levels. Thus, while generally only one administrative level stands between the leader and the primary producers and consumers in chiefdoms, at least two or three levels intervene in state societies (cf. Adams 1966; Service 1971, 1975; Flannery 1972; Wright and Johnson 1975; Peebles and Kus 1977; Wright 1977, 1978; Johnson 1978).

Many of the processes that led to the initial increased complexity of emergent states continue to operate in subsequent evolution. For example, many of the early state societies expanded beyond their original territorial boundaries, and thereby brought new groups of people under their control. The incorporation of new territories and peoples into the state leads to new administrative positions, and possibly a restructuring of the administrative networks by adding new levels to the hierarchy. The Inca, for example, reorganized in this way immediately after the first significant expansion of the empire; furthermore, the capital of Cuzco was rebuilt to reflect these changes (Rowe 1946:204–208, 1967c).

The purpose of this chapter is to examine the administrative organization of one of the antecedents of the Inca empire, the Chimu empire (A.D. 900–1470) on the north coast of Peru. Like the Inca, the Chimu expanded their control well beyond their original boundaries. The propositions to be tested are that the Chimu administrative network changed as a result of the expansion, and that the changes in administration are reflected in the architectural remains found in the capital, Chan Chan.

Administration in the Chimu Empire

Chan Chan is located in the Moche Valley, some 560 km north of Lima (Figure 1). According to historic information recorded after the Spanish conquest, the expansion of the

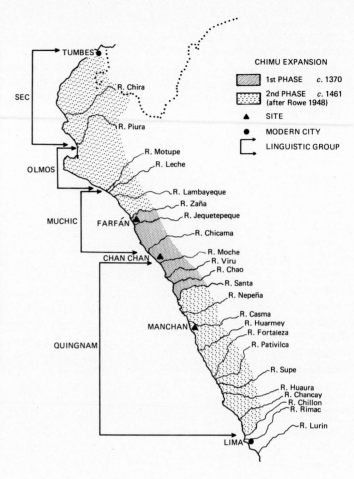

Fig. 1. Chimu expansion

empire occurred in two stages. The first stage is said to have occurred during the reign of the grandson of the founder of the dynasty, and the second stage during the reign of the last of the ten rulers mentioned in the accounts (Anonymous History of 1604 in Rowe 1948; Calancha 1638; Cabello Valboa 1951). The results of recent excavations in the southern part of the empire, however, indicate that the second stage of expansion probably occurred somewhat earlier than stated in the ethnohistoric documents (Mackey and Klymyshyn 1981; see chapter by Mackey, this volume). Nevertheless, until the chronology of the Chimu empire can be refined on the basis of further research, the expansion still can be divided into only two main stages.

In spite of the paucity of ethnohistoric records on the Chimu, certain administrative activities can be identified on the basis of the archaeological record and other lines of evidence. Perhaps the most easily identifiable are the administrative activities related to the construction and maintenance of irrigation canals and other monumental constructions – especially those in and around the capital (Day 1973:130–131; Moseley 1975c, 1975d; Ortloff *et al.* 1982; T. Pozorski and S. Pozorski 1982). Evidence for other administrative activities related to irrigation agriculture has been derived from the rural administrative centers (Keatinge and Day 1973, 1974; Keatinge

1974; see chapter by T. Pozorski, this volume), state villages whose inhabitants cultivated specialized crops (Keatinge 1975) and state-planned field systems (Kus 1980). Excavations of middens in other Chimu villages have yielded evidence of additional specialization in food-growing and procurement which resulted in the need for the distribution of these products among the various settlements (S. Pozorski 1976, 1982). Ethnohistoric sources indicate that the regulation of local production, control of labor for construction and maintenance, and redistribution of products were the responsibility of middle-level administrators in their role as 'local level lords' (Netherly 1977). From the capital, evidence exists for the distribution of raw materials and tools to the craft specialists (J. Topic 1977, 1982), and for the role of administrators in the storage of goods.

None of the types of artifacts, such as cylinder seals, counters, knotted recording devices or *quipus*, associated with administrative tasks in other early state societies, have been found in Chimu sites. Chimu artifacts which can be associated with administration include carved wooden staffs, which were indicators of status and/or position within the hierarchy, and vessels used in dispensing *chicha* (a maize beer), one of the duties of nobles and administrators (Netherly 1977). However, the staffs are rarely found in controlled contexts where they would be indicative of function; and the ceramic vessels associated with dispensing *chicha* are not sufficiently discrete in shape to allow for the specific identification of administrative tasks. Consequently, the identification of rooms as administrative in function is based almost entirely on their form and association with other architectural remains.

Chan Chan

Chan Chan, over 20 sq km in area (Moseley 1975b:219), consists primarily of ten monumental compounds, 34 elite compounds, and numerous small irregular agglutinated rooms (SIAR). This classification is based on differences in size, internal layout, and construction materials and techniques. The ten monumental compounds are enclosed by adobe walls over 9 m high, 1 to 5 m thick, and up to 600 m long. Although no two of these compounds are identical, five of them follow the same basic plan. With some exceptions discussed below, the compounds have large open plazas with benches and ramps, auxiliary plazas with a variety of architectural details, courts and storerooms, courts with U-shaped structures, burial platforms, and open areas containing structures with cobble foundations and walls of perishable materials. These monumental compounds have been identified as the palaces of the Chimu rulers (Day 1973, 1982a).

The 34 elite compounds are characterized by a high degree of variability. They are similar to the monumental compounds in that they are enclosed by adobe walls and contain similar plazas, courts, and rooms; however, they are considerably smaller, do not have the same internal layout as the monumental compounds, and lack burial platforms. These

elite compounds have been identified as the residences of the Chimu nobility (Klymyshyn 1976, 1982).

The SIAR, which constitute the bulk of the residential architecture at Chan Chan, are constructed of cobbles and perishable materials. The average size of the rooms is approximately 3×5 m, with several rooms composing a single dwelling. Storage facilities within the SIAR consist of small bins and pits rather than the formal storerooms found in the compounds. Craft specialists occupied at least some of these dwellings, and similar kinds of structures were used as craft workshops. The SIAR as a whole are more densely packed together than the elite and monumental compounds (J. Topic 1977, 1982).

Structures specifically associated with administrative functions are found only in the monumental and elite compounds. Since virtually no remains were found in these administrative rooms which could be used to identify their function, a functional interpretation must be based on the form and context of these structures. These administrative structures are described below, along with changes in their frequency and context in individual monumental compounds. These changes are then correlated with the chronology of Chan Chan and of the expansion of the Chimu empire. The final section is a discussion of the evidence for the reorganization of the Chimu administrative hierarchy in the Late Intermediate period as a result of this expansion.

Rooms associated with administrative functions

In the monumental and elite compounds, plazas, U-shaped structures and storerooms have been associated with administrative activities. Since the activities performed in the plazas were more generalized in nature, the discussion is limited to the U-shaped structures and storerooms.

Storerooms

Identification of the function of storerooms rests mainly on their formal characteristics and context. Further evidence comes from the results of excavation in these rooms. Rooms that have been identified as storerooms are arranged in rows within courts. Access to these courts is restricted in some way, and can be gained either through a narrow corridor, through a court containing a U-shaped structure, or through another court with storerooms. Access to individual storerooms is also restricted, in that the threshold entry is up to 1 m high and 1 m wide (Day 1973:184). The size of storerooms within a row is almost always identical (except in isolated cases where a smaller one was squeezed in at one end). The size of storerooms within a court is also usually the same.

While there is little direct evidence that these structures were indeed used for storage purposes, a number of indirect lines of evidence point to storage as their probable function. (1) The raised entries and generally restricted access indicate the rooms were not entered with great frequency. (2) Some of the rooms are as small as 1.5 m × 1.5 m. (3) There is great uniformity of these structures within a single room complex and

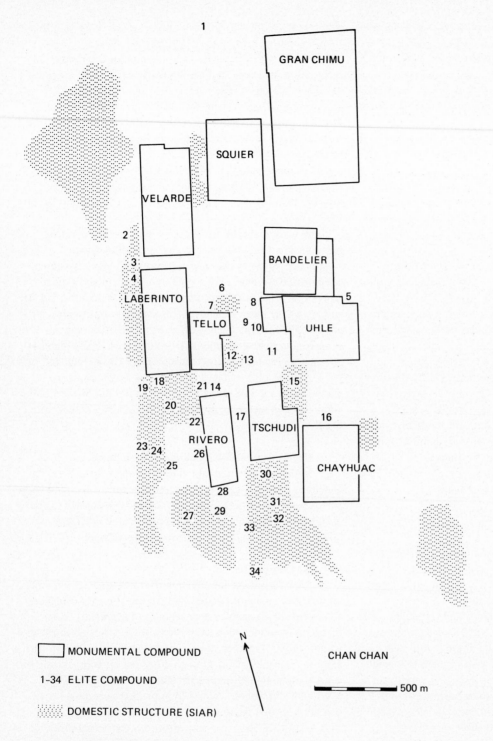

Fig. 2. Chan Chan

indeed within the site as a whole. (4) Though artifacts of any kind are rarely found in these rooms, sherds of possible storage vessels were found in several storerooms in elite compounds (Klymyshyn 1976). Thus, although it is remotely possible that these rooms were used as habitations, workshops or barracks, storage is a *much* more likely function.

Since the storerooms were empty, there is no way of knowing what was stored in them. The suggestion has been made that since the storerooms are so consistently empty and access to them is restricted, their valuable contents were probably systematically removed (Keatinge and Day 1973:283–284; Conrad 1974:76; Kolata 1978:252; Day 1982a:338). This, however, should not be construed to mean that all storerooms held exclusively high-status goods. Since archaeological (Keatinge and Day 1973, 1974; S. Pozorski 1976, 1982; J. Topic 1977, 1982) and ethnohistoric (Netherly 1977) evidence points to a redistributive Chimu economic system, storerooms would have held commodities (e.g. foodstuffs, raw materials and finished crafts) that were being redistributed, in addition to high-status goods. It is primarily this association of the storerooms with redistribution and control of goods which is the basis for the identification of the function of U-shaped structures.

U-shaped structures

Across the site, the frequency of association between storerooms and U-shaped structures is very high. In the monumental compounds, access to over 70% of the storeroom courts is controlled by one or more U-shaped structures; conversely, 64% of the U-shaped structures are located so that they control access to storeroom courts. 'Control' in this context means that access can be gained to the storeroom court only by going through a court containing a U-shaped structure. This frequency of association between U-shaped structures and storerooms led to the identification of U-shaped structures as loci of administrative activities, especially those activities associated with the storage of goods (Andrews 1972, 1974; Day 1973).

Like storerooms, U-shaped structures are located within courts with restricted access. Several types of U-shaped structures have been identified and seriated. Of these types, standard *audiencias* with two niches in each of three walls, as well as their variants, are found mainly in the monumental compounds (Andrews 1972, 1974; Kolata 1978, 1982). Two types of U-shaped structures are found in the elite compounds: standard *audiencias* and *arcones*. *Arcones* differ from *audiencias*, in that they are smaller and have bins rather than niches in the three walls. In addition to the presence of *arcones*, the main difference between U-shaped structures in the monumental and in the elite compounds is their association with storerooms: in the elite compounds, a maximum of 34% of the *audiencias* and almost none of the *arcones* control access to storerooms (Klymyshyn 1976, 1982). Of the various types of U-shaped structures, so far only *arcones* have been found in association with domestic structures or SIAR. In this context, *arcones* are isolated structures not associated with storerooms (J. Topic 1977, 1982).

Chronology

As mentioned above, the ethnohistoric documents record two stages of expansion in Chimu history. As yet, it has not been possible to refine this chronology or to date the Chimu expansion into specific areas, other than in terms of these two stages (cf. Mackey and Klymyshyn 1981; Keatinge and Conrad 1983). For this reason and because it is not possible to correlate changes in the distribution of storerooms and U-shaped structures with the finer chronological sequences proposed for Chan Chan on the basis of architectural differences (Kolata 1978, 1982) and ceramic seriations (Keatinge 1973; J. Topic, 1977; Mackey 1979), the monumental and elite compounds can

simply be divided into two phases, early and late, correlating with the two stages of expansion.

The most widely accepted chronological sequence for Chan Chan is based on the seriation of adobe bricks (Kolata 1978, 1982). On the basis of the brick seriation, the monumental compounds were constructed in the following order (Figure 2): Chayhuac, Uhle, Tello, Laberinto, Gran Chimu, Squier, Velarde, Bandelier, Tschudi, and Rivero. This seriation, however, while effective for dating the construction of the compounds, is inadequate for dating the full span of the use of individual compounds.

The division of the monumental compounds into an early and a late phase is based on the correlation of the brick sequence, the occurrence of a major flood, and ethnohistoric records. There is some disagreement on the timing of the flood relative to the construction of Gran Chimu. According to Kolata (1978:201) and Moseley and Deeds (1982:43), the flood occurred either during or after the construction of Gran Chimu. According to T. Pozorski (see chapter by T. Pozorski, this volume), the flood occurred prior to the construction of this compound. Both of these possibilities are taken into account in the discussion of changes in the administrative system in relation to the two stages of imperial expansion.

Ethnohistoric sources indicate that the Chimu conquest of the Lambayeque Valley occurred in the second stage of expansion (Anonymous History of 1604 in Rowe 1948) after a catastrophic flood (Cabello Valboa 1951). If the flood mentioned in this document and the one indicated by the archaeological record in Chan Chan are the same, then the early compounds in the capital correspond to the first stage of imperial expansion and the late compounds to the second stage. The early compounds would include Chayhuac, Uhle, Tello, Laberinto and possibly Gran Chimu, while the later compounds would include Squier, Velarde, Bandelier, Tschudi, Rivero, and again possibly Gran Chimu (Table 1).

Of the early compounds, Uhle has been associated with the start of the first stage of expansion. This dating is based on architectural and ceramic similarities between Uhle and Farfán, the major Chimu center in the Jequetepeque Valley (Kolata 1978:190–193; Keatinge 1982:206–209; Keatinge and Conrad 1983). Also, according to the chronicles (Anonymous History of 1604 in Rowe 1948; Calancha 1638), the Jequetepeque Valley was conquered in the first stage of expansion (Figure 1).

On the basis of the existing data it is not possible to determine which of the early compounds may have continued in use during the late phase. As mentioned, the brick seriation is not applicable to this problem. While there is a ceramic seriation (Keatinge 1973; J Topic 1977; Mackey 1979), it also cannot be used to date the length of occupation of individual monumental compounds, since there are few diagnostic sherds in the collections from the monumental compounds.

The only compound for which there is evidence of use in both phases is Laberinto. The construction of the outer walls of this compound occurred during the early phase, prior to construction at Gran Chimu. Construction of the interior walls

Table 1. *The chronology of the construction of monumental and elite compounds*

Stage of expansion	Phase of occupation	Monumental compounds*	Elite compounds†
First	Early	Chayhuac Uhle Tello	7
Second	---------?---------‡	Laberinto Gran Chimu Squier Velarde	---------?---------
	Late	Bandelier Tschudi Rivero	27

* After Kolata 1982:72.
† Klymyshyn 1976: Appendix VII.
‡ The dating of the beginning of the second stage of expansion and the problem of relating it to the construction of Gran Chimu
 and to the beginning of the late phase of occupation are discussed in the text.

of Laberinto, however, continued during the building of Gran Chimu. Furthermore, in the eastern extension of Laberinto, construction on both the outer and the interior walls continued much later, perhaps even after the construction of Rivero, the last monumental compound to be built (Kolata 1978:Ch. 3). Ceramics from both the main part and the extension of Laberinto also suggest that the compound continued in use during the late phase (Mackey 1979).

Although there is no complete construction sequence for the elite compounds, the brick seriation has been applied to 25 of the 34 compounds. On this basis, seven of the compounds were built in the early phase and eighteen during the late phase. Three others are closely associated with other elite compounds built in the late phase and/or with domestic structures dated to the late phase on the basis of ceramics. Of the seven early compounds, at least six continued in use during the late phase. The nine compounds for which there are no brick measurements are all associated with late phase compounds or domestic structures, and thus were probably in use during the late phase (though some might have been built earlier) (Table 1).

While the chronological sequence for Chan Chan certainly needs refinement, sufficient data are available to correlate the construction of the compounds with the two stages of imperial expansion. On this basis, it is then possible to correlate differences in the distribution of storerooms and U-shaped structures in the compounds with the expansion of the empire.

Storage in Chan Chan

Variations in the distribution of storerooms indicate significant differences among the monumental compounds. These differences lead to conclusions about changes in the concentration of wealth and redistribution in correlation with the expansion of the empire.

Distribution of storerooms

Data on the distribution of storerooms in the monumental compounds are presented in Tables 2 and 3. Table 2 is a tabulation of the quantitative data with the compounds listed in alphabetical order. Table 3 presents a ranking of the compounds on the basis of several indicators of storage capacity in correlation with the construction sequence. Several comments should be made on the variables and the quantitative data before proceeding to a discussion of their implications.

First, in both tables, storage capacity is given in terms of two sets of data – those based on storeroom courts and those based on storerooms only. The figures based on storerooms alone are a more accurate measure of actual storage capacity, especially since the function of the open areas within storeroom courts is not known. However, the measurements were made from the published maps of Chan Chan (Moseley and Mackey 1974), and since storerooms are both smaller and more numerous than courts, there is more potential for cumulative error in calculating total area on the basis of the storerooms. The figures based on the storeroom courts thus are given as a check on the figures based on the storerooms alone.

Second, in Table 2, the areas of storerooms and of storeroom courts are given for those located inside the main part of a compound, those located in either the annex or extension of a compound, and the combined total. Several compounds – Bandelier, Chayhuac, Tello, Squier and Uhle – do not have an annex or extension. Thus, in order to be able to compare all compounds, only the main part of a compound was considered in calculating the percentage of space allocated to storerooms or storeroom courts.

Third, perhaps the most significant indicator of the

Table 2. *Distribution of storerooms in the monumental compounds*

	Compounds (in alphabetical order)	Bandelier	Chayhuac	Gran Chimu	Laberinto	Rivero	Squier	Tello	Tschudi	Uhle	Velarde
Main part of compound	Number of storeroom courts	14	—	10	28	14	—	21	22	14	15 (20)
	Area of storeroom courts*	17 900	4200	31 100	35 300	9100	600	7200	17 400	8700	23 400 (31 200)
	Percentage of area of compound taken up by storeroom courts†	14%	2.3%	13%	23%	13%	0.4%	10%	14%	5%	18% (24%)
	Number of storerooms	175	67	259	641	180	28	260	242	175	297 (396)
	Area of storerooms	1840	1800	7620	7010	1730	110	1680	3020	1830	3200 (4270)
	Percentage of area of compound taken up by storerooms	1.8%	1.1%	3.3%	4.5%	2.4%	0.1%	2.3%	2.4%	0.9%	2.5% (3.3%)
Annex or extension	Area of storeroom courts	n.a.	n.a.	11 700	8200	4100	n.a.	n.a.	1100	n.a.	3600
	Area of storerooms	n.a.	n.a.	2360	1650	1020	n.a.	n.a.	100	n.a.	550
Combined total	Total area of storeroom courts	17 900	4200	42 800	43 500	13 200	600	7200	18 500	8700	27 000 (34 800)
	Total area of storerooms	1840	1800	9980	8660	2750	110	1680	3120	1830	3750 (4820)

* All measurements of area are given in square meters. The areas of storeroom courts have been rounded off to the nearest 100, and the areas of storerooms to the nearest 10.

† The percentages have been rounded off to the nearest one-tenth of one per cent.

relative differences among the compounds in terms of storage capacity is the percentage of the area of a compound allocated to either storerooms or storeroom courts. Taken together, these two figures indicate the importance of storage in individual compounds relative to other activities and functions. For this reason, these two variables are weighted more heavily than the others in the discussion below.

Fourth, Squier will not be considered in the discussion of the implications of differences in storage capacity. There are few storerooms of any kind in Squier, and those present are not enclosed in a court. More importantly, however, neither the outer walls nor the interior structures of Squier were ever completed. Thus, it is not possible to use Squier in drawing inferences about changes in the distribution of wealth and its control through time.

Fifth, in Table 2, two sets of figures are given for Velarde, which has been partially destroyed by the building of roads and looting. Based on the area destroyed in Velarde and the layout of the preserved interior rooms and courts, the preserved storerooms represent at least 75% of the potential storage capacity of this compound. In Gran Chimu, the potential storage capacity is much more difficult to reconstruct.

Thus, 25% has been added in an attempt at a reasonable reconstruction of the potential storage capacity. This 25% increase is a maximum and the actual storage capacity may well have been smaller. The figures given in parentheses represent the reconstructed potential storage capacity. Each compound is ranked in Table 3 on the basis of its potential storage capacity, rather than its preserved storage capacity. The main reason for doing so is that the preserved storage capacity distorts the difference between Velarde and the other compounds. Since the annex of Velarde is not as destroyed as the main part of the compounds, only the preserved storage capacity is used.

Taking these general clarifications into consideration, a number of patterns become apparent. As can be seen from Table 3, there is not a one-to-one correlation between the construction sequence of the monumental compounds and any of the indicators of storage capacity. Storage capacity generally increases from Chayhuac through Gran Chimu and decreases thereafter (cf. Day 1973:264–266; Conrad 1974:75–80; Kolata 1978:242–252, 1982:84).

Stating the trend in such general terms is somewhat misleading, however, since it obscures some of the changes in the distribution of storage capacity, particularly as they

Table 3. *The ranking of monumental compounds based on storage capacity in correlation with the construction sequence*

Construction sequence	Total area of storeroom courts*	% of area of compound in storeroom courts†	Total area of storerooms*	% of area of compound in storerooms†
Chayhuac	Chayhuac‡	Chayhuac‡	Tello‡	Uhle‡
Uhle	Tello	Uhle	Chayhuac	Chayhuac
Tello	Uhle	Tello	Uhle	Bandelier
Laberinto	Rivero	Gran Chimu/Rivero§	Bandelier	Tello
Gran Chimu	Bandelier		Rivero	Rivero/Tschudi§
Velarde	Tschudi	Bandelier/Tschudi§	Tschudi	
Bandelier	Velarde‖		Velarde‖	Velarde/Gran Chimu§
Tschudi	Gran Chimu	Laberinto	Laberinto	
Rivero	Laberinto	Velarde‖	Gran Chimu	Laberinto

*The total area of storeroom courts and of storerooms includes those in annexes and extensions.

†The percentage of the total area of a compound allocated either to storeroom courts or to storerooms is based on the main part of the compound only, i.e., excluding the annexes and extensions.

‡The compounds are listed in the order of increase in area and percentage of storeroom courts and storerooms.

§Compounds separated by an oblique stroke have the same ranking.

‖The ranking of Velarde is based on the reconstructed storage capacity (see text).

correlate with the expansion of the empire. The three earliest compounds, Chayhuac, Uhle and Tello, all have the smallest storage capacity, averaging less than 1800 sq m in storeroom area. Though these compounds have similar storage capacities, the percentage of the total area of the compound taken up by storerooms in Tello is twice that found in either Chayhuac or Uhle.

Storage capacity increases significantly in Laberinto, which has over four times the storeroom area of Tello and twice the percentage of space allocated to storage. Even though not all of the storerooms in Laberinto were built during the early phase and at the same time, these figures are indicative of a major change in storage capacity, especially since Gran Chimu shows a similar increase in storerooms over Tello. In comparison with these differences, the storeroom area in Gran Chimu is about the same as that of Laberinto, though the percentage of space allocated to storage differs.

Velarde reflects the start of a decrease in storage capacity, which appears to continue in the later compounds; however, it is difficult to make a direct comparison between Velarde and compounds built later in the sequence. The maximum total storeroom area in Velarde is approximately half of that in Gran Chimu and approximately 2.6 times larger than that of Bandelier. Both of these differences are smaller than the differences between Tello and Laberinto. Further, Bandelier presents a problem similar to Squier, in that many of the interior courts and rooms appear never to have been finished. The reason for this is unknown, though the relatively smaller storage capacity of Bandelier seems to be an isolated case rather than indicative of an overall trend (cf. Conrad 1974:75–80), especially since storage capacity increases again in Tschudi and Rivero.

It has been suggested that storerooms in elite compounds make up the difference between the storage capacity in the later compounds and that of Gran Chimu (e.g., Kolata 1978:251–252). However, only eight of the thirty-four elite compounds contain storerooms, with a combined area of only 4200 sq m (Klymyshyn 1976: Appendix VII). Adding this total to the storage capacity of Rivero still does not bring the total up to the peak storage capacity of Gran Chimu, but it does change the difference from approximately 0.3 to 0.7 times the capacity of Gran Chimu.

Three elite compounds abut Rivero or its annex and therefore must have been built after Rivero and its annex. The total area of storerooms in these elite compounds is 2860 sq m. On the other hand, the elite compounds in the immediate vicinity of or abutting Tschudi do not contain any storerooms (Klymyshyn 1976: Appendix VII). On this basis, the storage capacity during the occupation of Rivero is 1.8 times the capacity during the occupation of Tschudi. The percentage of space allocated to storage is the same in these two compounds, but smaller than that of Gran Chimu.

To summarize, the most significant change in storage capacity occurs between Laberinto and Tello, with the three earliest compounds having the lowest storage capacity. Of the three, Tello has the highest percentage of interior space allocated to storage. There is relatively little difference in storage capacity between Gran Chimu and Laberinto. However, after Gran Chimu there is a decrease, though not as great as the increase after Tello. Finally, storage capacity increases during the occupation of Rivero, as a result of the building of three elite compounds with storerooms in the immediate vicinity of Rivero. The importance of storage as a function in individual compounds also changes. The first significant increase in the percentage of space allocated to storage occurs in Tello. The highest percentage of storage space is in Laberinto. The percentage of storage space then decreases through the later compounds, though it is never again as low as in the earliest compounds.

Implication of the distribution of storerooms

As mentioned above, the monumental compounds in Chan Chan have been identified as the palaces of Chimu kings. This identification of function is based on several criteria, including the sequential building of the compounds and the presence of burial platforms. The interior layout of the palaces from Gran Chimu on follows a standardized plan, consisting of three sectors. The two north sectors are quite similar and contain entry plazas, auxiliary plazas, courts with storerooms, courts with U-shaped structures, and a burial platform. The south sector generally contains the remains of rooms similar to the domestic structures outside of the compounds. For this reason the south sector has been identified as housing the retainers of the residents of the north sectors (McGrath 1973). The compounds built after Laberinto (except for Squier and Bandelier) have a north annex, which guards the main entry and contains courts with storerooms and U-shaped structures. There are, however, significant differences among the monumental compounds, which will be examined below in conjunction with the implications of the differences in storage capacity.

Chayhuac, the first of the compounds to be built, shows a change in the context and location of storerooms from that in the pre-Chimu settlements in the Moche Valley. For the first time, storerooms are found inside of a compound (Bawden 1982a:304–307; T. Topic 1982:274–275). All of the Chayhuac storerooms are located in the same court as the burial platform. In Uhle, storerooms are found in the two courts with burial platforms, and, for the first time, in courts with U-shaped structures. However, fewer than half of the storerooms in Uhle are located away from the burial platforms. The function of storage in Uhle and Chayhuac was thus associated with the royal burial structures. This pattern differs from the other monumental compounds, in which few (if any) storerooms are located in courts with burial platforms.

Tello differs significantly from most of the other compounds in that it does not contain a burial platform and has a different internal layout. For these reasons, Tello is not considered one of the palaces. The suggestion has been made that Tello was built to house administrators who were not members of the royal family (Kolata 1978:185–187, 249). However, Tello has very few U-shaped structures (Table 4), which are associated with administrators. Moreover, the presence of a much higher number of U-shaped structures in Uhle points to more administrators in Uhle than Tello (Table 4). The high frequency of storerooms and low frequency of U-shaped structures indicate that Tello probably functioned primarily as a storage facility rather than as a residence for administrators.

Table 4. *Distribution of U-shaped structures in the monumental compounds in correlation with the construction sequence*

	Number of U-shaped structures		
Compounds*	Main part of compound	Annex and/or extension	Combined total
Chayhuac	0	n.a.†	0
Uhle	22	n.a.	22
Tello	3	n.a.	3
Laberinto	13	14	27
Gran Chimu	8	1	9
Velarde	11	7	18
Bandelier	10	n.a.	10
Tschudi	19	2	21
Rivero	11	6	17

* After Kolata 1982:72; Squier is not included in this table because it was never completed and because the only U-shaped structure it contains may be part of an intrusive elite compound.

† Chayhuac, Uhle, Tello and Bandelier do not have either an annex or an extension. Though Uhle was built in several sections, these are all considered as the main part of the compound, because of the internal layout.

Since the first stage of imperial expansion is contemporaneous with the occupation of Uhle, it seems highly likely that Tello, the next compound to be constructed, was built to accommodate goods accumulated during the expansion and afterwards through tribute. Though goods stored in Tello were still no doubt under royal control, the building of a separate storage facility apart from the palace points to the separation of goods directly allocated for use by the king, his family and attendants, from those intended for more general use. It is no coincidence that the building of a separate storage facility should coincide with the initial expansion of the empire. More goods were coming in; and the redistributive network had been increased, resulting in a change in the way in which goods were stored and allocated. The building of Tello as a separate storage facility marks the start of the allocation of more goods to general circulation through redistribution than to the royal funerary rites. Evidence for further changes in the distribution of storage can be seen in both Laberinto and Gran Chimu.

Laberinto probably had the same function as Tello (Figure 3). It differs from the palaces in that it does not contain a burial platform, the presence of which is perhaps the most important criterion used in identifying the monumental compounds as palaces (Day 1973; Conrad 1974, 1982). There are surface indications in the south part of Laberinto that space had been allocated for a burial platform, but a platform was never built. There are two funerary structures in the eastern extension of Laberinto. One of these, however, is quite different from the burial platforms in other compounds, and has not been classified as such (Conrad 1974, 1982). The second

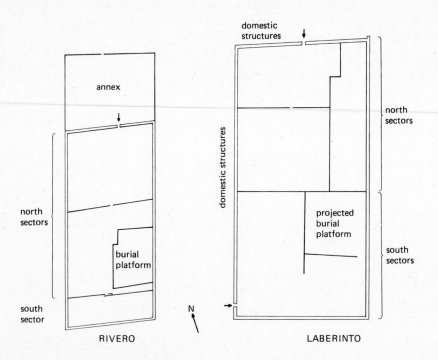

Fig. 3. Rivero and Laberinto

does conform to the architectural pattern of burial platforms, but appears to have been built after the construction of Rivero (Kolata 1978: Ch. 3). Because of its late chronological placement and its location outside of the main part of the compound, it does not seem probable that this second platform is associated with a king who ruled from Laberinto. Nonetheless, the indication that space may have been allocated in the main part of the compound for a burial platform points to the possibility that Laberinto originally may have been intended as a palace, but was actually used for other purposes.

In addition to the lack of a burial platform, Laberinto differs from the palaces in several respects. Of these, the lack of a north annex and differences in access patterns are most relevant to this discussion. All palaces completed after Laberinto (except for Bandelier), have a north annex, which restricts access into these compounds. Since Laberinto has no annex, its north entry is far more accessible than the entries of the compounds with annexes. Related to the lack of a north annex is a difference in access patterns. While the other monumental compounds all have a single north entry, Laberinto appears to have two: one in the north wall and one at the south end of the west wall. Both of these entries are accessible from the neighboring area with domestic structures. This increased accessibility, particularly from areas of domestic structures, is a significant difference between Laberinto and the palaces, since the architectural patterns in both the monumental and elite compounds indicate that control of access was one of the primary concerns in the planning of the compounds.

The internal access patterns in Laberinto are also different. Most relevant to this discussion is the total lack of access between the south sector of Laberinto and the north sectors. There is also less evidence for domestic structures in the south sector of Laberinto than in the later compounds. These differences indicate that the south sector of Laberinto probably did not house the retainers of the inhabitants of the north part of the compound. There is an area in the north part of Laberinto that probably did house retainers; however, this area is much smaller than the south sectors of the palaces, which indicates that there were fewer retainers in Laberinto. Separating the south sector from the rest of Laberinto made this area available for other functions, perhaps related to the accessibility of this part of the compound from the neighboring domestic structures through the southwest entry.

There are at least two possible explanations for the differences between Laberinto and the palaces. Laberinto may simply have been built before the plan for palaces had become standardized – as were Chayhuac and Uhle. On the other hand, it may have served a different function. Since there is no burial platform, and given that it has the highest percentage of storage space of all of the compounds, Laberinto probably served as a storage facility similar to Tello. Furthermore, the use of Laberinto as a storage facility probably correlates with the start of the second stage of expansion.

As mentioned, Laberinto was started before Gran Chimu, but rooms in both the main part of the compound and in the extension continued to be built well after Gran Chimu was finished. Though the temporal relationship between the building of Gran Chimu and the start of the second stage of expansion is not well defined, of all of the compounds the construction of Gran Chimu was closest in time to the start of this stage of expansion. Whether Gran Chimu was built just before or just after the start of the second stage of expansion, the large storage capacity of this palace can be explained as related to the increase in the flow of goods to the capital as a result of the expansion.

On the basis of the preceding discussion, the following sequence of events is suggested: (1) The building of Laberinto as a palace was started some time after the building of Tello. (2) The construction of Laberinto was then interrupted by the flood. (3) After the Chimu recovered from the flood, the second stage of expansion was initiated. (4) As a result of the increase in wealth and possible increase in available manpower, construction started on a new palace, Gran Chimu, which was larger and more elaborate than Laberinto. Gran Chimu thus replaced Laberinto as a palace. (5) The construction of Laberinto was then resumed, but it was converted into a storage facility. (6) The construction of additional storerooms in Laberinto, especially in the extension, continued as late as the building of Rivero. If this sequence of events is correct, then the decrease in storage capacity in the individual palaces built after Gran Chimu was the result of a reorganization of the distribution of storage in Chan Chan, rather than the result of a decrease in wealth (cf. Kolata 1982:84; see chapter by T. Pozorski, this volume).

As discussed above, this reorganization of storage began with the building of Tello. At that time, the Uhle palace contained goods allocated primarily for the royal funerary rites, while the storage facilities of Tello contained goods intended for redistribution. Given the storage capacity of Gran Chimu and the location of storerooms both in association with the burial platform and away from it, this palace contained both types of goods. Further, since there are large areas of Tello which are not built up, this compound does not appear to have continued in use.

The change between Tello and Gran Chimu did not represent a reversion to an earlier pattern. Although both Uhle and Gran Chimu contained both types of goods, in Uhle the majority of the storerooms are directly associated with the burial platform; whereas in Gran Chimu, the majority of the storerooms are not associated with the burial platform. The storage of both types of goods, and the management of redistribution only from the palace during the occupation of Gran Chimu proved inefficient, however. For this reason, Laberinto was converted to a storage facility. At the same time, the palaces continued to contain both goods allocated to the royal funerary rites and some of the goods allocated to redistribution. The evidence for this is to be seen in the continued presence in the later palaces, from Velarde up through Rivero, of storerooms located both in the immediate vicinity of the burial platform and away from it. Since the storerooms in Laberinto and its extension continued to be built during the construction of Rivero, there was a gradual shift of more and more goods to the storage facility accompanied by a reduction of the storage capacity of individual palaces.

However, there was no reduction in overall storage capacity in Chan Chan. For example, the combined storage capacity of Rivero, Laberinto, and the elite compounds abutting Rivero is 1.4 times the storage capacity of Gran Chimu.

The period between the building of Tello and the conversion of Laberinto into a storage facility can thus be seen as a period of experimentation with different ways of organizing and managing storage and distribution of goods within Chan Chan. The final separation of tasks related to storage between the palace and the storage facility could have been accomplished along several lines. (1) Different types of commodities may have been stored in the two types of monumental compounds. The palaces may have contained a higher percentage of elite goods, and the storage compounds a greater percentage of less prestigious goods. (2) Goods from different parts of the empire may have been stored in the two types of compounds. The palaces, for example, may have contained goods from the outlying provinces while the storage compounds housed goods from the immediate hinterland. (3) Alternatively, the separation of tasks may have related to the destination of the goods. The palaces may have contained goods intended for the royal funerary rites and for distribution to the nobles, while the storage compounds contained goods destined to be distributed to the commoners. The accessibility of Laberinto from the neighboring areas with domestic structures seems to support this separation of tasks related to storage.

These three ways of organizing the management of storage are not, of course, mutually exclusive. Determination of the specific manner in which goods were distributed and managed requires data which are not available. The data which are available, however, indicate that there was both a reorganization in the management of storage and a greater specialization and separation of related tasks as a result of both stages of imperial expansion.

Administrative hierarchy

Changes in the distribution of storage resulting from imperial expansion are paralleled by changes in the distribution of U-shaped structures and elite compounds at Chan Chan. The changes in the distribution of U-shaped structures and elite compounds indicate the same kind of specialization and separation of administrative tasks as do the changes in the distribution of storerooms. Specifically, the first stage of expansion was accompanied by the initial appearance of U-shaped structures and elite compounds, both of which were new architectural forms related to administration. The second stage of expansion was accompanied by an increase in the number of U-shaped structures and elite compounds and by the appearance of a new *type* of elite compound.

Differences among monumental compounds in the distribution of U-shaped structures are presented in Table 4. As can be seen from this table, Uhle is the earliest compound containing U-shaped structures and, except for Laberinto, it also has the highest number of U-shaped structures. As

Table 5. *Distribution of storerooms and* audiencias *in the elite compounds*

Phase of occupation	Number of elite compounds	Number of elite compounds with storerooms	Number of elite compounds with *audiencias*	Total number of *audiencias* in elite compounds
Early	7	2	3	6
Late*	33	8	14	42†

* All of the totals given for the late phase include both the newly built compounds and those which continued in use.
† *Arcones* were first built during the late phase of occupation. There are six *arcones* in the elite compounds in addition to the *audiencias* listed above (Klymyshyn 1976: Appendix VII) and seven in the areas with domestic structures (J. Topic 1982:155–156).

mentioned above, the occupation of Uhle coincides with the first stage of expansion. The appearance of U-shaped structures in association with storage in Uhle and then in Tello indicates that the primary task of the administrators in these two compounds was the management and control of storage.

There are, however, significant differences between these two compounds. In Uhle, each administrator controlled a smaller number of storerooms than in Tello. Since the administrators in Uhle were located inside the palace, they were probably related to the king, whereas those in Tello may not have been. Thus, in addition to the creation of new positions in the administrative hierarchy, the first stage of expansion may have also resulted in the recruitment of administrators from outside of the group of persons related to the king. Furthermore, since these two monumental compounds contained goods intended for different purposes, we also see a specialization of administrators with respect to different tasks related to the management of goods. Therefore, it can be argued that a reorganization of the administrative hierarchy, similar to that seen in the Inca (Rowe 1946), occurred early in the history of the Chimu as a result of imperial expansion. In both cases, the reorganization reflects the change from a localized state society to an expanding empire.

Since the construction and use of all of the U-shaped structures in Laberinto and its extension cannot be dated conclusively in relation to the start of the second stage of expansion, it is also not possible to calculate precisely the increase in late phase U-shaped structures on the basis of those located in monumental compounds. However, the fact that there *was* a significant increase is indicated by the increase of U-shaped structures in the elite compounds. If the number of U-shaped structures in the monumental and elite compounds are combined, the number of U-shaped structures during the late phase of occupation is about twice the number in the early phase (Tables 4 and 5). This increase indicates the recruitment of additional personnel into the administrative hierarchy. The location of at least half of the late phase U-shaped structures outside of the palaces indicates an augmentation in the recruitment of administrative personnel from outside of the royal family and their immediate attendants. However, the

main evidence for the creation of a new level in the administrative hierarchy comes primarily from the elite compounds rather than from the U-shaped structures.

As mentioned earlier, seven elite compounds were built in the early phase of occupation and twenty-seven in the late phase, and of the early compounds, at least six probably continued in use during the late phase. Though it is possible that some early compounds may have been destroyed as a result of the construction of later compounds, the concentration of fully 75% of the elite compounds around Rivero and Tschudi, the last two palaces to have been built, confirms that there was a significant increase in elite compounds during the late phase.

All but one of the early elite compounds are located within areas of domestic structures (SIAR). Only two of the early elite compounds contain storerooms and in both cases the percentage of storage space is less than 1%. Given the low storage capacity in these units and their location in association with domestic structures, it is probable that the primary role of the administrators in these compounds was the supervision of the inhabitants of the domestic structures. Since the majority of the inhabitants of these domestic structures were craftsmen (J. Topic 1977, 1982), the main tasks of the administrators in the early elite compounds were probably related to craft production.

The building of elite compounds at the time of the first expansion indicates the creation of a new administrative level between the administrators in the palaces and the lower-class residents. By the time of the first expansion, the administrative hierarchy in Chan Chan would have consisted of the following groups in addition to the king: the king's immediate assistants or palace administrators, the administrators in the storage compound (Tello), and the administrators in the elite compounds. The hierarchical relationship between these groups is presented in Figure 4. The relative statuses of these groups are based on architectural criteria indicative of the control of resources, such as storerooms and the amount of labor required to build the individual compounds. Furthermore, as discussed above, the administrators in the palaces more likely would have been relatives of the king than would those in Tello. There is no evidence to indicate whether the administrators in the elite

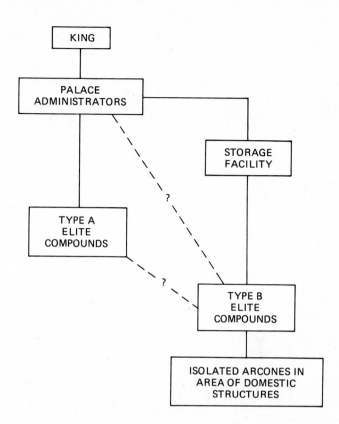

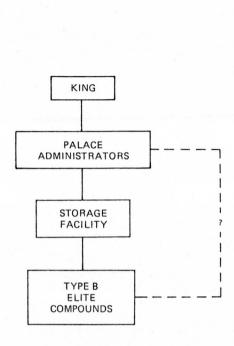

Fig. 4. Administrative hierarchy in Chan Chan during the early phase of occupation

Fig. 5. Administrative hierarchy in Chan Chan during the late phase of occupation

compounds reported to superiors in Tello, or directly to residents of the palaces. If administrators in Tello were responsible for redistribution of goods to inhabitants of the domestic structures, then it is likely that the administrators in the elite compounds reported to Tello rather than directly to the palace.

As can be seen in Table 5, there was a tremendous increase in the construction of elite compounds during the late phase of occupation. Though it is not possible to date precisely the construction of individual elite compounds, at the end of the late phase of occupation over 400% more elite compounds were in use than before the start of the second stage of expansion. This increase indicates yet another increase in administrative personnel. More important, however, is the appearance of both a new type of elite compound and isolated *arcones* in the areas of domestic structures. These two new features point to the creation of two new levels in the administrative hierarchy.

The new, 'Type A,' elite compounds are similar to the monumental compounds in their interior rooms and layout, but they are smaller and do not contain burial platforms. 'Type B' elite compounds, which are not similar to monumental compounds, also continued to be built. Since Type A compounds generally contain both *audiencias* and storerooms, and are located in proximity to the monumental compounds, their function was probably related more to the monumental compounds. Type B compounds all appear to have had a

function similar to the early elite compounds. That the administrators in the Type B elite compounds had a lower status than those in the Type A compounds is evidenced by their lesser degree of control over goods and other resources. On the basis of the location of the *arcones* in the areas of domestic structures and the artifacts found in them, the administrators in these U-shaped structures controlled the wells located in these areas and/or supervised craft production (J. Topic 1982:155–156).

Thus, during the late phase of occupation the administrative hierarchy in Chan Chan consisted of two new groups in addition to those discussed for the early phase of occupation: the administrators in the Type A elite compounds and those in the isolated *arcones*. The hierarchical relationships between these groups of administrators are presented in Figure 5. The administrative chain of command as it relates to the lower-class residents passes from the palace administrators, who were probably relatives of the king, through the storage facility (Laberinto) and the Type B elite compounds to the isolated *arcones* in the area of domestic structures. These last two ranks, the administrators in the Type B elite compounds and those in the *arcones*, had primarily supervisory duties related to craft production. The administrators in Laberinto were responsible for the management of stored goods and possibly for the distribution of goods to the inhabitants of the domestic structures. As discussed for the early phase, it is not possible to determine whether the administrators in the two lowest ranks reported directly to the palace or through the storage facility. However, clustering of several Type B elite compounds in the vicinity of Laberinto appears to support the suggestion that the administrators in these compounds reported to Laberinto rather than directly to the palace. Thus, the administrators in Laberinto also acted as the major link between the decision-making administrators in the palace and the lower-class residents.

Since the Type A elite compounds are located in proximity to the monumental compounds rather than to either Type B elite compounds or domestic structures, it is difficult to associate the function of the administrators in these elite compounds with either craft production or the lower-class residents. Further, the location of three of the Type A elite compounds indicates that they may have been responsible primarily for the sunken gardens at the south end of the capital or the special fields at the north end (T. and J. Topic 1980). Elsewhere (Klymyshyn 1976), I have suggested that the Type A elite compounds may have been the residences of administrators from the outlying provinces. Though this particular interpretation cannot be tested on the basis of existing data, the probability that the administrators in Type A elite compounds had responsibilities related to the provinces is supported by the appearance of this type of elite compound only *after* the second stage of expansion. Also, after the second stage of expansion, administrators in the palaces may have had responsibilities other than the direct management of goods. The fact that many of the U-shaped structures in Rivero, the last palace, are located away from courts with storerooms further supports this idea. The new responsibilities of the palace administrators might also have been related to the administration of a greatly expanded empire.

The preceding discussion has focused on evidence for changes in the administrative network in Chan Chan resulting from the two stages of Chimu expansion. The first change examined was the reorganization of the management of stored goods in Chan Chan resulting from the increased flow of goods into the capital from the provinces. Based on differences in the distribution of storerooms and storage capacity, two of the monumental compounds were identified as storage facilities from which goods may have been distributed to the lower-class residents. The existence of these storage facilities formed the basis for an examination of the manner in which tasks related to the management of stored goods became increasingly specialized through time. The second change discussed was the increased internal differentiation of the administrative hierarchy. The main data presented were the appearance of new architectural forms related to administration in correlation with both the first and the second stage of expansion and the increase in the number of these architectural forms through time.

Many of the conclusions and interpretations are necessarily speculative, given both the subject under discussion and the nature of available data. Nevertheless, there are sufficient data to determine that the administrative hierarchy in the Chimu capital responded to the increase in administrative tasks brought about by the expansion of the empire, by creating new positions and recruiting new personnel. These changes, which made the administration of the Chimu empire more effective and efficient, are correlated with the two stages of expansion, and are reflected in changes in the architectural patterns in the capital.

Acknowledgments

The information in the article is based on research conducted by members of the Peabody Museum–Harvard University Chan Chan–Moche Valley Project, directed by Drs Michael E. Moseley and Carol J. Mackey. This project was funded by the National Science Foundation and the National Geographic Society. Additional research was conducted by the author while on a Fulbright Collaborative Teaching/Research Grant in 1983. I would like to thank Jeff Serena and Hill Gates for comments on earlier drafts of this article. Edwin Chavez Farfán prepared the figures in their final form, for which I am especially grateful.

Chapter 11

**Changing priorities within the Chimu
state: the role of irrigation agriculture**

Thomas Pozorski

Introduction

Ancient Peru was one of the areas of the world where irrigation agriculture clearly was associated with the evolution of state forms of organization. Unfortunately, the *origins* of irrigation agriculture in Peru remain obscure because of the lack of physical evidence of canals and fields predating the Early Intermediate Period (200 B.C. to A.D. 600) (Lanning 1967:109). Thus, on the coast of Peru, for example, the existence of early irrigation agriculture going back to the Initial Period (1800 to 900 B.C.) is inferred only on the basis of indirect evidence. Specifically, this inference is based on (1) extreme dryness of the climate, which necessitates the use of canal irrigation to farm areas outside very restricted areas of river flood plain and (2) the change in settlement pattern of major sites from locations along the Pacific coastline during the preceding Cotton Preceramic Period to locations many kilometers inland during the Initial Period. Also, the Initial Period site locations are topographically advantageous for the construction, maintenance and use of canal intakes and associated fields. Since the origins of irrigation agriculture in Peru are obscure, its exact relationship to the rise of central leadership and social organization and ultimately the beginnings of state formation is likewise obscure and must be determined by means other than actual physical evidence of canals in association with early sites.

Regardless of the role of irrigation agriculture in the initial rise of Peruvian states, it is undeniable that irrigation agriculture played a major role in the growth and maintenance of state organization in coastal Peru since the Initial Period. This was particularly true for the various coastal states that existed from the late Early Intermediate Period through the Late Horizon (A.D. 400 to 1532).

On the north coast between the Motupe and Moche Valleys, physical remains of prehistoric canals are the largest and most complex of all the Peruvian coast (Kosok 1965:14; Moseley 1978c:17). Though much work needs to be done to establish a firm chronology, most of these surface remains probably date to the late Early Intermediate Period or later (A.D. 500 to 1500). This is certainly the case for the Moche Valley, which was the subject of an intensive investigation of prehistoric canal systems from 1976 to 1979 by the 'Programa Riego Antiguo,' directed by Michael Moseley, Shelia Pozorski, and myself. Survey and excavation of canals, fields, and associated structures in the Moche Valley and on the south side of the neighboring Chicama Valley showed that it is possible to obtain a detailed sequence of canal construction and relate that sequence to major archaeological sites and processes in the area. A survey of canal systems within and between other valleys north of Moche (Jequetepeque, Zaña, and Lambayeque) suggests that some aspects of these systems can be tied in with the Moche–Chicama canal sequence.

Other valleys to the south of Moche, such as Viru,

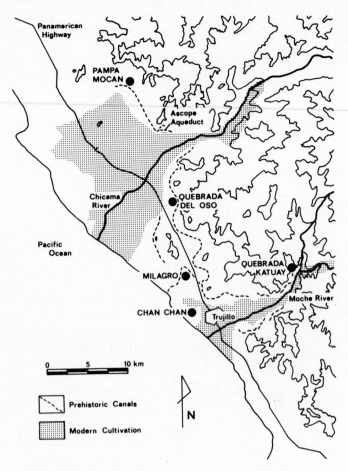

Fig. 1. Map of the Moche and Chicama Valleys showing the
limits of modern cultivation, areas of prehistoric canal remains,
and locations of prehistoric sites associated with canal remains

state. This detailed sequence of events can be tied in with other
areas to the north for a more complete reconstruction of the
development of the Chimu state during the Late Intermediate
Period.

The Moche Valley and the 3-Pampa canal sequence

Of all the zones of prehistoric canals and fields within the
Moche Valley, the large area on the north side of the valley,
known as the '3-Pampa' area and consisting of Pampas
Esperanza, Rio Seco and Huanchaco (Figure 2), provided the
most detailed sequence of canal construction – a sequence
which can be directly related to the construction sequence of
Chan Chan. This area has been described previously
(Farrington 1974; Deeds *et al*. 1978; Moseley and Deeds 1982),
but these descriptions were based only upon preliminary survey
and excavation information; new data have been incorporated
in the revised canal chronology presented below. Other parts of
the valley flanks, including Pampa Arenal, Cerro Orejas, and
Pampa Cacique, contain prehistoric canal remains, but these
areas are less complicated, show less time depth, and probably
all date to the period of maximum Chimu canal expansion
discussed below.

contain prehistoric canal remains, some of which probably date
to the Early Intermediate Period (Willey 1953:363); however,
surveys and excavations have not been conducted with
sufficient intensity in these valleys to date most remains
accurately. Based on a personal reconnaissance in these valleys,
similarities to canals and fields in Moche and Chicama suggest
a Late Intermediate Period date (A.D. 1000 to 1470) for most
of the canals that lie outside modern cultivation. More specific
dating is not possible without further work.

The remainder of this chapter is devoted to a discussion
of the relationship between canal irrigation and the Chimu state
during the Late Intermediate Period. The proposition that
maximum canal expansion is correlated with the height of
development of the Chimu state is tested and found not to be
true. Instead, maximum agricultural expansion was attained by
the end of the first phase of Chimu expansion (about A.D.
1300), after which agricultural limits contracted to more or less
modern limits of agriculture. It was during the post-1300 period
that the Chimu expanded their state through a second phase of
military conquest and developed into the empire that by A.D.
1470 provided the most serious challenge to the expanding Inca

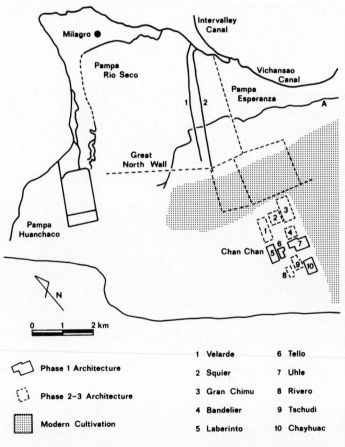

Fig. 2. Map of the '3-Pampa' area depicting the distribution of
prehistoric canal remains and their relationship to Chan Chan

Table 1. *Radiocarbon dates from canals in the Moche and Chicama Valleys**

Radiocarbon years	Calendar age	Location
720±90 (WSU–2171)	A.D. 1230±90	Moche, Vichansao canal, Pampa Rio Seco
570±80 (WSU–2170)	A.D. 1380±80	Moche, Vichansao canal, Pampa Rio Seco
580±60 (WSU–2172)	A.D. 1370±60	Moche, Vichansao canal, Pampa Esperanza
800±70 (WSU–2186)	A.D. 1150±70	Moche, Vichansao canal, Pampa Arenal
710±70 (WSU–2187)	A.D. 1240±70	Moche, Vichansao canal, Pampa Arenal
1400±80 (WSU–2175)	A.D. 550±80	Moche, canal A, Pampa Esperanza
910±80 (WSU–2184)	A.D. 1040±80	Chicama, Intervalley canal, Quebrada del Oso
890±80 (WSU–2177)	A.D. 1060±80	Chicama, Intervalley canal, Quebrada del Oso
870±80 (Kus 1972:227, UCLA–1711H)	A.D. 1080±80	Chicama, Intervalley canal, Quemazon
840±50 (WSU–2178)	A.D. 1110±50	Chicama, Intervalley canal, Quebrada del Oso
830±70 (WSU–2181)	A.D. 1120±70	Chicama, Intervalley canal, Quebrada del Oso
820±60 (Kus 1972:226, UCLA–1711G)	A.D. 1130±60	Chicama, Intervalley canal, Quemazon
790±70 (WSU–2176)	A.D. 1160±70	Chicama, Intervalley canal, Quebrada del Oso
780±110 (Kus 1972:227, UCLA–1711I)	A.D. 1170±110	Chicama, Intervalley canal, Quebrada del Oso
730±70 (WSU–2180)	A.D. 1220±70	Chicama, Intervalley canal, Quebrada del Oso
720±70 (WSU–2182)	A.D. 1230±70	Chicama, Intervalley canal, Quebrada del Oso
690±80 (WSU–2183)	A.D. 1260±80	Chicama, Intervalley canal, Quebrada del Oso
640±110 (WSU–2179)	A.D. 1310±110	Chicama, Intervalley canal, Quebrada del Oso
950±60 (WSU–2189)	A.D. 1000±60	Chicama, Ascope aqueduct

* All dates are uncorrected based upon the Libby half-life (5570±30 years).

The 3-Pampa canal sequence

The earliest physical evidence of canals in the Moche Valley is found on Pampa Esperanza which is located directly north of Chan Chan (Figure 2). The earliest channel of two canals uncovered during excavations, canal A and the prehistoric Vichansao canal, uncovered during excavations, dates to Moche III–IV times (c. A.D. 500; see Table 1), indicating that most of Pampa Esperanza was irrigated at that time. These two canals continued to be used well into Chimu times.

The first recognizable change in canal distribution is the extension of the Vichansao canal out across Pampa Rio Seco and Huanchaco during the early part of the Late Intermediate Period (Figure 2). A carbon 14 date of A.D. 1230±90 (Table 1), obtained from a cross section excavation on the upper branch of the Vichansao canal on Pampa Rio Seco, is associated with this phase of Chimu canal expansion. Two other dates of A.D. 1150±70 and A.D. 1240±70 (Table 1), from excavations on Pampa Arenal, are also associated with this canal expansion phase.

The next major change was a remodeling of the Vichansao canal on Pampas Esperanza and Rio Seco. Most of this remodeling consisted of the creation of a new stone-lined channel that closely followed the course of the generally unlined older canal. One significant difference, however, was the construction of canals 1 and 2, which led off from the Vichansao canal and crossed over the course of canal A (Figure 2), rendering it useless. Terminal dates of A.D.

1380±80 and A.D. 1370±60 respectively (Table 1) for this remodeling phase come from excavations in the Vichansao canal on Pampas Rio Seco and Esperanza.

At a certain point during the remodeling phase, estimated by bracketing radiocarbon dates to have been about A.D. 1300 (Table 1), a major flood, caused by unusually heavy *El Niño* rains which hit the Peruvian coast once or twice every century, damaged much of the canal system (Nials *et al.* 1979). An attempt was made to rebuild the system, as evidenced by scattered reconstructed canal segments on each of the pampas, but it was a greatly reduced effort, for the reconstructed channels are very small in comparison with earlier canals. No water was ever carried in the reconstructed canal segments, and it appears that irrigation limits essentially contracted to modern cultivation limits about this time. There are a few much later abortive canals on Pampa Esperanza, but these are definitely late features postdating the abandonment of Chan Chan and do not concern us here.

Pampa Esperanza canals and their relationship to Chan Chan

The above canal sequence, which is detailed particularly well on Pampa Esperanza, can be directly correlated with the compound construction sequence for Chan Chan. (See chapter by Klymyshyn, this volume, for a discussion of the Chan Chan compounds.) Following Kolata's sequence based on seriation of adobe bricks and *audiencias*, the four compounds of Chayhuac, Uhle, Laberinto, and Tello belong to the first construction

Table 2. *Radiocarbon dates from Chan Chan compounds and El Milagro de San José**

Radiocarbon years	Calendar age	Location
730±150 (Conrad 1974:741, GX–3253)	A.D. 1220±150	Chan Chan, Uhle
725±155 (Conrad 1974:741, GX–3251)	A.D. 1225±155	Chan Chan, Gran Chimu
680±120 (Conrad 1974:741, GX–3250)	A.D. 1270±120	Chan Chan, Tschudi
670±160 (Conrad 1974:741, GX–3245)	A.D. 1280±160	Chan Chan, Laberinto
620±155 (Conrad 1974:741, GX–3255)	A.D. 1330±155	Chan Chan, Squier
615±155 (Conrad 1974:741, GX–3244)	A.D. 1335±155	Chan Chan, Velarde
595±160 (Conrad 1974:741, GX–3254)	A.D. 1355±160	Chan Chan, Uhle
560±120 (Conrad 1974:741, GX–3246)	A.D. 1390±120	Chan Chan, Squier
510±180 (Conrad 1974:742, GX–3252)	A.D. 1440±180	Chan Chan, Gran Chimu
450±150 (Conrad 1974:742, GX–3247)	A.D. 1500±150	Chan Chan, Bandelier
405±160 (Conrad 1974:742, GX–3249)	A.D. 1545±160	Chan Chan, Rivero
345±155 (Conrad 1974:742, GX–3248)	A.D. 1605±155	Chan Chan, Rivero
695±80 (Keatinge 1980:286, I–9711)	A.D. 1255±80	El Milagro de San José, Pampa Rio Seco
625±80 (Keatinge 1980:287, I–7910)	A.D. 1325±80	El Milagro de San José, Pampa Rio Seco

* All dates are uncorrected based upon the Libby half-life (5570±30 years).

phase. The main constituents of the second phase are Gran Chimu and its annexes, including the Great North Wall which delimits the northern boundary of the site (Figure 2). The third and final phase consists of the compounds Squier, Velarde, Bandelier, Tschudi and Rivero. Though there may be questions about the ordering of individual compounds within these phases, the general ordering of the three groups is supported by ceramic evidence (Mackey, personal communication), radiocarbon dates (Table 2; Conrad 1974:741–748), a burial platform sequence (Conrad 1980:229; 1982:109), and evidence from the SIAR (small irregular agglutinated rooms) (J. Topic 1982:165–167) and elite compounds (Klymyshyn 1982:131–133) within Chan Chan. If this general ordering of the compounds is accepted, then the importance of the sequence for the present discussion is the chronological placement of Gran Chimu and the Great North Wall.

The canal sequence on Pampa Esperanza is directly tied in with the Chan Chan sequence by the relationship of canal 2 to the Great North Wall (Figure 2). This canal, which is part of the remodeling phase of the canal system, contains in its bed evidence of the 'great flood' that damaged the canal system. The Great North Wall is built over both this canal and the flood sediments it contains, indicating that its construction dates after the flood, and took place either during or after the final ineffective attempt to reconstruct the canal system. Therefore, according to this stratigraphic sequence, it is evident that all major canal construction and use in the 3-Pampa area occurred *before* the building of the Great North Wall and during the first construction phase of compounds in Chan Chan (this would correspond to the early phase of Klymyshyn, this volume). Moreover, it shows that the Moche Valley irrigation system had shrunk to about its modern limits before half of Chan Chan was built. Significantly it was the later phases of construction at

Chan Chan (Kolata's second and third phase, which Klymyshyn, this volume, combines into a single late phase), following the canal contraction, that saw the building of increasingly standardized monumental compounds with a tripartite layout and associated burial platforms (Conrad 1982:114–115; Kolata 1982:84–85), and standardization of *audiencias* (Kolata 1980:153, 1982:83). This was also a time of proliferation of great expanses of SIAR, artisan workshops (J. Topic 1980:275, 1982:165–166) and elite compounds (Klymyshyn 1980:266, 1982:131–133, 142–143). These patterns reflect the trend toward increased redistribution, bureaucracy, and focus on craft production that characterized Chan Chan during its height of power in the mid-fifteenth century A.D.

Rural administrative sites

Rural administrative centers containing *audiencias* have received considerable attention in the last few years as the result of investigations carried out in the Moche and Chicama Valleys in the early 1970s (Keatinge 1974, 1980; Keatinge and Day 1973, 1974). These rural *audiencia* sites, constructed by the Chimu during the Late Intermediate Period, are located in rural desert settings away from large urban centers, but in direct association with prehispanic canals and field systems. They are postulated to have served both as administrative centers for initial canal and field construction and later as centers for maintenance of canals and fields and control of crop production (Keatinge 1974:79–80; Keatinge and Day 1973:292). However, the point to be made here is that these rural *audiencia* sites were *primarily* established as administrative centers to oversee initial canal and field construction. As such, they represent the expansion of the Chimu state into desert areas previously unexploited. Only in a few cases did these planned fields actually produce enough crops for the associated *audiencia* sites ever to function in the administration of crop production. This pattern is well illustrated in a comparison of examples from both the Moche and Chicama Valleys.

Rural administrative sites within the Moche Valley

Within the Moche Valley, two major rural Chimu administrative structures containing *audiencias* are associated with canals and field systems: El Milagro located on Pampa Rio Seco and Quebrada Katuay situated about 28 km inland (Figures 1 and 2) (Keatinge 1974, 1980; Keatinge and Day 1974:233–234).

The site of El Milagro is located on Pampa Rio Seco between the upper and lower branches of the Vichansao canal (Figure 2). Several much smaller buildings are located within a few hundred meters of this site, but it is clearly the major structure which dominates this sector of Pampa Rio Seco. The site is within Pampa Rio Seco, the first expanse of land to have been incorporated as Chimu irrigation expanded beyond the cultivation limits established by the preceding Moche. Major feeder canals and fields surround the structure on all sides, but are not overlain by El Milagro structures; therefore, it is evident that El Milagro served as a headquarters during the initial construction of the Vichansao canal and the layout of the adjoining fields and feeders on Pampa Rio Seco (Keatinge 1974:79).

The main structure at El Milagro measures 55 m × 45 m and is constructed principally of waterworn cobbles from the nearby dry bed of Rio Seco. The architecture of the site is similar to that seen in Chan Chan with interior courts, tortuous passageways, *audiencias*, and small rooms, often with banks of niches (Keatinge 1974:677–672, Figure 21, 1980:285–287, Figure 3). Although Mackey (see chapter by Mackey this volume) does not ascribe a storage function to tertiary centers such as El Milagro, the five *audiencias* are closely associated with niched rooms, which are believed to be storage facilities. While Keatinge (1974:71) did not find any items stored in these niches in the course of his excavations, the likelihood that they were used for at least temporary storage of agricultural products is supported by relatively isolated location of the site surrounded by agricultural fields and by the definite association of the niches with *audiencias*, which control access to storerooms within Chan Chan (Andrews 1974; Keatinge and Day 1974:231–232). Beyond storage, control and redistribution of the agricultural products, including both food plants and industrial plants such as cotton, would have been important functions of the site of El Milagro. It also follows that since the fields and canals near the site are somewhat marginal and removed from Chan Chan and other habitation sites, El Milagro probably served as a center for maintaining the fields and canals, as well as redistributing the crops produced by them.

Two radiocarbon dates are associated with El Milagro and its nearby structures. One date of A.D. 1255±80 (Table 2) comes from the kitchen area of the main structure and another date, A.D. 1325±80 (Table 2), comes from an outbuilding next

to the lower branch of the Vichansao canal (Keatinge 1980:286–287). These dates agree well with those obtained from cross section excavations of canals on Pampas Rio Seco, Esperanza and Arenal (see above) and indicate that El Milagro spans both the expansion and remodeling phases in the 3-Pampa area.

Like El Milagro, the site of Quebrada Katuay, located about 28 km inland on the north side of the Moche Valley, is situated in an isolated area in association with prehistoric canals and fields (Keatinge 1974:76–78, Figure 24, 1980:294–296, Figure 6). Though part of the site has been destroyed by modern road construction and obscured by fallen wall debris, it appears to be somewhat similar to El Milagro. Quebrada Katuay measures 47.5 m × 20.2 m and has entry courts, small side courts, and probably once had an *audiencia* located at the rear of the compound (Keatinge 1974:76–77, 1980:294–296). It is much less complicated than El Milagro, but bears a close resemblance to rural administrative sites north of the Moche Valley.

Its simplicity may be due to the likelihood that the associated canal carried little, if any, water. Many canals, some with associated fields, in other marginal areas in the lower Moche Valley never carried water or did so only very briefly. If the same pattern held true for the Quebrada Katuay area, as seems likely, it could explain the simple undeveloped layout of the Quebrada Katuay administrative site. While this site served initially to administer canal construction, no storage areas were necessary and, since the zone failed to produce, architectural features, such as niches which functioned as storage and redistribution facilities, were never incorporated into the site plan. In comparison, the relatively complicated nature of the site of El Milagro may be in part due to its continued use as a center for field maintenance and crop production. These would have necessitated some alteration of an original, simpler layout which might be expected in an administrative headquarters established initially for supervising canal construction.

Rural administrative sites and canal systems outside the Moche Valley

In the Chicama Valley north of the Moche Valley, two rural administrative sites, Quebrada del Oso and Pampa Mocan, are associated with prehistoric and field systems. Quebrada del Oso is well known (Kus 1972:144–63; Keatinge 1974:72–76, Figure 23, 1980:288–292, Figure 5). Pampa Mocan is described here for the first time.

The site of Quebrada del Oso is located some three km southeast of the edge of modern cultivation in the Chicama Valley (Figure 1). The site consists of three structures, of which only the main one is the focus of this paper. The layout of this structure (Keatinge 1974:72–76, Figure 23, 1980:288–295, Figure 5) is similar to but less complex than that of El Milagro, and similar to but more complex than Quebrada Katuay. Typical Chimu architectural patterns common in Chan Chan are present at Quebrada del Oso, including two entry courts entered by means of indirect tortuous passageways, associated side courts and rooms flanking the entry courts, and a centrally placed *audiencia* near the rear of the structure. Unlike El Milagro, but like Quebrada Katuay, there are no niches present in any of the walls.

Quebrada del Oso is associated with the Chicama–Moche Intervalley canal which lies just 320 m north of the site. Fields associated with the penultimate construction phase of the Intervalley canal surround the site on all sides. As Keatinge (1974:75–76, 1980:293–294) has noted, the site structures were extant before the field system was laid out, since the furrows and feeder canals veer around the structures and do not pass under any of the walls. Since the Intervalley canal and associated field systems never carried water (T. Pozorski and S. Pozorski 1982:865), the function of the site must have been something other than the administration of field systems and the redistribution of crops grown in those fields. It is here at Quebrada del Oso that the original purpose of rural *audiencia* sites is most clear; namely, administration of the construction of a major canal system, in this case the Chicama–Moche Intervalley canal. Supervision of production in the surrounding fields may have been intended as a later function of the site, as was the case at El Milagro, but this was never realized. This may explain why there are no niches in the rooms at Quebrada del Oso.

Chronologically, Quebrada del Oso ties in well with the canal sequence of the '3-Pampa' area and the construction sequence at Chan Chan. The ceramics of the site are similar to

those found at El Milagro (Mackey, personal communication), and the *audiencia* is identical to an *audiencia* at El Milagro (Keatinge 1974:75, 1980:288); both of these *audiencias* are similar to types found in the Uhle, one of the earliest compounds at Chan Chan (Kolata 1980:153, 1982:83–84). The associated Intervalley Canal was constructed to provide water for the entire 3-Pampa area, as indicated by its looping around the base of Cerro Cabras and by its junction with the Vichansao canal above Pampa Esperanza (Figure 2). A series of twelve radiocarbon dates from excavations of the Intervalley canal, ten from the Quebrada del Oso area and two from further upstream, range from A.D. 1040±80 to A.D. 1310±110 (Table 1). These dates indicate that the Intervalley canal construction is contemporary with the maximum expansion of the canal and field systems in the Moche Valley, and probably overlaps with the remodeling phase as well.

The site of Pampa Mocan is located on the north side of the Chicama Valley, about 3.7 km northeast of the limits of modern cultivation (Figure 1). It is situated just outside the maximum limits of prehistoric irrigated land reclamation. As with Quebrada del Oso, there are other smaller structures in the area, but only the largest has an *audiencia*.

The *audiencia* structure of Pampa Mocan (Figure 3) bears a striking resemblance to that of Quebrada del Oso. It also has two entry courts and indirect tortuous passageways, and the *audiencia* is centrally placed near the rear of the building. Unlike Quebrada del Oso and Quebrada Katuay, but similar to El Milagro, it has three rooms with niches which probably served in association with the *audiencia* as areas for temporary storage. While the canal systems in the vicinity of Pampa Mocan have not been intensively investigated or excavated, survey in the area, especially in *quebrada* areas where canals have been cut by washes, has revealed some evidence of possible canal use. Clearly, however, some of the small feeder canals near the end of the system never carried water. By contrast, some of the larger canals, especially nearer modern cultivation limits, probably did function. Distribution of crops from fields watered by these canals would have been regulated by the Pampa Mocan *audiencia*. Therefore, this site probably served two functions: first as an administrative center for canal and field construction and later as an administrative center to oversee maintenance and crop production for the functioning canals and fields. The presence of niches in some of the rooms confirms this continuing secondary function as a storage and redistribution center.

Primarily because of its architectural similarities to *audiencia* sites further south, especially Quebrada del Oso, the Pampa Mocan site is probably contemporaneous with the other *audiencia* sites mentioned previously. Another radiocarbon date, however, can be indirectly tied in with the Pampa Mocan site and reinforces the relative dating based on architectural patterning. The Ascope aqueduct, located several kilometers inland and east of Pampa Mocan (Figure 1), once carried water to Pampa Mocan. A break in this aqueduct due to past flooding has exposed a profile showing a progressive buildup of canal

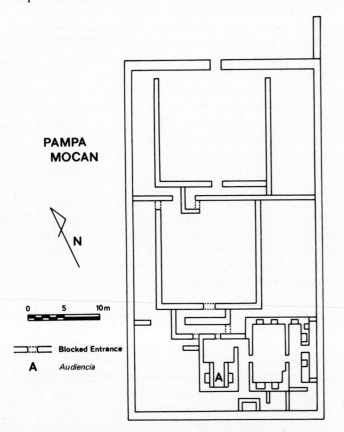

PAMPA MOCAN

N

0   5   10m

⊏·:⊏·⊏ **Blocked Entrance**

A   *Audiencia*

Fig. 3. Plan map of the *audiencia* site of Pampa Mocan

beds and sediment. A sample taken from a point 8.5 m below the top of the aqueduct yielded a date of A.D. 1000±60 (Table 1). This date correlates well with the early dates from the Chicama–Moche Intervalley canal as well as with the stratigraphy of the aqueduct, indicating that canal expansion on to Pampa Mocan was contemporary with at least the early part, if not the entire major canal expansion phase documented for the 3-Pampa area in the Moche Valley.

In summing up the relationship among the rural *audiencia* sites in the Chicama and Moche Valleys, it appears that the four rural *audiencia* sites (Pampa Mocan, Quebrada del Oso, Quebrada Katuay, and El Milagro) are all contemporary and associated with a phase of maximum canal and field expansion dating between A.D. 1050 and 1300. The *audiencia* sites of Quebrada del Oso and Quebrada Katuay, which do not contain niched rooms, reflect the original function of rural *audiencia* sites, namely, the administration of initial construction of canal and field systems. Since the canals associated with these sites did not carry water, no niched rooms used for the storage of crops were ever constructed. In contrast, El Milagro de San José and Pampa Mocan, which contain niched rooms, not only served as administrative centers for canal construction but also subsequently acted as centers of control for crop production and redistribution.

Irrigation expansion and the Chimu state

The relationship of Chimu agricultural expansion to the development of the Chimu state is examined in this section. In doing so, the nature and extent of the preceding Moche state during the Early Intermediate Period and Middle Horizon (A.D. 600–1000) is briefly reviewed as a background for subsequent discussion of the Chimu state. The examination of the role of irrigation and the Chimu state is divided into two sections. The first concerns the expanding role of irrigation during the early growth of Chan Chan and the first phase of Chimu state expansion. The second section deals with the contraction of irrigated land to essentially modern limits, an event which is somewhat paradoxically correlated with the maximum second phase expansion of the Chimu state.

The Moche state

Traditionally the Moche state is viewed as having controlled the coastal area from Lambayeque or Jequetepeque to Nepeña (Lanning 1967:121; Mason 1969:75; Willey 1971:132; T. Topic 1982:261), with possible connections either by trade or colonization as far north as Piura and as far south as Huarmey (Benson 1972:9; Donnan 1976:2, 1978:3; Shimada 1982:150–152; T. Topic 1982:261). The Moche state was centered at the site of Moche in the Moche Valley and flourished during Moche I–IV times (T. Topic 1982:276–277).

By Moche V times (*c.* A.D. 600–750), during the early part of the Middle Horizon, the site of Moche was abandoned and a new capital, Pampa Grande (Shimada 1978, 1981a; Day 1982b:333–335), was established in the Lambayeque Valley. Pampa Grande and the smaller contemporaneous site of

Galindo (Bawden 1982a, 1982b) in the Moche Valley were both established at points that were crucial for control of the irrigation systems of the lower parts of their respective valleys. It is likely that this Middle Horizon shift in site location was due to unrest further south (Bawden 1982a:319–310; Shimada 1982:155–156). This is not to say that Wari invaders conquered these valleys (Rowe 1963:19; Schaedel 1966a:343; Willey 1971:164), for there is almost no archaeological evidence for their presence on the north coast (Cardenas 1978:64; Bawden 1982a:320; Mackey 1982:329; Shimada 1982:169). However, sufficient unrest existed at that time to cause major populations to shift to more defensible locations.

More important for this study, however, is the fact that for the first time in several centuries, a major polity was not centered in the Moche Valley. It appears that the leaders within Lambayeque took advantage of unrest during early Middle Horizon times to break away from the Moche Valley and establish their own power center. The beginning of this trend is seen at Pampa Grande. During the next few hundred years, the Lambayeque Valley became more and more independent of the Moche Valley as manifested by the rise of other large sites in that valley such as Batán Grande, Apurlé, and Túcume (Shimada 1981a:169–188). Meanwhile, in the Moche Valley, the site of Galindo (Bawden 1982a, 1982b) was the main center during Moche V times.

The early Chimu state

Following the abandonment of Galindo (Bawden 1982a:320), the site of Chan Chan was established, though its original extent and characteristics have been obscured by later constructions. The 10 compounds that are still visible today were begun fairly early and built in sequential order. Evidence suggests that this compound sequence began in the late eleventh or early twelfth centuries and continued until the Inca conquest of the Chimu around A.D. 1470.

The irrigation canal sequence for the 3-Pampa area adjacent to Chan Chan is tied in both relatively and absolutely with the sequence of compound construction. The two sequences can be correlated in the following manner. (1) During the early stages of growth at Chan Chan (A.D. 1050 to 1300), including construction of the first four monumental compounds, the Moche Valley irrigation system reached its maximum extent, covering most of Pampas Rio Seco and Huanchaco as well as expanding into other marginal areas of the valley. (2) Toward the end of the maximum expansion period, much of the canal system was remodeled. (3) At about A.D. 1300, a large *El Niño* rain washed out much of the system. (4) After this flood, the compound of Gran Chimu and the Great North Wall of Chan Chan were built concurrently with, or shortly after, a partial reconstruction of the canal system, which never again carried water. (5) Five compounds, comprising about one-half of Chan Chan, were built after the unused reconstructed canal system, and irrigated land contracted essentially to modern limits.

In the Chicama Valley north of Moche, little is known

about total settlement pattern during the Middle Horizon and Late Intermediate Period. However, available evidence from both rural *audiencia* sites and radiocarbon dates suggests that maximum agricultural expansion on the north and south side of that valley was contemporary with expansion in the Moche Valley.

The Chicama evidence suggests that after a period of disruption during the Middle Horizon, this valley and probably at least as far north as Jequetepeque Valley and the Viru, Chao, and Santa Valleys to the south were conquered by a rejuvenated Moche Valley polity, the Chimu, centered in the Moche Valley. The Chimu thus reclaimed land traditionally governed by a Moche Valley polity since early Moche times. These conquered valleys were incorporated almost immediately into a vigorous plan of agricultural expansion as a means of increasing agricultural productivity and expanding the power base for the Moche-based polity. This physical evidence of Chimu intrusion lies well within the bounds of the maximum extent of the first phase of Chimu expansion described by the chronicles (Anonymous History of 1604 in Rowe 1948; Calancha 1638; Cabello Valboa 1951; Kosok 1965), and correlates well with Mackey's (see chapter by Mackey, this volume) assessment of the scope of archaeological evidence attributable to Phase I of the Chimu empire.

The postflood Chimu state

In view of this reconstructed time frame for the maximum extent of agricultural fields in the Chicama and Moche area, it is necessary to examine conditions surrounding the flood of about A.D. 1300, which damaged the Moche Valley canal system, and presumably affected systems in the other valleys.

It is evident in the Moche Valley system that most of the preserved fields are in marginal areas which received relatively little water, and functioned, at best, only seasonally and probably not every year. Some areas never received water at all, and therefore never aided the Chimu in their agricultural expansion efforts. Part of the reason lay with the lack of water that is endemic to most of the north-coast valleys; part lay with the poor engineering capabilities of the Chimu (see T. Pozorski and S. Pozorski 1982); and part lay with windblown sand and silt, which continually filled canals (especially during seasonal periods of disuse) and necessitated constant maintenance. In other words, the amount of crop yield from marginal lands in the Moche and Chicama Valleys and other conquered valleys north and south of Moche was probably barely enough to justify the maintenance needed to keep the fields viable during the early growth of the Chimu state. They thus became much less attractive as the Chimu consolidated their position and power base.

The crippling of the canal system by flooding apparently acted as a catalyst for a change in Chimu strategy. The canal system within modern cultivation limits was undoubtedly totally rebuilt and used after the flood, because that part of the system could be cultivated year-round, was relatively easy to maintain,

and produced good crop yields. However, the marginal areas were rebuilt, but not used. Instead of expending large amounts of labor on maintaining fields in marginal land, the Chimu apparently formed additional military units and set about to conquer coastal land to the north and south from which tribute could be exacted. Agricultural products lost because of the abandonment of marginal lands in the Jequetepeque to Santa Valleys were more than compensated for by the acquisition of tribute in products from lands outside this preflood core area.

Ethnohistorically, a great flood is supposed to have killed a ruler in Lambayeque called Fempellec (Cabello Valboa 1951:328–329; Rowe 1948), an event estimated as happening around A.D. 1300 (Kosok 1965:73). After his death, an interregnum occurred that lasted 'many days' (Cabello Valboa 1951:329), and did not end until a new ruler was set up in the Lambayeque Valley by the Chimu. On the basis of documents, primarily that of the Anonymous Trujillano (Vargas 1936:229–239), Kosok (1965:73–74) ties in the conquest of Lambayeque as happening sometime between the reign of Ñancenpinco, the Chimu ruler who governed the area between Jequetepeque and Santa, and that of Minchançaman, who was the Chimu ruler at the time of the Inca conquest of the Chimu. Between these two rulers were six or seven other rulers whose reigns spanned an unknown length of time estimated to have been between 100 (Rowe 1948) and 150 years (Kosok 1965:73). If the ethnohistorical flood is the same as that documented in the archaeological record, which seems likely (Nials *et al.* 1979; Moseley and Deeds 1982:48), then the remaining archaeological evidence coincides well with the ethnohistory. From A.D. 1300, the postulated time of the flood, to A.D. 1470, the time of the Inca conquest, six compounds, Gran Chimu, Squier, Velarde, Bandelier, Tschudi, and Rivero, were built at Chan Chan, most of which were probably built by different rulers as their palaces and final burial places (Conrad 1981:14–16, 1982:104–115; see chapter by Klymyshyn, this volume).

The standardization of the layout of the later compounds and of *audiencias* within those compounds (see chapter by Klymyshyn, this volume) indicates that the Chimu bureaucratic structure was becoming very formalized in response to a vastly increased redistributive network (Klymyshyn 1982:141; Kolata 1982:83–85). The artisans' quarters and workshops which made up the majority of the SIAR at Chan Chan undoubtedly furnished many of the goods, such as textiles, carved wood, worked shell, metal tools and ornaments, that were placed in the storerooms within the large compounds (J. Topic 1982:172–173). However, many goods and much agricultural produce also probably came from outside of Chan Chan in the form of tribute, which was eventually redistributed among the various classes of people inside and outside Chan Chan. Furthermore, it is likely that many of the artisans residing in Chan Chan were brought in from increasingly remote parts of the Chimu empire, particularly as it expanded to the north and south.

Conclusions

The archaeological and ethnohistorical data from Chan Chan and the canal and field systems studied in the Moche and Chicama Valleys reveal two important features of the Chimu state. The first is that from about A.D. 1000 to 1300, after a period of disruption during the Middle Horizon, Chan Chan developed as the center of an intervalley state controlling the area from Jequetepeque to Santa (see chapter by Mackey, this volume). This was an area which had been previously governed by the Moche state (T. Topic 1982:261). The desire and need for agricultural products (both industrial plants and food cultigens) to consolidate and expand the Chimu power base was satisfied by a vigorous program of canal and field expansion within each of the valleys under control. At the same time, there was an attempt to construct an intervalley canal to take water from the Chicama Valley to water fields above Chan Chan in the Moche Valley.

Second, from shortly after A.D. 1300, the time of a great flood that washed out the canal systems, to A.D. 1470, the time of the Inca conquest of the Chimu, the Chimu empire expanded enormously. It conquered territory as far north as Tumbes near the Ecuador border and as far south as the Chillon Valley on the central coast (Rowe 1948; see chapter by Mackey, this volume). This expansion, however, denotes a marked change in Chimu strategy. Apparently, after their canal system was damaged, the Chimu rulers began to realize that the marginal canals were not worth the labor investment needed to restore and maintain them.

The general implications of the above statements are readily apparent. Though the extent of prehistoric canals and fields on the north coast of Peru has always been highly regarded as a hallmark of the success of prehispanic adaptation and cultural development (Kosok 1965:15–20; Lanning 1967:180–182; Mason 1969:27; Price 1971:30; Moseley 1978c:17; Moseley and Deeds 1982:150–155), such was not the case. Parts or whole areas of these systems functioned only marginally or not at all. From the present study, it is clear that almost all of these marginal systems, at least from Jequetepeque south to Santa, predate about A.D. 1300. The extensive intravalley and intervalley systems in the Lambayeque region (Motupe Leche–Lambayeque–Zaña) are neither well known nor well dated, but parts of them are likely to predate A.D. 1300 as well (Nolan 1980:21–111; Shimada 1982:180). Indeed, most of these systems probably also predate A.D. 1300 simply because of ongoing contact between the Lambayeque area and valleys further south.

Moreover, on the basis of personal observations as well as those of Shimada (1982:180) it appears that many sections of the canal systems in the Lambayeque area, like those of systems further south, were used only briefly, sporadically, or not at all. It is likely that the construction of massive intravalley and intervalley systems was related to maintaining a high status. It is not inconceivable that competition for political power among various coastal rulers of the type seen in aboriginal Hawaii (Earle 1978:174) was a principal driving force in the construction of many large irrigation systems in marginal areas where chances of good crop yields were minimal. It is also possible that the Chimu administrative structure, much as in the Valley of Mexico (Sanders *et al.* 1979:395), had grown to such an extent that decisions were made on a self-serving basis and had little to do with meeting the subsistence needs of the population. Regardless of the motivation, the height of sociopolitical development on the north coast, represented by the fully expanded Chimu empire, was reached some 150 years *after* most of these canal systems fell into disuse. Clearly, maximum extent of irrigated land did not correlate with maximum development of the sociopolitical system.

What probably led to the second phase of Chimu expansion was a desire not so much for tribute from agricultural lands, but rather to gain access to and control over the production of artisan goods, especially metalworking, that had been so successfully controlled by Batán Grande and possibly other sites in the Lambayeque area for hundreds of years (Shimada 1982:178–179). Traditionally, control of land and its produce had formed the economic foundation for sociopolitical organization from the beginnings of state development in the Moche Valley and surrounding area. During the early development of the Chimu state, from A.D. 1000 to 1300, the Chimu elite consolidated their position by this traditional means while also being aware of the developments in the Lambayeque region. While there was certainly craft production in the earliest occupation of Chan Chan, it was probably not as developed as it was at Batán Grande, which had become a prominent religious and craft production center in the Lambayeque region by A.D. 800 (Shimada 1982:178–179). Once the rulers of Chan Chan had enough military force to challenge seriously and defeat these rich and powerful neighbors to the north, they did so with amazing rapidity. Control of craft production for Lambayeque, which meant not only obtaining artisan work as tribute but also the physical transfer of artisans from Lambayeque to the SIAR workshops at Chan Chan, provided a new source of wealth and power for Chan Chan and in turn fueled further conquest of other coastal areas. The intense competition for political power on the coast, which had stimulated the Chimu to build Chan Chan and expand their irrigation network, further induced the Chimu to gain wider control over craft production and develop it to the highest degree ever attained by an ancient Peruvian society. This is physically manifest by the proliferation of storerooms, *audiencias*, elite compounds, and SIAR within the Chan Chan. Within the short span of about 150 years, the Chimu more than quadrupled their zone of control and became the single most serious threat to the expanding Inca empire in the south.

Thus, while it can be said that irrigation agriculture definitely provided the subsistence base and fostered a certain level of state development on the Peruvian north coast, it is not true that great expansion of canal systems, both on an intravalley and intervalley level, generated, or is even correlated with, further state development. The limits of modern irrigation on the north coast as of about 1940, prior to extensive use of pumps or development of modern reclamation projects, are close to the limits of agriculture that were productively maintained during the Late Intermediate Period. Development of the Chimu state from a relatively small system controlling a few coastal valleys to the level of an empire controlling over 1300 kilometers of the coastline rested mainly on the manipulation and control of craft production and human labor, which, in turn, served to bolster the political power and status of the Chimu kings. The control of these two factors (Day 1982b:349) contributed to the development and refinement of governmental and administrative principles that were later adopted by the Incas (Rowe 1948) after they conquered the Chimu in A.D. 1470.

Acknowledgments
Funding for the Programa Riego Antiguo was provided by National Science Foundation grants BNS76–24538 and BNS77–24901. Permission for survey and excavation in the Moche and Chicama Valleys was granted by the Instituto Nacional de Cultura. Special appreciation is extended to Eric Deeds, who contributed significantly to the interpretations of canal cross sections.

Chapter 12

Chimu administration in the provinces

Carol J. Mackey

Introduction

A number of chapters in this volume deal with the reasons why states begin expanding and evolve into empires, and with the central governmental organization of such imperial states (see chapters by Schreiber, Klymyshyn and Isbell, this volume). Another aspect of the organization of empires concerns the administration of conquered provinces that are incorporated into the imperial state organization. The present chapter will focus on the administrative organization of the Chimu empire on the Peruvian north coast, and will look specifically at the extension of the administrative network beyond Chan Chan, the Chimu capital, out to the provinces of the empire. Since the expansion of the Chimu empire occurred from *c.* A.D. 1150 to 1470, a period of over 300 years, this is an ideal period for studying the long-term policies of imperial expansion.

While the archaeological record for many regions of the Chimu empire is still incomplete and heavily weighted to administrative centers built during the first wave of Chimu expansion, it is nevertheless adequate for the goals of this chapter. One of the main goals is to begin to define and rank Chimu administrative centers. However, as Wright and Johnson (1975) point out, a settlement hierarchy alone implies little about administrative organization. It is necessary to include evidence of administrative function as well as the distribution of these centers (see also Isbell and Schreiber

1978). Thus, the second goal of this chapter is to define the function of the Chimu administrative centers on the basis of architectural and spatial variables. Finally these data will be used to assess Chimu administrative policies in the provinces.

Chimu expansion

Prior to addressing the major goals of this chapter, it is necessary to review the background of Chimu expansion in terms of: (1) the chronology and extent of Chimu expansion; (2) the pre-existing polities prior to Chimu control and (3) the visibility of Chimu political control. The data used in this section are drawn from both Spanish chronicles and archaeological remains.

The chronology and extent of Chimu expansion

At the height of Chimu expansion, the Chimu Empire is said to have spread over some 1300 km of the coast of Peru from Tumbes in the north to the Chillon Valley (Figure 1). According to accounts in the Spanish chronicles, the Chimu launched two major phases of expansion from their capital, Chan Chan, in the Moche Valley (Anonymous History of 1604 in Rowe 1948; Calancha 1638; Cabello Valboa 1951). Rowe (1948) suggested a date of approximately A.D. 1370 for the first phase of expansion which encompassed the area from Zaña in the north to Santa Valley in the south. The second phase is said to have occurred almost 100 years later (A.D. 1460). This

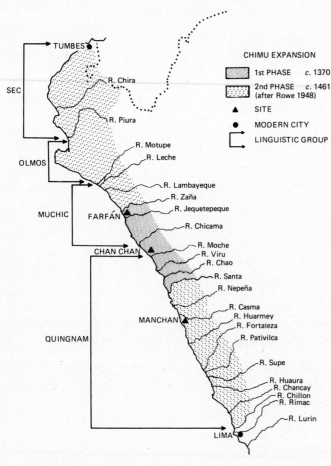

Fig. 1. Chimu expansion

with the understanding that the dates of these phases are earlier than indicated on the basis of ethnohistoric sources. This chronological assessment is based on both absolute radiocarbon assays and relative dating methods. The primary basis for the relative dating is the sequence for Chimu ceramics based on the sequence established for the Moche Valley (Keatinge 1973; Topic 1977; Donnan and Mackey 1978) and the seriation of the *audiencias* from Chan Chan (Andrews 1972; Kolata 1978, 1982).

Pre-existing polities prior to Chimu control

Now that the extent of the empire has been discussed, it is possible to turn to what is known about pre-existing polities preceding Chimu control. These groups will be discussed in terms of both their linguistic and sociopolitical affiliations. The chronicles agree that there were at least four linguistic groups incorporated into the Chimu empire (Figure 1). However, differences between these linguistic groups may not have been very great, since the linguistic distinctions on the coast appear to be at the dialect rather than the language level (Netherly 1977:100). The sociopolitical groups which were included within the Chimu empire do not necessarily correlate with the linguistic groups.

The Chimu incorporated large, multi-valley polities into their empire, especially during the second phase of expansion. These affiliations have been established through ethnohistoric, architectural and archaeological similarities. The first of these polities, Sicán (see Shimada, this volume), encompassed many of the valleys south of the Leche Valley. It would appear that at the time of the Chimu conquest, the Zaña and Jequetepeque Valleys would have been part of the Sicán complex. The evidence for this polity is based on the five-valley canal system which linked the valleys from Motupe to Jequetepeque into one economic unit (Kosok 1965). These valleys also share similarities in ceramic styles as well as in some of the features found in monumental architecture. The Chimu established administrative centers in the Jequetepeque Valley (Keatinge and Conrad 1983), and possibly in the Zaña Valley during their first phase of expansion, thereby establishing a foothold in the Sicán polity. It was not until the second expansion that the rest of the Sicán polity as well as the territory north of the Leche came under Chimu influence.

Prior to the Chimu conquest it appears that the largest political group south of the Moche Valley was the Casma polity, which included the valleys from Santa to Huarmey. The evidence for this polity, which would have existed since the latter part of the Middle Horizon, is based on similarities in ceramic styles and certain architectural features (Tello 1956; Collier 1962).

The capitals of these two polities, Sicán and Casma, were incorporated into the empire during the second phase of expansion. Although I am not yet certain about the Casma polity, it appears that there was a long-term relationship between Sicán and the Chimu capital prior to the

phase incorporated the areas between Tumbes and Zaña in the north and between Santa and Chillon in the south (Figure 1).

However, recent evidence indicates that both the first and second phases of expansion were earlier than had previously been thought. Radiocarbon assays from the Jequetepeque Valley indicate that the first phase of expansion to the north took place at approximately A.D. 1200 (Keatinge and Conrad 1983).

It is not clear from the ethnohistorical records whether, during the second expansion, the empire expanded to the north and south at the same time. Since three Chimu governors are listed for Lambayeque and none is listed for the southern region (Rowe 1948), it is possible that the Lambayeque area was incorporated prior to the Nepeña to Chillon area in the south. However, the date given by Shimada for the Chimu occupation of the Lambayeque region is A.D. 1400 (Shimada *et al.* 1982). The incorporation of the Casma Valley is clearly placed in the second Chimu expansion. Ceramic data from the Casma Valley correspond to the late ceramic phases in the Moche Valley, making the incorporation of this area around A.D. 1300. For the purpose of this paper the major chronological distinction between administrative centers will be whether they fall into the first or second phase of expansion,

Chimu conquest since similar stylistic and iconographic features occur in both cultural assemblages.

The north central coast, the area south of Huarmey to the Chillon Valley, is still relatively unknown in terms of its political alliances from the time of the Middle Horizon. Based only on similarity of pottery styles, mention has been made of the Fortaleza–Pativilca–Supe complex as well as Chancay and its neighboring valleys, but it is not yet clear whether these similarities indicate political unity of these valleys (Kosok 1965, Rowe 1948).

The visibility of Chimu political control

Chimu political control was limited to the north coast of Peru. This is not to say that the Chimu did not have alliances with the highlands. For example, there was a strong alliance between the Chimu and the Cajamarca state in the northern highlands (Rowe 1948, Topic and Topic 1982). However, within this coastal empire it appears that the Chimu exercised differing degrees of control. In particular, there appears to be a difference between the total area conquered and the area actually occupied by the Chimu as evidenced by the presence of state architecture and ceramics. As Schreiber (see chapter by Schreiber, this volume) has noted, Chimu political organization is characterized by an intensive form of control. Within each valley under direct Chimu control, the intensive level of their control is physically manifested by visible structures. Given this premise, it can be argued that direct control by the Chimu did not extend over the total area of their empire. On the basis of the known administrative centers, therefore, the area under direct Chimu control appears to have extended from the Leche Valley in the north to the Fortaleza Valley in the south (Schaedel 1951a; Willey 1953; Collier 1955; Tello 1956; Thompson 1961; Kosok 1965; Proulx 1968, 1973; Keatinge 1974; Cardenas 1976, 1977; Mackey 1979; Mackey and Klymyshyn 1982; Keatinge and Conrad 1983; Deeds n.d.). There is no known evidence of administrative centers in the north from the Leche to the Ecuadorian border. From the Fortaleza Valley south to the Chillon Valley, the only possible Chimu center is located in the Huaura Valley (Kosok 1965). There is, however, evidence of Chimu ceramics in many of the valleys which do not have Chimu centers (Rowe 1948; Lanning 1963; Menzel 1977, James Richardson, personal communication).

Therefore, large areas which were considered part of the total Chimu empire were never under direct administrative control. This could be due to the fact that these areas were conquered in the second phase of expansion and consequently were never fully incorporated into the empire before the Inca conquest of the Chimu in the fifteenth century. An alternative explanation is that the provincial administrative policies of the Chimu had changed from an intensive to an extensive level of control during their second phase of expansion (Schreiber, this volume). More information is needed about the type of control exerted by the Chimu in these areas which do not have a visible administrative network.

Defining and ranking Chimu administrative centers

Before moving to a discussion of the function of Chimu administrative centers, it is necessary first to define the architectural variables used in identifying an administrative center and second to rank these centers. Characteristics used to define a state administrative center are derived from the Chimu capital, Chan Chan, where the major architectural classes and the repetitive architectural patterns linked to administrative functions have been identified (Moseley and Mackey 1974).

There are three major classes of architecture at Chan Chan: monumental compounds, elite compounds and SIAR (see chapter by Klymyshyn, this volume for discussion of these three). The compounds are built of adobe and tapia by means of corporate labor groups; the domestic structures, on the other hand, are constructed of cane and reed matting walls over cobble foundations and were probably constructed by the inhabitants. Repetitive architectural patterns identified within the monumental compounds include: (1) niched and non-niched patios with benches and ramps identified as possible areas for public ceremonies and/or redistributive activities (Netherly 1977); (2) U-shaped structures, or *audiencias*, that have been identified as both residences and offices of the administrators, who were nobles (Andrews 1972, 1974; Day 1973); (3) storeroom complexes, used for the storage of wealth and commodities and associated with courts and/or *audiencias*; and (4) burial platforms, used to inter the kings and their retainers. Access to rooms and patios in the majority of compounds is through either pilastered doorways, tortuous passageways or baffled entries.

Elite compounds, identified as the residences of lower nobility at Chan Chan, differ from the monumental compounds in being less formally planned and allocating a smaller percentage of interior space to courts, *audiencias* and storage complexes. Furthermore, elite compounds do not contain burial platforms, nor do they all contain *audiencias* (Klymyshyn 1976, 1982, and see chapter by Klymyshyn, this volume).

Using these architectural variables it is possible both to identify administrative centers outside Chan Chan and to rank them. However, these architectural variables alone are not sufficient for ranking the sites, and additional variables are discussed below.

Ranking

In most state societies the administrative network is indicated by a settlement system consisting of at least three levels or ranks of administrative centers (Johnson 1973). In the case of the Chimu, the data indicate that the empire is characterized by a settlement hierarchy of at least four administrative ranks above the village level.

Though grouping the Chimu administrative centers on the basis of the architectural variables discussed above is important in determining the function of the centers, these variables result in only two settlement ranks. Therefore, in order to discriminate further, both between and within ranks, it is necessary to quantify the above mentioned variables (Table

Table 1 *Architectural and quantitative variables*

Rank	Site	Valley	Compounds				Domestic habitation	Number of compounds	Size of compound†	Size of patio
			Audiencias	Patios	Storerooms	Burial platform	Perishable structures			
Primary	Chan Chan	Moche	×	×	×	×	×	45*	608 × 282 m 171 456 sq m	72 × 72 m 5184 sq m
Secondary	Manchan	Casma	×	×	×	×	×	12	360 × 240 m 86 400 sq m	140 × 80 m 11 200 sq m
	Farfán	Jequetepeque	×	×	×	×	×	6	350 × 115 m 40 250 sq m	60 × 60 m 3600 sq m
Tertiary	V–124	Viru	×	×				1	67 × 112 m 7504 sq m	?
	H–360485 Pampa Esperanza	Moche	×	×				1	76 × 63 m 4788 sq m	10 × 15 m 150 sq m
	Talambo	Jequetepeque	×	×				1	66 × 44 m 2904 sq m	24 × 34 816 sq m
	El Milagro	Moche	×	×				4‡	55 × 45 m 2475 sq m	16 × 11 m 176 sq m
	Quebrada del Oso	Chicama	×	×				3‡	62.5 × 33 m 2062 sq m	18 × 18 m 324 sq m
	Mocan	Chicama	×	×				1	51 × 29 m 1479 sq m	18 × 16 m 288 sq m
Quaternary	Quebrada Katuay	Moche	×	×				1	47.5 × 20 m 950 sq m	10 × 10 m 100 sq m
	H–186436 Pampa Rio Seco	Moche	×	×				1	23 × 22 m 506 sq m	10 × 10 m 100 sq m
	H–192483 Pampa Rio Seco	Moche	×	×				1	20 × 16 m 320 sq m	7 × 8 m 56 sq m
	H–394544 Pampa Esperanza	Moche	×	×				1	17 × 12 m 204 sq m	5 × 9 m 45 sq m

*includes monumental and elite compounds
†Size refers to one compound only
‡includes main compound and auxiliary structures

1). The first quantifier is the number of compounds and/or auxiliary structures at an administrative center. However, this can be used only to differentiate among higher ranking centers, since tertiary and quaternary centers generally have only one main compound. Therefore, it is necessary to look for other qualifiers to discriminate between the lowest ranks. The two qualifiers used are: (1) size of the compound and (2) size of the principal patio. The quantification of these architectural variables discriminates between the ranks and indicates the amount of corporate labor invested as well as site complexity (Table 1).

Besides Chan Chan, which is the primary or highest ranked settlement, the ranking indicates two secondary, six tertiary and four quaternary centers. This sample is severely limited, since it only includes sites where the architectural features are apparent; consequently, the 13 centers include only those which have been excavated and/or mapped. The 13 centers (shown in Table 1) are located in five valleys: Jequetepeque, Chicama, Moche, Viru and Casma. Within these valleys there are Chimu centers which are *not* included in this sample because they have not been excavated or mapped (Willey 1953; Kosok 1965; Netherly 1977; Rogger Ravines, personal communication). For example, ten lower-ranked Chimu centers have been identified in the Casma Valley (Thompson 1961), but there are sufficient data available on only two of these sites for the present analysis. Other Chimu centers outside of these five valleys are also not included because of insufficient data.

As stated above, the ceramic and *audiencia* seriations have been used to assign these centers to either the first or second Chimu expansion (Andrews 1972; Keatinge 1973; Topic 1977; Donnan and Mackey 1978; Kolata 1978, 1982). It should be noted that the current sample of administrative centers is heavily weighted toward those sites built during the first phase of Chimu expansion. Of the sites discussed, only the Casma Valley represents the second wave of expansion. The following discussion begins with the secondary centers, since the characteristics of the primary center, Chan Chan, have been discussed.

Secondary centers

As of this date, besides the capital, Chan Chan, the two largest and most complex centers are Farfán in the Jequetepeque Valley (Schaedel 1951a; Keatinge *et al.* 1975; Keatinge 1982; Keatinge and Conrad 1983) and Manchan in the Casma Valley (Schaedel 1951a; Thompson 1961; Mackey 1980; Mackey and Klymyshyn 1981). Farfán is dated to the first expansion while Manchan is dated to the second phase of expansion.

Both centers consist of compounds, six at Farfán and nine at Manchan, constructed of adobe. The type of administrative architecture identified at Chan Chan is found in the compounds at these centers, including patios with benches and ramps, *audiencias*, and storerooms. In the case of Manchan, though the *audiencias* differ from those found in other Chimu centers in their morphology, they are, nonetheless, equivalent in function (Andrews 1972, 1974; Kolata 1978, 1982). Both secondary centers contain rows of unadorned rooms, identified as storerooms by their uniform size, contiguous arrangement, and lack of domestic remains (Mackey and Klymyshyn 1981, 1982; Keatinge and Conrad 1983). Further, access to rooms and patios in several compounds at both centers is through pilastered doorways, tortuous passageways and baffled entries.

There are, however, major differences between Farfán and Manchan in (1) the burial of the administrators, (2) the existence of domestic perishable structures, and (3) the overall site plan. One of the six Farfán compounds has a burial platform similar to those associated with royal burials in Chan Chan (Conrad 1974, 1982; Keatinge and Conrad 1983). Manchan, on the other hand, has separate burial compounds containing high-status burials in subterranean chambers (Mackey and Klymyshyn 1982).

Only Manchan has evidence of a second socioeconomic class, as manifested by areas of perishable domestic structures (Moore 1981). Finally, both administrative centers differ in site plan. The compounds at Farfán are separated one from

another, as at Chan Chan (Keatinge 1982; Keatinge and Conrad 1983) while four of the nine compounds comprising Manchan are agglutinated and the remainder are separated. The overall site plan, as well as other architectural features, may indicate an incorporation of local building styles at Manchan (Mackey and Klymyshyn 1981).

Tertiary centers

A total of six sites identified as tertiary centers are known in the Jequetepeque, Chicama, Moche and Viru Valleys. These centers were all built during the first expansion of the empire. Four of the six consist of a main compound and two consist of a main compound and auxiliary structures (Table 1). These centers vary in construction materials. The Viru Valley center is constructed of adobe, while the remaining five are of masonry construction (Collier 1955; Keatinge 1974; Keatinge and Conrad 1983; Deeds n.d.; see chapter by T. Pozorski, this volume).

Only two of the architectural characteristics defined at Chan Chan are found in these centers: *audiencias* and patios. At El Milagro, one of the auxiliary structures also has an *audiencia*, but *audiencias* are restricted to the main compounds at other tertiary centers (Keatinge 1974). While the *audiencias* conform closely to the characteristics of those identified for the monumental and elite compounds at Chan Chan, the patios differ in size and ornamentation. At Chan Chan, a patio is a large enclosed area which may be ornamentally niched and often has benches and a ramp. Only two of the tertiary centers, Talambo in the Jequetepeque Valley and V–124 in the Viru Valley, have large patios. Except for El Milagro, which has a patio with a ramp and niched walls, the patios at the other tertiary centers are small and do not have ramps. Several of these centers have pilastered doorways (e.g., El Milagro) and most all have baffled entries. Talambo, Quebrada del Oso and Mocan (see chapter by T. Pozorski, this volume) are especially similar in site plan. None of the tertiary centers in this sample contains formalized storerooms or a burial platform. Perishable structures are found only at El Milagro. These are small windbreaks located in the fields surrounding the site. Though these are temporary structures they provide evidence for the presence of agricultural laborers at the center.

Quaternary centers

A total of four quaternary centers, dating to the first expansion of the empire, have been described within various areas of the Moche Valley (Deeds n.d.). Each consists of a single compound and all are constructed of stone. These sites are uniform in terms of their lack of elaboration and small size (Table 1). As with the tertiary centers only two architectural characteristics are noted: *audiencias* and patios. Each center has only one patio adjacent to the *audiencia*, whereas in the tertiary center there were often two patios. Patios in the quaternary centers are much smaller than in the tertiary centers, and none have ramps or niches. Only the two sites on the Pampa Rio Seco in the Moche Valley have baffled entries from the patio into the *audiencia*.

To summarize, the data indicate that the minimal definition for an administrative center is the presence of at least one compound with an *audiencia*, or its functional equivalent, and a patio. Though this definition applies to this sample, it may be altered when a larger sample is available. In terms of architectural patterning, there are similarities between the primary and secondary centers and between the secondary and tertiary centers. With regard to the settlement hierarchy, there are at least four administrative ranks; however, there does not seem to be a uniform distribution of ranks within each valley. Of the valleys under discussion, Jequetepeque, Chicama, Moche, Viru and Casma, only the Moche and Casma Valleys have three ranks represented; Jequetepeque has at least two ranks, while the Viru Valley may have only one rank. To date, quaternary centers have been identified in the Moche and Casma Valleys. More research is needed to determine the causes of this distribution pattern.

Function of administrative centers

The variables discussed in the last section were used to define different ranks of administrative centers. However, as stated above, additional information other than settlement hierarchy is needed to understand the administrative organization. This information primarily concerns administrative functions.

In the Andean literature pertaining to administrative centers, a variety of functions have been discussed. These include: (1) the housing of administrators (cf. Morris 1972); (2) the control of other settlements (Isbell and Schreiber 1978; see chapter by Schreiber, this volume); (3) the administration of natural resources such as land and water (Keatinge 1974, 1982; Keatinge and Conrad 1983); (4) the control of manpower for either economic or military purposes (Morris 1972; Netherly 1977; Julien 1978; D'Altroy 1981); (5) the collection and storage of goods as well as their shipment (Julien 1978; D'Altroy 1981); (6) the performance of ceremonial or religious activities (Morris 1972; Netherly 1977); and (7) the control of craft production for the state (Morris 1974; Moore 1981).

Many of these functions have been identified at the Chimu centers under discussion. In addition to the variables presented in Table 1, the location of administrative centers in relation to other centers and resources has been used in identifying their function. The following synchronic discussion correlates function with the hierarchical rank of the center.

Facilities for administrators

All centers have the function of providing housing for administrators. This is manifested by the *audiencias* which have been identified as possible administrative residences and offices at Chan Chan (Andrews 1972, 1974; Day 1973; Moseley 1975b).

Manchan differs from the rest of the centers in that *audiencias* at the site do not conform totally to the formal characteristics identified at Chan Chan. However, *audiencias* at Manchan do share the function of guarding access to storerooms (see chapter by Klymyshyn, this volume). In addition to *audiencias*, residential areas have been identified in association with compounds at Manchan. Such rooms, with solely a residential function, have not been identified in the monumental compounds at Chan Chan, where residential and administrative functions do not appear to involve separate architectural facilities. Alternative explanations for the residential rooms at Manchan could be that these rooms were for lower-level administrators.

Judging by the number of *audiencias*, the number of administrators in the secondary centers was low. At Manchan, there are three *audiencia* equivalents and four residential units identified for the whole center (Mackey and Klymyshyn 1982), while Farfán has three *audiencias* identified for two of the six compounds (Keatinge and Conrad 1983). El Milagro, a tertiary center, has five *audiencias* in one compound (Keatinge 1974). The number of *audiencias* within one administrative compound, therefore, does not seem to be correlated with either the size of the compound or the rank of the center within the administrative hierarchy.

Ceremonial and religious functions

Two architectural components may be correlated with ceremonial and religious functions: (1) patios and (2) burial platforms or structures. It is well documented that providing food and drink, especially *chicha*, was a major responsibility of a lord toward his subjects on the north coast (Netherly 1971:211). This function may well have been carried out in the large patios, such as those found in the primary, secondary and perhaps some of the tertiary centers.

Excavations in the patios at Manchan have revealed large vessels used to hold *chicha* sunken in the patio floor. Further, one of the major production activities carried out in the domestic structures at Manchan was the brewing of *chicha* at a scale beyond the level of family consumption (Moore 1981; Mackey and Klymyshyn 1982). Excavation at Manchan also revealed evidence of ceremonial activities within the patio in the form of a cache of common foods consisting of whole plants, such as maize, *pacae*, and animals, including a whole bird and parts of a llama.

Whether patios in all ranks of administrative structures functioned in this manner cannot be determined at this time, but it is possible that patio size correlates with function. Large patios are found in primary, secondary and in the two tertiary centers of Talambo in the Jequetepeque Valley and V–124 in the Viru Valley. The patios in both these tertiary centers are approximately 900 sq m in area, making them larger than the patios in other tertiary and quaternary centers (Table 1). It is possible that Chan Chan assumed domain over social functions within the Moche and Chicama Valleys, since no lower-ranking center in these valleys has a large patio. Although its patio size is only 176 sq m, the center of El Milagro may be an exception since it contains an elaborately niched patio similar to those found in some of the compounds at Chan Chan (Keatinge 1974).

The other architectural component with a ceremonial or religious function is the burial platform or structure. One of the manifestations of rank is the type of interment and the associated burial goods. At Chan Chan there are two kinds of burial platforms: the larger ones for royalty found in the monumental compounds, and smaller ones outside the compounds which could have been used for the nobility (T. Pozorski 1971, 1979; Conrad 1974). Both of these burial practices point to important religious ceremonies honoring the lords at their death. This is further attested to by the labor involved in the construction of the mortuary structures and the conspicuous consumption of goods and human sacrifice.

One of the Farfán compounds contains a burial platform similar to those found in the monumental compounds at Chan Chan. It has been suggested that the conquering military commander, Pacatnamú, became the first governor of this new Chimu territory and was interred in the platform (Keatinge 1982; Keatinge and Conrad 1983). Two alternative explanations are possible for the existence of the burial platform at Farfán. One is that the commander was a member of the royal dynasty, and the second is that he was given special permission by the Chimu ruler.

At the site of Manchan, built at least 100 years later than Farfán, there is a different pattern for the burials awarded high-ranking officials. Instead of a burial platform, elite burials are located in burial structures, which are separate compounds devoted only to interments. These burials are in prepared subterranean chambers or tombs, and are associated with fine textiles, ceramics and carved wooden staffs (Mackey and Klymyshyn 1982). As Netherly states (1977), lords of certain rank enjoyed the privilege of being carried in a litter. Such a litter, made of wood, with a woven fiber seat, was found in one of the burial structures and further attests to the high status of the nobles who were buried there.

Storage facilities

Storage facilities have been identified thus far only at primary and secondary centers. Since the storerooms contain the goods being controlled by the administrators, it is significant that this function is greatly curtailed at the secondary centers. A total of 49 storerooms have been identified in five of the nine compounds at Manchan. Of these 49 storerooms, eight are small and of uniform size (1.2 × 1.8 m). Of the remaining storerooms, 15 are in the medium range (4×2 to 6×5 m) while 26 are in the large range (6×6 to 11×12 m). The medium-range storerooms all have access guarded by *audiencias*, whereas the majority of the small and large types can be entered directly from an open patio. This pattern of unguarded storerooms does not occur at the capital. While the guarded access in the medium-range storerooms may suggest storage of elite goods, storerooms with unguarded access could have been used for storage of more mundane items.

The number of storerooms identified thus far at Farfán is 42 though others may exist within unexcavated compounds. These are of two sizes, 2.2×2.2 m and 5×5 m, comparable to the small- and medium-size storerooms respectively at Manchan. Twenty-two storerooms of both sizes are located behind the burial platform at Farfán. This pattern of storage associated with a burial platform has precedent in the earlier monumental compounds in Chan Chan (see chapter by Klymyshyn, this volume). The remaining twenty storerooms are all medium-size and have access guarded by an *audiencia* (Keatinge and Conrad 1983). Both types of storerooms at Farfán could have been used for elite goods and/or comestibles. However, since Farfán has only guarded storage this may emphasize the storage of elite goods over comestibles.

The number of storerooms found at each of the secondary centers is but a small fraction of the number of storerooms contained in any single compound at Chan Chan (see chapter by Klymyshyn, this volume). It is apparent that long-term stockpiling of either elite goods or comestibles was not a major function of the secondary centers, and has not been identified at all at tertiary and quaternary centers.

Control of labor

All administrative centers controlled a labor force. The difference among the centers was whether this labor force was permanent or temporary, and employed in craft and/or agricultural pursuits. In the present sample, control of a permanent lower-class population, including both craftsmen and agriculturalists, is found only at the primary center and at the secondary center of Manchan. Concentrated areas of domestic structures are located throughout both Chan Chan and Manchan. At both sites these structures are constructed of perishable materials; however, they differ in size, construction technique and materials. The number of permanent residents at Chan Chan was approximately 20 000–30 000, whereas the lower-class residents at Manchan probably never exceeded 2000. The majority of these residents at both centers consisted primarily of artisans (J. Topic 1977, 1982; Moore 1981).

One responsibility of the administrators was the recruitment of manpower for temporary or *corvée* labor which was performed either at the center or in nearby areas. Centers of all ranks utilized *corvée* labor for construction of the compounds; lower-order centers utilized it primarily in the construction and maintenance of canals and fields (see chapter by T. Pozorski, this volume). All of the centers probably employed a temporary labor force to construct the compounds. At Chan Chan and Manchan, additional laborers were necessary since the majority of the resident labor force were engaged in craft production. As Farfán and the lower-ranked centers lacked a permanent labor force, workers must have been brought in for the construction of the compounds.

In addition to the construction of the compounds, a temporary labor force was utilized at tertiary and quaternary centers during the construction of nearby canals and fields and during the agricultural cycle (Keatinge and Day 1973, 1974; Keatinge 1974, 1982; Keatinge and Conrad 1983; Deeds n.d.;

see chapter by T. Pozorski, this volume). Two lines of evidence at the tertiary centers support this notion. First, there are remains of temporary shelters in the fields surrounding El Milagro. These remains consist of small U- or L-shaped piles of stones which would have served as foundations for windbreaks (Keatinge 1974). The second line of evidence consists of the large quantity of broken bowls found in the fields around Quebrada del Oso. As Keatinge (1974) observes, these would appear to be the remains of vessels used to feed a temporary work force during construction of the nearby Intervalley canal. Since quaternary centers have a similar location in regard to canals and fields, it is assumed that they controlled a temporary labor force as well.

Control of production for the site

The type of production carried out by a center is correlated with both the rank of the center and the type of labor force it employed. Of the primary and secondary centers, both Chan Chan and Manchan controlled craft production for the state through a permanent resident artisan population. However, recent reports from the Batán Grande complex (Shimada *et al.* 1982) and from Chotuna (Christopher Donnan, personal communication) indicate that these centers, located in the Leche and Lambayeque Valleys respectively, contain evidence of copper production associated with the Chimu occupation. Since data are not yet available on these centers it is only possible to suggest that other centers in the empire may have also controlled craft production for the state. The lower-ranked centers controlled agricultural production through a temporary labor force.

Both Chan Chan and Manchan engaged in similar types of craft production, including metalworking, woodworking, weaving and spinning. At both centers textile production was carried out primarily in the domestic structures while metalworking was carried out in both domestic structures and workshops. It would appear that the majority of high quality items were produced at Chan Chan. There presently is no evidence for the production of high-status metal items at Manchan. The copper artifacts, such as needles, produced at Manchan were utilitarian in nature, and were used in the production of other items, such as textiles. High-status textiles produced at the site may have been used by resident nobles, or they may have been distributed to other nobles within the Casma Valley, or possibly exported to Chan Chan as part of tribute. Evidence was also found at Manchan in several of the domestic structures for large-scale production of *chicha*. It would appear that *chicha* was brewed in the domestic structures for use by the administrators during public ceremonies. At Chan Chan the focus of *chicha* production has not been determined; however, vessels used in its production have been found in both the compounds (Klymyshyn 1976) and domestic structures (J. Topic 1977).

Both tertiary and quaternary centers were directly involved in all stages of agricultural production, from canal construction and field preparation to planting and harvesting

(Keatinge and Day 1973, 1974; Keatinge 1974, 1982; Keatinge and Conrad 1983; Deeds n.d.). Evidence for the control of agricultural resources by these centers comes primarily from their location. All the tertiary and quaternary centers in the present sample, with the possible exception of V–124 in the Viru Valley, are located away from densely populated areas, but in close proximity to canals and fields. With the exception of Talambo in the Jequetepeque Valley and Katuay in the Moche Valley, the tertiary and quaternary centers are in the lower portion of their respective valleys. Both Talambo and Katuay are located further inland (12 km and 28 km respectively) and are near the maximum elevation canals in each valley (Keatinge 1974; Keatinge and Conrad 1983).

The tertiary center of V–124 in the Viru Valley commands access to both marine resources and extensive areas of sunken gardens or *wachaques* (Mackey 1979). It is therefore probable that this center supervised the construction and intensive farming associated with these gardens. A similar function has also been noted for La Muenga, one of the tertiary centers in the Casma Valley (Mackey and Klymyshyn 1982; T. Pozorski *et al.* 1983). Like V–124, La Muenga is located close to marine and agricultural resources, but was not involved in canal construction.

Summary and conclusions

At its peak the Chimu empire was composed of people who at the time of the Chimu conquest spoke different languages and had attained different degrees of political centralization. The degree to which such political and/or cultural differences affected the function and distribution of Chimu administrative centers remains to be demonstrated. All primary and secondary centers share two functions: control of storage and ceremonial activities. Only two of the highest-ranking centers, Chan Chan and Manchan, controlled a permanent resident population and craft production for the state.

There are, however, major differences in complexity between the primary and secondary centers. These differences emphasize the political and economic centralization of the empire, and the focus on the capital of Chan Chan. Chan Chan appears to have controlled the amount of goods which could be amassed by the secondary centers. Though there was sufficient local storage capacity to maintain these centers, the main concentration of stored goods was at the capital. Centers of all ranks may have acted as shipment points in funneling goods to other centers or directly to the capital.

Though more data are needed from other secondary centers, it appears that Chan Chan held the monopoly on elite goods, and, in the case of Manchan, regulated the kinds of goods which could be produced. This regulation of both the amount and type of goods would have kept the provincial nobility dependent on the capital for most luxury goods. The data also indicate that the lower-ranked centers specialized in control of land and water (Keatinge and Day 1973, 1974). With such a limited function, these lower-ranked centers would have had minimal need for administration (Wright and Johnson 1975). As was pointed out, administrators at the higher ranking centers are permanent, while those at the centers of lower rank may not be. In the tertiary and quaternary centers the lack of permanent administrators is correlated with the utilization of a temporary labor force and seasonal resource exploitation.

Finally it would appear that differences between the two secondary centers, Manchan and Farfán, may represent changes in administrative policies between the two expansion phases of the Chimu empire. The three changes indicated are: (1) differing functions for secondary centers; (2) integration of the local lords; and (3) change in the status of the administrators.

Farfán, in comparison to Manchan, does not appear to have had an equal role in the state's economic system, since it did not oversee a permanent labor force or administer production for the state. Like the Manchan elite, the resident administrators at Farfán must have played a role in the shipment of goods to the capital, but that appears to have been their only direct economic concern. After the second phase of expansion, secondary centers, such as Manchan, may have had a different role in the economic structure of the empire. There also appear to be other centers, dating to the second expansion, which were concerned with production (Shimada *et al.* 1982; Christopher Donnan, personal communication).

The second major policy change appears to have been in the relationship between Chan Chan administrators and the local lords. The architectural patterns of the secondary center and lower-level centers, constructed during the first phase of expansion, adhere strongly to the architectural canons of Chan Chan. On the other hand, the architectural patterns at Manchan appear to be a result of the blending of local and Chimu styles, since the Manchan patterns differ from Chan Chan in terms of architectural detail, internal use of space and construction. This blending of architectural styles seems to indicate that local traditions were not totally supplanted by imperial Chimu ones. Given this evidence, it seems that the policy in the second phase, at least as manifested by Manchan, was not to impose totally the state's pattern on the newly acquired territory. This evidence conforms to ethnohistoric sources on the Chimu which indicate that local lords were incorporated into the Chimu network (Rostworowski 1961; Netherly 1977).

There may have been a change in the policy regarding the rank of administrator sent to govern the provinces during the second expansion. This inference is based primarily on the type of burial facility found at the two secondary centers. Since burial platforms were reserved for royalty at Chan Chan, it is of interest that the provincial administrator at Farfán would be awarded this privilege. The lack of the burial platform and perhaps the absence of the true *audiencia* at Manchan could indicate that lower-ranked nobles were sent to govern in the provinces during the second phase of expansion. Further work is needed in other areas within the Chimu empire to identify the variation in the administrative network and the changes between the two phases of expansion.

Acknowledgments

The research carried out at Manchan was conducted as part of the Proyecto Chimu Sur, directed by the author and A. M. Ulana Klymyshyn. This project was funded by the National Science Foundation Grant No. BNS 8023639 (1981–82) and the Center for Field Research (Earthwatch) and National Geographic Society (1982). The excavations were authorized by the Instituto Nacional de Cultura Acuerdo No. 02/26.02.81. I thank Edwin Chavez Farfán for preparing the map used in Figure 1.

Chapter 13

**Horizontal and vertical dimensions
of prehistoric states
in north Peru**

Izumi Shimada

Introduction

The central Andes typically have been characterized as a land of environmental diversity and extremes, and Andean civilization as a whole embodies a wide repertoire of biocultural adaptations. Cardich (1975, 1980) and Rhoades and Thompson (1975) have remarked on the importance of the intense semitropical sunlight and notable diurnal temperature fluctuation for dense, permanent human occupation and cultivation at very high altitudes in the central Andes. Numerous authors have emphasized the relative importance of altitudinal over latitudinal differences in understanding Andean ecology. Yamamoto (1982) and others (e.g., Brush 1977, 1982; Thomas 1976; Webster 1971; cf. Duviols 1973) have noted the wide distribution, stability, and/or productivity of predominantly camelid-potato agropastoralism and sectorial farming.

Other significant environmental and cultural features that distinguish the central Andes from other alpine regions of the world include: the diversity and complexity of ecological zones and patterns created by vertically and horizontally condensed topography, extreme altitudinal differences, the climatic and economic importance of the nearby Pacific, and the wide distribution of (both coast and highlands) and diverse functions served by domesticated camelids (Masuda 1981; Shimada 1985a).

The preceding is not meant to be exhaustive but serves as an effective reminder of the complexity, significance and pervasiveness of dynamic interplay between the Andean environment with its peculiarities and the Andean human population. A notable culmination of this creative dynamism in the Andes has come to be called 'verticality' (see Murra 1968, 1972, 1975, and particularly 1985; Shimada 1985a). During the 1970s, 'verticality' became the symbol of a heightened awareness among students of Andean civilization of dynamic and interzonal, complementary interaction and perception. However, research into biocultural adaptations to the 'linearly oriented, non-repetitive, vertical dimension' (Patterson 1973) was too often conducted without a proper, concurrent assessment of co-existing 'horizontality' (Shimada 1982), which has been inappropriately stereotyped as 'repetitive and redundant' (Carneiro 1970; Patterson 1973). It is my impression that when 'verticality' is invoked as a descriptive, analytical or explanatory device, alternative or other variables and perspectives are not adequately explored. Just as there is a diverse range of resources and production zones along the vertical dimension of the central Andes, a similar range of variation is found horizontally (e.g. Netherly 1977; Rostworowski 1979a, 1981; Shimada 1982, 1985a, 1985b). For any given Andean population, there is a wide range of complementary arrangements that can be generated by a similarly diverse range of political and economic mechanisms.

In addressing the 'origins and development of the

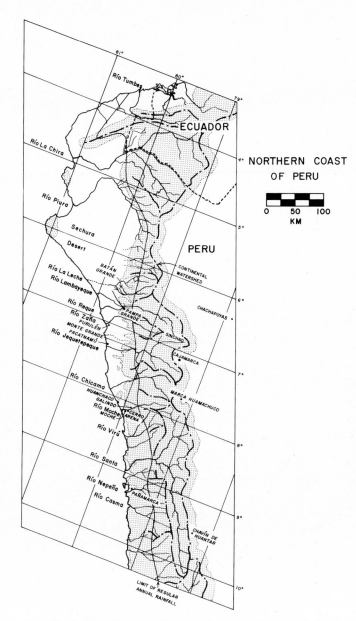

Fig. 1. Map of northern Peru showing some of the principal sites mentioned in the text

Andean state' one of our primary tasks is to identify specific complementary permutations and associated organizational forms, as well as the natural and cultural conditions and factors that gave rise to them. In this chapter, I address this issue in the context of the late Moche (Phases IV and V; *c.* A.D. 450–700) and Middle Sicán (*c.* A.D. 900–1100) cultures on the north coast of Peru (Figure 1; Table 1). These polities developed significantly different management strategies and organizational forms.

Horizontality of the late Moche polity
Political and territorial expansion

In spite of the precocity of chronological, stylistic and iconographic research and understanding, our knowledge of the variability and organization of Moche site structure and activities at the individual site and settlement system levels, as well as the associated sociopolitical organizations, is still in its infancy. Systematic or extensive excavations of Moche sites have been disturbingly scarce; there has been disproportionate emphasis on funerary and high-order ceremonial/administrative sites. Thus, the following discussion unavoidably stresses settlement pattern data typically unaccompanied by excavation data and vaguely defined 'coastal valley' or study areas (see Shimada 1982:185–187).

For the first two phases of the five-phase Moche chronology, not enough is known to speak of their culture in any detail. Even the spatial distribution of Phase I and II ceramics has not been adequately defined. These early ceramics have been reported from the Chicama and Moche Valleys of the north coast, as well as the Cerro Vicús region of the far north coast (e.g., Donnan 1978; Donnan and Mackey 1978; Larco 1948, 1963; T. Topic 1982). There have been various unverified reports of discoveries of Phase II vessels from the Leche and Zaña Valleys situated between the two extremes mentioned above.

The Viru Valley project has shown site-unit intrusion and Moche territorial expansion during Phase II into the valley from the neighboring Moche and/or Chicama Valleys to the north (e.g., Collier 1955; Strong and Evans 1950; Willey 1953). Schaedel (1972:21) believes the site of Huancaco was the regional administrative–ceremonial center with the site of Huaca Verde serving as a secondary regional center. By this time the site of Moche had emerged as a principal site, if not the capital, of the emergent intervalley polity. Hastings and Moseley (1975) have established that construction of the solid adobe Pyramid of the Sun began during Phase III and gradually expanded until Moche occupation of the site basically ceased by the end of Phase IV, around A.D. 500–550.

When we turn our attention to regions south of the Viru Valley, we find settlement pattern data that suggest a variable degree of territorial control and political integration to the south bank of the Nepeña Valley during Phases III and IV. Surveys of the Santa Valley by Donnan (1973) and Wilson (1983; this volume) clearly show extensive Moche occupation below the valley neck. The intrusive character of Moche occupation is apparent in data collected by Wilson: the sudden appearance of Moche ceramics, disruption of the local style, and shifts in settlement pattern and population distribution toward fewer, more dispersed, and larger sites (also T. Topic 1982).

Unlike the thorough territorial control and political integration of the Chicama, Moche, Viru and Santa Valleys by the Moche, surface survey data for the Nepeña Valley resemble that described for the Lambayeque and Leche Valleys to the north. Thirty-seven sites with Phase III and IV ceramics recorded by Proulx (1983) seem to form three loose clusters. We find 12 sites within a 6 km radius of the Moche regional center of Pañamarca (Figure 2). Beyond this radius, the site density drops sharply until one approaches the second cluster,

Table 1. *Regional cultural chronologies*

Lambayeque Valley (Nolan 1980)		Relative chronology (Rowe and Menzel 1967)	Batán Grande	Moche Valley (Donnan and Mackey 1978)
Colonial	1600			Colonial
		Colonial		Chimu-Inca
Chimu-Inca (A.D. 1450–1550)	1500	Late Horizon (1476–1534)	Chimu-Inca	
	1400		Chimu	
Lambayeque C (A.D. 1250–1450)				
	1300		Late Sicán (A.D. 1100–1350)	
	1200	Late Intermediate (900–1476)		Late
Lambayeque B (A.D. 1000–1250)				
	1100			Middle Chimu
	1000			
	900		Middle Sicán (A.D. 900–1100)	Early
Lambayeque A (A.D. 700–1000)		4 (800–900)		
	800			
		3 (750–800) Middle Horizon	Early Sicán (A.D. 700–900)	
	700	2B (700–750)		
		2A (650–700)		V
	600	1B (600–650)		
		1A (550–600)	Late Moche (A.D. 450–700)	IV
Late Moche (A.D. 450–700)	500			III Moche
	400			
				II
	300	Early Intermediate (400 B.C.–A.D.500)		
				I
	200			
	100			
	A.D.			Gallinazo

which includes eight sites within 6 km of the Nepeña and Vinchamarca River confluence. The last cluster is roughly 40–45 km inland around the confluence of the Nepeña and Salitre Rivers. Seven sites form this cluster and Proulx's Figure 1 shows three of them yielding both Recuay and Moche ceramics. Overall, Moche occupation focused on the 'middle valley;' control of the upper valley was tenuous (Proulx 1983:90; Daggett, this volume).

Northward expansion during Phase III may well have reached the south bank of the Zaña Valley and by the end of Phase IV the Moche intervalley polity appears to have established continuous territorial control as far north as the north bank of the Leche Valley.

The site of Pacatnamú situated on the north bank of the Jequetepeque Valley at the mouth of the Jequetepeque River has various Moche monumental adobe constructions and apparently served as a major religious–political center that included elite burial structures (Ubbelohde-Doering 1967). Eling's (1978) surveys and excavations revealed extensive Moche III and IV field and irrigation systems in Talambo on the northern edge of the Jequetepeque Valley. Moche ceramics and burials are also found at the sites of San José de Moro (Disselhoff 1959) and near the south base of Cerro Farfán.

Walter Alva (1982: personal communication; Alva and Alva 1985) reports that in the Zaña Valley, Moche III and IV occupation extends from mid-valley to the Pacific coast. The well-known 'Inca' trunk road that passes through the middle sectors of the Zaña, Lambayeque and Leche Valleys is likely to have been formalized, if not constructed, during Phases III and IV by the intruding Moche (Figure 3). Sites yielding Phase IV ceramics are closely associated with the road on both sides north of the Zaña Valley. For example, an unnamed site with various platform mounds and one pyramid immediately northwest of the village of Palomino occupies the south end of the Rinconada de Collique which links the Zaña and Lambayeque Valleys. At the north end of the Rinconada is the major site of Collique-Cipan (see Kosok 1959, 1965; Nolan 1980; Schaedel 1951a, 1966b, 1972; Shimada 1976, 1982), occupying a strategic location for operation of the intervalley Collique Canal.

Further north along the road we find some bichrome Moche ceramics (Phase IV?) at Cerro Patapo and Tres Tomas, both strategic in respect to the Antigua Taymi Canal. Evidence of Moche (Phases IV and V) habitations and burials is found at various sites in the mid-Leche Valley (e.g., Huacas del Pueblo Batán Grande, Facho, Soledad, Chepa, La Merced, and Lucia-Cholope; Shimada 1981b, 1982). The north–south road and associated Moche settlements, as well as a

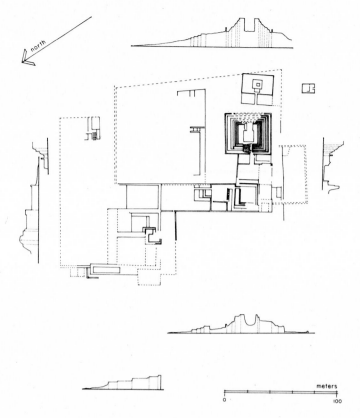

Fig. 2. Architectural drawing of the site of Pañamarca in the Nepeña Valley (redrawn from Schaedel 1951b)

three-level settlement hierarchy with the capital at Moche, form a strong basis for arguing state status for the Moche polity during Phase IV.

In the Lambayeque and Leche Valleys, however, the Moche occupation appears to have been limited to the middle portion. For example, the site of Cerro Boró (Rodriguez 1967) with its concentric masonry walls and major platforms atop a rugged hill in the middle of the valley bottom land was the westernmost Moche settlement of Phase IV. Schaedel (1951a) suggests that the presence of an indigenous polity center at the site of Colluz just south of the modern settlement of Pomalca effectively prevented coastward expansion by the Moche population. More extensive mid-valley occupation in the Leche, then, may imply the absence of a strong local policy.

Overall, Moche occupation north of the Zaña Valley suggests concern with north–south movement and control of water. At the same time, among the sites mentioned for this region none are clearly distinguished as regional administrative centers. I suspect, however, that the sites of Collique-Cipan and Huaca Soledad are likely candidates.

Moche horizontality and discontinuous territoriality

Here I consider a series of hypothesized colonies in the Vicús region of the far north coast, the Huarmey Valley on the north-central coast, and the Chincha Islands off the south coast of Peru, serving needs of the subsistence and political economy of the Moche on the north coast (compare this distribution with the map in Donnan 1978, p. 1).

The Vicús region has been an archaeological enigma. Larco (1967:7) laments that no scientific excavation has yet been conducted. This is partly due to the peculiar mixture of ceramic styles, techniques, and forms that suggest contact with areas to the south. Larco (1967, his figures 4 and 5, for example) illustrates double spout-bridge, double stirrup spout, and modelled jars closely resembling those of the Paracas, Nazca and Moche cultures. Recent analyses of artifacts looted from tombs in Loma Negra highlighted the problematical nature of the true cultural identity and the chronological significance of those artifacts with stylistic, morphological, and technical affiliations with coastal cultures to the south (e.g., Disselhoff 1971, 1972; Horkheimer 1965; Jones 1979; Lanning 1963; Lapiner 1976; Lechtman *et al.* 1982; Matos 1965–66).

Donnan (quoted by Lechtman *et al.* 1982:5), looking from the north-coast Moche perspective, argues that what Lumbreras (1979) calls 'Vicús/Mochica' ceramics from Loma Negra are attributable to Phase I and II, while the sheet metal objects from there show 'artistic canons that are most similar to the fineline drawing of Moche III or IV.' He also suggests that this apparent chronological difference may be due to the possibility that 'the stylistic canons of sheet metal representations were somewhat ahead of the fineline ceramic tradition' (quoted in Lechtman *et al.* 1982:5).

Based on his study of the Banco Popular del Peru collection of ceramics from the Vicús region, Lumbreras (1979), on the other hand, distinguishes the Vicús/Vicús local and Vicús/Moche styles, arguing that the latter is a product of a colony of selected artisans established and controlled by the Moche polity centered in an area farther south. He (1979:118–144) notes significant iconographic divergence between Vicús/Moche and north-coast Moche ceramics and questions the applicability of a stylistic/chronological scheme based on the latter for the former. The Vicús/Moche ceramics in the Banco Popular collection show a mixing of features that are individually effective chronological markers in north-coast Moche ceramics. Thus, Lumbreras (1979:33) assigns a wide time span of 100 B.C. to A.D. 600 to the Vicús/Moche materials. Matos' (1965–66) survey suggests that the Vicús/Moche may have persisted until *c.* A.D. 650–700 (Phase V; also see Rowe 1942).

In spite of some chronological ambiguity, what is evident about the Vicús/Moche is that its style is Moche and its metal objects display impressive metallurgical mastery, productivity, and morphological variation (Figure 4; e.g., Disselhoff 1971, 1972; Jones 1979; Lapiner 1976; Lechtman *et al.* 1982). Although 'Questions about extraction of raw materials from the environment, the organization of production, and craft specialization' cannot be readily answered (Lechtman *et al.* 1982:29), the quantitative and qualitative features of the Loma Negra metal objects point to the considerable political and/or economic importance of the Vicús region to the Moche intervalley polity as a whole. I concur with Lumbreras in

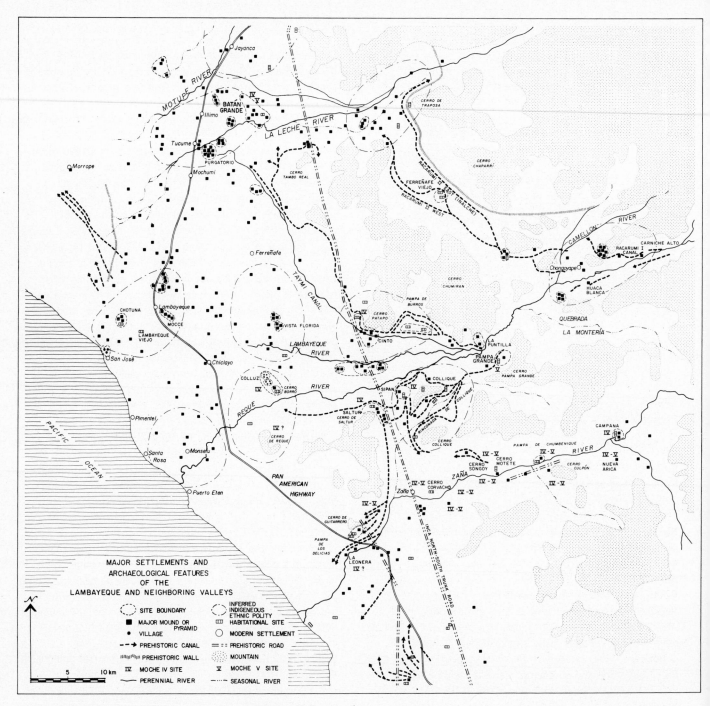

Fig. 3. Distribution of major sites in the Lambayeque Valley complex

arguing that the Vicús/Moche products were locally manufactured by a closely supervised colony of Moche artisans. However, the inferred presence of a Moche colony does not imply that the vast expanse that separates the Batán Grande region in the Leche Valley and the Vicús region (170 km) was under Moche control; rather, we are speaking of horizontally discontinuous territoriality (Shimada 1982; also see Ramírez 1985; Rostworowski 1985). Although it is tempting to suggest that the luxurious metal objects were part of a

mutual agreement between local and Moche elites that allowed the latter access to certain resources and/or production zones, the available data neither support nor refute the idea.

Available evidence suggests southern examples of Moche discontinuous territoriality in the Huarmey Valley on the north-central coast and the Chincha Islands off the south coast. The Huarmey Valley is over 100 km south of the Moche regional center of Pañamarca in the Nepeña Valley. There is only a minimal amount of evidence attesting to contact with the

Fig. 4. A Vicus/Moche copper artifact from the site of Loma Negra. Reprinted with the Permission of the Museo Chileno de Arte Precolombino, Artifact No. 0361

Moche in the intervening area. The Casma Valley, just 30 km south of Pañamarca, thus far has yielded few ceramics that are recognizably Moche in style. At the same time, the paucity of evidence for the Moche presence may relate to the general problem of identification of Early Intermediate Period occupation in that valley.

Evidence for Moche occupation of the Huarmey Valley some 70 km south of the Casma is considerably stronger and varied. Thus far Duccio Bonavia (personal communication) has identified seven sites with Moche IV ceramics, with one site having Phase III ceramics as well. Tabio (1977:112–113) also attests to the presence of definite Moche ceramics at sites on both banks of the Huarmey River. Overall, these sites cover much of the lower and middle valley, although no sites near the coast have yielded Moche ceramics. Tabio (1977:113) reports a site (his H–100B) near the confluence of the Huayup and Yanaparin Rivers, *c.* 35 km inland, yielding fine Moche ware. Unlike the northern counterpart in the Vicús region, Moche ceramics in the Huarmey show no readily apparent regional idiosyncrasies. However, there may well be some iconographic differences.

In addition to the ceramics and tombs, Conklin (1978) describes high-quality Moche textiles (Phase V) from the Huarmey Valley. The textile pieces, taken together, show a close similarity in design to those from the central region of the Moche polity, while, at the same time, there are some technical differences (Conklin 1978:313, 324).

The above lines of evidence are suggestive of political control over much of the Huarmey Valley by the Moche polity that perhaps expanded originally in Phase III. Whether this expansion was military in nature remains to be seen. Conquest and political integration may have been preceded by the establishment of missionary or exchange/trade outposts (Shimada 1981b:441–442), somewhat reminiscent of the *pochtecas* in the Aztec world.

The extent of the Moche effort to gain access to as broad a range of resources and production zones along the Peruvian coast as possible is dramatically illustrated by the Moche artifacts recovered from guano deposits found on some of the 30-odd offshore (5–20 km) islands, including the Chincha Islands off the south coast (Kubler 1948; G. E. Hutchinson [described in Kubler 1948]; T. J. Hutchinson 1873). Colonial writers also attest to the prehispanic use of guano as an agricultural fertilizer. Diez de San Miguel (1964:245), Cieza de León (1946:232–2) and others emphasize the importance of guano for maize cultivation in southern Peru and the considerable distance people travel to procure it. Julien (1985) notes that guano adds valuable phosphate and nitrogen to the arid far south-coast soil deplete in organic nutrients and may increase maize harvest by as much as two- to three-fold. For the north coast, Netherly (1977:50) reports that, although colonial descriptions are rare, the prehispanic exploitation of guano for agricultural uses is certain.

These guano islands may have had additional economic significance serving as fishing/processing bases and hunting grounds for penguins, seals and sea lions. Hutchinson (quoted by Kubler 1948:49) questions the value of badly leached guano on the Islas de Lobos off the Lambayeque coast. Fonseca and Richardson (1978) suggest that sea lions rather than guano may have been the object of prehistoric expeditions to these offshore islands. Donnan (1978:136) describes the sea lion as a 'significant animal in Moche art,' often painted or modelled in ceramics, and believes their stomach stones are an important part of the Moche curing process (also see Gillin 1945:124; Rostworowski 1981:113). Larco (1938:97) reports their teeth accompanying human burials and M. Shimada (Shimada and Shimada 1981) has identified their bones in refuse at the site of Pampa Grande (Phase V), Lambayeque Valley.

As much as the northern offshore islands such as Lobos de Afuera and Lobos de Tierra were used as processing bases (salting and/or drying fish) by fisherman from different communities taking advantage of the surrounding fishing grounds (Netherly 1977:47–48; also Murphy 1925), the Chincha and other southern islands could have accommodated fishermen and guano miners from various coastal regions. In regard to the northern offshore islands, Netherly (1977:45) envisions them to have been multifunctional (fishing stations and sanctuaries), available to different 'ethnic groups or social divisions.'

However, the significance of the data from these islands to this paper derives from (1) their dispersed nature, particularly to the south, (2) the availability of immense quantities of guano and other marine resources to the Moche, and (3) the absence of any readily recognizable evidence attesting to their exploitation by populations on the south and central coast contemporary with the Moche. Kubler (1948:40–41) remarked:

> That the ceramics of Nazca and Ica valleys should be lacking is astonishing, in the presence of Moche artifacts that are usually supposed not to extend so far south. In any case, a revision of our concepts of Moche extension is clearly indicated ... Such a revision at once suggests the hypothesis that the success of the Moche cultural pattern may have depended in part upon a technique of guano fertilization of arid coastal valleys.

Clearly, given its well-known beneficial effects, guano could have been a vital part of agricultural intensification and/or expansion into marginal zones (see, e.g. Eling 1978) and as such would have been of considerable concern to the Moche polity. Moche exploitation of a number of large guano deposits (presumably contemporaneous) off the north coast (e.g., Macabí and Guañape Islands) as well as on the Chincha Islands argues a large and widespread demand. We must consider the distinct possibility of the Moche as a prehistoric 'naval force' monopolizing *access* to the offshore islands. Under these conditions, guano mining, fishing and/or hunting rights might have been granted to varied ethnic groups of different geographical base (both Moche and non-Moche) in exchange for a portion of the guano production or some other tribute such as elite sumptuary goods much like the late prehispanic arrangement described by Ramírez (1985). This situation differs from the resource sharing described for the late prehispanic central coast (Dillehay 1979), where some material indications of concurrent occupation or exploitation have been found.

What I have described thus far contrasts significantly with Schaedel's (1972:20) earlier view that 'The Moche polity at its maximum expansion would have had a capital in the Moche, complete occupation of the Chicama, Viru and Santa Valleys, and strategically located centers in the Nepeña, Jequetepeque and Lambayeque (with no trace as yet in the intervening valley of Zaña), and possible outlying centers in the Leche.' The horizontal extent of the polity and the concepts of horizontal archipelago and discontinuous territoriality mark the difference.

The Moche V transformation

The impressive horizontality achieved during Phase IV was significantly eclipsed during the relatively brief Phase V, which may have begun as early as A.D. 550 or as late as A.D. 600 and lasted to A.D. 650–700. This is a period when many parts of the central Andes saw the collapse of the old and establishment of new social and political orders. Moche occupation of the site of Moche essentially ended by the end of Phase IV (Mackey and Hastings 1982; Moseley and Deeds 1982; T. Topic 1982) and concurrently we see a series of major, nucleated Moche V settlements at valley necks (e.g., Galindo, Ventanilla, and Pampa Grande in the Moche, Jequetepeque and Lambayeque Valleys respectively), strategic for control of the best agricultural lands, water, and intake points for major canals and coast–highland movements. T. Topic and J. Topic (1982) note that Moche V sites of the middle Moche Valley were heavily fortified and clustered at points which could have controlled coast–highland and Moche–Viru traffic. The demographic and political centers of Phase V shift inland and northward with the extensive (*c.* 6 km) ceremonial city of Pampa Grande emerging as the last capital of the Moche intervalley polity (Figure 5). Although diagnostic Phase V ceramics have been reported from the southern half of the north coast, the viability of Moche political control of the southern north coast is questionable (see Donnan 1973; Schaedel 1951b). On the other hand, Matos (1965–66) reports finding Moche V ceramics at various sites in the Vicús–Piura region and my recent excavations (Shimada 1982; Shimada 1981b) have revealed Phase V Moche burials, and domestic as well as elaborate adobe 'ceremonial' constructions in central Leche Valley. Moche V was essentially a northern north-coast phenomenon.

Fieldwork at Pampa Grande in 1973, 1975 and 1978 revealed that accompanying the above settlement and territorial shift was a wide range of material, organizational and ideological changes most likely systemic in nature: (1) unprecedented architectural expanse, diversity (in form, size and location) and nucleation, implying attendant population concentration and functional differentiation, (2) the appearance of large-scale, standardized storage facilities with controlled access, (3) new construction techniques, including 'chamber-and-fill,' 'fitted tiles,' 'log roofing/flooring' and 'encased columns,' (4) cursory treatment of sacrificial burials, (5) decrease in the range and overall frequency of ceramic representations of earlier Moche 'mythological' figures, and (6)

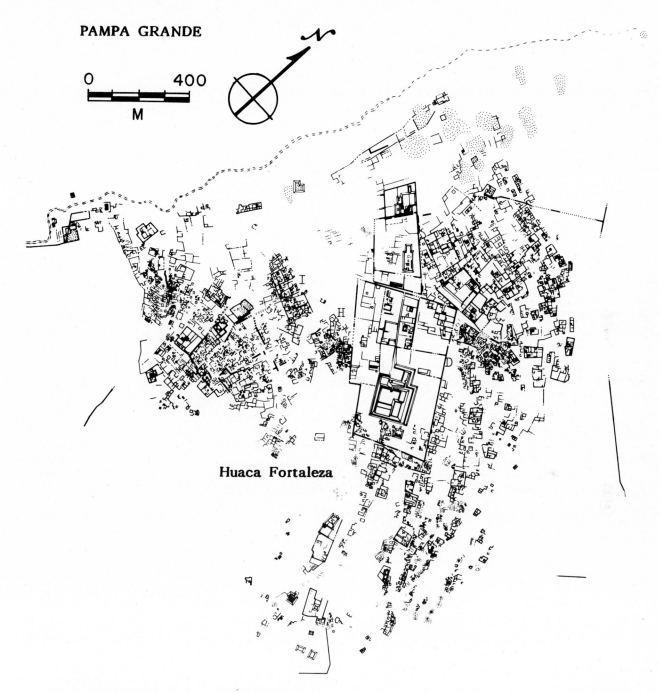

PAMPA GRANDE

0   400

M

Huaca Fortaleza

Fig. 5. Architectural map of the site of Pampa Grande

new ceramic forms and popularity of blackwares, including bowls and plates (Anders 1977, 1981; Haas 1985; Shimada 1976, 1978, 1982; Shimada and Cavallaro 1986; Shimada and Shimada 1981). The blackwares include those that suggest revival of Early Horizon ceramics and imitation of forms introduced from the south. Fine blackware bowls emerge as a major status item.

At least a three-level administrative hierarchy within the site of Pampa Grande is suggested by (1) the roughly concentric distribution of rectangular walled enclosures and irregular

agglutinated habitational structures away from the centrally situated, enormous enclosure (600×400 m) which houses the Huaca Fortaleza [Huaca Grande] pyramid (basal dimensions of *c*. 275×180 m and 55 m high; Figure 6), and (2) the supervisory requirements of spatially dispersed, segmentary or small incremental craft production (e.g., metalworking, weaving, figurine manufacture), documented through extensive excavations (Shimada 1978, 1982; Shimada and Shimada 1981). While small-scale copper working and weaving were carried out in the middle of the industrial sector, the production of

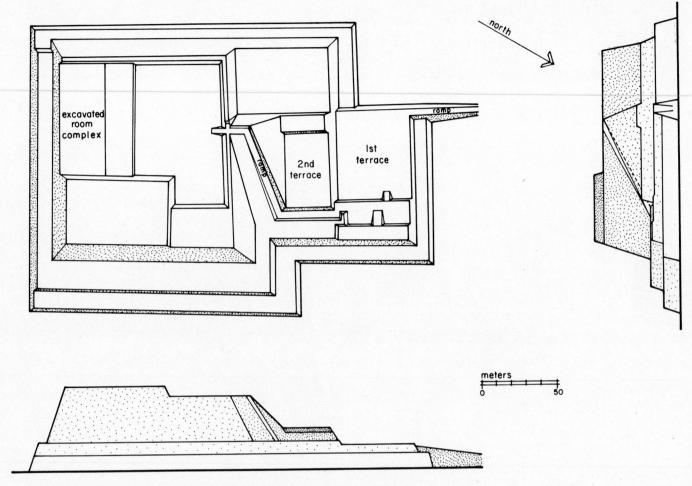

Fig. 6. A reconstruction drawing of the Huaca Fortaleza pyramid at Pampa Grande

sumptuary *Spondylus* artifacts was carried out adjacent to a major pyramidal platform within a spacious walled enclosure (Figure 7; Shimada 1982; Shimada and Shimada 1981). Large-scale cotton processing seems to have occurred in a large courtyard surrounded by a niched wall with a bench, drum frames and racks of complete deer antlers within a formal adobe enclosure. Daily administration was undoubtedly improved by the extensive network of streets throughout the site. Overall, a strong case can be made for a state-level urban society at Moche V Pampa Grande. Emergence of the urban Moche V state at Pampa Grande, however, must be seen within the context of transitory social and, to a lesser degree, geographical circumscription. It was an unprecedented situation: a new capital was rapidly established while its dominion and perhaps even ideological base were undergoing significant change.

The nature and extent of the impact of the erosion of the southern half of the Moche coast-wide horizontality are difficult to assess. Although the inventory of subsistence and nonsubsistence resources present at Pampa Grande is impressive (Shimada 1982; Shimada and Shimada 1981), we do not have a comparable list or any reliable measure of the total resource extractive/productive capability of the Moche IV polity (see, T. Pozorski 1976; Shimada and Shimada 1985:10, 19).

Although we cannot directly ascertain access to offshore islands, the presence of a wide range and large quantities of marine products, including penguin, sea lion, and deep-sea fish at such inland sites as Pampa Grande (50 km inland) and Galindo argues that the Moche polity retained much of its traditional maritime orientation and power.

At the same time, based on the population structure, diet and varied functions inferred from large quantities of camelid remains recovered at Pampa Grande and other contemporaneous sites, together with ethnohistorical, ethnographic and physiological data, we can strongly argue that llamas (and perhaps even alpacas) were bred and herded on the north coast during Moche V and most likely considerably earlier (Shimada 1982; Shimada and Shimada 1981, 1985). In discussing the verticality and horizontality of the Moche polity, we must not ignore llama caravans originating out of the north coast under the control of the Moche polity. The inferred horizontal archipelagos may have been linked by sea and land. In addition to those Moche ceramic representations of llamas with cargo illustrated elsewhere (Shimada and Shimada 1985),

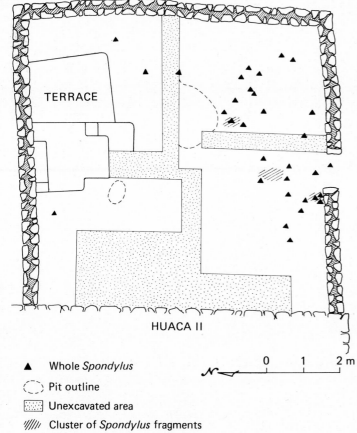

▲ Whole *Spondylus*

⬭ Pit outline

▦ Unexcavated area

▨ Cluster of *Spondylus* fragments

Fig. 7. *Spondylus* workshop adjacent to a major pyramid (Huaca II) at Pampa Grande

we should note others that illustrate llamas with basket loads of fish (Museo Amano, Lima) and *Strombus* sp. (Figure 8). Imported *Spondylus* sp. and *Strombus* sp. from coastal Ecuador may have been carried by coastal llama caravans under Moche control.

Moche verticality

Reliable archaeological evidence attesting to large- or small-scale Moche intrusion inland beyond the coastal *yunga* zone or the highest intake point of the coastal irrigation system (see Shimada 1982:185–187) is quite limited for Moche phases. Terada and Matsumoto (1985) point to the discovery of a fragment of a Moche stirrup spout vessel in a layer corresponding to their Cajamarca Media Sub-Phase A (final portion of the Early Intermediate Period ?) in their excavation in the Cajamarca Basin. Conversely, for this time, I know of no significant cluster of Cajamarca, Huamachuco or Recuay artifacts in the coastal region below the *yunga* zone (see Proulx 1982; Tello 1956; J. Topic and T. Topic 1983a; cf. T. Topic 1982:274) that may indicate their enclaves.

The best-known evidence for some form of contact between the Moche and its highland-based neighbor, Recuay, are iconographic elements (e.g., 'dragon' or 'moon monster' or 'crested animal') found on decorated ceramics (e.g., Bankmann 1980; Bruhns 1977; Reichert 1982). On the basis of his study of Recuay and Moche ceramics depicting a 'crested animal,' Reichert (1982:290) concludes that the 'contact' between these two populations was 'quite limited' and 'superficial.' He observes that 'The misinterpretation of rigid Recuay artistic canons by Moche artists suggests that these coastal people were not intimately aware of the nature of highland society.'

Although sharing of some basic ideological concepts and features between Moche and contemporaneous north highland populations is likely, specific behavioral or organizational implications and correlates have not yet been defined. Although localized, small-scale barter between coastal and neighboring highland communities and elite gift exchange of prestigious items probably existed during this time, I do not see evidence for large or specialized exchange or trade. I suspect the Moche polity was more concerned with control (or at least sharing) of the *yunga* or *chaupiyunga* zone where mineral

Fig. 8. Moche drawing depicting llama carrying *Strombus* shells (redrawn from Kutscher 1983: Figure 305)

resources, coca cultivation, San Pedro cactus stands and the intake for coastal irrigation systems occur. In fact, the establishment of major Moche V settlements may well have been partially conditioned by the threat of coastward expansion by the emergent Cajamarca polity in the north highlands.

Essentially I see a coast-centric resource base with minimal or limited vertical complementarity continuing throughout the Moche sequence. Cajamarca expansion toward the coast, as discussed later, seems to have occurred during a period of sociopolitical destructuring on the coast.

The Sicán polity and its changing verticality and horizontality

Middle Cajamarca – Early Sicán articulation: verticality
With the collapse of the Moche polity *c*. A.D. 700, we see a significantly different coast–highland relationship. Our understanding of the relevant times in the Cajamarca Basin has been greatly improved by recent Japanese excavations. As noted earlier, the phase crucial to our discussion is the Cajamarca Media with its Sub-Phases A and B, roughly equivalent to Reichlens' (1949) Cajamarca II (Terada and Matsumoto, 1985). During Sub-Phase A (prior to Middle Horizon 1b or the arrival of Wari influence in Huamachuco), they see the Classic and Floral Cursive decoration coexisting in time and space, and characterize it as a time of regional integration. The former, however, disappears by Sub-Phase B, during which kaolin Cajamarca ceramics with Floral Cursive decoration spread out into a wide area (e.g., Chachapoyas and *ceja de montaña*, Batán Grande, some Moche sites, Wari and the surrounding area, and Callejón de Huaylas). A large kaolin sherd of the Cajamarca Floral Cursive style was found atop Huaca Fortaleza [Huaca Grande] at Pampa Grande.

The spread of Floral Cursive ceramics, however, must be seen within the context of the fluctuating sociopolitical and perhaps even natural conditions of the Middle Horizon, i.e., Moche V transformation and collapse, as well as expansion and collapse of the Wari 'empire.' My reading of the above is that Cajamarca Media Sub-Phase A dates up to the end of Moche IV and that Sub-Phase B corresponds to Moche V and the following Early Sicán (see below). I hypothesize that coastward expansion of the Cajamarca population (Floral Cursive; Sub-Phase B) closely coincided with the Moche IV and V transition and was significantly curtailed by the expansion of the Middle Sicán polity (see below) toward the end of the Middle Horizon.

The post-Moche V cultural tradition centered in the Batán Grande region of Lambayeque is designated as Sicán. It is subdivided into three phases (Table 1). Early Sicán (*c*. A.D. 700–900) is poorly known. No population center or physical expression of a centralized polity has been identified. Middle Sicán (*c*. A.D. 900–1100) corresponds to the classic period during which artifacts bearing its distinct art style and iconography spread so far south as Pachacamac (Figure 9). It is also known for large-scale arsenical copper production,

unprecedented funerary practices and offerings and numerous monumental pyramids constructed in the chamber-and-fill format (e.g., Carcedo and Shimada 1985; Shimada 1981b, 1982, 1985a, 1985b; Shimada and Cavallaro, 1986; Shimada and Elera 1984; Cavallaro 1982). Other than ceramics, little is known of the Late Sicán (*c*. A.D. 1100–1350). Here we are concerned with the Early (*c*. A.D. 700–800) and Middle Sicán (*c*. 800–1000).

Crucial data on the Cajamarca–Sicán relationship come from the 5 m stratigraphy at Huaca del Pueblo Batán Grande that spans nearly 1100 years of the regional prehistory starting *c*. A.D. 450. The stratigraphy and associated radiocarbon dates (Table 2) show that, without any significant hiatus, Moche V occupation was succeeded by those associated with (1) *paleteada* (paddled ware), (2) blackware showing strong iconographic and morphological similarities to Pachacamac and Wari artifacts of Middle Horizon 2 (Shimada and Elera 1984), and (3) what have been popularly called 'Coastal Cajamarca' ceramics dominated by painted plates with annular bases

Fig. 9. Middle Sicán blackware with hallmark 'Sicán lord' representation

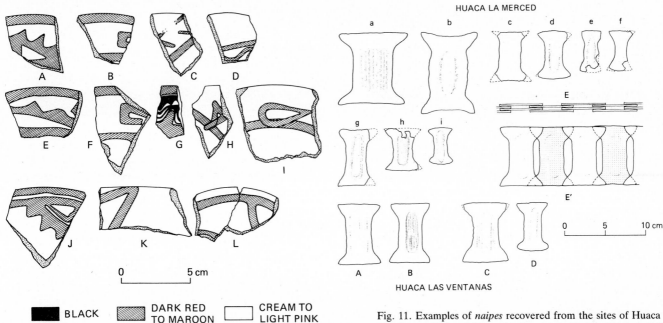

Fig. 10. Examples of Coastal Cajamarca ceramics excavated from Huaca del Pueblo Batán Grande

Fig. 11. Examples of *naipes* recovered from the sites of Huaca La Merced (1-i) and Huaca Las Ventanas (A-D). drawings E-E' illustrate how *naipes* were found stacked together at Huaca Menor

(Figure 10; Shimada 1982, 1983, 1985b; Shimada *et al.* 1981; Shimada and Elera 1984).

'Coastal Cajamarca' ceramics, characterized by forms, decorative styles and motifs that resemble Cajamarca plates, are found widely from the Jequetepeque (Ravines 1982) to Leche Valleys. The oxidized paste with mica suggests local coastal manufacture. In spite of their continuity until the end of Middle Sicán and the wide range of contexts in which they occur, they remain conservative in decorative style and design, and forms, and never seem to approach the technical quality seen in the prestigious Sicán blackware.

The conservatism and relatively low quality craftsmanship may relate to the rapid expansion of the Middle Sicán polity into the *yunga* zone and attendant diminution of the Cajamarca sphere of influence and territorial control. Significantly, Terada and Matsumoto (1985) note the reduced distribution of Cajamarca Tardía (Semi-Cursive) Cajamarca ceramics. Although Middle Cajamarca Sub-Phase B ceramics have been recovered from Middle Sicán construction fill, thus far no Cajamarca ceramics have been excavated from Middle Sicán floor or primary contexts in Batán Grande.

Middle Sicán horizontality

Sicán verticality focused on sharing with Cajamarca population(s) or controlling the *yunga* or *chaupiyunga* zones. Horizontality may have achieved a significant new dimension with a hypothesized maritime trade system linking coastal Ecuador and Peru using some standardized medium of exchange (Shimada 1985b, 1985c). This paper discusses only the *naipes* used in the hypothesized system (for fuller discussion of horizontality see Shimada 1985c).

Over the course of seven field seasons in Batán Grande, we have encountered a wide range of metal objects in looted and scientifically excavated Middle Sicán burials. What interests us are I- or double T-shaped hammered and cut sheet metal (arsenical copper) objects called *naipes* (Figure 11). The largest cache of *naipes* recorded for Batán Grande comes from an enormous Middle Sicán (C-14 date of 915±50 BP; GrN–5474) shaft tomb at Huaca Menor in the Sicán Precinct (Figure 12) that measured 14 m to a side and at least 20 m in depth (Pedersen 1976). Grave offerings included 17 human sacrifices, one layer each of *Spondylus* sp., lapis lazuli and cinnabar, large quantities of 'laminitas de oro,' an estimated 500 kg of 'copper' artifacts such as spear points and hoe blades, as well as a large quantity of *naipes* orderly arranged and stacked according to different shape–size categories (Pedersen 1976:64). Each stack contained some 500 specimens. The 25 specimens measured by Pedersen (1976:65) varied in length and width from 7.3 to 5.0 cm and 5.3 to 3.2 cm respectively.

Naipes are quite common in Middle Sicán tombs; a small tomb excavated in 1981 atop the Huaca La Ventanas pyramid revealed, along with diagnostic Middle Sicán blackware and tri-color jars, a package of some 20 *naipes*, each about 4.2×2.1 cm in size, placed in front of a seated, cross-legged adult body. A partially looted tomb at the western base of the principal pyramid of Huaca La Merced salvaged by C. Elera, M. Paredes and V. Pimentel (Elera 1984) contained at least four packages of small (*c.* 4.7×1.5 cm) *naipes*, as well as lesser numbers of specimens of at least four larger shape–size categories (up to 10 cm in length, 8.5 cm in width and 44 g in weight). We suspect that this tomb originally contained many more *naipe* specimens. The associated ceramics belong to early

Table 2. *Relevant radiocarbon dates*

Sample context and material	Laboratory no.	Date (f = fractionation corrected; p = preliminary)
Pampa Grande		
burnt wooden post atop platform mound (Huaca 18), Sector H	A–1704	1280±70 B.P.; A.D. 670
charred cotton, floor of elite compound ('Deer House'; Unit 14)	SMU–399	1300±60 B.P.; A.D. 650
charred cotton, floor of burnt platform mound in rectangular enclosure (Unit 16)	SMU–644	1300±55 B.P.; A.D. 650
burnt cane, roof of *Spondylus* workshop, rectangular compound (Unit 15)	SMU–682	1380±40 B.P.; A.D. 570f
burnt wooden post, floor of multi-terraced room, Unit 45, Sector H	A–1705	1380±70 B.P.; A.D. 570
Huaca Las Ventanas		
charcoal from firepit immediately below Wall 1, Eastern Sector	Beta–3403	1090±60 B.P.; A.D. 860
wooden beam of shaft tomb roof, Southern Sector	SMU–1070	1050±70 B.P.; A.D. 900p
burnt roof, adobe enclosure overlying shaft tomb (SMU–1070)	Beta–3402	980±50 B.P.; A.D. 970
Huaca Menor		
wooden bow from gravelot of looted shaft tomb	GrN–5474	915±50 B.P.; A.D. 1035
Huaca El Corte		
charcoal from burnt roof atop Platform Mound 1	Beta–1802	985±65 B.P.; A.D. 965

All dates are uncorrected.

Middle Sicán with an estimated age of *c.* A.D. 900–950.

In western Mexico and coastal Ecuador, similar objects, typically inverted-T and to a lesser extent I or double-T in shape and labelled 'copper axe money,' have been long known (e.g., Easby *et al.* 1967; Estrada 1957, 1961; Holm 1966–67, 1975). Most of the Ecuadorian specimens have been recovered from caches and tombs in the middle and lower reaches of the Guayas River dating from *c.* A.D. 800–900 to the time of Spanish conquest (Huancavilca–Manteño and Milagro–Quevedo cultures; Holm 1966–67:141, 1971:11). Holm (1975:2–3) argues that 'copper axe money,' much like modern coins, with portability, durability, standardized shape, size and probably weight, as well as intrinsic value, served as a medium of exchange. Importantly, he (1966–67:140–41, 1975:9–10) believes the metal for axe money production or the money itself to have been *imported* to coastal Ecuador from elsewhere as the region consists of recent alluvial and fluvial formations with very little ore potential. The distribution of axe money suggests that it was highly valued and differentially accessible to different sectors of the society. This hypothesized tradition of long-distance trade using some standardized medium of exchange is reasonable in the light of the recent ethnohistorical documentation of *mindalá* traders in late prehispanic Ecuador (Salomon 1978).

In contrast to the Ecuadorian situation, in Peru historical data preceded archaeological indications of possible standardized tokens of exchange ('copper'). The *Aviso* published in 1970 by Rostworowski (also see 1975a, 1977b; cf. Pease 1985 and Ramírez-Horton 1982) speaks of 6000 Chincha *mercaderes* on the south coast of Peru during Inca domination of the Andes. These *mercaderes* described as travelling by sea to and from coastal Ecuador were reported to have bought and sold using copper. The Lambayeque region is said to have participated in this maritime economic system.

On the basis of close similarities (e.g., size, shape, weight, manufacturing techniques, packaging, contexts, dating, and composition), I have argued elsewhere (Shimada 1984a, 1985b) that both coastal Ecuadorian 'copper axe money' and *naipes* served similar functions, and that the Middle Sicán

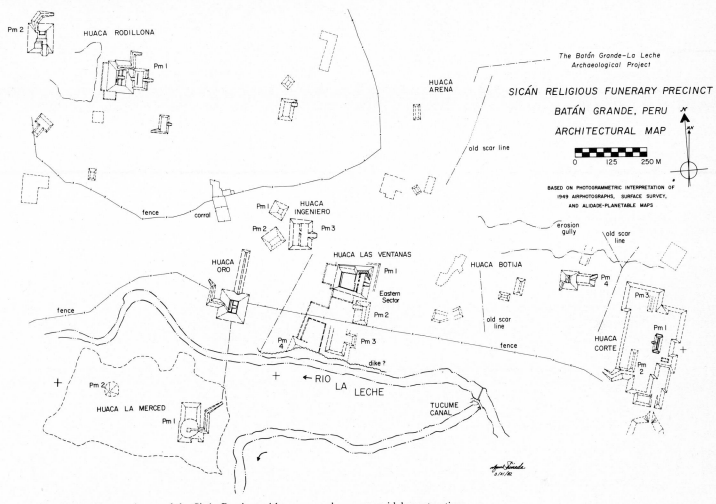

Fig. 12. Architectural map of the Sicán Precinct with over one dozen pyramidal constructions

participated in a coastal Ecuadorian–Peruvian maritime exchange system. Further, closer similarities in the elemental composition of (1) *naipe* specimens from the Sicán Precinct, and (2) primary metallurgical products (e.g., prills, ingots) from *documented local contemporaneous* smelting sites (all arsenical copper with very similar trace element composition) argue that the *naipes* were locally produced under Middle Sicán control. Reliability of the compositional data was assured by (a) cross-checking the proton-induced X-ray emission results with those of atomic absorption spectrometry and neutron activation, and (b) analysis of *naipe* specimens representing different size–shape categories and burials, as well as those of the same size–shape category derived from a single, package. The consistency of the data derived from these analyses and the quantity and diversity of *naipe* specimens recovered from Middle Sicán tombs suggest that *naipes* were *standardized* in various respects, including the metal supplied for their production, and produced on a *large scale*.

The above offers significant new insights into the evolution of the Middle Sicán polity (see Shimada 1983) and nature of its economy. One persistent question has concerned the mechanisms involved in the accumulation of the impressive quantities and variety of sumptuary and exotic goods found in Middle Sicán elite shaft-tombs. A single tomb in the Sicán Precinct yielded some 200 gold and silver artifacts (e.g., *tumi* knives, repoussé vases, masks, necklaces) with shell, turquoise, lapis lazuli and emerald inlays and adornments (Carcedo and Shimada 1985; Pedersen 1976; Tello 1937a, 1937b; Valcárcel 1937). I hypothesize (see also Shimada 1985b) that the Middle Sicán polity participated in Ecuadorian–Peruvian trade and profited from its contribution of, if not control over, the production and distribution of standardized tokens or *naipes*. The polity could also have exported raw materials (blanks, ingots) and implements (e.g., agricultural tools) to be used elsewhere, for example, on coastal Ecuador, in exchange for various exotic and sumptuary goods (e.g., gold nuggets, *Spondylus* sp., precious and semiprecious stones). I consider large-scale arsenical copper production beginning around A.D. 850 to have been a key variable that *promoted* (as opposed to initiated; see Shimada 1983) the evolution of the Middle Sicán state.

The above model of Ecuadorian–Peruvian coastal trade may need to incorporate a north highland population, much as Rostworowski's (1970, 1975a, 1977b) ethnohistorical model of late prehispanic coastal Ecuador–Chincha trade includes the participation of a contiguous *altiplano* population. On the basis of the recently transcribed *visita* of Cajamarca (carried out between 1571 and 1572) and 'patronyms' found therein, Rostworowski (1985) argues for the presence of well-acculturated pre-Inca enclaves of north-coast populations (*yunga*) in the north highlands. Although my recent survey has shown various local prehistoric mines that apparently yielded copper oxide and arsenical pyrite ores (Shimada 1984b, 1985b), the north highlands were rich in copper and arsenic-bearing ores (perhaps charcoal fuel as well?) and could well have augmented local supplies for the Middle Sicán metallurgists. Lechtman (1976, 1979; cf. Netherly 1977; Shimada 1985b) sees the north highlands as the primary source of arsenic-bearing ores. In addition to coastal agricultural produce, marine resources and arsenical copper products, the Middle Sicán polity could have offered goods from the inferred Ecuadorian–Peruvian coastal trade.

Discussion and conclusion

The preceding discussion raises the possibility that the Middle Sicán polity occupied the crucial nexus in an interregional economic system that spanned both horizontal (north–south along the coast) and vertical (east–west or coast–highland) dimensions. According to this conception, the power, wealth and prestige of the Middle Sicán polity was largely based on its organization and technology or its ability to procure raw materials from various coastal and highland regions without colonization, and process and distribute the resultant products (together with its distinct art style and iconography). Its territorial base seems to have been even more restricted than that of the Moche V polity. Yet it achieved remarkable material wealth and a state level of sociopolitical integration within a 200-year span.

We must keep in mind, however, its ascendency closely correlated in time with the rapid decline of the Wari and Pachacamac polities to the south (Shimada 1983). Menzel (1977) sees 'influence' moving south to north in the early Middle Horizon but north to south during Middle Horizon Epoch 3. The collapse of the Wari polity and attendant decline of Pachacamac may well have allowed the establishment of new or the revival of old political and economic alliances and communication routes, as well as greater population movement.

Another important consideration in future elaboration or verification of the ambitious economic model presented here is the inadequacy of our current understanding of Middle Sicán manifestations outside the northern north coast. Further research may well show that the Middle Sicán ceramics found at such dispersed areas as Isla La Plata (coastal Ecuador), Ancón and Pachacamac derived from actual colonial occupation rather than limited elite gift exchange or trade, and consequently we may have to revise the extent of the Middle Sicán discontinuous

territoriality or resource base and production zones.

As noted elsewhere (Shimada 1982, 1985a), our knowledge of 'culturally valued resources' in the Andes is poor. This point was illustrated in regard to the ambiguity surrounding the source location(s) of arsenic-bearing ore for Sicán metallurgy and how different sources (local coastal mines or importation from distant north highland mines) would significantly affect our view of the nature of associated economic and political institutions (Shimada 1985a, 1985b). Different perceptions of coastal resources and production zones also bear directly on the horizontal archipelago model discussed in respect to the Moche polity during Phase IV. Conventionally, Moche territorial expansion (e.g., Carneiro 1970; Patterson 1973) has been seen as spatially continuous and aimed at control of additional land and water; i.e., more of the same 'scarce' resources. This view is based on the rather restricted perception of coastal resources and production zones as essentially 'redundant' or 'repetitive.' I believe the preceding explains only half of the situation at hand. The impressive distance spanned by the hypothesized Moche colonial enclaves or 'sharecroppers' would in fact argue that *horizontality was in part, if not largely, an attempt to overcome the constraints of this 'redundancy' and achieve resource diversity.* Clearly, documentation of resource diversity or the presence of valuable natural resources must go hand in hand with documentation of their cultural exploitation and importance. However, we need many more intensive microenvironmental studies in all parts of the Andes.

Moche horizontality seems to have been motivated by what could be called political circumscription, in addition to the above. It can be said with a fair degree of confidence that the Moche polity did not encounter opposing or competing groups with comparable levels of sociopolitical integration horizontally along the coast north of Lima. In contrast, vertical expansion may have been constrained by the presence of the Cajamarca, Huamachuco and Recuay polities.

It should be clearly noted that in this chapter verticality and horizontality are treated as analytically discrete. In reality, they could well coexist in time and space and, more importantly, be organizationally and ecologically complementary.

Lastly, this chapter should serve to drive home the point that the issues at hand should be formulated and assessed in terms of Andean data before 'universally applicable' theories and models of state origin prejudice our perception and search for 'relevant data.' The interplay of concepts and phenomena such as 'discontinuous territoriality,' llama caravans, diverse permutations of ecological complementarity, localized resources such as guano and *Spondylus* sp., pairing of small and large river valleys (Schaedel 1951a; Shimada 1985c), large-scale arsenical copper production, and coast-wide maritime trade with standardized tokens must be taken into account in modeling the evolution of prehispanic states in northern Peru.

Chapter 14

**Implications of Andean verticality
in the evolution of political complexity:
a view from the margins**

Charles M. Hastings

Introduction

The emergence of incipient states in certain areas of the central Andes undoubtedly had far-reaching ramifications in the political development of the region. It did not, however, induce a uniform transformation to state organization throughout the Andes. Processes of state formation were set in motion relatively early in some areas, but only belatedly, if at all, in others. Despite the great antiquity of complex society in the central Andes, some native groups may not have fallen under state rule until confronted by the imperial armies of the Inca in the fifteenth century. The transition to state organization was a locally variable process barely completed on a pan-Andean scale by the time of the Spanish invasion.

Explanatory models of this transition should account for the durability of relatively less complex sociopolitical systems in certain areas and the emergence of incipient states in others. The general purpose of the following discussion is to examine how this regional variability relates to two cultural variables: (1) 'verticality,' which refers to cultural adaptations of a society to the vertical ecology of the Andes, and (2) ethnicity, the fragmentation of a population into culturally recognized divisions. Neither verticality nor ethnicity is necessarily a primary cause of highland state formation, but both should be taken into consideration in explanations of the cultural processes leading to state formation.

The interplay of ecological factors and ethnic boundaries may be partially responsible for some of the variability in highland evolutionary processes. The transition to state-level society in the highlands is related to the problem of coastal state origins, but need not be explained by an identical set of causal factors. The apparent resistance of some highland areas to changes associated with state formation would seem to indicate a highly adaptive cultural system capable of withstanding the profound and disruptive influence of state formation and expansion in neighboring areas. The persistence of such systems as viable alternatives to state organization affords a different perspective on state origins; 'negative' cases of this sort are needed to evaluate better the causes and directions of evolutionary change.

The concept of Andean verticality subsumes a number of ecological relationships relevant to problems of highland state formation. As used here, 'verticality' refers simply to the means of access to vertically dispersed resources of the Andean landscape. The units of regional analysis selected for this discussion are cultural groupings antecedent to the ethnic divisions of Tawantinsuyu. The verticality of specific groups will be examined not necessarily as a cause of state formation, or the lack thereof, but as one of many aspects of culture and ecology affecting the course of sociopolitical change.

Evolutionary changes in political organization may alter ecological relationships of highland societies to each other and to their natural environment. Conversely, certain sets of ecological relationships may retard the indigenous development of particular political systems. The position taken here is that structural changes toward state-level society were unlikely within cultural groups which were (1) in control of a highly diverse range of ecological zones, and (2) settled in zones which could not sustain a massive concentration of population. This view predicts that the political economy of vertically dispersed, low-density cultural groups will stabilize at relatively low levels of organizational complexity. Economic transactions confined within cultural groups are expected to be more secure and less dependent upon political mediation than those which cross-cut culturally recognized boundaries.

On the other hand, the potential for structural changes in political economy may be greater among groups with less secure access to dispersed resources. Groups confined to a relatively narrow range of zones may experience deficiencies in their resource base due to changes in population size within groups or in political relations among them. The development of greater societal complexity is stimulated by expanding and maintaining access to a broader ecological base. In the midst of a large population this process may generate an increasingly more centralized system of administration and redistribution. Evolutionary implications of verticality will be assessed with the understanding that population growth is a requisite condition but not necessarily the primary impetus in state formation.

This argument will be illustrated for the Late Intermediate Period (A.D. 1000 to 1465) with an example of the 'nonemergence' of highland states, or rather the persistence of less complex political systems. Ethnohistoric and archaeological data will be reviewed for a broad regional transect through the central and eastern highlands of Peru. Prior to the Late Horizon, or period of Inca rule between about 1465 and 1532, the archaeological remains in this area bear little resemblance to what would normally be expected from prehistoric states.

Ethnohistoric documentation identifying two ethnic groups, the Chinchacocha and Tarama, will be contrasted with archaeological evidence of cultural divisions. This comparison illustrates a need for caution in delimiting cultural groups and raises questions on the meaning of ethnicity in an Andean context. The configuration of these groups and their settlement patterns will be examined with respect to the level of political complexity attained in this region during the Late Intermediate Period.

Ecological zonation

The combined territories of the Tarama and Chinchacocha covered much of the Junín Plateau and the valleys to the east within the present-day departments of Junín and Pasco (Figure 1). The Junín Plateau is a high, vast grassland about 100 km long by 50 km wide between two snowcapped mountain ranges exceeding 5700 m in a few places. The western of these ranges, the Cordillera Occidental, is the continental divide. Passes through this bleak, frigid zone lead to the headwaters of several coastal valleys, particularly the

Huaura, Chancay, Chillon, and Rimac. The eastern range, the Cordillera Oriental, is much more discontinuous and is penetrated by some of the eastern valleys. The plateau between these ranges terminates on the north in the upper branches of the Huallaga Valley and tapers southeastward into the broad Mantaro Valley.

Lake Junín (also known as Chinchaycocha) is a large shallow body of water with marshy shores about 4100 m above sea level. The lake occupies much of an extensive plain surrounded by rolling hills 300 to 400 m higher, which in turn are flanked on either side by the *cordillera*. The lake plain and low hills around it are referred to as the Junín *puna*. The *puna* is primarily a pastoral zone between 4000 and 4500 m which formerly sustained enormous herds of domesticated camelids, llamas and alpacas, as well as smaller numbers of the wild vicuña. It is too cold for most agricultural crops other than the hardiest tubers, notably *maca* (*Lepidium meyenii* Walp.) and a few especially rugged varieties of potatoes. Salt springs are found in three locations on or just below the plateau.

On the eastern margins of the plateau are isolated segments of Cordillera Oriental, known locally as the *janca*.

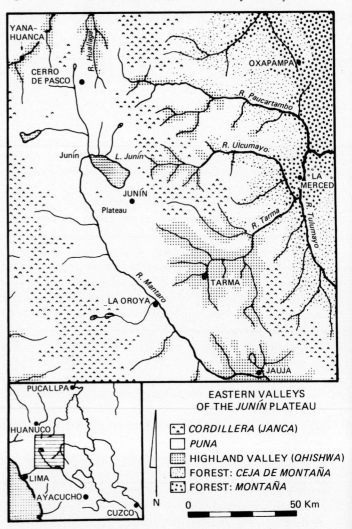

Fig. 1. Eastern valleys of the Junín Plateau

This is a zone of extremely mountainous terrain with hundreds of small, glacially formed lakes and numerous peaks above 4800 m. Three river systems drain eastward through broad gaps in the *cordillera*. The largest and southernmost is the Tarma, fed by several tributaries originating in the Junín *puna*. These tributaries are divided by long ridges 4000 to 4300 m in elevation projecting outward from the plateau. The upper Tarma and its many branches flow through steep-sided valleys with narrow floors 800 to 1200 m below the ridges. These upper valleys are in a weak rainshadow and have a relatively dry climate compared to the plateau and eastern zones. The two river systems to the north, the Ulcumayo and Paucartambo, are less widely branching and do not quite break through the *cordillera* into the Junín Plateau.

The upper drainages of all three rivers juxtapose limited grazing land on the ridgecrests with agriculturally fertile slopes and bottomlands of the valleys, often referred to as the *qhishwa* zone. The *qhishwa* is the agricultural heartland of the region where the great bulk of staple Andean crops is grown. The most important are the Andean tubers, potatoes and smaller quantities of *oca*, *ulluco*, and *mashua*, grown seasonally on the upper slopes, and maize produced on or near valley floors, which in some areas are irrigated.

Farther east the valleys steepen their descent into deep canyons and narrow gorges of the *ceja de montaña*, the transitional zone between the sierra and eastern lowlands. Canyons attain depths of 2000 m below adjacent ridges leading back to the *cordillera*. Eastward extensions of the *cordillera* form a direct, high-elevation linkage of the Junín Plateau to the *ceja de montaña*. Mountainsides are covered with dense forest up to 3600 m, and are kept moist throughout the year by a foggy, drizzly and cool climate. Toward the east, the lower elevations and greater exposure to tropical air masses have an ameliorating effect on the climate, permitting cultivation of a broader variety of crops and earlier harvests than are possible in the highland valleys.

The Tarma, Ulcumayo, and Paucartambo Rivers converge between 600 and 800 m in the *montaña*. This is a subtropical to tropical zone of steep foothills and intermittently wider valleys leading into the Amazon basin. Apart from upper ridges rising into the *ceja de montaña* and sierra, the *montaña* is mostly peripheral to the region of prehispanic occupation by the highland population.

Verticality

The concept of verticality is concerned with how resources of some or all of these zones were integrated into the regional economy of any particular period. While there may have been little if any economic interdependence between zones during the earliest phases of occupation in the Junín region (Pearsall 1980; Rick 1980), plant and animal domestication were probably responsible for an overall restructuring of economic demand and regional economic organization during later periods. By early colonial times the *puna* population had to 'provide for its necessities from those

adjoining' (Vázquez de Espinosa 1942 (1628):490). There is little doubt that the Late Intermediate Period population was dependent for subsistence purposes on the resources of a number of zones below the *puna*. This dependence raises questions about the economic strategies of exploiting such resources, and how they related to the ethnic, political, communal and kin-based divisions of society.

On a simplified level, a multizonal resource base may be exploited through strategies of specialization and exchange, economic diversification, or some combination of these two (Service 1975). A regional economy emphasizing specialization and exchange within the Junín Plateau and eastern valleys might be associated with socioeconomic groups confined to narrow ranges of environmental zones. Accordingly, resident groups of the *puna* would be the herders, weavers, llama drivers for caravans, and salt workers of the region. Those in the upper valleys would be farmers cultivating highland crops such as maize, beans, squash, quinoa, potatoes, and other tubers. Others based in the lower *ceja de montaña* might specialize in growing coca and chili peppers or in gathering honey, wax, feathers, fruits, wood, and medicinal plants from the forests. Traditional exchange among specialized occupants of each of these zones could still be observed throughout much of this region as recently as a few decades ago (see Farfán 1949; Andrews 1963; Hastings n.d.).

An emphasis on economic diversification, as opposed to specialization, entails exploitation of resources dispersed in a number of ecological zones. Such diversification is illustrated today on the community level in the lower Tarma *ceja de montaña*, where households are guaranteed access to herding, agricultural, and forest resources spanning more than 2500 m elevation. On a yet broader scale, Murra (1972) noted a tendency for late prehispanic groups to maximize the diversity of zones under their control and minimize dependence on exchange with other groups. His general model of 'verticality' describes the utilization of outlying zones by groups based in a 'nucleus of dense population and political power' (Murra 1981:6). It is well documented for ethnohistoric examples of nuclear or core areas in the *puna* and highland valleys and is most problematical for those hypothetically in coastal valleys or the *ceja de montaña* (see chapter by Shimada, this volume). His model is visualized as an 'archipelago' in that groups could exploit resource areas territorially remote from their core area, and a number of groups might share access to the same outlying resources.

The contrast drawn here opposes the economic interdependence of locally specialized groups and the self-sufficiency of diversified groups sustained by the resources of multizonal territories. Such territories might be geographically continuous, as discussed by Espinoza (1975:39), or discontinuous, as in Murra's vertical archipelago, or some combination of both. The applicability of these different conceptualizations of regional economic organization to the Late Intermediate Period occupation of the Junín Plateau and eastern valleys will be considered below. This will be done in part by examining the geographical distribution of ethnic groups relative to the *puna*, highland valleys, and *ceja de montaña*. First, the problem of group definition must be considered.

Ethnicity: ethnohistoric perspectives

Sixteenth-century Tawantinsuyu might be thought of as an enormous cultural medley of disparate parts subsumed into an empire. The components of the empire were ethnically distinct groups readily identifiable by their style of headdress or other aspects of personal adornment (Cieza de León 1946: Ch. XLV; 1973: Ch. XXIII; Cobo 1890 (3):231). Administrative provinces were constituted from one or more ethnic groups originating in cultural divisions that predate the Inca conquest (Rowe 1946:185, 262). These groups were perceived in 1532 as culturally meaningful entities and presumably were similarly regarded a century earlier. Their political and economic integrity, however, remains obscure. In the Junín area, this problem is well illustrated for the groups known as Tarama and Chinchacocha, names alternatively applied to indigenous groups of people, provinces or geographical areas, and state settlements.

Specific records of settlement distributions are not available until the general population had already been resettled into a small number of easily accessible *reducciones* under the jurisdiction of the Corregimiento de Tarama y Chinchacocha. A surviving summary of a general *visita* of Peru conducted between 1570 and 1575 lists five villages occupied by more than 1900 households (10 797 persons) in the Repartimiento de Chinchacocha, and six villages occupied by about 1000 households (5757 persons) in the Repartimiento de Tarama (Miranda 1925:203–204). These *reducciones* were probably formed in part from villages in separate valleys and different zones, partially obscuring the configuration of earlier

territorial units. Even so, it is noteworthy that the Repartimiento de Tarama was confined to two or three upper branches of the Tarma Valley and that most of Chinchacocha was on the central plateau (Figure 2).

Early descriptions of these provinces or *repartimientos* reveal a contrasting association of Chinchacocha with herding and Tarama with agriculture, especially maize. Estete (1946:101) and Cieza de León (1946: Ch. LXXXIII) were impressed by the enormous herds of camelids and abundant wildlife around Lake Junín. The Chinchacocha population was commonly listed as a source of livestock, fresh meat, *charqui* (dried meat), fish, and wool in exchange relations with ethnic groups of the upper Huallaga (Ortiz de Zúñiga 1967:63, 179; 1972:43, 58). Cieza contrasts the harsh environment of Chinchacocha, where only certain root crops can survive, with the temperate valleys of Tarama ideal for maize and other cultigens. Pachacuti Yamqui (1950:253) supports this association between Tarama and maize with an anecdote about a fifteenth-century Tarama ruler. This *curaca* was so renowned for his consumption of maize beer that the Inca dispatched him throughout the empire to partake in rituals intended to improve agricultural production.

The Chinchacocha and Tarama were only two of many ethnic groups in the central highlands, each of varying size and economic potential. The task at hand is to examine the relationship between the Tarama and the Chinchacocha in the context of this broad regional array of interacting groups. An especially close relationship between these two may be suspected simply from the frequency with which they are named together in early Spanish documents. Cieza de León (1946: Ch. XC) at one point lumps them into a single province, and a few decades later crown authorities followed suit by merging them into a single, jointly named *corregimiento*.

The implied close relationship between occupants of the

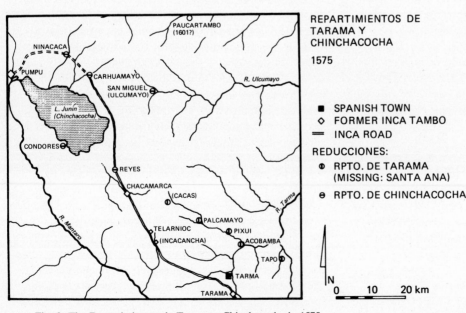

Fig. 2. The Repartimientos de Tarama y Chinchacocha in 1575

Junín *puna* and the *qhishwa* zone of the eastern valleys is substantiated by several sixteenth-century sources. One of Pizarro's earliest grants of *encomienda* treats the Chinchacocha and Tarama as a single province on the basis of the existing administrative apparatus, in which the *curaca* Taparas was recognized as ruler of both groups. By 1549 the *curaca* of Chinchacocha was Runato, who, according to a tax record from the same period, was also ruler of the Paucartambo Valley (Figure 2; Pedro de Gasca 1549 in Rostworowski 1975b:79, 81). Runato's Paucartambo domain, as described shortly thereafter, bore no resemblance to the *puna*: 'This place has a temperate climate and they raise excellent fruit; nearby are sugar mills, and to the east, many heathen' (Vázquez de Espinosa 1942:489). The Chinchacocha were evidently also established in another eastern valley, the Ulcumayo. By 1575 native occupants of this valley had been resettled into the village of San Miguel, one of the six initial *reducciones* of the Chinchacocha (Figure 2; Miranda 1925). Territorial continuity from the plateau into both of these valleys could explain why

coca leaf, maize, and wooden troughs, all of which had to be obtained below the *puna*, were listed among tribute obligations of the Chinchacocha in 1549. Such continuity could provide communities on the *puna* with access to these and other eastern products and would be contrary to the 'vertical archipelago' pattern inferred by Rostworowski (1975b:75) from this same tribute list.

Sixteenth-century Tarama and Chinchacocha *reducciones* were all on the Junín Plateau or in upper sections of the eastern valleys, leaving unknown the ethnic, *encomienda* and *repartimiento* affiliations of settlements in the *ceja de montaña*. Ethnohistoric insights into this problem come from later sources on access routes and parish extensions into the eastern zones, suggesting a close connection between the main plateau and the lower Tarma. The lower Tarma *ceja de montaña* can be surprisingly accessible from the central *puna*, because of eastern prongs of high terrain extending far beyond the main plateau. One of the earliest known trails into the Tarma lowlands was a direct route from the *puna* via one such arm of the *cordillera*, circumventing most of the highland valley zone of the upper Tarma (Camino de Suárez in Figure 3; Hastings 1981).

This east–west axis is also evident in eighteenth-century parish divisions linking several *puna* villages to settlements in the eastern valleys, notably Ninacaca with Huachón, Carhuamayo with Ulcumayo, and Reyes (Junín) with Racas, Cacas, and Huasahuasi (Figure 3; Ruiz 1952:85–86). Yet Huasahuasi, which is marginally within the Tarma *ceja de montaña*, is much nearer the parish of Acobamba in the upper Tarma than to Reyes in the *puna*; its ecclesiastical association with the upper parish suggests that affairs of the lower Tarma population in the *ceja de montaña* may traditionally have been at least as great a concern in the *puna* as in the upper Tarma.

In review, the ethnohistoric sources leave little doubt that the Chinchacocha were politically linked to settlements in the upper Paucartambo and Ulcumayo Valleys at the time of Spanish contact, providing communities based in the *puna* with access to products of the *quichua* zone and possibly also the *ceja de montaña* in these same valleys. Evidence of ethnic ties to the *ceja de montaña* of the lower Tarma at this same time is rather more tenuously based on later sources but is consistent with this same general pattern of Chinchacocha continuity across zones to the east. The applicability of these observations to prehispanic regional organization, and especially to periods preceding the Inca conquest, will now be examined with archaeological data.

Ethnicity: archaeological perspectives

Archaeological evidence bearing on the verticality and cultural boundaries of the Chinchacocha and Tarama has been gathered during the past ten years in regional surveys spanning environmental transitions from the *puna* to the *montaña* (Parsons and Hastings 1977; Bonnier and Rozenberg 1978; Hastings 1981). Systematic surveys provide a substantial data base for the southeast section of the Junín Plateau and much of

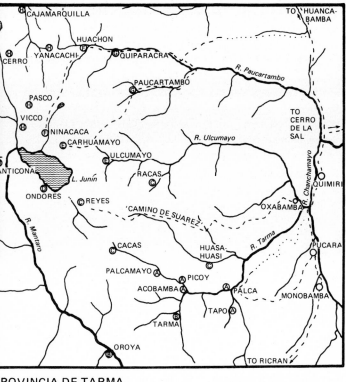

ROVINCIA DE TARMA
IGHTEENTH-CENTURY PARISHES:
3 OF 13)

- - - - EIGHTEENTH-CENTURY
TRAIL TO THE *MONTAÑA*
········· ROUTE UNCERTAIN

N

0 10 20 30 40 50 Km

A. *ACOBAMBA*
B. *VILLA DE TARMA*
C. *REYES*
D. *ONDORES*
E. *CARHUAMAYO*
F. *NINACACA*
G. *PAUCARTAMBO*
H. *VILLA DE PASCO*

Fig. 3. Eighteenth-century parishes of the Provincia de Tarma

the Tarma drainage area, supplemented by spotty
reconnaissance in the Ulcumayo Valley.

Settlement patterns

In general, Late Intermediate Period residential sites
within this survey area are small, dense clusters of architectural
remains and surface pottery in high, relatively inaccessible
locations. Sites typically cover 0.5 to 2.5 ha and contain about
20 to 60 building foundations. Approaches to most sites are
partially blocked by any combination of ditches, earthworks,
walls and other fortifications. It is inferred from these structural
remains that defense was a major consideration underlying the
placement of settlements during this period (see chapter by J.
Topic and T. Topic, this volume).

Late Intermediate Period sites in the surveyed section of
the Junín Plateau are found primarily on hilltops and ridges
above 4200 m, rather than on the floor of the *pampa*. Parsons
reports a great abundance of ancient corral remnants which by
themselves are difficult to date, but in many cases are
associated with Late Intermediate Period settlements (Parsons
and Hastings 1977:34–35). Several relatively large settlements
with associated corrals are situated in the margins of the main
puna just inside the Tarma watershed.

Beyond the *puna* margins, sites are typically found on
narrow, steep-sided ridges dividing branches of the Tarma
River. Most are between 3800 and 4200 m and afford access to
limited grazing land above and agricultural land below. Corral
foundations are generally less numerous if present at all,
whereas agricultural terrace remnants may be extensive on

adjacent mountainsides. Most sites are tightly nucleated and
well fortified. A few are located on relatively low mountain
spurs deep within the valleys, but in general the *qhishwa* zone
seems to have been exploited primarily from settlements just
above it.

In the *ceja de montaña*, site locations continue to be
defensive, but fortifications are less elaborate. Variability in site
size is greater, ranging from nine hectares down to a small
fraction of one hectare. A multi-tier settlement pattern is
evident within a greatly expanded vertical range encompassing
ecological zones between 4200 and 1600 m elevation. Upper
tier sites are those of the *altura*, a high grassland comparable to
the *puna* but much more moist. Lower tier sites occupy steep
spurs deep within the forested canyons, or *yunca* zone. The
outer tier refers to sites in the *montaña* margins at the tips of
long ridges from the sierra.

Based on a sample size of nearly 200 sites from about
1400 sq km, the Late Intermediate Period population
distribution between Lake Junín and the upper *montaña*
appears to have been quite uneven. The frigid *janca* and parts
of the cloud forest in the *ceja de montaña* probably were settled
only sparsely and ephemerally, if indeed they were occupied at
all. Settlement was densest in and near the transition between
the Junín Plateau and upper valleys of the Tarma drainage. The
largest sites are primarily in this interface between *puna* and
quishwa, and secondarily in the *altura* along the eastern rim of
the Andes. The greatest proliferation of very small sites, some
barely large enough for a few households, is in lower zones of
the *ceja de montaña*.

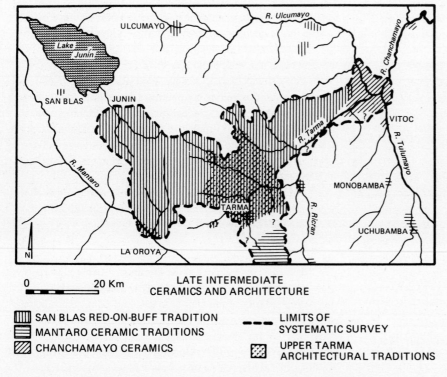

Fig. 4. Distributions of Late Intermediate Period ceramics and architecture

Ceramics

The most characteristic component of Late Intermediate Period ceramic assemblages from the southern *puna* and Tarma valleys is a fine, elaborately decorated ware known variously as San Blas Red-on-Buff, San Blas Pintado, and Palcamayo (Parsons and Hastings 1977:19, 34; Matos and Parsons 1979:166; Bonnier and Rozenberg 1978:67). This pottery and a coarser, undecorated ware constitute the great bulk of the ceramic assemblages of most Late Intermediate Period sites. Also present in many sites are trace amounts of ceramics generally associated with the Huanca ethnic group in and near the Mantaro Valley to the south. Most of this exotic pottery falls within the Mantaro Base Roja tradition (LeBlanc 1981:138–141), and probably represents some form of widespread interethnic exchange.

San Blas Red-on-Buff pottery emerges as a major if not dominant component of Late Intermediate Period sites in the *puna*, on ridges between the highland valleys, and in the *ceja de montaña* (Figure 4). It is widespread throughout the Tarma drainage except in the far southern tributaries, which are mainly within the Mantaro traditions, and near the mouth of the river, where Amazonian traditions of the *montaña* are prevalent. Surface pottery on the few known sites of the upper and lower Ulcumayo Valley is also predominantly San Blas Red-on-Buff. In the southern *puna* Red-on-Buff pottery has been found in the survey area southeast of Lake Junín and in the initial type site of San Blas, a former salt quarry about five km southwest of the lake.

This region of Late Intermediate Period San Blas ceramics can thus be delimited on the south and east by partially known stylistic boundaries with ceramic traditions of neighboring Huanca and Amazonian groups respectively. The northern limit is undefined at present, but must lie south of the Yacha sites examined by Thompson (1968, 1972) in the Huallaga headwaters and probably also the little-known Yaros sites in the northern *puna*. The western stylistic boundary is even more speculative, although no painted San Blas ceramics have yet been reported west of the Cordillera Occidental. The geographical extent of the San Blas ceramic region demonstrable from existing data measures about 80 km east–west by 60 km north–south, but these dimensions might be enlarged to at least 100 km × 80 km if the regional data base were to be expanded.

Within such a large and ecologically diverse ceramic region San Blas painted pottery is strikingly uniform. High degrees of similarity among even the most distant collections cannot yet be quantitatively demonstrated but are apparent in the clay quality, firing technology, vessel shapes and design motifs.

Architecture

Whereas San Blas ceramics appear geographically undifferentiated throughout their region of distribution, stone architecture is much less uniform. Variability in building design and site layout has not been systematically studied, but regional patterning is evident in three categories of stone architecture: simple circular buildings, rectangular structures with two or more stories, and fortifications.

Residential structures in all parts of the San Blas ceramic region are round, single-story buildings generally four or five m in interior diameter with a single doorway and rarely any windows or wall niches. Roofs were presumably conical or hemispherical and constructed of poles and *ichu* grass thatch. These buildings rarely abut against one another, and are scattered throughout a site in accordance with local relief, terracing, and, in some cases, patio configurations.

A second building type is a square or rectangular structure two or three stories high with a window-like entrance to each floor and a flat roof of stone slabs and sod. The ground story ceiling is rarely preserved and appears only as a row of slab supports projecting from the walls. Inner dimensions of the basal story range from about 2 m × 1 m to 3 m × 2 m. The proportion and distribution of these buildings within sites are extremely variable. Most are freestanding or conjoined in pairs (Bonnier and Rozenberg 1978: Plate 4; Parsons and Matos 1978: Fotos 3 to 5). These may be scattered irregularly throughout a site or clustered around one or two well-defined patios. Alternatively, a larger number of two- or three-story units may be merged into a single complex structure (Matos and Parsons 1979: Foto 4). In a few sites this complex appears as a series of contiguous rooms against the inside of a massive wall on the site perimeter.

Site fortifications constitute the third category of construction to be considered here. Most settlements were fortified, but some were more securely fortified than others. The defensive advantages of a high, limited access site location were usually augmented by concentrated defensive works across the ridgecrest approach to one or both ends of the site. The simplest fortifications consist of a single wall or a paired wall and ditch across the ridgecrest. At the opposite extreme are much more elaborate, extensive or repetitive fortifications. The principal approach to a site may cross as many as three dry moats and adjacent walls in succession. Some defensive walls attained heights greater than 7 m. Walls may be flanked by high towers or by a series of bastions and in some cases are elaborated into parapets (Bonnier and Rozenberg 1978: Plate 1, Figure 1).

Rectangular, multilevel structures and exceptional fortifications have approximately the same geographical distributions. Sites with multistory buildings do not correspond on a fully one-to-one basis with especially well-fortified sites, but both are restricted primarily to the upper Tarma drainage. On this basis, the architecture of the upper Tarma may be treated as a distinct tradition in which round buildings, two-story structures, and elaborate defenses co-occur within the same area and often within the same sites. This tradition defines a subarea of the San Blas ceramic region that is concentrated in the *qhishwa* zone and the intervalley ridges just above it (Figure 4). It is notably absent from the *ceja de montaña* and most surveyed areas of the main *puna*. Nor has it been detected in the Ulcumayo drainage, but too little is known of the Ulcumayo to infer its presence or absence. One or two sites with multistory buildings in the *puna* margins of the Mantaro Valley above La Oroya may represent the western limits of the tradition and are uncharacteristically remote from the *qhishwa* zone (Jeffrey Parsons, personal communication).

The multistory buildings might plausibly have functioned as storage facilities for agricultural crops from the *qhishwa*, especially maize. Of special interest in this regard is the local name 'Pirhuayoc' for one particularly well-fortified site with exclusively rectangular, two-story buildings. In Tarma Quechua, 'pirwa' translates into 'storeroom' or 'granary' and can also be modified to mean 'multistoried' or 'one above the other' (Adelaar 1977:464).

Two factors may account for the absence of multistory structures in the *ceja de montaña*. First, the eastern climate is so damp that it may have been prudent to dispose of production surpluses beyond local needs through regional economic channels, rather than attempting long-term storage of great quantities of perishable goods. The second factor takes into consideration the economic potential of the eastern slopes in a broader, regional context. In much of the *ceja de montaña*, the climate is too wet, the slopes too steep, or the soil too acid for successful long term agriculture. Slash-and-burn agriculture and weeding below timberline also require greater labor inputs than does agriculture in the *qhishwa* zone of the sierra. The regional economic advantages of the eastern zones lie in the relatively early harvests of traditional sierra cultigens and the great diversity of crops and nonagricultural forest resources. The potential role of the *ceja de montaña* in the regional economy is related more to this diversity and timing of production than to bulk production in any one crop. It should therefore not be surprising that specialized facilities for long-term, bulk storage of agricultural goods are concentrated in the densely settled highland valleys and are virtually absent from the eastern slopes.

The upper Tarma architectural tradition implies an association between defensive concerns and massed storage, and this association emerges in the highland valleys rather than the *puna* and *ceja de montaña*. From a broad regional perspective, the agricultural productivity of the *qhishwa* might be the most limited of highly valued resources in the central Peruvian highlands. There is a regional scarcity of land in which the full range of sierra crops, such as maize, *quinoa*, squash, potatoes, *ocas*, and *ullucos*, can be grown in large quantities. The upper valleys of the Tarma drainage represent the greatest concentration of such farmland within a 180 km section of sierra between Jauja and Yanahuanca (Figure 1). The value of the Tarma *qhishwa* is further enhanced by its ample productive potential for maize, a crop of special significance in Andean social and ceremonial contexts.

The archaeological record and oral histories leave little doubt that warfare was a major problem during the Late Intermediate Period. Native testimonies explicitly single out competition for scarce agricultural land as a primary cause of

armed conflict among the neighboring Huanca (Toleda 1940). Under these conditions, the agricultural surpluses of the Tarma valleys would seem particularly vulnerable, especially if intermittent raiding was more common than total conquest in the *modus operandi* of warfare in the Tarma region. Given this vulnerability, the special emphases on defense in upper Tarma sites may be proposed to have been functionally related to the regionally scarce production and concentrated storage of *qhishwa* crops.

In contrast, the *puna* is a far more extensive ecological zone in which the primary resource, livestock, is inherently mobile and at any point in time may be scattered over great distances. In this same regard, the preceding arguments against massed, long-term storage in the *ceja de montaña* might also account for the seemingly lesser preoccupation with defense in eastern settlements. Occupied areas of the highland valleys, *puna*, and *ceja de montaña* were all threatened by potential outbreaks of hostilities, but the danger appears to have been greatest in settlements within the upper Tarma architectural tradition.

Cultural unity

The differentiation and distribution of ethnic groups in the Junín *puna* and eastern valleys are interrelated problems concerning the degree of regional cultural unity. The most conspicuous visual clues to ethnic identity at the time of Spanish contact were stylistic differences in headdresses and other aspects of personal adornment not likely to survive in the archaeological record. Investigations of Late Intermediate Period ethnicity must therefore rely on alternative and perhaps less reliable criteria than those elicited from sixteenth-century native informants. The problem of Tarama and Chinchacocha ethnicity will be addressed here with respect to (1) regional aspects of style in preservable material culture; (2) political relationships implicit in documentary sources; and (3) regional economic organization.

Style

Ethnic costume may have been the most conscious symbol of ethnic identity, but other components of material culture probably functioned in a similar capacity. The most abundant class of artifacts that might be stylistically related to ethnic divisions is pottery, though the ethnic implications of ceramic style areas are not at all clear. Thompson's (1968) preliminary study of Huánuco ceramics suggests with reservations that pottery may be of some use in differentiating ethnic groups. Similarly, the San Blas stylistic boundary with Mantaro traditions to the south and Amazonian traditions to the east is believed to correspond approximately to the southern and eastern ethnic frontiers of the Tarma Valley population.

The San Blas ceramic region is troublesome in that it spans areas of both Tarama and Chinchacocha occupation and other areas of unknown ethnicity. One explanation for this situation would be that pottery in this area simply does not function as a meaningful medium for differentiating ethnically separate groups. However, this would be inconsistent with the obvious contrasts of the San Blas tradition with pottery of the surrounding Huanca, Yacha and Amazonian groups. Alternatively, the San Blas tradition shared by the Tarama and Chinchacocha may be indicative of a closer relationship between two groups having more in common with each other than with their other neighbors. If so, these two groups were not as separate as the chroniclers lead us to believe.

Architectural differentiation of subareas of the San Blas ceramic tradition will be discussed below as a manifestation of internal economic and ecological contrasts within the region. On a different level, patterns of building design and construction serve to distinguish the entire ceramic region from other areas with different architectural traditions. For example, architectural styles of both the Yacha, Chupachu and Wamalí ethnic groups to the north are completely different from those that have been described here (Thompson 1972). Also, while Huanca residential architecture is similar in many respects to that of the Tarama and Chinchacocha, the multistory rectangular buildings, towers, and bastions of the upper Tarma drainage clearly are not part of the Huanca architectural tradition.

Political units

The Late Intermediate Period settlement pattern data are not supportive of any large-scale political unification in the area of the Tarama and Chinchacocha. Settlement size is the best index of political centralization that is measurable from available data. A centralized, hierarchical political structure might be inferred if there were a well-defined hierarchy of site sizes with certain sites categorically much larger than others. This is not the case for the site survey of the Tarma valleys and adjacent *puna* (Figure 5a). All sites are smaller than ten ha, and even within this low size range there is no clear category of size-dominant sites. Sites larger than 2.5 ha may be considered relatively large, but sizes of 'large' sites are distributed relatively evenly up to nine ha. As previously noted, the relatively large sites tend to be near the interface between *puna* and valley, or in the *altura* of the *ceja de montaña*.

One of the largest sites was discovered in the *altura* of the lower Tarma survey, and aerial photographs reveal one or two possibly comparable sites in similar but unsurveyed zones of the lower Ulcumayo. The site–size histogram of a group of 24 sites surveyed in the Tarma *ceja de montaña* illustrates the categorical distinctiveness of this one site, which is named Paraupunta (Figure 5b). The same contrasts emerge if settlement size is measured by building counts; more than 150 buildings stood within Paraupunta, whereas all other sites had fewer than forty structures each.

It can be argued that political authority within subareas such as this was concentrated within a single dominant site (Hastings n.d.). This same pattern is not evident on a broader scale for large areas of the Tarma drainage and Junín Plateau. Consequently, there is no archeological basis for inferring higher orders of Late Intermediate Period political centralization at all comparable to the regional administration established under Inca control. On a long-term basis the available data favor a higher degree of fragmentation in the regional political structure.

Regional economy

The documentary sources suggest, with varying degrees of confidence, prehispanic ties between the Chinchacocha on the *puna* and people of undesignated ethnicity in the Paucartambo, Ulcumayo and lower Tarma Valleys. These ties are apparent only in an administrative context, and published ethnohistoric materials reveal nothing about their socioeconomic correlates. However, this administrative linkage in combination with a shared pre-Incaic ceramic tradition constitutes firmer grounds for postulating a broader relationship of greater antiquity between *puna* and valley populations.

Strong similarities in San Blas pottery suggest frequent contact and a degree of shared culture across a broad series of ecological zones from the *puna* to the *ceja de montaña*. This same area appears fragmented if settlement patterns and nonresidential architecture are considered. Such variability is explicable in functional terms by regional economic differentiation. Sites of the upper Tarma, which has the greatest area of *qhishwa* farmland, are distinguished by specialized structures argued to have been agricultural storage facilities. Exceptional fortifications around some of these sites indicate a local preoccupation with defense that may be causally related to the production and storage of sierra crops. Sites of the main

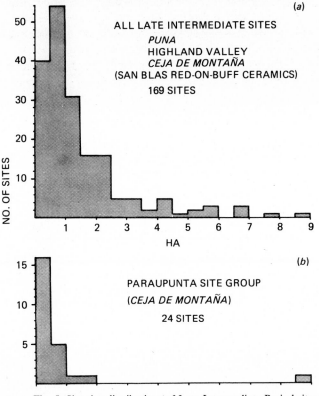

Fig. 5. Site size distributions of Late Intermediate Period sites

puna are characterized by their association with extensive corrals, as would be expected in a predominantly herding zone. Settlements of the *ceja de montaña* were dispersed in multiple tiers, allowing occupants to take advantage of extreme ecological diversity rather than concentrating production and storage within a narrower range of products.

The inferred contrasts within the regional economy may be better described as differing subregional economic emphases, rather than full economic specialization. Within the constraints of the local environment, some degree of economic diversity was maintained in each occupied subregion. Pastoralism on the *puna* was complemented by cultivation of the hardiest tubers and root crops, as noted by Cieza de León and still evident in visible furrows of ancient fields (Jeffrey Parsons and Ramiro Matos, personal communications). Sites in the upper Tarma were suitably located to exploit *qhishwa* farmland as well as ridgecrest pasturage; ancient terraced fields and small numbers of corrals imply a partially mixed economy in many of these sites. As noted, the greatest potential for economic diversification lay in the *ceja de montaña*, where llama herds and fields of frost-resistant tubers could be tended only a day's travel from coca fields and *chonta* palms.

Viewed as a whole, the San Blas ceramic region appears organizationally intermediate between an interdependent system of fully specialized parts and an aggregate of wholly self-sufficient independent parts. Subareas were differentiated by partially overlapping ranges of economic activities practical in each. Economic self-sufficiency may have been sought, but could never be fully realized by individual settlements or small groups of settlements; local economic deficiencies required cooperation on a higher level among subareas of the San Blas ceramic region.

Tarama and Chinchacocha ethnicity

Spanish records are relatively unambiguous on the ethnicity of the upper Tarma and Lake Junín subareas of the San Blas ceramic region. The Paucartambo and Ulcumayo Valleys are administratively linked by sixteenth-century sources to the Chinchacocha in the *pampa* around Lake Junín. The strongest ethnohistoric evidence of prehispanic ties between the Tarama in the upper Tarma valleys and these same Chinchacocha is their fealty to a single *curaca* during the Late Horizon, at which time they formed a single province of Tawantinsuyu. Archaeologically, these groups are differentiated primarily by an abundance of corrals in one, and two-story rectangular structures in the other. Both differences can be explained in terms of contrasting economic orientations.

This information does not resolve a fundamental question concerning the ethnic unity of *puna* and valley occupants. Ethnicity should ideally be defined by a broad range of customs, beliefs, ritual practices, linguistic differences, and other cultural criteria correlated with recognized social boundaries. The ethnicity of a group whose identity is not specified historically must be sought through other criteria that are less than ideal. Ethnicity may also be correlated in some

degree with variations in political structure, regional economy, artistic design, technological development and, according to Lumbreras (1974c:74–75), the 'forces of production.' Some of these variables are more amenable to archaeological and/or ethnohistoric investigation, but their relationships to consciously recognized ethnicity are poorly understood.

There is a danger of circular reasoning in defining ethnic groups by criteria that are also the subject of investigation, and this danger is applicable to studies of Tarama and Chinchacocha. Based on archaeological appearances on the ground, one might regard their shared ceramic tradition, architectural contrasts with other groups, and the spatial continuity of settlement across their common border as evidence of cultural unity. If the concept of ethnicity can be considered in relative rather than absolute terms, then the combined Tarama–Chinchacocha population within the *puna*, and the Tarma, Ulcumayo, and Paucartambo Valleys, might constitute a single group of the central highlands (Figure 6). The identities 'Tarama' and 'Chinchacocha' could designate subsections of the larger group that were geographically and to a large extent economically differentiated from each other. A high degree of ethnic continuity among subsections would also explain why Inca administrators decided to merge them into a single province after the conquest.

This interpretation of existing data, however, cannot be confirmed or rejected without a more informative ethnohistoric comparison of hypothetical subsections and a better understanding of their material correlates in the archaeological record. It is quite possibly an oversimplification of interrelationships among ethnicity, economy, and spatial patterning that were already complex in the Late Intermediate Period and were confounded even further by the *mitmaq* resettlement policies of the Inca.

Conclusions

The Junín Plateau and eastern valleys have been described as an ecological diverse region of extensive high-elevation pastures, prime agricultural land, luxuriant cloud forests, and subtropical foothills. Highland agricultural land was most extensive in the upper Tarma Valley and its several tributaries. These were farmed and occupied by a cultural group identified as the Tarama, whose settlements can be distinguished by possible storage facilities and, in some cases, by especially formidable fortifications. Tarama population densities were greatest just below the margins of the Junín *puna*, in close proximity to settlements thought to have been occupied by the Chinchacocha. The Chinchacocha were the predominant, if not exclusive population of the Junín Plateau south of the Yaros and Yanamate near Cerro de Pasco. Though widely known as a *puna* population, they also appear to have occupied lower zones to the east, including the upper Paucartambo and Ulcumayo Valleys. These lower settlements represent a monoethnic expansion of vertical control into the valleys and are not part of a multiethnic vertical archipelago.

It is more problematical to determine the ethnic status of

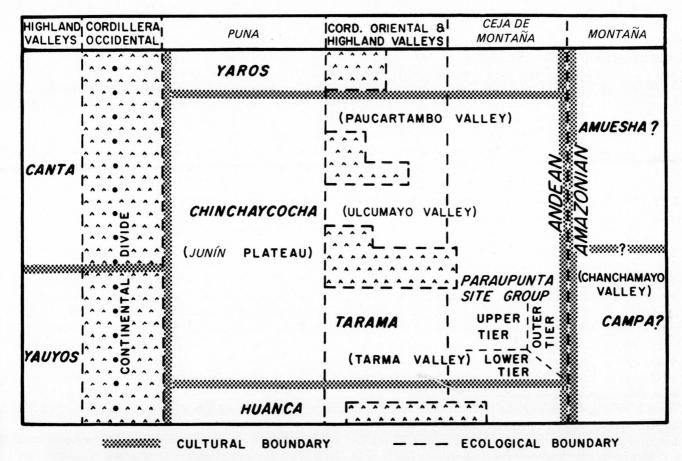

Fig. 6. Ecological context of Late Intermediate Period cultural groups

the lower Tarma occupation with respect to the Tarama and Chinchacocha. The available data are inconclusive but raise the possibility of stronger ties to the Chinchacocha in the *puna* than to the Tarama in the upper Tarma. However, the known historical references are perhaps too late to assume continuity from prehispanic periods, and architectural contrasts in the archaeological remains of the upper and lower Tarma may not be a good index of ethnicity. Settlements in the Tarma *ceja de montaña* could have been reached from the Junín *puna* via a direct route that avoids the apparent 'core area' of Tarama occupation in the upper valleys. This accessibility casts further doubt on the likelihood that ethnic lands were intermingled as an archipelago, even if the lower Tarma was a colony of the Chinchacocha.

This usage of the term 'ethnic' requires considerable caution, for the ethnic status of the Tarama and Chinchacocha is unclear. In one sense they are separate groups identified as such by the chroniclers and settled in ecologically distinct zones. Yet these ecological contrasts are at best applicable only to conceptual core areas of Tarama and Chinchacocha occupation described by the early Spaniards. The earliest documentary sources are less informative on the full and

potentially overlapping vertical range of exploitation by these groups. Nor do they provide much insight into degrees of ethnic differentiation, apart from implying that the Tarama and Chinchacocha had been joined into a single province of Tawantinsuyu.

From an archaeological perspective, the ethnic differentiation between these two groups does not appear to be so great as between either one and any other groups of the central highlands. It may be that the preservable material correlates of ethnicity as perceived in 1532 are too subtle or too poorly understood to be discernible in the current state of archaeological research. The ceramic and architectural variability discussed above is meaningful as a measure of cultural similarity, but the prehispanic ethnic implications of such similarity are difficult to interpret without better ethnohistoric data on the ethnic categories themselves.

Surveyed sites on the southern *puna* and in the eastern valleys may be characterized archaeologically as a culturally distinct group by their San Blas pottery, residential architecture and architectural contrasts in nonresidential structures with other groups. Archaeological variability within this group is interpretable in terms of economic differentiation. The corrals around *puna* sites, multistory structures near the upper Tarma agricultural land, and vertically dispersed settlement pattern in the *ceja de montaña* can all be related to ecological contrasts favoring differing economic strategies. Even so, some degree of economic diversification appears to have been sought on a local level. Within the constraints of local zonation, however, this diversification results in economic differentiation on a regional scale.

The *ceja de montaña* is the only subarea in which centralized control over a number of settlements may be inferred from the settlement pattern. The full range of resources of the eastern slopes spans a vertical series of zones too far apart to be efficiently exploited from a single settlement. The Late Intermediate Period response to this problem appears to have been the formulation of a settlement group of numerous small sites dispersed in distant zones beneath a dominant, centrally located site in the *altura*. Total population size in the *ceja de montaña* was never very great, however, and probably limited the development of local political systems.

On a broader scale, the political organization of the plateau and eastern valley populations evidently failed to develop into a highly centralized, hierarchical system of control for any extended period prior to the Inca conquest. Late Intermediate Period site size is generally much smaller and less variable, for example, than site size in the adjacent area of Huanca occupation in the Yanamarca and upper Mantaro Valleys (Parsons and Hastings 1977; Earle *et al.* 1980:20–23). It is very likely that the Huanca attained a higher level of sociopolitical complexity than did the Tarama or Chinchacocha, regardless of whether or not they ever became a state. Differences in the political trajectories of these groups are inferred largely from very high population densities among the Huanca, which may in turn be causally related to the capacity of local production to sustain a large and dense population. The relatively low level of sociopolitical complexity inferred for the Tarama and perhaps the Chinchacocha may be a function of the distribution of population near the interface between *puna* and valley, which calls into question the role of verticality in political development.

This role is partially attributable to the significance of verticality as a determinant of population density and distribution. Mutual access to herding and agricultural land appears to have been a major concern in the selection of settlement locations, resulting in relatively high site densities in the upper reaches of the valleys and along the outer margins of the plateau. Had access to the *qhishwa* been the sole determinant, site density could probably have attained higher levels near the bottomlands and junctions of the largest valleys. The interface between *puna* and valley affords access to multiple resource zones, but is linearly distributed around each side valley of the Tarma drainage. Settlements conforming to a multizonal economic strategy are consequently dispersed throughout the upper watershed rather than concentrated in one or a few central locations.

Relatively low levels of sociopolitical complexity in the Junín Plateau and eastern valleys may also have been maintained in part by the relationship between political authority and access to remote resources. As it appears archaeologically, the Late Intermediate Period occupation of this region was culturally continuous from *puna* to cloud forest. Exchange among households or other low-level socioeconomic units might theoretically have been a viable means of procuring distant products within such a region of high stylistic homogeneity, especially if such homogeneity can be correlated with high levels of socioeconomic cooperation. Should this be a tenable position, then political leadership need not have been strongly developed or highly centralized to assure widespread access to vertically dispersed resources.

Under different circumstances such leadership in political mediation and diplomatic maneuvering would be advantageous in arranging the colonization of remote enclaves and in maintaining these detached and fragmented territories. It might figure less prominently, however, in an ecologically diverse region with widespread household level exchange (Mayer 1974:42–43). The failure of a strong, highly centralized and hierarchically structured political system to emerge among the Tarama and Chinchacocha thus may be due as much to the viability of exchange within their combined territories as to their propensity for settlement in zones where high population concentrations were not feasible.

Archaeological and ethnohistoric data have been presented here to describe a negative case of state formation in the Andean highlands. Negative cases require explanations for the persistence of society at nonstate levels of organization, or for the failure of potential causal mechanisms to precipitate state formation. It would not be justifiable to draw conclusions about 'prime movers' of state formation from such cases, since any number of critical conditions might not have been met. The pre-Incaic political economy of the Tarama and Chinchacocha populations appears to have been a durable and possibly widespread system eclipsed only by the overwhelming military might of Tawantinsuyu.

Population size and density were discussed as critical factors at least partially responsible for the persistence of society at a nonstate level in this area. Yet population alone is an insufficient explanation, since a 'critical mass' for political change might conceivably have been attained had settlements been concentrated near the valley bottoms. The fact that they were not, and that population densities remained relatively low, is explicable in part through the economic priorities of verticality.

Access to vertically dispersed resources in turn requires consideration of the geographical limits and ecological diversity of areas controlled by ethnic units. It has been argued that ethnic units, continuously spread across a wide range of zones, might concentrate less power than those that were more fragmentary and confined within narrower ecological limits. Yet the meaning of ethnicity and its recognition from archaeological materials remain in the forefront of problems that are poorly understood but crucial to the study of political evolution in the Andean highlands.

Acknowledgments

Material pertaining to the eastern part of this region, especially the districts of Huasahuasi and San Ramón, is based upon work conducted in 1979 and 1980 with support by the National Science Foundation under Grant BNS79–20055 and by a Rackham Dissertation Grant from the University of Michigan.

Chapter 15

Comment

Betty J. Meggers

Explaining the emergence of states has been a major concern among anthropologists for several decades, yet we are no closer to a consensus. The participants of this symposium have cited habitat diversity, environmental conscription, powerful integrative forces, warfare, limited access to prestige goods, concentrated control over production, and charismatic leaders as critical in the cases they have investigated. Other catalysts often suggested include trade, religion, population pressure, redistributive exchange systems, and regional specialization (e.g. Jones and Kautz 1981). Some anthropologists have approached explanation in terms of concepts such as segregation and centralization (Flannery 1972) and scale, integration, and complexity (Blanton *et al.* 1982).

The emergence of states is part of the general process of cultural evolution, which itself is subject to divergent explanations at almost every level. Whether we regard it as a global phenomenon ('unilinear evolution') or a recurrent localized process ('multilinear evolution'), most of us agree that there has been increasing organizational complexity that is resolvable into a sequence of stages with diagnostic features. The effort to move from this kind of descriptive statement to explanation provokes the diversity expressed in this symposium. There is no doubt that cultural configurations have been transformed, intensified, and destroyed by local historical events, both natural (earthquakes, droughts, epidemics, and so on) and cultural (conquests, overexploitation of subsistence resources, technological and ideological innovations, and so on). It is equally evident that identifying particular agents in local situations has not brought us the understanding prerequisite to formulating explanatory principles.

We might break this stalemate by turning the situation around and viewing local expressions as unique products of a general process of evolution buffeted by unpredictable historical events. Growing receptivity to applying evolutionary principles developed by biologists to cultural evolution is a positive trend for two reasons: (1) it provides us with a large body of theory and (2) it exposes anthropocentric biases inculcated by our immersion in the phenomena we are trying to study.

An example of the value of 'borrowing' from biologists is provided by Thomson's (1982) analysis of three distinct meanings for the term 'evolution,' whose confusion has led to misunderstandings among biologists, and which similarly impede understanding among anthropologists. The first is simply 'change over time,' a statement of the pattern observable in the geological record and among living organisms. The biological statement that 'fishes precede amphibians' is comparable to the cultural statement that 'chiefdoms precede states.' The second meaning introduces process. In this sense, the relationship is more than chronological. 'Fishes gave rise to amphibians;' similarly, 'Chiefdoms gave rise to states.' At this level, the explanation is general and based on the premise that all living things (and cultural traits) emerge from pre-existing forms rather than being newly and independently created fully developed. The presence among amphibians of features compatible with their derivation by modification from fishes and their later appearance in the fossil record are consistent with this conclusion. Similar logic applies to cultural phenomena. Few anthropologists would dispute the derivation of states from chiefdoms; both the continuities in various sociocultural expressions and the chronological evidence from the archaeological record support this interpretation.

Among biologists as well as anthropologists, the arguments derive mainly from the third meaning of the term 'evolution:' the specific ways in which changes arise and are perpetuated. In biology, the Darwinian explanation, natural selection, which involves differential survival of randomly generated variations, has demonstrated great resilience and flexibility. The discovery of genes and methods of their modification provided the mechanism for producing the variations. Recent advances in knowledge of the molecular structure and composition of genes have revealed new methods of variation and accumulation of diversity, which appear to permit more rapid and drastic transformations than traditional Darwinian theory has recognized. What is important from our standpoint is that these discoveries have not caused biologists to reject the general principle of natural selection. On the contrary, they clarify previously puzzling situations. In particular, they imply that gaps in the fossil record may reflect quantum changes rather than inadequate preservation of intermediate forms.

Of particular interest to the problem of understanding cultural change is Thomson's use of a threshold model to reconcile accumulation of genotypic diversity with maintenance of phenotypic uniformity:

> threshold models . . . produce the maximum potential change in a system with the minimal proximate disturbance . . . The situation could build up until the potential exists for a small further genetic change . . . or even an external environmental cue suddenly to cause a threshold to be crossed . . . In such a model, potentially a whole subpopulation can be at the same threshold and can be pushed over together by the spread of a single new allele or the same change in the environment, or both.
>
> (1982:531)

Substituting 'cultural' for 'genetic' change and 'cultural innovation' for 'allele' provides a potential explanation for rapid cultural change. Indeed, Boserup's analysis of the transformation of Europe during the Industrial Revolution fits the threshold model very well. In her view, Europe was for millennia unable to assimilate technological innovations developed earlier in Middle Eastern and Asiatic societies because of insufficient population density and dispersed settlement pattern. When this situation changed,

> when the density needed for urbanization was reached and transport facilities improved, the way was opened for

all the urban-linked, advanced technologies and intellectual achievements which had accumulated in other parts of the world. The initiative and creativeness which accompanied the concentration of the elite in urban centers in many ancient societies assumed revolutionary strength in Europe. Europe could import the inventions and scientific achievements which ancient societies had to think out.

> (1981:101)

Conversely, the absence of threshold conditions can account for the failure of innovations to be adopted among groups who are aware of them, and to whom they might appear to us beneficial (although other factors may also be involved).

Boserup and most of the participants in this symposium confine themselves to cultural instruments of change, either internally developed or introduced. Little attention is paid to the other principal factor cited by Thomson; namely, changes in the environment. Yet the Pacific coast of South America is endowed with multiple sources of drastic and unpredictable long- and short-term perturbations. Both abrupt phenomena such as volcanic eruptions and earthquakes and gradual changes such as continental uplift and climatic oscillations must have had significant impacts on human populations and cultures. Indeed, recent investigations on the north coast of Peru indicate that tectonic uplift and shifts in El Niño rendered inoperative extensive irrigation systems, with consequent reduction in subsistence productivity (Moseley *et al.* 1983). In the highlands, terraces and other remnants of cultivation above the present upper altitudinal limit attest to more benign conditions in the past and imply periodic stress on populations living at high elevations (Cardich 1975). The dramatic changes in weather and vegetation wrought by recent shifts in El Niño make it possible to observe one kind of catastrophe to which precolumbian groups also had to adapt. The gaps and discontinuities in the archaeological record may often reflect responses to such stresses and opportunities.

To see cultural events as the expression of evolutionary principles rather than conscious human initiative, we must discard our anthropocentric perspective. Rather than invoking the prestige of an elite to explain the emergence of state organization, we should ask how an elite enhanced a society's competitive advantage. What circumstances make centrally regulated redistribution more advantageous than reciprocity between kin and trading partners? What makes specialization in manufacturing goods or securing raw materials superior to local self-sufficiency among groups or regions with equal access to the required resources? Under what circumstances is the coexistence of autonomous societies more adaptive or less adaptive than their political integration? Are cultural configurations specialized to exploit particular habitats vulnerable when circumstances change? Does the replacement of theocratic by secular systems of integration reflect competitive superiority, comparable to the replacement of marsupials by placental mammals?

Following the tenets of the threshold model, we should

examine whether incipient structures or 'preadapted' cultural behavior is essential to social elaboration. If not, how are drastic transformations accomplished? What are the impacts of similar perturbations of cultural and natural origin on societies at the same or different levels of complexity or possessing the same or different forms of sociopolitical organization? Are departures from stable conditions, whether negative or positive, essential for significant cultural changes to take place? Asking these kinds of questions forces us to perceive specific situations as manifestations of basic processes, in which charismatic leaders, population pressure, warfare, and other 'prime movers' become the instruments rather than the causes of change.

These comments may appear unrelated to the reason I was asked to serve as a discussant, which is to provide a perspective from Amazonia. However, they derive directly from that perspective. Many of the mechanisms cited as conducive to state formation in the central Andes exist in the tropical forest, among them long-distance trade, localized specialization in manufacturing, warfare, and charismatic leaders. Incipient forms of occupational specialization, social stratification, and other 'preadaptations' also occur. The failure of configurations of the complexity achieved in the Andean region to emerge in the lowlands thus cannot be attributed to the absence of cultural potential. Rather, it seems to reflect constraints preventing fulfillment of that potential.

Our situation can be compared to that of the medieval alchemists, who sought in vain to transmute mercury into gold, frustrated by their ignorance of the structures of chemical elements and the rules for their alteration. Acquiring this knowledge made it possible to transmute gold into mercury and propelled us into the Atomic Age. The likelihood that a similar breakthrough in understanding the behavior of cultural elements will be equally significant for the future of our species provides a formidable challenge to spur on the search.

Chapter 16

Broader perspectives on Andean state origins

M. C. Webb

At the start of this disussion I would like to say that all of the contributions contained herein have been of exceptionally high quality and have provided very useful data – and raised highly interesting questions – relevant to the origins and evolution of the prehispanic Andean state. My comments will, however, largely be concerned with those topics which focus upon the beginnings and early stages of pristine or primary state development, primarily on the Peruvian coast, both because these involve questions upon which my own interest has largely been concentrated and because it was for these papers that I was given primary responsibility in the symposium from which this volume had its inception. Also, in no case will I presume to take serious issue with the archaeological facts as presented – matters upon which the regional specialist obviously possesses much more control than I. While I am fully conscious of the problem of the specialist versus the generalist ('the specialist must know more and more about less and less, while the generalist can only know less and less about more and more – so that soon no one will know anything about anything'), my role falls into the latter category. Accepting the data base as given, supplemented by such recent general syntheses as Lanning (1967), Willey (1971) and Lumbreras (1974a) and an interested outsider's knowledge of the journal literature, the discussion which follows will attempt to relate the views presented in the individual contributions to general questions of state origin.

These presentations can in fact be taken collectively as variations upon a general theme which appears to be emerging in recent discussions of that question. This theme represents a possible reconciliation – a moving together – of certain previously divergent views to the point that now (perhaps) serious disagreement mainly centers upon the question of which factors in a multivariant process were most critical at what point in the development. This possibility of agreement stems in large measure from the growing recognition that the search for primary state origins (indeed, for the origins of any state system) must be seen as the specification of a gradual, though surely accelerating, developmental trend rather than as a search for the moment at which, so to speak, some divine – or anthropological – authority rang the gong in heaven and declared, 'the state now exists.'

At the risk of some oversimplification, the theories commonly raised in regard to state origins may be classified for convenience in terms of two contrasts. The first is that between coercive militaristic explanations (the 'blood and iron' approach) and cooperative voluntaristic explanations (the 'sweetness and light' approach). The second contrast is between ecological explanations (adaptation primarily in the sphere of political economy) and explanations in terms of information processing (adaptation primarily in the ideological sphere). While these differences of approach probably reflect possibly irreconcilable differences of philosophy and mind-set, it does seem to be the case that the coercive and the ecological views typically go together, as do the voluntaristic and information processing approaches. Among figures associated with the former package may be noted: Carneiro (1961, 1970, 1978); Sanders and Price (1968); Harris (1977, 1979); Webster (1975), and myself (Webb 1968, 1975). Associated with the latter are such names as: Wittfogel (1957); Braidwood (1975); Flannery (1972); Johnson (1973); Kottak (1972, 1974, 1977); Brunfiel (1983) and Wilson (1983). While these lists are by no means exhaustive (omitting, for example, the name of Fried [1967, 1978], one of the key figures with whom all modern discussions of the topic must start), a perusal of the works cited (and their bibliographies) provide a reasonably good picture of the range of current opinion.

That there are, however, complicating factors is clearly indicated by the work of scholars who have taken a somewhat more eclectic view, such as Service (1975, 1978) or Haas (1982), or who have shifted their position with more empirical data, such as Wright (1972, 1977, 1978), significantly, in the latter case, from an almost purely information processing approach to one in which militarism plays a prominent part. It is, however, important to note that the value of such multiform approaches lies not in any facile and fashionable rejection of 'prime movers,' perhaps accompanied by an unfortunate refusal to specify in any useful fashion the relative strengths of factors operative at various points in the process, but precisely in the fact that the forces in question undoubtedly were continual, both logically and in space and time. Thus, as Marx and Engels recognized a century ago (Engels 1942), economic power is surely coercive, although less overtly so than naked armed force or fully developed hydraulic controls. In the same way, the emic reality of a ritual system that makes it a reliable information processing device would almost certainly give coercive power – at least up to a point (cf. Childe 1951). Obviously, too, these considerations apply whether the key items to be regulated are arable land or critical trade goods, or both (Sahlins 1958, 1963, 1972; Webb 1965, 1974, 1975). In my view, the really critical point is that what we see in state origins is an epochal though gradual shift from voluntaristic processes to coercive ones as interlocking aspects of one unitary (and probably inevitable, once events have moved far enough) development. This is not really surprising since, after all, this shift has always been the key problem.

In a very real sense, the question at issue often seems to be, not what caused the state but at what point in the developmental shift one chooses to call the polities in question 'state.' In other words, what you look for is what you get. If one wishes to characterize the system as a state at a relatively early point in the process, the system will almost certainly appear less coercive (and smaller in scale and less heterogeneous in nature) and a differing mix of causes will be seen – indeed, will be – operative; at a later point the whole situation will be more coercive. The important question is not the semantic debate (although this has not been without value in clarifying the issues), but rather the examination of the shifting proportions of factors within the general trend. It would seem, in other words, that there are conditions which in lesser intensity or in particular proportions lead to ranked societies – that is, to chiefdoms, with their reliance on information processing and theocratic sanctions, but also with the ability to force the issue of obedience (up to a point and upon occasion) – but which later in an appropriate setting can, indeed must, so intensify as to lead in turn from these to polities in which direct, open, militarily based coercive force was present, that is to societies which unquestionably were states.

Moreover, it would appear that Peru represents a prime example of just such developments. However, since I still prefer to restrict the use of the term 'state' to a relatively advanced point in the state formation process due to (or giving rise to?) my view that the emergence of coercive armed force was the final critical issue (in so far as one can be defined), I should probably deal at the outset with an area of disagreement with Haas, with whom clearly my views are otherwise much in accord. Considering such large late Initial Period and Early Horizon sites as La Florida and Las Haldas to be the work of states, he naturally considers state origins in these cases (at least) to be the consequences of theocratic power supplemented by this leadership group's evolving control of irrigated land – what one might call the classic Wittfogel scenario; warfare, while important, functioned primarily in the further consolidation and development of the state (the same processes are seen as working; the characterization of the stages differs). Are the sites of this time realistically to be regarded as indicators of states? With 400 000 cu m of construction at Huaca La Florida or even the 41 000 cu m at T. Pozorski's site of Huaca de los Reyes (T. Pozorski 1980), they are big – far larger, as Haas notes, than monuments typically reported in ethnographic accounts of chiefdoms.

Some comparisons may be germane at this point. The largest *marae* temple on Tahiti, that of Mahaiatea, had an approximate volume of only 14 000 cu m (26 m × 81 m on the base by 13 m high), although located within an extensively filled and leveled court of 114 m × 81 m (Ferdon 1981:52–56; Bellwood 1979:339–342). To my surprise, the largest ceremonial platform in the Hawaiian Islands, the *heiau* temple of Puukohola in the Kohala district of Hawaii at under 15 000 cu m (42.5 m × 103 m on the base by 3 m high at the tallest portion with a 2 m × 24 m wall about the top) was no larger (DeVarigny 1981:95–96; Kamakau 1961:145, 154–155). These are not in the same league at all.

At the same time, however, there is the question of cultural decision as to the activities chosen for ritual elaboration. David Malo (1951:170–174) reported that at the dedication of one of these large *luakini* temples well over 2200 pigs were slaughtered. Translating pigs into people is not easy, but Rappaport's data for the Maring of New Guinea suggest that caring for pigs is about as difficult as caring for people (Rappaport 1968:153–165; cf. Harris 1974:48–56). Putting these efforts into the support of 1500 extra builders working for one-third of the year (122 days), at 10 loads of 20 kg per worker per day, one gets 1 830 000 loads, totaling 36 600 000 kg. Allowing 140 loads per cu m (this from the specific gravity of limestone), one calculates to 13 000 cu m additional. In other words, people, not pigs would nearly double the size of an Hawaiian temple in one season's work. I have calculated that the 3000 men of a large-scale chiefdom (population of 15 000) working in 10 shifts of 300 men each (each shift lasting for one-tenth of the year or 36 days) could accumulate 400 000 cu m in slightly over 50 years, a figure which essentially agrees with T. Pozorski's calculations for Huaca de los Reyes. People are of course more difficult to raise than pigs, but they can support themselves, as the figures just given allow them to do. It is, moreover, clear that at the time of Cook an Hawaiian chiefdom was devoting essentially half a year's activity and a quite considerable quantity of goods to the ritual cycle (Webb 1965). In other words, the population of chiefdoms might typically put their efforts into activities other than monument building. (One thinks too of the undoubted kingdoms of East Africa, whose constructional activity was minimal.) It all depends on what one likes: Haas and I, as New World archaeologists, enjoy hauling rocks about in the hot sun; the Polynesians favored feasting on pig and dancing.

But was this proposed potential for building by chiefdoms ever actually realized? The answer appears to be yes, although not commonly. About one km off the east coast of the Micronesian island of Ponape (with an area 334 sq km and an estimated aboriginal population of perhaps 20 000 or a little more) is the well-known site of Nan Madol, the largest megalithic construction in the Pacific (Riesenberg 1968:1–6). Covering an area of perhaps 70 ha, the site consists of about 90 artificial islands of earth and coral with retaining walls of columnar basalt blocks (some of them ranging up to 45 m in length and 50 cm in thickness, with weights of over five metric tons). Some of the islands are about one ha in size and the total constructed surface is probably in excess of 200 000 sq m. Since the islands rise at least 2.5–3 metres above the lagoon floor and one open-air 'temple' alone may bulk 40 000 cu m, the total mass probably exceeds 600 000 cu m (Ayres and Haun 1978: Figure 2; Bellwood 1979:288–292; Karig 1948;51, 54, 67, 84–92; John Fischer, personal communication). Although there is no clear evidence that the work was planned in advance, the regularity of size and alignment of the constructions strongly indicates a continuity of tradition and authority throughout the process.

In West Carroll Parish in northeastern Louisiana stands the famous terminal Archaic site of Poverty Point, dating to the early first millennium B.C. Construction at the site consists of three large earth mounds and a semicircular earthwork made up of six concentric ridges extending 1.25 km north–south and 1 km east–west. The total volume of the large mound called Mound A and of the smaller Motley Mound and Mound B together is roughly 275 000 cu m. Since the original height and precise mode of construction of the ridges are still unclear, volume estimates for these features inevitably are very

imprecise, but their bulk is likely to have been on the order of 500 000–800 000 cu m, which gives a total for the site of over 750 000 cu m (C. H. Webb 1977:16–19). At the Middle Mississippian site of Cahokia, near East St Louis in southern Illinois, Monks Mound, measuring 308 m × 216 m and with a height of approximately 30 m, is the largest aboriginal construction north of Mexico. It was built in fourteen stages between the tenth and fourteenth centuries, and its bulk is estimated at 615 000 cu m (Fowler 1974:6, 13; Reed 1973). Despite previous larger estimates, current views as to the site's population are in the 10 000 range (James B. Griffin, personal communication). It will be recalled that the site once contained scores of other mounds, some quite large.

Turning to the Old World, one may note some examples from the Wessex region in southern England. Renfrew (1973a) provides an estimate of 181,136 cu m (6 500 000 cu ft) of bulk for the Dorset Cursus and estimates 9 000 000 man hours for its construction – by his estimates of available population and probable labor expenditure about 25 years of activity (my calculations for a 15 000 person chiefdom noted above would give a duration of 23.5 years for the project). For Silbury Hill, a great earthen mound 40 m high and 167 m in diameter with an estimated bulk in artificial construction of 247 875 cu m, the estimated labor investment is 18 000 000 man hours over a period of perhaps 15 years (Renfrew 1973a; 1973b; Balfour 1980:152–153). For the nearby site of Avebury, with its reported 200 000 English tons of chalk embankment (64 500 cu m to 96 000 cu m, depending on the density of the chalk) and 4000 tons of stone, the labor estimate is 1 500 000 man hours (Renfrew 1973a; Burl 1976:326–332). For Stonehenge 18 mi to the south, the labor estimate is over 30 000 000 man hours, although, since this was largely required to haul in the various great stones (up to 50 English tons in weight), it was probably expended in relatively short bursts rather than steadily over an extended period (Renfrew 1973a; 1973b:218–219; Burl 1976:302–316).

These are, indeed, considerable – and unusual – expenditures of sustained effort and vivid testimonies (in some cases) to enduring plans. (For comparison it may be noted that the Great Pyramid of Giza has a volume of about 2 526 000 cu m.) But, as Renfrew, among others, has noted, chiefdoms possess both the technological means and the organizational skills to achieve them (Renfrew 1973b:129–131, 214–233, 1983), provided they wish to work at this scale. One may, in fact, wonder if the failure of any more recent chiefdoms to achieve comparable works may not reflect the fact that in recent centuries states have occupied the areas best suited to produce primary states and otherwise tended to control the prime resources of the continental land masses, so that optimal conditions for chiefly efforts no longer existed.

These points have been pursued at some length because it is critical not to underestimate the possible upper range of chiefdom-level activity, thereby creating an unnecessarily great contrast between state and prestate systems, which in turn leads to our thinking in terms of almost certainly overly abrupt transitions. This mistake (a kind of semantic trick played upon ourselves) of placing the time of state origins at too early a point may well obscure the nature of the processes operative in the truly transitional era. The key question may in fact be the nature of these exceptional, unusual, 'non-bona fide' chiefdoms. There clearly is something going on at a stage between the typical chiefdom and the Great Pyramid, but what?

In my view, it is precisely in the structure and operation of chiefdoms when expanded to exceptionally great size and intensity of activity – because of a set of circumstances which is indeed rare – that the origins of the primary state may be found. In a very real sense, chiefdoms are the 'natural' culmination of sociocultural evolution, wherever conditions of technology and environment produce a productivity sufficient to support relatively large, dense and stable populations (Webb 1975). Thus chiefdoms have arisen in a fairly broad range of environmental types located (in contrast to the six to eight primary or largely primary state areas, all of which are environmentally similar) where these conditions of demography and settlement pattern have created the demand for persons with the access to information and the authority needed to allocate and develop productive resources, secure desirable or essential exotic goods, deal with possibly competitive and hostile neighbors, and insure reasonable internal harmony in relatively large communities. Although the leaders of these kinds of societies provide valuable and even critical services of an organizational, administrative, adjudicatory and prognosticating sort, their authority in large measure depends on operations superficially at some remove from real-world issues – that is, upon the provision of supernatural benefits (rainmaking, insuring fertility), religious sanctions (mana and taboo, bewitching or cursing) or the accumulation of goods which serve ritual or ideological as opposed to immediately utilitarian ends (Kula goods, tapa cloths, coppers). The fact that these powers (which as Sahlins [1963, 1972] noted, in large measure represent a consolidation, stabilization and centralization of the role of the egalitarian tribal big man) function through the deployment of prestige and religious powers, that is on the ideological level, rather than through the use of more directly coercive measures, is what makes controls in these polities more 'voluntaristic' than in states, as usually defined.

One can imagine three kinds of circumstances which singly or – more probably – in combination would push large chiefdoms in the direction of major transformations, of changes in scale and gravity of operation, creating both dangers and opportunities. The first would be significant and rapid population growth, with the consequence both that the subsistence base would have to be expanded – and protected from others in similar circumstances – and that greater effort would have to be made to secure foreign goods, again possibly in competition with other like-minded groups. The second would be a patchy environment with a mosaic distribution of those resources which were becoming more critical. The third

would be a relationship between the technology and the environment in which, finally, the expansion of extensive as opposed to intensive systems of production became impossible or at least very difficult so that continued growth required a high investment of labor and other capital – the expansion of hydraulic agriculture in arid or semiarid regions being the most developmentally clear-cut case. This, it seems to me, is the essential feature of 'circumscription' (perhaps not the best term for the situation, but one which has entered the literature). In other words, the critical issue is not severe overcrowding, per se, or abrupt environmental boundaries (difficulty of definition), but rather the onset of conditions which would pin down the populations of vigorous, growing ranked societies into a crisis situation in which the already ongoing powers of an existing centralized elite group would expand to the point of full reliance upon overt coercion. (A moment's reflection brings the realization that all of the exceptional chiefdoms mentioned above, to some degree 'failed states,' although located in very productive settings, lacked either sufficient circumscription, an expandable and controllable subsistence base or room for further expansion.)

By this view, the powers of the state would become added on to the prerogatives of the already existing chiefs, and in a very real sense the state would emerge from the top down rather than beginning from the bottom up in fractious intervillage squabbles. On this point Wilson's objections on the basis of his Santa Valley data to the circumscription hypothesis as usually understood (or misunderstood) are well taken, although they do not, really, cancel the valid contribution of the theory. And, in fairness to Carneiro, it must be noted that he never implied that the state emerged in some sort of Calcutta-like situation by the struggle of the last starving survivors of a famine; on the contrary, the state was the achievement of prosperous, vigorous, expanding societies which happened to find themselves in a setting in which they were unable to back out of a situation of growing conflict. Indeed, as S. Pozorski (1979b) pointed out a few years ago, the introduction of irrigation would at first increase the available land, thereby reducing population pressure in the simple sense – but at the cost of compelling the population to stay in place. One could also imagine other circumstances which would have similar effects, for example the support of early cultural elaboration on highly productive marine resources, either as a substitute for cultivated plants or as an essential protein source, since the availability of such resources from a limited zone would also represent circumscription in this more sophisticated sense. Unusually productive lacustrine resources may in fact have been the key factor in the emergence of the Poverty Point site (Jon Gibson, personal communication). Therefore, I have absolutely nothing invested in the debate concerning the relative role of marine resources versus cultigens in the support of the great preceramic sites of Peru (e.g. Moseley 1975a; Lanning 1967; Patterson 1971; Parsons 1970; Raymond 1981; Wilson 1981), except to doubt that in the long run anything could match agriculture in terms of its implications for population expansion, capital investment and administrative control, so that a moderate or qualified stance such as that of Quilter and Stocker (1983) is most likely to be correct for long-term trends.

It is probably the case that the situation outlined above is simply an expansion and intensification under special demographic and ecological conditions of those factors which must have given rise to ranked societies in the first place. Moreover, as suggested above, chieftains do put the arm on their followers, at times quite severely, war extensively among themselves and behave in all sorts of feisty ways. Kamakau's account of aboriginal Hawaii contains numerous examples (Kamakau 1961; cf. Sahlins 1972), while as recently as the 1970s a *Nahnmwarki* (paramount) of Ponape, in the course of construction activities, without any appeal to American colonial sanctions, had his people and his subordinate chiefs literally trembling for their titles (Martha Ward, personal communication). In this sense neighboring groups on the chiefdom level can handle their relationships in a 'voluntaristic' (note the quotes) fashion, with the 'arm' and military force nevertheless present. What (or who) lies within the territory of a given paramount is not always clear, since it depends on conditions at any given moment. Relations between potential contenders for the paramountcy or between a paramount and a subordinate may shift rapidly between obedience and hostility. In this way the coercive mechanisms may develop upward through the chiefdom level even though generally chieftains get the job done without the use of overt force (Davenport 1964).

Viewed in this light, Wilson's data actually fit the proposed scheme quite well (cf. Wilson 1983). I would gather that at the relevant periods the lower Santa Valley had 50–90 sq km of irrigated crop land and a population of about 30 000 persons. On Tahiti the larger of the two main divisions of the island had 100 sq km (Ferdon 1981:29, 179–180). Cook estimated the aboriginal population for the whole island as 100 000 (probably too high a figure), although in 1797, after severe depopulation, the estimate was only 16 000 (Goldman 1970:172); in the 1950s the population was about 36 000. In the larger portion of the island two or three chiefdoms were somewhat shakily controlled by a paramount, so the situation seems quite similar to that reconstructed for the Santa Valley. Some internal fighting took place, but the really critical conflicts were with the other portion of the island and with the other islands of the Society Island group (I doubt that artifact differences would reveal the internal divisions). The situation in Hawaii was generally similar (Webb 1965). Perhaps in the Santa Valley these sorts of processes – organization to enforce internal control and to fight other valley polities along the coast (and the loot resulting from the latter efforts, if successful) – would in time have led to the emergence of the state, had not the Moche beaten them to it.

Ranking – as indicated for example by restricted access to the most holy places on analogy with observed chiefdom practice – would of course have started much earlier. Feldman's paper on Aspero illustrates this point especially clearly, as well

as most of the other features one might expect to occur in rather large and well-organized chiefdoms – chiefdoms appearing, moreover, at about the time and place one would predict. S. Pozorski's study of the Casma Valley then demonstrates the next stage of the process, one or more major chiefdoms (her simple state) forging ahead under optimum conditions in the Initial Period to peak in one of these polities capable of truly extraordinary monument construction (Sechin Alto) later in the period, and then the emergence of relatively unrestrained militarism at the start of the Early Horizon. One almost has the impression of a final boiling over of coercive force from a previously confining theocratic container (her theocratic state) – appropriately, in the context of inter-valley and inter-regional rivalries – so that hereafter evidence for warfare is unmistakable. The developments in Moche are also of considerable interest, suggesting as they do that the more evolved a theocratic, voluntaristic polity becomes – that is, the longer it toys with and elaborates 'chiefly' mechanisms of centralization before switching over to newer, more overtly violent controls – the more effectively it may be able finally to apply such force at that later stage, provided, of course, that it had not been destroyed in the mean time (or, better yet, that most of its rivals had been weakened or eliminated by early and more premature militarism).

Daggett's work in Nepeña would of course also be illustrative of the process, perhaps marked in this case by more (or more obvious) intra-valley war building up throughout the Early Horizon. In this context one may also note the Topics' very apt comments concerning the degree to which evidence for militarism is uncertain, this uncertainty being much more likely to result in underestimates than overestimates of warfare (in reading S. Pozorski's remarks about the 'mound-dominated' sites of Early Intermediate Period Moche, I could not help thinking about Mesoamerica, where the city temple mound was universally recognized as the defenders' last redoubt – the symbol for the fall of a city being a temple in flames – or about conceptions of the Classic Maya prior to the discovery of the Bonampak murals).

In regard to war, one may suspect that an 'archaeologically conspicuous' (so to speak) force may not have been required. The papers by T. Pozorski, Klymyshyn and Mackey indicate just how small the controlling group might have been even as late as Chimu times. Evidently in the operation of even quite militaristic states (and both the Chimu and the earlier Moche have reputations as very tough customers indeed) the critical mass need not be large; presumably this could be true in earlier periods as well. This is not too surprising in the context of pre-industrial war. The Battle of Bosworth Field (1485), which set the Tudor dynasty on the English throne for 120 years, probably did not involve a total of 15 000 men on both sides. At the Battle of Sedgemoor (1685), where the force of James II defeated the Duke of Monmouth, the total number engaged probably did not exceed 12 000. In the evolution from chiefdom to state an even smaller number might have been critical – and a single alliance group among the

Dani of New Guinea could in theory have fielded forces of from one-sixth to one-third the size of the figures just cited (of course, that the Dani almost certainly would do no such thing is the key question, but see below).

The precise circumstances might well vary from place to place as long as the critical general condition of large groups with effective centralized leadership coming into serious competition in situations of economic binding or fastening down prevailed, sustained population growth being the obvious variable which would create and increase this through time. (And, in fact, such population growth seems to have been present in all of the primary state areas at least before the culmination of the development, although in most cases clearly not to the extent of occupying all arable land.) In world perspective one may in fact see such broadly differing factor mixes. On the Peruvian coast, possibly because of relatively small rivers controllable at the head, the picture does rather look more like Wittfogel's scheme than does the situation in many areas, even though warfare was clearly also a major factor. In regard to Mesoamerica, I once shocked an advanced seminar with the statement, 'There are no real states till the Postclassic.' Looking back, what I was trying to say was that, although states clearly were there in some degree by the Protoclassic, their continued strongly theocratic cast does remind one of greatly magnified chiefdoms (a characteristic, incidentally, which created problems for Mesoamericanists from Morgan to Vaillant), with the result that this region seems the closest to exemplifying Childe's (1951) view that the state in large measure arose through theocratic sanctions (cf. Webb 1968). In Mesopotamia a relatively high utilization of highly valuable materials and products may have caused them to be the critical resource, with the result that trade and information processing were more prominent – a feature perhaps reflected in unusually strong and early development of city life (although even here there seems to have been considerable population growth at the critical periods (Adams 1972, 1981; Wright 1977). In Egypt, on the other hand, Butzer's recent (1976) study suggests no serious shortage of land and local control of irrigation until a fairly late date, so that, very much in the manner outlined above, the Nile ecology seems to have served primarily to pin down the local nome populations as they fought for a variety of reasons – a point worth returning to shortly.

Although space precludes discussion of other, less well-reported primary state areas, the essential point, clearly, is that in all cases one starts with a set of societies with centralized direction achieved by 'voluntary' means and ends with them facing one another in circumstances of severe and inevitable military competition, a competition which, moreover, must in time put such naked coercive power into the hands of the rulers that local independence and the liberties of the commoners will be severely curtailed even in victorious societies. Both the previous centralization and the emerging strife are essential, and the lack of the former may be one reason that the Dani (who may have had dense population and labor-intensive

agriculture in a somewhat 'circumscribed' setting for centuries) did not develop beyond an advanced big-man system (Heider 1970, 1979). Shimada's work on occupational and regional integration, although dealing with later periods when the state was relatively well developed, also brings out the importance of centralized direction (cf. Shimada 1978).

In a sense, as I once suggested in an unpublished paper (Webb 1972), it is not so much that the state makes civilization as that civilization, or rather its roots – all that ritualism, art, legend, genealogy, prestige manufacturing, cultus and so forth that one associates with chiefdoms – makes the state. A somewhat similar point has been made in the engineer Mendelssohn's argument – probably rather overstated – that it was the organization required for pyramid building that finally consolidated the Egyptian state in the Old Kingdom (Mendelssohn 1974). However, this ancient civilization does this (or reaches its culmination), acquiring an aspect vital to its consolidation, expansion and survival, only when the back and forth fighting reaches an intensity that both causes the general population to accept discipline and also places free wealth – loot, tribute or the labor power of actually conquered populations – into the hands of the leadership (all processes noted by S. Pozorski for the later Early Horizon and later periods). Only this level of intensity (which need not at first involve the gobbling up by one polity of all the others, since all the competing elites would benefit both from the fruits of victory and from the imposition of the discipline required to avoid or to recover from defeat) gives the leadership sources of power untrammeled by the kinship bonds, ceremonial obligations and traditional restraints that tie the hands of chieftains. It is apparently this critical level of intensity – commonly a reflection of population distribution – that the groups described by Hastings lacked, despite their having, in some cases, rather productive agriculture and a tendency to frequent raiding; they were simply too spread out.

My views have been moving in the direction of such a compound or two-tiered view of state origins for some time (Webb 1978). In this regard, just as there is no need to suppose a final struggle of the last bleeding survivors of prestate struggles, so there is no need to suppose planned wars to take over scarce resources. In fact, at first there were probably not wars of conquest at all. The evidence of history and the ethnographic record pretty clearly indicates that neighboring peoples concerned to exploit the resources of the same environmental zones can be relied upon to fight over all kinds of things; quarrels do occur and, once the people out there have things worth taking, such robbery will become a significant part and, increasingly, a prime motive for warfare. Just put a group of large, prosperous, expanding chiefdoms together in a pressure cooker of environmental–subsistence technology limitation and it should happen. Like the convict's explanation to a shocked Richard Pryor that he had murdered the entire household because, after all, they were all at home, so too in our projected scenario the potential enemies, victims and sources of loot would be very much 'at home.' (Probably not because of social circumscription [Carneiro 1970] in most cases, because already existing states previously formed in some other region where developments were more rapid on account of real ecological fixing in place – regular circumscription – would have moved in first and taken them all over.) The fact that even in the Inca era the need for such wealth was in considerable measure created by an ideological system – by a sort of theological box into which the ruling class had locked itself – certainly does not negate this point (Conrad and Demarest 1984). Human motivations are always a complex mix of the practical, the emotional and the frankly irrational. Whatever the specific reasons, leaders (and others) on all but the simplest societal levels tend to want more.

Once a point is reached at which it is actually easier to take the desired items from one's neighbors than to produce them oneself, the consequences are fairly predictable. In this regard, the situation reported by T. Pozorski for the Chimu, although also a late case, is most instructive – and so typical as to be almost amusing. When, after years of effort, they were finally unable to get their great inter-valley canal to carry water (T. Pozorski and S. Pozorski 1982), at the first opportunity provided by the chaos consequent upon an ecological catastrophe they marched forth and took over much of the surrounding coast. One can scarcely doubt that this was simply a replay on a larger scale of processes of long duration in the Andean area – and indeed in every primary state area (cf. Steward 1956). When these activities had gone on long enough, the state had evolved.

The question still remains of what to call such polities, working as they do with mechanisms typical of the chiefdom stage but only under exceptional circumstances, and clearly immediately ancestral to the state as usually recognized by the historians, social scientists and politicians. I have used the terms 'super chiefdom' and 'conditional state' (so-called because obedience is still to some degree conditional and because events are often much conditioned by external factors because of the elite's still relatively weakly developed freedom of action), but neither seems particularly apt. I therefore now suggest the term 'regional polity' as a reasonably neutral designation of this type or stage – exemplified in Peru by the developments of the Initial Period and the Early Horizon. I hope thereby to do full justice to all aspects of the process of state formation, from its voluntaristic beginnings to its fully coercive conclusion, while looking to high-quality regional investigations of the type reported herein to elucidate the precise mix of factors operative in given conditions at any specific point in a given regional sequence.

REFERENCES CITED

Adams, Richard N.
1975 *Energy and Structure: A Theory of Social Power*. University of Texas Press, Austin.

Adams, Robert McC.
1966 *The Evolution of Urban Society*. Aldine, Chicago.
1972 Demography and the 'Urban Revolution' in Lowland Mesopotamia. In *Population Growth: Anthropological Implications*, edited by Brian Spooner, pp. 60–63. MIT Press, Cambridge.
1981 *Heartland of Cities: Surveys of Ancient Settlement and Land Use of the Central Floodplain of the Euphrates*. University of Chicago Press, Chicago.

Adelaar, Willem F. H.
1977 *Tarma Quechua*. The Peter de Ridder Press, Lisse.

Alarco, Eugenio
1971 *El Hombre Peruano en su Historia*, Vol. 1. Editorial Ausonia Tallares Gráficos, Lima.
1975 *Las Piedras Grabadas de Sechin*. Editorial Ansonia Tallares Gráficos, Lima.

Alva, Walter
1978 Las Salinas de Chao: Un Complejo Precerámico. In *El Hombre y la Cultura Andina*, edited by Ramiro Matos, pp. 275–276. III Congreso Peruano, Actas y Trabajos, Vol. 1. Lima.

Alva, Walter L., and Susana Meneses de Alva
1985 Los Murales de Ucupe en el valle de Zaña, Norte del Peru. *Beitrage zur Allgemeinen und Vergleichenden Archaologie* 5(1983):335–60.

Amat, Hernan
1976 Estudios Arqueológicos en la Cuenca del Mosna y en el Alto Marañón. *41st International Congress of Americanists* 3:532–544.

Anders, Martha B.
1975 Formal Storage Facilities in Pampa Grande, Peru: A Preliminary Report of Excavations. Unpublished manuscript in possession of the author.
1977 Sistema de Depósitos en Pampa Grande, Lambayeque. *Revista del Museo Nacional* 43:243–279.
1981 Investigation of State Storage Facilities in Pampa Grande, Peru. *Journal of Field Archaeology* 8:391–404.
1982 Diseño para la Investigacion de los Funciones de un Sitio Wari. *Investigaciones* 2:27–44. Universidad Nacional San Cristobal de Huamanga, Ayacucho.

Andrews, Anthony P.
1972 *A Preliminary Study of U-shaped Structures in Chan Chan and Vicinity, Peru*. Unpublished B.A. thesis, Department of Anthropology, Harvard University, Cambridge.
1974 The U-shaped Structures of Chan Chan, Peru. *Journal of Field Archaeology* 1:241–264.

Andrews, David H.
1963 *Paucartambo, Pasco, Peru: An Indigenous Community and a Change Program*. Ph.D. dissertation, Department of Anthropology, Cornell University. University Microfilms, Ann Arbor.

Ayres, William S., and Allan E. Haun
1978 Ponape Archaeological Survey. Interim Report No. 77–2, Submitted to the Historic Preservation Committee, Ponape District, and Trust Territory of the Pacific Islands, Historic Preservation Program, Saipan, Micronesian Archaeological Survey.

Balfour, Michael
1980 *Stonehenge and Its Mysteries*. Charles Scribner's Sons, New York.

Bankes, George
1977 *Peru before Pizarro*. Phaidon Press, Oxford.

Bankmann, Ulf
1980 Moche und Recuay. *Baessler-Archiv* 27(1979, Heft 2):253–271.

Bawden, Garth
1977 *Galindo and the Nature of the Middle Horizon in Northern Coastal Peru*. Unpublished Ph.D. dissertation, Department of Anthropology, Harvard University, Cambridge.
1982a Galindo: A Study in Cultural Transition During the Middle Horizon. In *Chan Chan: Andean Desert City*, edited by Michael E. Moseley and Kent C. Day, pp. 285–320. University of New Mexico Press, Albuquerque.
1982b Community Organization Reflected by the Household: A Study of Pre-Columbian Social Dynamics. *Journal of Field Archaeology* 9:165–181.
Bawden, Garth, and Geoffrey W. Conrad
1982 *The Andean Heritage*. Peabody Museum Press, Cambridge.
Bellwood, Peter
1979 *Man's Conquest of the Pacific: The Prehistory of Southeast Asia and Oceania*. Oxford University Press, New York.
Benavides, Mario
1979 Notas Sobre Excavaciones en Cheqohuasi, Wari. *Investigaciones* 2:9–26. Universidad Nacional San Cristobal de Huamanga, Ayacucho.
Bennett, Wendell C.
1939 *Archaeology of the North Coast of Peru*. Anthropological Papers of the American Museum of Natural History, Vol. 37, Part 1, New York.
1943 The Position of Chavin in Andean Sequences. *American Philosophical Society Proceedings* 86:323–326.
1944 *The North Highlands of Peru*. Anthropological Papers of the American Museum of Natural History, Vol. 39, Part 1, New York.
1948 *A Reappraisal of Peruvian Archaeology*. Society for American Archaeology *Memoir* No. 4. (Editor)
1950 *The Gallinazo Group, Viru Valley, Peru*. Yale University Publications in Anthropology 43, New Haven.
1953 *Excavations at Wari, Ayacucho, Peru*. Yale University Publications in Anthropology 49, New Haven.
Bennett, Wendell C., and Junius B. Bird
1964 *Andean Culture History*. The Natural History Museum Press, Garden City, New York.
Benson, Elizabeth P.
1972 *The Mochica: A Culture of Peru*. Praeger Publishers, New York.
Berger, R., G. Ferguson, and W. F. Libby
1965 ULCA Radiocarbon Dates IV. *Radiocarbon* 7:347.
Bird, Junius B.
1948a America's Oldest Farmers. *Natural History* 57:296–303, 334–335.
1948b Preceramic Cultures in Chicama and Viru. In *A Reappraisal of Peruvian Archaeology*, edited by Wendell C. Bennett, pp. 21–28. Society for American Archaeology Memoir No. 4.
1951 South American Radiocarbon Dating. In *Radiocarbon Dating*, edited by Frederick Johnson, pp. 1–65. Society for American Archaeology Memoir No. 8.
Bird, Robert McK., and Junius B. Bird
1980 Gallinazo Maize from the Chicama Valley, Peru. *American Antiquity* 45:325–332.
Blanton, Richard E., Stephen A. Kowalewski, Gary Feinman, and Jill Appel
1982 *Ancient Mesoamerica; A Comparison of Change in Three Regions*. Cambridge University Press, New York.
Bonavia, Duccio
1974 *Ricchata Quellccani: Pinturas Murales Prehispánicas*. Editorial Ausonia, Lima.
Bonnier, E., and C. Rozenberg
1978 L'Habitat en Village, à l'Epoque Préhispanique, dans le Bassin Shaka-Palcamayo. *Bulletin de l'Institut Français d'Etudes Andines* 7(1–2):49–71, 7(3–4):59–60.
Boserup, Ester
1981 *Population and Technological Change: A Study of Long-term Trends*. University of Chicago Press, Chicago.
Braidwood, Robert J.
1975 *Prehistoric Men*. 8th edition. Scott, Foresman, Glenview, Illinois.
Bram, Joseph
1941 *An Analysis of Inca Militarism*. Monographs of the American Ethnological Society, No. 4. University of Washington Press, Seattle.
Brennan, Curtiss
1978 *Investigations at Cerro Arena, Peru: Incipient Urbanism of the Peruvian North Coast*. Ph.D. dissertation, Department of Anthropology, University of Arizona, Tucson. University Microfilms, Ann Arbor.
1980 Cerro Arena: Early Cultural Complexity and Nucleation in North Coastal Peru. *Journal of Field Archaeology* 7:1–22.
1982 Cerro Arena: Origins of the Urban Tradition on the Peruvian North Coast. *Current Anthropology* 23:247–254.
Brewster-Wray, Christine
1983 Spatial Patterning and the Function of a Huari Architectural Compound. In *Investigation of the Andean Past: Papers from the First Annual Northeast Conference on Andean Archaeology and Ethnohistory*, edited by Daniel H. Sandweiss, pp. 122–135. Cornell Latin American Studies Program, Ithaca.
Browman, David L.
1976 Demographic Correlations of the Wari Conquest of Junin. *American Antiquity* 41:465–477.
1982 Some Political and Economic Implications of the Wari–Tiwanaku Interface. Paper presented at the 44th International Congress of Americanists, Manchester.
Bruhns, Karen O.
1977 The Moon Animal in Northern Peruvian Art and Culture. *Ñawpa Pacha* 14(1976):21–39.
Brumfiel, Elizabeth M.
1983 The Aztec State Making: Ecology, Structure, and the Origin of the State. *American Anthropology* 85:261–284.
Brush, Stephen B.
1977 *Mountain, Field and Family: The Economy and Human Ecology of an Andean Valley*. University of Pennsylvania Press, Philadelphia.
1982 The Natural and Human Environment of the Central Andes. *Mountain Research and Development* 2(1):19–38.
Bueno, Alberto and Terence Greider
1979 Arquitectura Precerámica de la Sierra Norte. *Espacio* 1:5.
Bueno, Alberto, and Lorenzo Samaniego
1969 Hallazgos Recientes en Sechin. *Amaru* 11:31–38.
Burger, Richard L.
1978 *The Occupation of Chavin, Ancash, in the Initial Period and Early Horizon*. Ph.D. dissertation, Department of Anthropology, University of California, Berkeley. University Microfilms, Ann Arbor.
1979 Resultados Preliminares de Excavaciones en los Distritos de Chavin de Huantar y San Marcos, Peru. In *Arqueología Peruana*, edited by Ramiro Matos, pp. 133–155. Lima.
1981 The Radiocarbon Evidence for the Temporal Priority of Chavin de Huantar. *American Antiquity* 46:592–602.
1985 Concluding Remarks: Early Peruvian Civilization and its Relation to the Chavin Horizon. In *Early Ceremonial Architecture in the Andes*, edited by Christopher B. Donnan, pp. 269–89. Dumbarton Oaks, Washington, D.C.
Burger, Richard L., and Frank Asaro
1977 Análisis de Rasgos Significativos en la Obsidiana de los Andes Centrales. *Revista del Museo Nacional* 43:281–325.
Burger, Richard L., and Lucy S. Burger
1980 Ritual and Religion at Huaricoto. *Archaeology* 33(6):26–32.
1985 The Early Ceremonial Center of Huaricoto. In *Early Ceremonial*

Architecture in the Andes, edited by Christopher B. Donnan, pp. 111–138. Dumbarton Oaks, Washington, D.C.

Burl, Aubrey
1976 *The Stone Circles of the British Isles*. Yale University Press, New Haven and London.

Bushnell, G. W. S.
1963 *Peru*. Thames and Hudson, London.

Busto, José Antonio del
1970 *Peru Antiguo*. Librería Studium Editores, Lima.
n.d. *Peru Preincaíca*. Librería Studium Editores, Lima.

Butzer, Karl W.
1976 *Early Hydraulic Civilization in Egypt: A Study in Cultural Ecology*. University of Chicago Press, Chicago and London.

Cabello Valboa, Miguel
1951 *Miscelanea Antártica*, originally published in 1586. Universidad Nacional Mayor de San Marcos, Lima.

Calancha, Antonio de la
1638 *Crońica Moralizada del Orden de San Augustín en el Peru, Con Succesos Ejemplares de Esta Monarquía*. Pedro Lacvalleria, Barcelona.

Carcedo, Paloma, and Izumi Shimada
1985 Behind the Golden Mask: Sicán Gold Artifacts from Batan Grande, Peru. In *Art of Pre-Columbian Gold: Jan Mitchell Collection*, edited by Elizabeth P. Benson and Julie Jones, pp. 60–75. Weidenfeld and Nicolson, London.

Cardenas, Mercedes
1976 *Informe Preliminar del Trabajo de Campo en el Valle de Chao*. Instituto Riva-Agüero, Pontífica Universidad Católica del Peru, Lima.
1977 *Informe Preliminar del Trabajo de Campo en el Valle de Santa*. Instituto Riva-Agüero, Pontífica Universidad Católica del Peru, Lima.
1978 *Columna Cronológica del Valle de Santa: Sitios Arqueológicos del Valle Bajo y Medio*. Instituto Riva-Agüero, Seminario de Arqueología, Lima.

Cardich, Augusto
1975 Agricultores y Pastores en Lauricocha y Límites Superiores del Cultivo. *Revista del Museo Nacional* 51:11–36. Lima.
1980 El Fenómeno de las Fluctuaciones de los Límites Superiores del Cultivo en los Andes: Su Importancia. *Relaciones de la Sociedad Argentina de Antropología* XIV(1):7–31.

Carlevato, Denise C.
1979 *Analysis of Ceramics from the Casma Valley, Peru: Implications for the Local Chronology*. Unpublished M.A. thesis, Department of Anthropology, University of Wisconsin, Madison.

Carmichael, Patrick H.
1980 *Prehistorica Sociopolitical Evolution of Small Polities in the Northern Sierra, Peru*. Unpublished M.A. thesis, Trent University, Peterborough, Ontario.

Carneiro, Robert L.
1961 Slash and Burn Among the Kuikuru and Its Implications for Cultural Development in the Amazon Basin. In *The Evolution of Horticultural Systems in Native South America: Causes and Consequences*, edited by Johannes Wilbert, pp. 47–68. Sociedad de Ciencias Naturales La Salle, Caracas.
1967 On the Relationship Between Size of Population and Complexity of Social Organization. *Southwestern Journal of Anthropology* 23:234–243.
1970 A Theory of the Origin of the State. *Science* 169:733–738.
1978 Political Expansion as an Expression of the Principle of Competitive Exclusion. In *Origins of the State: The Anthropology of Political Evolution*, edited by Ronald Cohen and Elman R. Service, pp. 205–223. Institute for the Study of Human Issues, Philadelphia.
1981 The Chiefdom: Precursor of the State. In *The Transition to*

Statehood in the New World, edited by Grant D. Jones and Robert R. Kautz, pp. 37–39. Cambridge University Press, Cambridge.

Cavallaro, Rafael
1982 *Social and Religious Consideration of Variation in Marked Adobes in Monumental Architecture at Batan Grande*. Unpublished B.A. thesis, Department of Anthropology, Princeton University, Princeton.

Childe, V. Gordon
1951 *Man Makes Himself*. Paperback edition. Originally published in 1936. New American Library, New York.

Cieza de León, Pedro
1946 La Crónica del Peru, originally published in 1553. In *Crónicas de la Conquista del Peru*, edited by Julio le Riverend, pp. 125–497. Editorial Nueva España, S.A., Churubusco, Mexico.
1977 *La Segunda Parte de la Crónica del Peru que Trata del Señorio de los Incas*, originally published in 1554. Editorial Universo, S.A., Lima.

Cobo, Bernabé
1890 *Historia del Nuevo Mundo*, originally published in 1653. E. Rasco, Seville.

Collier, Donald
1955 *Cultural Chronology and Change as Reflected in the Ceramics of the Viru Valley, Peru*. Fieldiana: Anthropology 4. Field Museum of Natural History, Chicago.
1962 Archaeological Investigations in the Casma Valley, Peru. In *Akten des 34 International Amerikanistenkongresses*, pp. 411–417.

Conklin, William
1974 Pampa Gramalote Textiles. In *Irene Emery Roundtable on Museum Textiles, Proceedings: Archaeological Textiles*, edited by P. L. Fiske, pp. 77–92. The Textile Museum, Washington, D.C.
1978 Estructura de los Tejidos Moche. In *Tecnología Andina*, edited by Rogger Ravines, pp. 299–332. Instituto de Estudios Peruanos, Lima.
1982 The Information Systems of Middle Horizon Quipus. In *Ethnoastronomy and Archaeoastronomy in the American Tropics*, edited by Anthony F. Aveni and Gary Urton, pp. 261–281. Annals of the New York Academy of Sciences, Vol. 385. New York.

Conrad, Geoffrey W.
1974 *Burial Platforms and Related Structures on the North Coast of Peru: Some Social and Political Implications*. Unpublished Ph.D. dissertation, Department of Anthropology, Harvard University, Cambridge.
1980 Plataformas Funerarias. In *Chanchán, Metropolí Chimu*, edited by Rogger Ravines, pp. 217–230. Instituto de Estudios Peruanos, Lima.
1981 Cultural Materialism, Split Inheritance, and the Expansion of Ancient Peruvian Empires. *American Antiquity* 46:3–26.
1982 The Burial Platforms of Chan Chan: Some Social and Political Implications. In *Chan Chan: Andean Desert City*, edited by Michael E. Moseley and Kent C. Day, pp. 87–117. University of New Mexico Press, Albuquerque.

Conrad, Geoffrey W., and Arthur A. Demarest
1984 *Religion and Empire: The Dynamics of Aztec and Inca Expansionism*. Cambridge University Press, Cambridge.

Cook, Anita G.
1979 *The Iconography of Empire: Symbolic Communication in Seventh Century Peru*. Unpublished M.A. thesis, Department of Anthropology, State University of New York, Binghamton.

Coupland, Gary G.
1979 *A Survey of Prehistoric Fortified Sites in the North Highlands of Peru*. Unpublished M.A. thesis, Trent University, Peterborough, Ontario.

Czwarno, Robert M.

1983 *Ceramic Indications of Cultural Interaction: Evidence from Northern Peru*. Unpublished M.A. thesis, Trent University, Peterborough, Ontario.

Daggett, Richard E.
1980 The Trade Process and the Implications of Trade in the Bahamas. *The Florida Anthropologist* 33:143–151.
1982a The Nature of the Early Horizon in the Nepeña Valley, North Coast of Peru. Paper presented at the 47th annual meeting of the Society for American Archaeology, Minneapolis.
1982b Virahuanca Bajo: On Understanding Megalithic Sites in the Nepeña Valley. Paper presented at the First Annual Conference on Andean Archaeology and Ethnohistory, Ithaca.
1983 Megalithic Sites in the Nepeña Valley, Peru. In *Investigations of the Andean Past: Papers from the First Annual Northeast Conference on Andean Archaeology and Ethnohistory*, edited by Daniel H. Sandweiss, pp. 75–97. Cornell Latin American Studies Program, Ithaca.

D'Altroy, Terence N.
1981 *Empire Growth and Consolidation: The Xauxa Region of Peru under the Incas*. Ph.D. dissertation, Department of Anthropology, University of California, Los Angeles. University Microfilms, Ann Arbor.

Davenport, William
1964 Hawaiian Feudalism. *Expedition* 6:14–27.

Day, Kent C.
1973 *Architecture of Ciudadela Rivero, Chan Chan, Peru*. Unpublished Ph.D. dissertation, Department of Anthropology, Harvard University, Cambridge.
1982a Ciudadelas: Their Form and Function. In *Chan Chan: Andean Desert City*, edited by Michael E. Moseley and Kent C. Day, pp. 55–56. University of New Mexico Press. Albuquerque.
1982b Storage and Labor Service: A Production and Management Design for the Andean Area. In *Chan Chan: Andean Desert City*, edited by Michael E. Moseley and Kent C. Day, pp. 333–349. University of New Mexico Press, Albuquerque.

Deeds, Eric E.
n.d. Site Survey of the Moche Valley. MS in possession of the author.

Deeds, Eric E., James S. Kus, Michael E. Moseley, Fred Nials, Charles Ortloff, Lonnie Pippin, Shelia Pozorski, and Thomas Pozorski
1978 Un Estudio de Irrigación Prehispánica en Pampa Esperanza, Valle de Moche: Metodología y Resultados Preliminares. In *El Hombre y la Cultura Andina*, edited by Ramiro Matos, pp. 217–234. III Congreso Peruano, Actas y Trabajos, Vol. 1, Lima.

DeHetre, Deborah A.
1979 *Prehistoric Settlement and Fortification Patterns of La Libertad, Peru: An Aerial Photographic Analysis*. Unpublished M.A. Thesis, Trent University, Peterborough, Ontario.

DeVarigny, Charles
1981 *Fourteen Years in the Sandwich Islands, 1855–1868*. University of Hawaii Press, Honolulu.

Diez de San Miguel, Garci
1964 *Visita Hecha a la Provincia de Chucuito por Garci Diez de San Miguel en el año 1567*, edited by Waldemar Espinoza Soriano, pp. 3–287. Documentos Regionales para la Etnología y Etnohistoria Andinas, Vol. 1. Ediciones de la Casa de la Cultura del Peru, Lima.

Dillehay, Tom D.
1979 Pre-hispanic Resource Sharing in the Central Andes. *Science* 204:24–31.

Disselhoff, Hans D.
1959 Tumbas de San José de Moro (Provincia de Pacasmayo, Peru). *Proceedings of the 32nd International Congress of Americanists*, pp. 364–367. Copenhagen.
1971 *Vicús, eine Neu Entdecke Alteperuanische Kultur*. Monumenta Americana 3.

1972 Metallschmuck aus der Loma Negra, Vicús. *Antike* Walt 3, Jahrg. heft 2, Zurich.

Donnan, Christopher B.
1973 *Moche Occupation of the Santa Valley, Peru*. University of California Publications in Anthropology, no. 8, Los Angeles.
1976 *Moche Art and Iconography*. UCLA Latin American Center Publications, Los Angeles.
1978 *Moche Art of Peru*. UCLA Latin American Center Publications, Los Angeles.
1982 Dance in Moche Art. *Ñawpa Pacha* 20:97–120.

Donnan, Christopher B., and Carol J. Mackey
1978 *Ancient Burial Patterns of the Moche Valley, Peru*. University of Texas Press, Austin.

Drucker, Philip
1965 *Cultures of the North Pacific Coast*. Chandler, San Francisco.

Duviols, Pierre
1973 Huari y Llacuaz. *Revista del Museo Nacional* 39:153–191.

Earle, Timothy K.
1972 Lurin Valley Peru: Early Intermediate Period Settlement Development. *American Antiquity* 37:467–477.
1978 *Economic and Social Organization of a Complex Chiefdom: The Halelea District, Hawa'i, Hawaii*. Anthropological Papers, Museum of Anthropology, University of Michigan 63, Ann Arbor.

Earle, Timothy K., Terence N. D'Altroy, Catherine J. LeBlanc, Christine A. Hastorf, and Terry Y. LeVine.
1980 Changing Settlement Patterns in the Upper Mantaro Valley, Peru. *Journal of New World Archaeology* 4(1). Institute of Archaeology, University of California, Los Angeles.

Easby, Dudley T., Jr, Earle R. Caley and K. Moazed
1967 Axe-money: Facts and Speculation. *Revista Mexicana de Estudios Antropológicos* 21:107–148. Mexico City.

Elera, Carlos G.
1984 Características e Implicaciones Culturales en Dos Tumbas Disturbadas de Huaca La Merced, Complejo Arqueológico de Batán Grande, Lambayeque, Costa Norte del Peru. Informe presentado al Instituto Nacional de Cultura, Lima.

Eling, Herbert H., Jr
1978 Interpretaciones Preliminares del Sistema de Riego Antiguo de Talambo en el Valle de Jequetepeque, Peru. In *El Hombre y la Cultura Andina*, edited by Ramiro Matos, pp. 401–19. III Congress Peruano, Actas y Trabajos, Vol. 2, Lima.

Engel, Frederic A.
1957a Early Sites on the Peruvian Coast. *Southwestern Journal of Anthropology* 13:54–68.
1957b Sites et établissements sans Ceramique de la Côte Peruvienne. *Journal de la Société des Americanistes*, New Series 55:43–95.
1963 *A Preceramic Settlement on the Central Coast of Peru: Asia, Unit 1*. Transactions of the American Philosophical Society 53(3).
1966 *Geografía Humana Prehistórica y Agricultura Precolombina de la Quebrada de Chilca*. Universidad Agraria, Oficina de Promoción y Desarrollo, Departamento de Publicaciones, Lima.
1967 Le Complexe Preceramique d'el Paraíso (Perou). *Journal de la Société des Americanistes* 55:43–96.
1970 *Las Lomas de Iguanil y el Complejo de Haldas*. Departamento de Publicaciones, Universidad Agraria, Lima.

Engels, Friedrich
1942 *The Origin of the Family, Private Property and the State: In the Light of the Researches of Lewis H. Morgan*, originally published in 1884.

Espinoza, Waldemar
1975 Ichoc-Huánuco y el Señorio del Curaca Huanca en el Reino de Huánuco, Siglos XV y XVI, un Visita Inédita de 1549 para la Etnohistoria Andina. *Anales Científicos de la Universidad del Centro del Peru*, 4:5–88. Huancayo, Peru.

Estete, Miguel de
1946 La Relación del Viaje que Hizo el Señor Capitán Hernando Pizarro, originally published in 1563. In *Crónica de la Conquista del Peru*, edited by Julio le Riverend, pp. 90–108. Editorial Nueva España, Churubusco, Mexico.

Estrada, Emilio
1957 *Ultimas Civilizaciones Pre-Históricas de la Cuenca del Rio Guayas.*
1961 Correlaciones entre la Arqueología de la Costa del Ecuador y el Peru. *Humanitas* 2(2):31–61.

Farfán, J. M. B.
1949 Colección de Textos Quechuas del Peru Central. *Revista del Museo Nacional* 18:121–166.

Farrington, Ian S.
1974 Irrigation and Settlement Pattern: Preliminary Research Results from the North Coast of Peru. In *Irrigation's Impact on Society*, edited by Theodore E. Downing and McGuire Gibson, pp. 83–94. Anthropological Papers of the University of Arizona 25. University of Arizona, Tucson.

Feldman, Robert A.
1977 Life in Ancient Peru. *Field Museum of Natural History Bulletin* 48(6):12–17.
1978 Informe Preliminar Sobre Excavaciones en Aspero, Peru y sus Implicaciones Teóricas. *Investigación Arqueológica* 2:20–27.
1980 *Aspero, Peru: Architecture, Subsistence Economy, and Other Artifacts of a Preceramic Maritime Chiefdom*. Unpublished Ph.D. dissertation, Department of Anthropology, Harvard University, Cambridge.
1985 Preceramic Corporate Architecture: Evidence for the Development of Non-Egalitarian Social Systems in Peru. In *Early Ceremonial Architecture in the Andes*, edited by Christopher B. Donnan, pp. 71–92. Dumbarton Oaks, Washington, D.C.

Ferdon, Edwin N.
1981 *Early Tahiti as the Explorers Saw It, 1767–1797*. University of Arizona Press, Tucson.

Flannery, Kent V.
1971 The Cultural Evolution of Civilizations. *Annual Review of Ecology and Systematics* 3:399–426.

Flores, Isabel
1960 Wichqana, Sitio Temprano en Ayacucho. In *Antiguo Peru, Espacio y Tiempo*, edited by Ramiro Matos, pp. 335–344. Librería-Editorial Juan Mejía Baca, Lima.

Fonseca, Oscar and James B. Richardson, III.
1978 South American and Mayan Cultural Contacts at the Las Huacas Site, Costa Rica. *Annals of Carnegie Museum of Natural History* 47:299–317.

Ford, James A.
1949 *Cultural Dating of Prehistoric Sites in the Viru Valley, Peru*. Anthropological Papers of the American Museum of Natural History, Vol. 43, Part 1, New York.

Fowler, Melvin L.
1974 Cahokia: Ancient Capital of the Midwest. *Addison-Wesley Module in Anthropology* 48:1–38. Reading, Massachusetts.

Fried, Morton H.
1967 *The Evolution of Political Society: An Essay in Political Anthropology*. Random House, New York.
1978 The State, the Chicken, and the Egg; or, What Came First? In *Origins of the State: The Anthropology of Political Evolution*, edited by Ronald Cohen and Elman R. Service, pp. 35–47. Institute for the Study of Human Issues, Philadelphia.

Fung, Rosa
1969 Las Aldas: su Ubicación Dentro del Proceso Histórico del Peru Antiguo. *Dédalo* 5(9–10), Lima.

Fung, Rosa, and Carlos Williams
1977 Exploraciones y Excavaciones en el Valle de Sechin, Casma. *Revista del Museo Nacional* 43:111–155.

Gayton, Anna H.
1927 *The Uhle Collections from Nievería*. University of California Publications in American Archaeology and Ethnology, Vol. 21, No. 8, Berkeley.

Gayton, Anna H., and Alfred L. Kroeber
1927 *The Uhle Pottery Collections from Nazca*. University of California Publications in American Archaeology and Ethnology, Vol. 24, No. 1, Berkeley.

Gillin, John
1945 *Moche: A Peruvian Coastal Community*. Institute of Social Anthropology Publication No. 3. Smithsonian Institution, Washington, D.C.

Godelier, Maurice
1977 *Perspectives in Marxist Anthropology*. Cambridge University Press, Cambridge.

Goldman, Irving
1970 *Ancient Polynesian Society*. University of Chicago Press, Chicago and London.

Gorenstein, Shirley S.
1963 *The Differential Development of Military and Political Organization in Prehispanic Peru and Mexico*. Ph.D. dissertation, Department of Anthropology, Columbia University, New York. University Microfilms, Ann Arbor.

Grieder, Terence
1975 A Dated Sequence for Building and Pottery at Las Haldas. *Ñawpa Pacha* 13:99–112.

Grieder, Terence, and Alberto Bueno
1981 La Galgada: Peru before Pottery. *Archaeology* 34:44–51.
1985 Ceremonial Architecture at La Galgada. In *Early Ceremonial Architecture in the Andes*, edited by Christopher B. Donnan, pp. 93–109. Dumbarton Oaks, Washington, D.C.

Haas, Jonathan
1981 Class Conflict and the State in the New World. In *The Transition to Statehood in the New World*, edited by Grant D. Jones and Robert R. Kautz, pp. 81–102. Cambridge University Press, Cambridge.
1982 *The Evolution of the Prehistoric State*. Columbia University Press, New York.
1985 Excavations on Huaca Grande: An Initial View of the Elite at Pampa Grande. *Journal of Field Archaeology* 12:391–409.

Haley, Shawn D.
1979 *Late Intermediate Period Settlement Patterns on the Carabamba Plateau, Northern Peru*. Unpublished M.A. thesis, Trent University, Peterborough, Ontario.

Harris, Marvin
1974 *Cows, Pigs, Wars and Witches: The Riddles of Culture*. Random House, New York.
1977 *Cannibals and Kings: The Origins of Cultures*. Random House, New York.
1979 *Cultural Materialism: The Struggle for a Science of Culture*. Vintage Books, New York.

Hastings, Charles M.
1981 Prehistoric Vertical Economy in the Eastern Andes: The Tarama of Central Peru. Progress Report on Fieldwork Conducted in 1979–1980, Submitted to the National Science Foundation. MS on file, Museum of Anthropology, University of Michigan, Ann Arbor.
n.d. Highland Settlements in Eastern Forests: Late Intermediate Occupation of the Central Peruvian Ceja de Montaña. In *New Models for the Political Economy of Pre-Columbian Polities*, edited by Patricia J. Netherly and David Friedel, volume in preparation.

Hastings, Charles M., and Michael E. Moseley
1975 The Adobes of Huaca del Sol and Huaca de la Luna. *American Antiquity* 40:196–203.

Heider, Karl G.

1970 *The Dugum Dani: A Papuan Culture in the Highlands of West New Guinea*. Viking Fund Publications in Anthropology 49. Wenner-Gren Foundation for Anthropological Research, New York.

1979 *Grand Valley Dani: Peaceful Warriors*. Holt, Rinehart and Winston, New York.

Holm, Olaf

1966–67 Axe Money from Ecuador. *Folk* 8–9:135–143, Copenhagen.

1975 *La Pieza* No. 3. Casa de la Cultura Ecuatoriana, Guayas.

1981 *Cultura Milagro-Qeuvedo*. Museo Antropológico y Pinacoteca del Banco Central del Ecuador, Guayaquil.

Horkheimer, Hans

1961 *La Cultura Mochica. Las Grandes Civilizaciones del Antiguo Peru 1*. Ediciones Seguros y Reaseguros Peruano-Suiza, Lima.

1965 *Vicús*. Instituto de Arte Contemporáneo, Lima.

Huapaya, C.

1977–78 Vegetales como Elementos Antisísmicos en Estructuras Prehispánicas. *Arqueología PUC* 19–20:27–38.

Huntington, Richard, and Peter Metcalf

1978 *Celebrations of Death*. Cambridge University Press, Cambridge.

Hutchinson, Thomas J.

1873 *Two Years in Peru, with Exploration of its Antiquities*. Sampson, Low, Marston and Searle, London.

Isbell, William H.

1977 *The Rural Foundation for Urbanism: Economic and Stylistic Interaction between Rural and Urban Communities in Eighth Century Peru*. University of Illinois Press, Urbana.

1978 Environmental Perturbations and the Origins of the Andean States. In *Social Archaeology: Beyond Subsistence and Dating*, edited by Charles Redman *et al.*, pp. 303–313. Academic Press, New York.

1980 La Evolución del Urbanismo y del Estado en el Peru Tiwanakoide. *Estudios Arqueológicos* 5:121–132. Instituto de Investigaciones Arqueológicas y Restauración Monumental, Universidad de Chile, Antofagasta.

1982 The Huari Urban Prehistory Project. Paper presented at the 44th International Congress of Americanists, Manchester.

Isbell, William H., and Katharina Schreiber

1978 Was Huari a State? *American Antiquity* 43:372–389.

Ishida, Eiichiro, Koichi Aki, Taiji Yazawa, Seiichi Izumi, Hisashi Sato, Iwao Kobori, Kazuo Terada, and Taryo Obayahsi

1960 *Andes I: The Report of the University of Tokyo Scientific Expedition to the Andes in 1958*. Bijutsushuppansha, Tokyo.

Izumi, Seiichi

1971 Development of the Formative Culture in the Ceja de Montaña of the Central Andes. In *Dumbarton Oaks Conference on Chavin*, edited by Elizabeth P. Benson, pp. 49–72. Dumbarton Oaks, Washington, D.C.

Izumi, Seiichi, and Kazuo Terada

1972 *Excavations at Kotosh, Peru. A Report on the Third and Fourth Expeditions*. University of Tokyo Press, Tokyo.

Izumi, Seiichi, and Toshihiko Sono

1963 *Andes 2: Excavations at Kotosh, Peru, 1960*. Kadokawa Publishing Co., Tokyo.

Jimenez, Arturo

1969 El Estilo Sechin, *Amaru* 11:39–41.

Johnson, Gregory A.

1973 *Local Exchange and Early State Development in Southwestern Iran*. Anthropological Papers, Museum of Anthropology, University of Michigan 51. Ann Arbor.

1978 Information Sources and the Development of Decision-making Organizations. In *Social Archaeology: Beyond Subsistence and Dating*, edited by Charles L. Redman *et al.*, pp. 87–112. Academic Press, New York.

Jones, Grant D., and Robert R. Kautz (editors)

1981 *The Transition to Statehood in the New World*. Cambridge University Press, Cambridge.

Jones, Julie

1979 Mochica Works of Art in Metal: A Review. In *Pre-Columbian Metallurgy of South America*, edited by Elizabeth P. Benson, pp. 53–104. Dumbarton Oaks, Washington, D.C.

Julien, Catherine J.

1978 *Inca Administration in the Titicaca Basin as Reflected at the Provincial Capital of Hatunqolla*. Ph.D. dissertation, Department of Anthropology, University of California, Berkeley. University Microfilms, Ann Arbor.

1985 Guano and Resource Control in Sixteenth Century Arequipa. In *Andean Ecology and Civilization*, edited by S. Masuda, Izumi Shimada and Craig Morris, pp. 185–231. University of Tokyo Press, Tokyo.

Kamakau, Samuel M.

1961 *Ruling Chiefs of Hawaii*. Kamehameha Schools Press, Honolulu.

Kano, Chaki

1979 *The Origins of the Chavin Culture*. Studies in Pre-Columbian Art and Archaeology 24. Washington, D.C.

Karig, Walter

1948 *The Fortunate Islands: A Pacific Interlude*. Rinehart, New York.

Kauffmann, Federico

1980 *Manual de Arqueología Peruana*. Iberia, Lima.

Keatinge, Richard W.

1973 *Chimu Ceramics from the Moche Valley, Peru: A Computer Application to Seriation*. Unpublished Ph.D. dissertation, Department of Anthropology, Harvard University, Cambridge.

1974 Chimu Rural Administrative Centers in the Moche Valley, Peru. *World Archaeology* 6:66–82.

1975 Urban Settlement Systems and Rural Sustaining Communities: An Example from Chan Chan's Hinterland. *Journal of Field Archaeology* 2:215–227.

1980 Centros Administrativos Rurales. In *Chanchán: Metrópoli Chimu*, edited by Rogger Ravines, pp. 283–298. Instituto de Estudios Peruanos, Lima.

1981 The Nature and Role of Religious Diffusion in the Early Stages of State Formation: An Example from Peruvian Prehistory. In *The Transition to Statehood in the New World*, edited by Grant D. Jones and Robert R. Kautz, pp. 172–187. Cambridge University Press, Cambridge.

1982 The Chimu Empire in a Regional Perspective: Cultural Antecedents and Continuities. In *Chan Chan: Andean Desert City*, edited by Michael E. Moseley and Kent C. Day, pp. 197–224. University of New Mexico Press, Albuquerque.

Keatinge, Richard W., David Chodoff, Deborah P. Chodoff, Murray Marvin, and Helaine Silverman

1975 From Sacred to the Secular: First Report on a Prehistoric Architectural Transition on the Peruvian North Coast. *Archaeology* 28:128–129.

Keatinge, Richard W., and Geoffrey W. Conrad

1983 Imperialist Expansion in Peruvian Prehistory: Chimu Administration of Conquered Territory. *Journal of Field Archaeology* 10:255–283.

Keatinge, Richard W., and Kent C. Day

1973 Socio-economic Organization of the Moche Valley, Peru, during the Chimu Occupation of Chan Chan. *Journal of Anthropological Research* 29:275–295.

1974 Chan Chan: A Study of Precolumbian Urbanism and the Management of Land and Water Resources in Peru. *Archaeology* 27:228–235.

Kigoshi, K., Y. Tomidura, and K. Endo

1961 Gakushuin Natural Radiocarbon Measurements I. *Radiocarbon* 4:91–92.

Klymyshyn, Alexandra M. Ulana

1976 *Intermediate Architecture in Chan Chan, Peru*. Unpublished Ph.D.

dissertation, Department of Anthropology, Harvard University, Cambridge.

1980 Inferencias Sociales y Funcionales de la Arquitectura Intermedia. In *Chan Chán: Metrópoli Chimu*, edited by Rogger Ravines, pp. 250–266. Instituto de Estudios Peruanos, Lima.

1982 Elite Compounds in Chan Chan. In *Chan Chan: Andean Desert City*, edited by Michael E. Moseley and Kent C. Day, pp. 119–143. University of New Mexico Press, Albuquerque.

Knobloch, Patricia J.

1981 *A Study of the Andean Huari Ceramics from the Early Intermediate Period to Middle Horizon Epoch I*. Ph.D. dissertation, Department of Anthropology, State University of New York, Binghamton.

Kolata, Alan L.

1978 *Chan Chan: The Form of the City in Time*. Unpublished Ph.D. dissertation, Department of Anthropology, Harvard University, Cambridge.

1980 Chanchan: Crecimiento de una Ciudad Antigua. In *Chanchán: Metrópoli Chimu*, edited by Rogger Ravines, pp. 130–154. Instituto de Estudios Peruanos, Lima.

1982 Chronology and Settlement Growth at Chan Chan. In *Chan Chan: Andean Desert City*, edited by Michael E. Moseley and Kent C. Day, pp. 67–85. University of New Mexico Press, Albuquerque.

Kosok, Paul

1959 El Valle de Lambayeque. *Actas ye Trabajos del II Congreso Nacional de Historia del Peru: Época Pre-Hispánica* 1:69–76. Lima.

1965 *Life, Land and Water in Ancient Peru*. Long Island University Press, New York.

Kottack, Conrad P.

1972 A Cultural Adaptive Approach to Malagasy Political Organization. In *Social Exchange and Interaction*, edited by Edwin N. Wilmsen, pp. 107–128. Anthropological Papers, Museum of Anthropology, University of Michigan 46, Ann Arbor.

1974 *Anthropology: The Exploration of Human Diversity*. Random House, New York.

1977 The Process of State Formation in Madagascar. *American Ethnologist* 4:136–155.

Kroeber, Alfred L.

1925a *The Uhle Pottery Collections from Moche*. University of California Publications in American Archaeology and Ethnology, Vol. 21, No. 5, Berkeley.

1925b *The Uhle Pottery Collections from Supe*. University of California Publications in American Archaeology and Ethnology, Vol. 21, No. 6, Berkeley.

1926 *The Uhle Pottery Collections from Chancay*. University of California Publications in American Archaeology and Ethnology, Vol. 27, No. 7, Berkeley.

1930 *Archaeological Explorations in Peru, Part II: The Northern Coast*. Field Museum of Natural History Anthropological Memoirs, Vol. 2, No. 2, Chicago.

1944 *Peruvian Archaeology in 1942*. Viking Fund Publications in Anthropology No. 4. New York.

Kroeber, Alfred L., and William D. Strong

1924a *The Uhle Collections from Chincha*. University of California Publications in American Archaeology and Ethnology, Vol. 21, No. 1, Berkeley.

1924b *The Uhle Pottery Collections from Ica*. University of California Publications in American Archaeology and Ethnology, Vol. 21, No. 3, Berkeley.

Krzanowski, Andrzej

1977 Yuraccama: The Settlement Complex in the Alto Chicama Region (Northern Peru). *Polish Contributions in New World Archaeology* 16:29–58.

Kubler, George

1948 Toward Absolute Time: Guano Archaeology. In *A Reappraisal of Peruvian Archaeology*, edited by Wendell C. Bennett, pp. 29–50. Society for American Archaeology Memoir No. 4.

Kus, James S.

1972 *Selected Aspects of Irrigated Agriculture in the Chimu Heartland, Peru*. Ph.D. dissertation, Department of Geography, University of California, Los Angeles. University Microfilms, Ann Arbor.

1980 La Agricultura Estatal en la Costa Norte del Peru. *America Indígena* 40:713–729. Mexico City.

Kutscher, Gerdt

1954 *Cerámica del Peru Septentrional*. Casa Editora Gebr. Mann, Berlin.

Lanning, Edward P.

1963 *A Ceramic Sequence for the Piura and Chira Coast, North Peru*. University of California Publications in American Archaeology and Ethnology, Vol. 46. No. 2, Berkeley.

1967 *Peru before the Incas*. Prentice-Hall, Englewood Cliffs, New Jersey.

1974 Western South America. In *Prehispanic America*, edited by Shirley Gorenstein, pp. 65–86. St. Martin's Press, New York.

Lapiner, Alan

1976 *Pre-Columbian Art of South America*. H. N. Abrams, New York.

Larco, Rafael

1938 *Los Mochicas I*. Casa Editora La Crónica y Variedades S.A., Ltd, Lima.

1941 *Los Cupisniques*. Casa Editora La Crónica y Variedades, S.A., Ltd, Lima.

1948 *Cronología Arqueológica del Norte del Peru*. Sociedad Geográfica Americana, Buenos Aires.

1963 *Las Épocas Peruanas*. Museo Rafael Larco Herrera, Lima.

1967 *La Ceramica de Vicús y sus Nexos con las Demas Culturas*. Santiago Valverde, Lima.

Lathrap, Donald W.

1971 The Tropical Forest and the Cultural Context of Chavin. In *Dumbarton Oaks Conference on Chavin*, edited by Elizabeth P. Benson, pp. 73–100. Dumbarton Oaks, Washington, D.C.

LeBlanc, Catherine J.

1981 *Late Prehispanic Huanca Settlement Patterns in the Yanamarca Valley, Peru*. Ph.D. dissertation, Department of Anthropology, University of California, Los Angeles. University Microfilms, Ann Arbor.

Lechtman, Heather

1976 A Metallurgical Site Survey in the Peruvian Andes. *Journal of Field Archaeology* 3:1–42.

1979 Issues in Andean Metallurgy. In *Pre-Columbian Metallurgy of South America*, edited by Elizabeth P. Benson, pp. 1–40. Dumbarton Oaks, Washington, D.C.

Lechtman, Heather N., Antonieta Erlij, and Edward J. Barry, Jr

1982 New Perspectives on Moche Metallurgy: Techniques of Gilding Copper at Loma Negra, Northern Peru. *American Antiquity* 47:3–30.

Lumbreras, Luis G.

1970 *Los Templos de Chavin, Guía para el Visitante*. Publicación del Proyecto Chavin, Lima.

1971 Towards a Re-evaluation of Chavin. In *Dumbarton Oaks Conference on Chavin*, edited by Elizabeth P. Benson, pp. 1–28. Dumbarton Oaks, Washington, D.C.

1972 Los Estudios sobre Chavin. *Revista del Museo Nacional* 38:73–92.

1974a *The Peoples and Cultures of Ancient Peru*. Smithsonian Institution Press, Washington, D.C.

1974b Los Reinos Post-Tiwanaku en el Area Altiplánica. *Revista del Museo Nacional* 40:55–86.

1974c *La Arqueología Como ciencia Social*. Ediciones Histar, Lima.

1977 Excavaciones en el Templo Antiguo de Chavin (Sector R); Informe de la Sexta Campaña. *Ñawpa Pacha* 15:1–38.

1979 *El Arte y la Vida Vicús*. Banco Popular del Peru, Lima.

1981 The Stratigraphy of Open Sites. In *Prehistory of the Ayacucho Basin, Peru, Vol. II: Excavations and Chronology*, edited by Richard S. MacNeish *et. al.*, pp. 167–198. University of Michigan Press, Ann Arbor.

Lynch, Thomas F.
1972 Current Research: Highland South America. *American Antiquity* 37:274–278.

MacKenzie, Janet
1980 *Coast to Highland Trade in Precolumbian Peru: Dendritic Economic Organization in the North Sierra*. Unpublished M.A. thesis, Trent University, Peterborough, Ontario.
1985 Ancient Frontiers, Boundaries, and Defense: Great Walls and Little Walls in Northern Peru. In *Status, Structure and Stratification: Current Archaeological Reconstructions*. The Archaeological Association of the University of Calgary.

Mackey, Carol J.
1979 Archaeological Investigations in the Southern Part of the Chimu Empire. Report Submitted to the Instituto Nacional de Cultura, Lima. MS in possession of the author.
1980 A Preliminary Ranking of Chimu Sites. Paper presented at the 20th Annual Meeting of the Institute of Andean Studies, Berkeley.
1982 The Middle Horizon as Viewed from the Moche Valley. In *Chan Chan: Andean Desert City*, edited by Michael E. Moseley and Kent C. Day, pp. 321–331. University of New Mexico Press, Albuquerque.

Mackey, Carol J., and Charles Hastings
1982 Moche Murals from the Huaca de la Luna. In *Pre-Columbian Art History: Selected Readings*, edited by Alana Cordy-Collins, pp. 293–312. Peek Publications, Palo Alto.

Mackey, Carol J., and Alexandra M. Ulana Klymyshyn
1981 Construction and Labor Organization in the Chimu Empire. *Ñawpa Pacha* 19:99–114.
1982 Political Integration in Prehispanic Peru. Research Proposal Submitted to the National Science Foundation. MS in possession of the authors.

MacNeish, Richard S.
1981 Synthesis and Conclusions. In *Prehistory of the Ayacucho Basin, Peru, Vol. II: Excavations and Chronology*, edited by Richard S. MacNeish *et al.* pp. 199–257. University of Michigan Press, Ann Arbor.

MacNeish, Richard S., Angel G. Cook, Luis G. Lumbreras, Robert K. Vierra, and Antoinette Nelken-Turner
1981 *Prehistory of the Ayacucho Basin, Peru, Vol. II: Excavations and Chronology*. University of Michigan Press, Ann Arbor.

MacNeish, Richard S., Thomas C. Patterson, and David L. Browman
1975 *The Central Peruvian Prehistoric Interaction Sphere*. Papers of the R. S. Peabody Foundation for Archaeology No. 7.

Mair, Lucy
1977 *Primitive Government*. Indiana University Press, Bloomington.

Malo, David
1951 *Hawaiian Antiquities (Moolelo Hawaii)*. Bernice P. Bishop Museum Special Publication 2. Bishop Museum Press, Honolulu. Second edition.

Martins, R.
1976 *New Archaeological Techniques for the Study of Ancient Root Crops in Peru*. Unpublished Ph.D. dissertation, Department of Botany, University of Alabama, Birmingham.

Mason, J. Alden
1969 *The Ancient Civilizations of Peru*. Penguin Books, Harmondsworth, Middlesex.

Masuda, Shozo
1981 Introducción. In *Estudios Etnográficos del Peru Meridional*, edited by Shozo Masuda, pp. v–viii. University of Tokyo, Tokyo.

Matos, Ramiro
1965–66 Algunas Consideraciones Sobre el Estilo de Vicús. *Revista del Museo Nacional* 34:89–130.

1968 A Formative Period Painted Pottery Complex at Ancón, Peru. *American Antiquity* 33:226–232.

Matos, Ramiro, and Jeffrey R. Parsons
1979 Poblamiento Prehispánico en la Cuenca del Mantaro. In *Arqueología Peruana*, edited by Ramiro Matos, pp. 157–171. Universidad Nacional Mayor de San Marcos, Lima.

Matsuzawa, Tsugio
1978 The Formative Site of Las Haldas, Peru: Architecture, Chronology, and Economy. Translated by Izumi Shimada. *American Antiquity* 43:652–673.

Mayer, Enrique
1974 El Trueque y los Mercados en el Imperio Incaico. In *Los Campesinos y el Mercado*, edited by Enrique Mayer, Sidney W. Mintz, and G. W. Skinner, pp. 13–50. Pontifica Universidad Católica del Peru, Lima.

McCown, Theodore
1945 *Pre-Incaic Huamachuco: Survey and Excavations in the Region of Huamachuco and Cajabamba*. University of California Publications in American Archaeology and Ethnology, Vol. 39, No. 4. Berkeley.

McGrath, James E.
1973 *The Canchones of Chan Chan: Evidence for a Retainer Class in a Preindustrial Urban Center*. Unpublished B.A. thesis, Department of Anthropology, Harvard University, Cambridge.

Melly, Alfredo
1983 *Loma del Shingo: Un Sitio Fortificado en la Frontera Chimu*. Unpublished B.A. thesis, Universidad Nacional de Trujillo, Trujillo, Peru.

Mendelssohn, Kurt
1974 *The Riddle of the Pyramids*, Praeger, New York.

Menzel, Dorothy
1964 Style and Time in the Middle Horizon. *Ñawpa Pacha* 1:1–106.
1968 New Data on the Huari Empire in Middle Horizon Epoch 2A. *Ñawpa Pacha* 6:47–114.
1977 *The Archaeology of Ancient Peru and the Work of Max Uhle*. Lowie Museum of Anthropology, University of California, Berkeley.

Menzel, Dorothy, John H. Rowe, and Lawrence E. Dawson
1964 *The Paracas Pottery of Ica: A Study in Style and Time*. University of California Publications in American Archaeology and Ethnology, Vol. 50, Berkeley.

Middleton, John
1965 *The Lugbara of Uganda*. Holt, Rinehart and Winston, New York.

Miranda, Cristoval de
1925 Relación de los Corregimientos y Otras Officios que se Proveen en los Reynos e Provincias del Pirú. In *El Virrey Martín Enrique 1581–1583*, edited by D. Roberto Levillier, pp. 128–230. Gobernantes del Peru: Cartas y Papeles, Vol. 9. Imprento de Juan Pueyo, Madrid.

Moore, Jerry D.
1981 Chimu Socio-economic Organization: Preliminary Data from Manchan, Casma Valley, Peru. *Ñawpa Pacha* 19:115–128.

Morris, Craig
1967 *Storage in Tawantinsuyu*. Unpublished Ph.D. dissertation, Department of Anthropology, University of Chicago.
1972 State Settlements in Tawantinsuyu: A Strategy of Compulsory Urbanism. In *Contemporary Archaeology*, edited by Mark P. Leone, pp. 393–401. Southern Illinois University Press, Carbondale.
1974 Reconstructuring Patterns of Non-agricultural Production in the Inca Economy: Archaeology and Documents in Institutional Analysis. In *Reconstructing Complex Societies*, edited by Charlotte B. Moore, pp. 49–60. Supplement to American Schools of Oriental Research Bulletin, No. 20, Cambridge.
1976 Master Design of the Inca. *Natural History* 85(10):58–67.
1978 The Archaeological Study of Andean Exchange Systems. In *Social*

Archaeology: Beyond Subsistence and Dating, edited by Charles Redman *et al.*, pp. 315–327. Academic Press, New York.

Morris, Craig, and Donald E. Thompson
1970 Huánuco Viejo: An Inca Administrative Center. *American Antiquity* 35:344–362.

Moseley, Michael E.
1968 *Changing Subsistence Patterns: Late Preceramic Archaeology of the Central Peruvian Coast*. Unpublished Ph.D. dissertation, Department of Anthropology, Harvard University, Cambridge.
1972 Subsistence and Demography: An Example of Interaction from Prehistoric Peru. *Southwestern Journal of Anthropology* 28:25–49.
1974 Organizational Preadaptation to Irrigation: The Evolution of Early Water Management Systems in Coastal Peru. In *Irrigation's Impact on Society*, edited by Theodore E. Downing and McGuire Gibson, pp. 77–82. Anthropological Papers of the University of Arizona 25. University of Arizona Press, Tucson.
1975a *The Maritime Foundations of Andean Civilization*. Cummings Publishing Co., Menlo Park, California.
1975b Chan Chan: Andean Alternative of the Preindustrial City. *Science* 187:219–225.
1975c Prehistoric Principles of Labor Organization in the Moche Valley, Peru. *American Antiquity* 40:191–196.
1975d Secrets of Peru's Ancient Walls. *Natural History* 84:34–41.
1978a The Evolution of Andean Civilization. In *Ancient Native Americans*, edited by Jesse D. Jennings, pp. 491–541. W. H. Freeman and Co., San Francisco.
1978b Pre-agricultural Coastal Civilizations in Peru. *Carolina Biological Readers*, No. 90, J. J. Head, general editor. Carolina Biological Supply Co., Burlington, North Carolina.
1978c An Empirical Approach to Prehistoric Agrarian Collapse: The Case of the Moche Valley, Peru. In *Social and Technological Management in Dry Lands*, edited by Nancy L. Gonzalez, pp. 9–43. AAAS Selected Symposium 10. Westview Press, Boulder.
1983 Central Andean Civilization. In *Ancient South Americans*, edited by Jesse D. Jennings, pp. 179–239. W. H. Freeman and Company, San Francisco.
1985 The Exploration and Explanation of Early Monumental Architecture in the Andes. In *Early Ceremonial Architecture in the Andes*, edited by Christopher B. Donnan, pp. 29–57. Dumbarton Oaks, Washington, D.C.

Moseley, Michael E., and Kent C. Day (editors)
1982 *Chan Chan: Andean Desert City*. University of New Mexico Press, Albuquerque.

Moseley, Michael E., and Eric E. Deeds
1982 The Land in Front of Chan Chan: Agrarian Expansion, Reform, and Collapse in the Moche Valley. In *Chan Chan: Andean Desert City*, edited by Michael E. Moseley and Kent C. Day, pp. 25–53. University of New Mexico Press, Albuquerque.

Moseley, Michael E., and Robert A. Feldman
n.d. Fishing, Farming, and the Foundations of Andean Civilization. In *The Archaeology of Hunter-Gatherer Subsistence Economies in Coastal Environments*, edited by G. Bailey and J. Parkington. Cambridge University Press, in press.

Moseley, Michael E., Robert A. Feldman, Charles Ortloff, and Alfredo Narvaez
1983 Principles of Agrarian Collapse in the Cordillera Negra, Peru. *Annals of Carnegie Museum of Natural History* 52:299–327.

Moseley, Michael E., and Carol J. Mackey
1974 *Twenty-Four Architectural Plans of Chan Chan, Peru: Structure and Form at the Capital of Chimor*. Peabody Museum Press, Cambridge.

Moseley, Michael E., and Gordon R. Willey
1973 Aspero, Peru: A Reexamination of the Site and Its Implications. *American Antiquity* 38:452–468.

Mujica, Elias
1975 *Excavaciones Arqueológicas en Cerro de Arena: Un Sitio Formativo Superior en el Valle de Moche, Peru*. Unpublished B.A. thesis, Department of Anthropology, Pontífica Universidad Católica del Peru, Lima.

Murphy, Robert C.
1925 *Bird Islands and Peru*. G. Putnam's Sons, New York.

Murra, John V.
1964 Una Apreciación Etnológica de la Visita. In *Garci Diez San Miguel, Visita Hecha a la Provencia de Chucuito*, pp. 421–444. Casa de la Cultura, Lima.
1968 An Aymará Kingdom in 1567. *Ethnohistory* 15:115–151.
1972 El Control Vertical de un Máximo de Pisos Ecológicos en la Economía de las Sociedades Andinas. In *Visita de la Provincia de León de Huánuco*, edited by John V. Murra, pp. 429–476. Documentos para la Historia y Etnología de Huánuco y la Selva Central, Vol. 2. Universidad Nacional Hermilio Valdizan, Huánuco, Peru.
1975 *Formaciones Económicas y Politicas del Mundo Andino*. Instituto de Estudios Peruanos.
1981 The 'Vertical Control' of Maximum of Ecological Tiers in the Economies of Andean Societies. Translated by D. Chavin Escobar and revised by Gabriel Escobar. MS in possession of the author.
1985 'El Arcipelago Vertical' Revisited. In *Andean Ecology and Civilization*, edited by Shozo Masuda, Izumi Shimada and Craig Morris, pp. 3–13. University of Tokyo Press, Tokyo.

Netherly, Patricia
1977 *Local Level Lords on the North Coast of Peru*. Ph.D. dissertation, Department of Anthropology, Cornell University. University Microfilms, Ann Arbor.

Nials, Fred, Eric Deeds, Michael E. Moseley, Shelia Pozorski, Thomas Pozorski, and Robert A. Feldman
1979 El Niño: The Catastrophic Flooding of Coastal Peru. *Field Museum of Natural History Bulletin* 50(7):4–14; 50(8):4–10.

Nolan, James L.
1980 *Prehispanic Irrigation and Polity in the Lambayeque Sphere, Peru*. Ph.D. dissertation, Department of Anthropology, Columbia University, University Microfilms. Ann Arbor.

Olson, E., and W. S. Broecker
1959 Lamont Natural Radiocarbon Dates V. *American Journal of Science* 257:1–28.

O'Neale, Lila M., and Alfred L. Kroeber
1930 *Textile Periods in Ancient Peru*. University of California Publications in American Archaeology and Ethnology, Vol. 28, No. 2, Berkeley.

ONERN (Oficina Nacional de Evaluación de Recursos Naturales)
1972 *Inventario, Evaluación y Uso Racional de los Recursos Naturales de la Costa: Cuencas de los Ríos Santa, Lacramarca y Nepena*. 3 vols. ONERN, Lima.
1973 *Inventario, Evaluacion y Uso Racional de los Recursos Naturales de la Costa: Cuencas de los Ríos Virú y Chao*. 2 vols. ONERN, Lima.

Ortiz de Zúñiga, Inigo
1967 Visita de las Cuatro Waranqa de los Chupachu. In *Visita de la Provincia de León de Huánuco en 1562*, originally published in 1562, edited by John V. Murra, Vol. 1. Universidad Nacional Hermilio Valdizan, Huánuco, Peru.
1972 Visita de los Yacha y Mitmaqkuna Cuzqueños Encomendados en Juan Sanchez Falcón. In *Visita de la Provincia de León de Huánuco en 1562*, originally published in 1562, edited by John V. Murra, Vol. 2. Universidad Nacional Hermilio Valdizán, Huánuco, Peru.

Ortloff, Charles R., Michael E. Moseley, and Robert A. Feldman
1982 Hydraulic Engineering Aspects of the Chimu Chicama–Moche Intervalley Canal. *American Antiquity* 47:572–595.

Osborn, Alan J.
1977a Prehistoric Utilization of Marine Resources in Coastal Peru: How Much Do We Understand? Paper presented at the 76th annual meeting of the American Anthropological Association, Houston.
1977b Strandloopers, Mermaids and other Fairy Tales: Ecological Determinants of Marine Resource Utilization – the Peruvian Case. In *For Theory Building in Archaeology*, edited by Lewis R. Binford, pp. 157–205. Academic Press, New York.

Pachacuti Yamqui, Joan de Santacruz
1950 Relación de Antiquedades deste Reyno del Pirú, originally published in 1613(?). In *Tres Relaciones de Antiguedades Peruanos*. Editorial Guaraní, Asunción, Paraguay.

Parsons, Jeffrey R., and Charles M. Hastings
1977 Prehispanic Settlement Patterns in the Upper Mantaro, Peru: Progress Report for the 1976 Field Season. MS on file, Museum of Anthropology, University of Michigan, Ann Arbor.

Parsons, Jeffrey R., and Ramiro Matos
1978 Asentamientos Prehispánicos en el Mantaro, Peru. Informe Preliminar. In *El Hombre y la Cultura Andina*, edited by Ramiro Matos, pp. 539–555. III Congreso Peruano, Actas y Trabajos, Vol. 2, Lima.

Parsons, Mary H.
1970 Preceramic Subsistence on the Peruvian Coast. *American Antiquity* 35:292–302.

Patterson, Thomas C.
1968 Current Research. Highland South America. *American Antiquity* 33:422–424.
1971a Central Peru: Its Economy and Population, *Archaeology* 24:316–321.
1971b Chavin: An Interpretation of Its Spread and Influence. In *Dumbarton Oaks Conference on Chavin*, edited by Elizabeth P. Benson, pp. 29–48. Dumbarton Oaks, Washington, D.C.
1973 *America's Past: A New World Archaeology*. Scott Freeman Co., San Francisco.

Patterson, Thomas C., John P. McCarthy, and Robert A. Dunn
1982 Polities in the Lurin Valley, Peru, during the Early Intermediate Period. *Ñawpa Pacha* 20:61–82.

Paul, Anne
1982 The Symbolism of Paracas Turbans: A Consideration of Style, Serpents and Hair. *Ñawpa Pacha* 20:41–60.

Paulsen, Allison C.
1976 Environment and Empire: Climatic Factors in Prehistoric Andean Culture Change. *World Archaeology* 8:121–132.
1977 Review of *A Further Exploration of the Rowe Chavin Seriation and Its Implications for North Coast Chronology*, by Peter Roe. *American Anthropologist* 79:736–737.

Pearsall, Deborah M.
1980 Pachamachay Ethnobotanical Report: Plant Utilization at a Hunting Base Camp. In *Prehistoric Hunters of the High Andes*, by John W. Rick, pp. 191–231. Academic Press, New York.

Pease, Franklin
1985 Cases and Variations of Verticality in the Southern Andes. In *Andean Ecology and Civilization*, edited by Shozo Masuda, Izumi Shimada and Craig Morris, pp. 141–160. University of Tokyo Press, Tokyo.

Pedersen, Asbjorn
1976 El Ajuar Funerario de la Tumba de la Huaca Menor de Batan Grande, Lambayeque, Peru. *Actas y Memorias del XLI Congreso Internacional de Americanistas* 2:60–73. Mexico City.

Peebles, Christopher S., and Susan M. Kus
1977 Some Archaeological Correlates of Ranked Societies. *American Antiquity* 42:421–448.

Pickersgill, Barbara
1969 The Archaeological Record of Chili Peppers (*Capsicum* sp.) and the Sequence of Plant Domestication in Peru. *American Antiquity* 34:54–61.

Polanyi, Karl
1957 The Economy as Instituted Process. In *Trade and Market in the Early Empires*, edited by Karl Polanyi, C. M. Arensberg, and H. W. Pearson, pp. 243–270. H. Regnery Co., Chicago.

Pozorski, Shelia
1976 *Prehistoric Subsistence Patterns and Site Economics in the Moche Valley, Peru*. Ph.D. dissertation, Department of Anthropology, University of Texas, Austin. University Microfilms, Ann Arbor.
1979a Late Prehistoric Llama Remains from the Moche Valley, Peru. *Annals of Carnegie Museum of Natural History* 48:139–170.
1979b Prehistoric Diet and Subsistence of the Moche Valley, Peru. *World Archaeology* 11:163–184.
1982 Subsistence Systems in the Chimu State. In *Chan Chan: Andean Desert City*, edited by Michael E. Moseley and Kent C. Day, pp. 177–196. University of New Mexico Press, Albuquerque.
1983 Changing Subsistence Priorities and Early Settlement Patterns on the North Coast of Peru. *Journal of Ethnobiology* 3:15–38.

Pozorski, Shelia, and Thomas Pozorski
1979a Alto Salaverry: A Peruvian Coastal Preceramic Site. *Annals of Carnegie Museum of Natural History* 48:337–375.
1979b An Early Subsistence Exchange System in the Moche Valley, Peru. *Journal of Field Archaeology* 6:413–432.
n.d. Preliminary Results of Investigations in the Casma Valley, Peru. MS in possession of the authors.

Pozorski, Thomas
1971 *Survey and Excavation of Burial Platforms at Chan Chan, Peru*. Unpublished B.A. thesis, Department of Anthropology, Harvard University, Cambridge.
1975 El Complejo de Caballo Muerto: Los Frisos de Barro de la Huaca de los Reyes. *Revista del Museo Nacional* 41:211–251.
1976 *Caballo Muerto: A Complex of Early Ceramic Sites in the Moche Valley, Peru*. Ph.D. dissertation, Department of Anthropology, University of Texas, Austin. University Microfilms, Ann Arbor.
1979 The Las Avispas Burial Platform, Chan Chan, Peru. *Annals of Carnegie Museum of Natural History* 48:119–137.
1980 The Early Horizon Site of Huaca de los Reyes: Societal Implications. *American Antiquity* 45:100–110.
1982a The Caballo Muerto Complex: An Investigation of Cupisnique Culture. *National Geographic Society Research Reports* 14:523–532.
1982b Early Social Stratification and Subsistence Systems: The Caballo Muerto Complex. In *Chan Chan: Andean Desert City*, edited by Michael E. Moseley and Kent C. Day, pp. 225–253. University of New Mexico Press, Albuquerque.
1983 The Caballo Muerto Complex and Its Place in the Andean Chronological Sequence. *Annals of Carnegie Museum of Natural History* 52:1–40.

Pozorski, Thomas, and Shelia Pozorski
1982 Reassessing the Chicama–Moche Intervalley Canal: Comments on 'Hydraulic Engineering Aspects of the Chimu Chicama–Moche Intervalley Canal.' *American Antiquity* 47:851–868.

Pozorski, Thomas, Shelia Pozorski, Carol J. Mackey, and Alexandra M. Ulana Klymyshyn
1983 Prehispanic Ridged Fields of the Casma Valley, Peru. *Geographical Review* 73:407–416.

Price, Barbara J.
1971 Prehispanic Irrigation Agriculture in Nuclear America. *Latin American Research Review* 6(3):3–60
1977 Shifts of Production and Organization: A Cluster Interaction Model. *Current Anthropology* 18:209–234.

Proulx, Donald A.
1968 *An Archaeological Survey of the Nepeña Valley, Peru*. Department of Anthropology, Research Report No. 2. University of Massachusetts, Amherst.
1971 Headhunting in Ancient Peru. *Archaeology* 24(1):16–21.
1973 *Archaeological Investigations in the Nepeña Valley, Peru*.

Department of Anthropology, Research Project No. 13. University of Massachusetts, Amherst.

1976 The Early Horizon of North Coastal Peru. A Review of Recent Developments. *El Dorado* 1:1–15.

1982 Territoriality in the Early Intermediate Period: The Case of Moche and Recuay. *Ñawpa Pacha* 20:83–96.

Proulx, Donald A., and Richard E. Daggett

1980 Early Horizon Sites in the Nepeña Valley, Peru. Paper presented at the 45th annual meeting of the Society for American Archaeology, Philadelphia.

Quilter, Jeffrey, and Terry Stocker

1983 Subsistence Economies and the Origins of Andean Complex Societies. *American Anthropologist* 85:545–562.

Radiocarbon Dates Association, Inc.

n.d.a Radiocarbon Date for Chankillo, Sample Submitted by H. Reichlen.

n.d.b Radiocarbon Dates for Cerro Sechin, Samples Submitted by K. Terada.

Raimondi, Antonio

1873 *El Departamento de Ancachs: Sus Riquezas Minerales*. Lima.

Ramírez-Horton, Susan

1982 Retainers of the Lords or Merchants: A Case of Mistaken Identity. In *El Hombre y Su Ambiente en los Andes Centrales*, edited by Luis Millones and Hiroyasu Tomoeda, pp. 123–136. Senri Ethnological Studies 10. National Museum of Ethnology, Osaka.

1985 Social Frontiers and the Territorial Base of Curacazgos. In *Andean Ecology and Civilization*, edited by Shozo Masuda, Izumi Shimada and Craig Morris, pp. 423–442. University of Tokyo Press, Tokyo.

Rappaport, Roy A.

1968 *Pigs for the Ancestors: Ritual in the Ecology of a New Guinea People*. Yale University Press, New Haven and London.

Rathje, William L.

1971 The Origin and Development of the Lowland Classic Maya Civilization. *American Antiquity* 36:275–285.

1972 Praise the Gods and Pass the Metates: A Hypothesis of the Development of Lowland Rainforest Civilizations in Mesoamerica. In *Contemporary Archaeology*, edited by Mark P. Leone, pp. 365–392. Southern Illinois University Press, Carbondale.

Ravines, Rogger

1982 *Panorama de la Arqueología Andina*. Instituto de Estudios Peruanos, Lima.

Ravines, Rogger, and William H. Isbell

1975 Garagay: Sitio Ceremonial Temprano en el Valle de Lima. *Revista del Museo Nacional* 41:253–281.

Rawls, Joseph

1979 *An Analysis of Prehispanic Andean Warfare*. Ph.D. dissertation, Department of Anthropology, University of California at Los Angeles, University Microfilms, Ann Arbor.

Raymond, J. Scott

1981 The Maritime Foundations of Andean Civilization: A Reconsideration of the Evidence. *American Antiquity* 46:806–821.

Reed, Nelson A.

1973 Monks and Other Mississippian Mounds. In *Explorations into Cahokia Archaeology*, edited by Melvin L. Fowler, pp. 31–42. Illinois Archaeological Survey Bulletin 7. University of Illinois, Urbana.

Reichert, Raphael X.

1982 Moche Iconography – The Highland Connection. In *Pre-Columbian Art History: Selected Readings*, edited by Alana Cordy-Collins, pp. 279–291. Peek Publications, Palo Alto.

Reichlen, Henri, and Paule Reichlen

1949 Recherches Archeologiques dans les Andes de Cajamarca: Premier Rapport de la Mission Etnologique Française au Perou Septentrional. *Journal de la Société des Americanistes* 38:137–174.

Renfrew, Colin

1972 *The Emergence of Civilisation, the Cyclades and the Aegean in the Third Millennium B.C.* Methuen, London.

1973a Monuments, Mobilization and Social Organization in Neolithic Wessex. In *The Explanation of Culture Change: Models in Prehistory*, edited by Colin Renfrew, pp. 539–558. University of Pittsburgh Press, Pittsburgh.

1973b *Before Civilization: The Radiocarbon Revolution and Prehistoric Europe*. Knopf, New York.

1974 Beyond a Subsistence Economy: The Evolution of Social Organization in Prehistoric Europe. In *Reconstructing Complex Societies*, edited by Charlotte B. Moore, pp. 69–88. Supplement to American Schools of Oriental Research Bulletin No. 20, Cambridge.

Rhoades, Robert E., and Stephen I. Thompson

1975 Adaptive Strategies in Alpine Environments: Beyond Ecological Particularism. *American Ethnologist* 2(3):535–551.

Rick, John W.

1980 *Prehistoric Hunters of the High Andes*. Academic Press, New York.

Riesenberg, Saul

1968 *The Native Polity of Ponape*. Smithsonian Contribution to Anthropology 10. Smithsonian Institution Press, Washington, D.C.

Rodriguez Suy Suy, Victor Antonio

1967 Secuencia Cultural en el Valle de Lambayeque. Paper presented at the Primer Simposio de Arqueología de Lambayeque, Chiclayo.

Roe, Peter

1974 *A Further Exploration of the Rowe Chavin Seriation and Its Implications for North Central Coast Chronology*. Dumbarton Oaks Studies in Pre-Columbian Art and Archaeology 13. Dumbarton Oaks, Washington, D.C.

1978 Recent Discoveries in Chavin Art: Some Speculations on Methodology and Significance in the Analysis of a Figural Style. *El Dorado* 3:1–41.

Rosas, Hermilio

1976 Investigaciones Arqueológicas en la Cuenca del Chotano. *Proceedings of the 41st International Congress of Americanists* 3:137–174.

Rosas, Hermilio, and Ruth Shady

1970 Pacopampa: Un Complejo Temprano del Periódo Formativo Peruano. *Arqueología y Sociedad* 3:1–16.

Rostworowski, Maria

1961 *Curacas y Sucesiones: Costa Norte*. Imprenta Minerva, Lima.

1970 Mercaderes del Valle de Chincha en la Época Prehispánica: Un Documento y unos Comentarios. *Revista Española de Antropología Americana* 5:135–178, Madrid.

1975a Pescadores, Artesanos y Mercaderes Costeños en el Peru Prehispánico. *Revista del Museo Nacional* 41:311–349.

1975b La 'Visita' a Chinchacocha de 1549. *Anales Científicos de la Universidad del Centro del Peru* 4:71–88. Huancayo, Peru.

1977a *Etnia y Sociedad: Ensayos sobre la Costa Central Prehispánica*. Instituto de Estudios Peruanos, Lima.

1977b Coastal Fishermen, Merchants, and Artisans in Pre-hispanic Peru. In *The Sea in the Pre-Columbian World*, edited by Elizabeth P. Benson, pp. 167–186. Dumbarton Oaks, Washington, D.C.

1981 *Recursos Naturales Renovables y Pesca, Siglos XVI y XVII*. Instituto de Estudios Peruanos, Lima.

1985 Patronyms with the Consonant F in the Guarangas of Cajamaraca. In *Andean Ecology and Civilization*, edited by Shozo Masuda,

Izumi Shimada and Craig Morris, pp. 401–421. University of Tokyo Press, Tokyo.

Rowe, John H.
1942 A New Pottery Style from the Department of Piura, Peru. *Carnegie Institution of Washington, Division of Historical Research, Notes on Middle American Archaeology and Ethnology.* 1(8):30–34.
1946 Inca Culture at the Time of the Spanish Conquest. In *Handbook of South American Indians*, Vol. 2, Julian H. Steward, general editor, pp. 183–330. Bureau of American Ethnology, Bulletin 143. Smithsonian Institution, Washington, D.C.
1948 The Kingdom of Chimor. *Acta Americana* 6:26–59.
1954 *Max Uhle, 1856–1944: A Memoir of the Father of Peruvian Archaeology.* University of California Publications in American Archaeology and Ethnology, Vol. 46, No. 1, Berkeley.
1960 Cultural Unity and Diversification in Peruvian Archaeology. In *Men and Cultures, Selected Papers*, edited by A. F. C. Wallace, pp. 627–631. Proceedings of the 5th International Congress of Anthropological and Ethnological Sciences, University of Pennsylvania Press, Philadelphia.
1961 Stratigraphy and Seriation. *American Antiquity* 26:324–330.
1962a Stages and Periods in Archaeological Interpretation. *Southwestern Journal of Anthropology* 18:40–54.
1962b *Chavin Art: An Inquiry into Its Form and Meaning.* Museum of Primitive Art, New York.
1963 Urban Settlements in Ancient Peru. *Ñawpa Pacha* 1:1–27.
1967a An Interpretation of Radiocarbon Measurements on Archaeological Samples from Peru. In *Peruvian Archaeology, Selected Readings*, edited by John H. Rowe and Dorothy Menzel, pp. 16–30. Peek Publications, Palo Alto, California.
1967b Form and Meaning in Chavin Art. In *Peruvian Archaeology: Selected Readings*, edited by John H. Rowe and Dorothy Menzel, pp. 72–103. Peek Publications, Palo Alto, California.
1967c What Kind of a Settlement was Inca Cuzco? *Ñawpa Pacha* 5:59–76.

Rowe, John H., and Dorothy Menzel
1967 Introduction. In *Peruvian Archaeology, Selected Readings*, edited by John H. Rowe and Dorothy Menzel, pp. v–x. Peek Publications, Palo Alto, California.

Ruiz, Hipólito
1952 Relación Histórica del Viaje, que Hizo a los Reynos del Peru y Chile el Botánico D. Hipólito Ruiz en el Año de 1777 hasta el de 1788. Edited by Jaime Jaramillo-Arango. Talleres Gráficos de Candido Bermejo, Madrid.

Sabloff, Jeremy A., and Carl C. Lamberg-Karlovsky (editors)
1975 *Ancient Civilization and Trade.* University of New Mexico Press, Albuquerque.

Sahlins, Marshall D.
1958 *Social Stratification in Polynesia.* University of Washington Press, Seattle.
1963 Poor Man, Rich Man, Big Man, Chief: Political Types in Melanesia and Polynesia. *Comparative Studies in Society and History* 5:285–303.
1972 *Stone Age Economics.* Aldine-Atherton, Chicago.

Salomon, Frank L.
1978 *Ethnic Lords of Quito in the Age of the Incas: The Political Economy of North-Andean Chiefdoms.* Ph.D. dissertation, Department of Anthropology, Cornell University. University Microfilms, Ann Arbor.

Samaniego, Lorenzo
1973 *Los Nuevos Trabajos Arqueológicos en Sechin, Casma, Peru.* Larsen Ediciones, Trujillo, Peru.

Sanders, William T.
1973 The Significance of Pikillacta in Andean Culture History. *Miscellaneous Papers in Anthropology* No. 8. Pennsylvania State University.

Sanders, William T., Jeffrey R. Parsons, and Robert S. Santley
1979 *The Basin of Mexico.* Academic Press, New York.

Sanders, William T., and Barbara J. Price
1968 *Mesoamerica: The Evolution of a Civilization.* Random House, New York.

Sawyer, Alan
1968 *Mastercraftsmen of Ancient Peru.* Solomon R. Guggenheim Foundation, New York.

Schaedel, Richard P.
1951a Major Ceremonial and Population Centers in Northern Peru. In *Civilizations of Ancient America, Selected Papers of the XXIX International Congress of Americanists*, pp. 232–243. Chicago.
1951b Mochica Mural at Pañamarca. *Archaeology* 4:145–154.
1966a Incipient Urbanization and Secularization in Tiahuanacoid Peru. *American Antiquity* 31:338–344.
1966b Urban Growth and Ekistics on the Peruvian Coast. *Proceedings of the 36th International Congress of Americanists* 2:531–539.
1972 The City and the Origin of the State in America. *Actas y Memorias del XXXIX Congreso Internacional de Americanistas* 2:15–33. Lima.

Schreiber, Katharina J.
1978 *Planned Architecture of Middle Horizon Peru: Implications for Social and Political Organization.* Ph.D. dissertation, Department of Anthropology, State University of New York. University Microfilms, Ann Arbor.
1982 Changing Settlement Patterns in the South Central Highlands of Peru. Paper presented at the 47th annual meeting of the Society for American Archaeology, Minneapolis.
n.d. The Rise of the State in the Nasca Valley. In *Origin of the Prehistoric Andean State: An Evaluation of Theory, Method and Data*, edited by William H. Isbell, in preparation.

Service, Elman R.
1971 *Primitive Social Organization: An Evolutionary Perspective*, Second Edition. Random House, New York.
1975 *Origins of the State and Civilization: The Process of Cultural Evolution.* Norton, New York.
1978 Classical and Modern Theories of the Origins of Government. In *Origins of the State: The Anthropology of Political Evolution*, edited by Ronald Cohen and Elman R. Service, pp. 21–34. Institute for the Study of Human Issues, Philadelphia.

Shady, Ruth
1976 Investigaciones Arqueológicas en la Cuenca del Utcubamba. *41st International Congress of Americanists* 3:579–589.

Shady, Ruth, and Arturo Ruiz
1979 Evidence for Interregional Relationships during the Middle Horizon on the North Central Coast of Peru. *American Antiquity* 44:676–684.

Shimada, Izumi
1976 *Socioeconomic Organization at Moche V Pampa Grande, Peru: Prelude to a Major Transformation to Come.* Ph.D. dissertation, Department of Anthropology, University of Arizona. University Microfilms, Ann Arbor.
1978 Economy of a Prehistoric Urban Context: Commodity and Labor Flow at Moche V Pampa Grande, Peru. *American Antiquity* 43:569–592.
1981a Temples of Time: The Ancient Burial and Religious Center of Batán Grande, Peru. *Archaeology* 34(5):37–45.
1981b The Batán Grande–La Leche Archaeological Project: The First Two Seasons. *Journal of Field Archaeology* 8:405–446.
1982 Horizontal Archipelago and Coast–Highland Interaction in North Peru: Archaeological Models. In *El Hombre y su Ambiente en los Andes Centrales*, edited by Luis Millones and Hiroyasu Tomoeda, pp. 137–210. Senri Ethnological Studies 10, National Museum of Ethnology, Osaka.
1983 The Formation of the Middle Sicán Polity: The Highland Connection and Revitalization Movement. Paper presented at

the 48th Annual Meeting of the Society for American Archaeology, Pittsburgh.

1984a Llama and Cash Flow on the Prehispanic Coast. Paper presented at the 49th Annual Meeting of the Society for American Archaeology, Portland.

1984b Ancient Metallurgy and Mining on the Northern Coast of Peru. Paper presented at the Third Annual Meeting of the Northeast Conference on Andean Archaeology and Ethnohistory, Amherst.

1985a Introduction. In *Andean Civilization and Ecology*, edited by Shozo Masuda, Izumi Shimada and Craig Morris, pp. xi–xxxii. University of Tokyo Press, Tokyo.

1985b Perception, Procurement and Management of Resources: Archaeological Perspective. In *Andean Civilization and Ecology*, edited by Shozo Masuda, Izumi Shimada and Craig Morris, pp. 357–399. University of Tokyo Press, Tokyo.

1985c La Cultura Sicán: Caracterización Arqueológica. In *Presencia Histórica de Lambayeque*, edited by Eric Mendoza S., pp. 76–133. H. Falconi, Lima.

Shimada, Izumi, and Rafael Cavallaro
1986 Monumental Adobe Architecture of the Late Prehispanic Northern North Coast of Peru. *Journal de la Société des Americanistes* 71:41–78.

Shimada, Izumi, and Carlos Elera
1984 Batán Grande y la Complejidad Cultural Emergente en Norperu durante el Horizonte Medio: Datos y Modelos. *Boletín del Museo Nacional* 8:41–47.

Shimada, Izumi, Stephen Epstein, and Alan D. Craig
1982 Batán Grande: A Prehistoric Metallurgical Center in Peru. *Science* 216:952–959.

Shimada, Melody, and Izumi Shimada
1981 Explotación y Manejo de los Recursos Naturales en Pampa Grande, Sitio Moche V: Significado del Análisis Orgánico. *Revista del Museo Nacional* 45:19–73.

1985 Prehistoric Llama Breeding and Herding on the North Coast of Peru. *American Antiquity* 50:3–26.

Squier, Ephraim G.
1877 *Incidents of Travel and Exploration in the Land of the Incas*. Harper and Brothers, New York.

Steward, Julian H.
1956 Cultural Evolution. *Scientific American* 194:69–80.

Strong, William D.
1925 *The Uhle Pottery Collections from Ancón*. University of California Publications in American Archaeology and Ethnology, Vol. 21, No. 4, Berkeley.

1948 Cultural Epochs and Refuse Stratigraphy in Peruvian Archaeology. In *A Reappraisal of Peruvian Archaeology*, edited by Wendell C. Bennett, pp. 93–102. Society for American Archaeology Memoir 4.

1957 *Paracas, Nazca, and Tiahuanacoid Cultural Relationships in South Coastal Peru*. Society for American Archaeology Memoir No. 13.

Strong, William D., and Clifford Evans, Jr
1952 *Cultural Stratigraphy in the Viru Valley, Northern Peru*. Columbia University Studies in Archaeology and Ethnology, Vol. 4. Columbia University Press, New York.

Tabio, Ernesto
1977 *Prehistoria de la Costa del Peru*. Instituto de Ciencias Sociales de la Academia de Ciencias de Cuba, La Habana.

Tello, Julio C.
1929 *Antiguo Peru: Primera Época*. La Comisión Organizadora del Segundo Congreso Sudamericano de Turismo, Lima.

1930 Andean Civilization: Some Problems of Peruvian Archaeology. *Proceedings of the 23rd International Congress of Americanists*, pp. 259–290.

1937a Los Trabajos Arqueológicos en el Departamento de Lambayeque. *El Comercio*, January 29–31.

1937b El Oro de Batán Grande. *El Comercio*, April 18.

1939 Sobre el Descubrimiento de la Cultura Chavin del Peru. *Actas de la Primera Sesion del XXVII Congreso Internacional de Americanistas*, pp. 231–252. Mexico.

1942 Origen y Desarrollo de las Civilizaciones Prehistóricas Andinas. *Actas y Trabajos Científicos, XXVII Congreso Internacional de Americanistas*, pp. 589–720. Lima.

1943 Discovery of the Chavin Culture in Peru. *American Antiquity* 9:135–160.

1956 *Arqueología del Valle de Casma. Culturas Chavin, Santa o Huaylas Yunga y Sub-Chimu*. Publicación Antropológica del Archivo 'Julio C. Tello,' Vol. 1. Universidad Nacional Mayor de San Marcos, Lima.

1960 *Chavin, Cultura Matriz de la Civilización Andina. Primera Parte*. Publicación Antropológica del Archivo 'Julio C. Tello,' Vol. 2. Universidad Nacional Mayor de San Marcos, Lima.

Terada, Kazuo and Ryozo Matsumoto
1985 Sobre la cronologia de la tradición Cajamarca. In *Historia de Cajamarca*, ed. F. Silva, W. Espinoza, and R. Raunes, pp. 67–89. Instituto Nacional de Cultura, Cajamarca.

Thomas, R. Brooke
1976 Energy Flow at High Altitudes. In *Man in the Andes: A Multidisciplinary Study of High Altitude Quechua*, edited by Paul T. Baker and M. A. Litte, pp. 379–404. Dowden, Hutchinson and Ross, Stroudsburg, Pa.

Thompson, Donald E.
1961 *Architecture and Settlement Patterns in the Casma Valley, Peru*. Unpublished Ph.D. dissertation, Department of Anthropology, Harvard University, Cambridge.

1962a The Problem of Dating Certain Stone-Faced Stepped Pyramids on the North Coast of Peru. *Southwestern Journal of Anthropology* 18:291–301.

1962b Additional Stone Carving from the North Highlands of Peru. *American Antiquity* 28:245–246.

1966 Archaeological Investigations in the Huarmey Valley, Peru. *36th International Congress of Americanists* 1:541–548.

1968 Provincial and Imperial Inca Pottery. Paper read at the 33rd annual meeting of the Society for American Archaeology, Santa Fe.

1972 Peasant Inca Villages in the Huánuco Region. *Verhandlungen des XXXVIII Internationalen Amerikanistenkongresses*, band 4. Klaus Renner, Munich.

Thomson, Keith S.
1982 The Meanings of Evolution. *American Scientist* 70:529–531.

Toledo, Francisco de
1940 Información Hecha por Orden de Don Francisco de Toledo en su Visita de las Provincias del Peru, originally published in 1570. In *Don Francisco de Toledo, Supremo Organizador del Peru: Sus Informaciones sobre los Incas (1570–1572)*, edited by Roberto Levillier, pp. 14–37. Espasa-Calpe, S.A., Buenos Aires.

Topic, John R.
1977 *The Lower Class at Chan Chan: A Quantitative Approach*. Unpublished Ph.D. dissertation, Department of Anthropology, Harvard University, Cambridge.

1980 Excavaciones en los Barrios Populares de Chanchán. In *Chanchán: Metrópoli Chimu*, edited by Rogger Ravines, pp. 267–282. Instituto de Estudios Peruanos, Lima.

1982 Lower-Class Social and Economic Organization at Chan Chan. In *Chan Chan: Andean Desert City*, edited by Michael E. Moseley and Kent C. Day, pp. 145–175. University of New Mexico Press, Albuquerque.

Topic, John R., and Theresa L. Topic
1978 Prehistoric Fortification Systems of Northern Peru. *Current Anthropology* 19:618–619.

1982 Huamachuco Archaeological Project: Preliminary Report on the First Field Season, July–August 1981. MS on file, Department of Anthropology, Trent University, Peterborough, Ontario.

1983a Coast–Highland Relations in Northern Peru: Some Observations on Routes, Networks, and Scales of Interaction. In *Civilization in the Ancient Americas*, edited by Richard M. Leventhal and Alan L. Kolata, pp. 237–259. University of New Mexico Press, Albuquerque.

1983b Huamachuco Archaeological Project: Preliminary Report on the Second Season, June–August 1982. MS on file, Department of Anthropology, Trent University, Peterborough, Ontario.

1985 Coast–Highland Relations in Northern Peru: The Structure and Strategy of Interaction. In *Status, Structure and Stratification: Current Archaeological Reconstructions*. The Archaeological Association of the University of Calgary, Calgary.

Topic, Theresa L.

1982 The Early Intermediate Period and Its Legacy. In *Chan Chan: Andean Desert City*, edited by Michael E. Moseley and Kent. C. Day, pp. 255–284. University of New Mexico Press, Albuquerque.

Topic, Theresa L., and John R. Topic

1980 Agricultura en Chanchán. In *Chanchán: Metrópoli Chimu*, edited by Rogger Ravines, pp. 194–208. Instituto de Estudios Peruanos, Lima.

1982 Prehistoric Fortification Systems of Northern Peru. Preliminary Report on the Final Session January–December 1980. MS on file, Department of Anthropology, Trent University, Peterborough, Ontario.

1984 *Huamachuco Archaeological Project: Preliminary Report on the Third Season, June–August 1983*. Trent University, Occasional Papers in Anthropology No. 1. Department of Anthropology, Peterborough, Ontario.

Ubbelohde-Doering, Heinrich

1967 *On the Royal Highways of the Inca*. Thames and Hudson, London.

Ugent, Donald, Shelia Pozorski, and Thomas Pozorski

1981 Prehistoric Remains of the Sweet Potato. *Phytologia* 49(5):401–415.

1982 Archaeological Potato Tuber Remains from the Casma Valley of Peru. *Economic Botany* 36:182–192.

Uhle, Max

1903a *Pachacamac*. Department of Archaeology, University of Pennsylvania, Philadelphia.

1903b Ancient South American Civilization. *Harper's Monthly Magazine* 107:780–786.

Uhle, Max, and Alphons Stubel

1892 *Die Ruinenstaette von Tiahuanaco im Hochlande des Alten Peru*. Verlag von Karl W. Hiersemann, Leipzig.

Valcarcel, Luis E.

1937 Un Valioso Hallazgo Arqueológico en el Peru: Informe sobre los Hallazgos en los Yacimientos Arqueológicos de La Merced, La Ventana y Otros del Distrito de Illimo, Lambayeque. *Revista del Museo Nacional* 6:164–168.

Vargas, Ruben

1936 La Fecha de la Fundación de Trujillo. *Revista Histórica* 10:229–239. Instituto Histórico del Peru, Lima.

Vazquez de Espinosa, Antonio

1942 *Compendium and Description of the West Indies*. Originally published 1628. Translated by Charles U. Clark. Smithsonian Institute Miscellaneous Collections, Vol. 102. Washington, D.C.

Webb, Clarence H.

1977 The Poverty Point Culture. *Geoscience and Man* 17. School of Geoscience, Louisiana State University, Baton Rouge.

Webb, Malcolm C.

1965 The Abolition of the Taboo System in Hawaii. *Journal of the Polynesian Society* 74:21–39. W. W. Norton and Co., New York.

1968 Carneiro's Hypothesis of Limited Land Resources and the Origins of the State: A Latin Americanist's Approach to an Old Problem. *South Eastern Latin Americanist* 12:1–8.

1972 The Carrot and the Stick: Free Obedience and Coercive Force in the Rise of Civilization. Paper presented at the 71st annual meeting of the American Anthropological Association, Toronto.

1974 Exchange Networks: Prehistory. *Annual Review of Anthropology* 3:357–383.

1975 The Flag Follows Trade: An Essay on the Necessary Interaction of Military and Commercial Factors in State Formation. In *Ancient Civilization and Trade*, edited by Jeremy A. Sabloff and Carl C. Lamberg-Karlovsky, pp. 155–209. University of New Mexico Press, Albuquerque.

1978 Toward a Compound or 'Multi-Layered' Theory of State Origins. Paper presented at the 14th annual meeting of the Southern Anthropological Society, Lexington.

Webster, David

1975 Warfare and the Evolution of the State: A Reconsideration. *American Antiquity* 40:464–470.

Webster, Stephen

1971 An Indigenous Quechua Community in Exploitation of Multiple Ecological Zones. *Actas y Memorias del 39 Congreso Internacional de Americanistas* 3:174–183.

Wendt, W. E.

1964 Die Prakeramische Seidlung am Rio Seco, Peru. *Baessler Archiv* 11:225–275.

Willey, Gordon R.

1945 Horizon Styles and Pottery Traditions in Peruvian Archaeology. *American Antiquity* 11:49–56.

1946 The Viru Valley Program in Northern Peru. *Acta Americana* 4:224–238.

1951 The Chavin Problem: A Review and Critique. *Southwestern Journal of Anthropology* 7:103–144.

1953 *Prehistoric Settlement Patterns in the Viru Valley, Peru*. Bureau of American Ethnology, Bulletin No. 155. Washington, D.C.

1971 *An Introduction to American Archaeology, Volume Two: South America*. Prentice-Hall, Englewood Cliffs, New Jersey.

Willey, Gordon R., and John M. Corbett

1954 *Early Ancón and Early Supe Culture: Chavin Horizon Sites of the Central Peruvian Coast*. Columbia University Studies in Archaeology and Ethnology, Vol. 3. Columbia University Press, New York.

Willey, Gordon R., and Philip Phillips

1958 *Method and Theory in American Archaeology*. University of Chicago Press, Chicago.

Williams, Carlos

1978–80 Complejos de Pirámides con Planta en U: Patrón Arquitectónico de la Costa Central. *Revista del Museo Nacional*: 41:95–110.

1985 A Scheme for the Early Monumental Architecture of the Central Coast of Peru. In *Early Ceremonial Architecture in the Andes*, edited by Christopher B. Donnan, pp. 227–240. Dumbarton Oaks, Washington, D.C.

Wilson, David J.

1981 Of Maize and Men: A Critique of the Maritime Hypothesis of State Origins on the Coast of Peru. *American Anthropologist* 83:93–120.

1983 The Origins and Development of Complex Prehispanic Society in the Lower Santa Valley, Peru: Implications for Theories of State Origins. *Journal of Anthropological Archaeology* 2:209–276.

1985 *Prehispanic Settlement Patterns in the Lower Santa Valley, North Coast of Peru: A Regional Perspective on the Origins and Development of Complex Society*. Ph.D. dissertation, Department of Anthropology, University of Michigan. University Microfilms, Ann Arbor.

Wittfogel, Karl A.

1955 Developmental Aspects of Hydraulic Societies. In *Irrigation Civilizations: A Comparative Symposium*, edited by Julian H. Steward, pp. 43–52. Pan American Union, Washington, D.C.

1957 *Oriental Despotism: A Comparative Study of Total Power*. Yale University Press, New Haven.

Wobst, H. Martin

1977 Stylistic Behavior and Information Exchange. In *Research Essays in Honor of James B. Griffin*, edited by Charles Cleland, pp. 317–342. Anthropological Papers, Museum of Anthropology, University of Michigan 61, Ann Arbor

Wright, Henry T.

1972 A Consideration of Interregional Exchange in Greater Mesopotamia: 4000–3000 B.C. In *Social Exchange and Interaction*, edited by Edwin N. Wilmsen, pp. 95–105. Anthropological Papers, Museum of Anthropology, University of Michigan 46, Ann Arbor.

1977 Recent Research on the Origin of the State. *Annual Review of Anthropology* 6:379–397.

1978 Toward an Explanation of the Origin of the State. In *Origins of the State: The Anthropology of Political Evolution*, edited by Ronald Cohen and Elman R. Service, pp. 49–68. Institute for the Study of Human Issues, Philadelphia.

Wright, Henry T., and Gregory A. Johnson

1975 Population, Exchange and Early State Formation in Southwestern Iran. *American Anthropologist* 77:267–289.

Yamamoto, Norio

1982 A Food Production System in the Southern Central Andes. In *El Hombre y Su Ambiente en los Andes Centrales*, edited by L. Millones and H. Tomoeda, pp. 39–62. Senri Ethnological Studies 10. National Museum of Ethnology, Senri.

Zaki, Andrzej

1978 *Ayangay: Polskie Odkrycia Archeologiczne W Peru*. Polski Uniwersytet Na Obczyznie, London.

INDEX

Peer Polity Interaction and Socio-political Change

Edited by Colin Renfrew and John F. Cherry

Thirteen leading archaeologists have contributed to this innovative study of the socio-political processes – notably imitation, competition, warfare, and the exchange of material goods and information – that can be observed within early complex societies, particularly those just emerging into statehood. The common aim is to explain the remarkable formal similarities that exist between institutions, ideologies and material remains in a variety of cultures characterised by independent political centres yet to be brought under the control of a single, unified jurisdiction.

A major statement of the conceptual approach is followed by ten case studies from a wide variety of times and places, including Minoan Crete, early historic Greece and Japan, the classic Maya, the American Mid-West in the Hopewellian period, Europe in the Early Bronze Age and Early Iron Age, and the British Isles in the late Neolithic.

Contributors: GINA L. BARNES; RICHARD BRADLEY; DAVID P. BRAUN; SARA CHAMPION; TIMOTHY CHAMPION; ROBERT CHAPMAN; JOHN CHERRY; DAVID A. FREIDEL; RICHARD HODGES; COLIN RENFREW; JEREMY A. SABLOFF; STEPHEN SHENNAN; ANTHONY SNODGRASS.

New Directions in Archaeology

0 521 22914 6

Hunters in Transition

Mesolithic Societies of Temperate Eurasia and their Transition to Farming

Edited by Marek Zvelebil

This book analyses one of the crucial events in human cultural evolution: the emergence of postglacial hunter-gatherer communities and the development of farming. Traditionally, the advantages of settled agriculture have been assumed and the transition to farming has been viewed in terms of the simple dispersal of early farming communities northwards across Europe. The contributors to this volume adopt a fresh, more subtle approach. Farming is viewed from a hunter-gatherer perspective as offering both advantages and disadvantages, organisational disruption during the period of transition and far-reaching social consequences for the existing way of life. The hunter-gatherer economy and farming in fact shared a common objective: a guaranteed food supply in a changing natural and social environment. Drawing extensively on research in eastern Europe and temperate Asia, the book argues persuasively for the essential unity of all postglacial adaptations whether leading to the dispersal of farming or the retention and elaboration of existing hunter-gatherer strategies.

Contributors: TAKERU AKAZAWA; PAUL DOLUKHANOV; CLIVE GAMBLE; STEFAN KAROL KOZLOWSKI; JANUSZ KOZLOWSKI; JAMES LEWTHWAITE; GERALD MATYUSHIN; PETER ROWLEY-CONWY; SLAVOMIL VENCL; MAREK ZVELEBIL.

New Directions in Archaeology

0 521 26868 0

The Archaeology of Contextual Meanings

Edited by Ian Hodder

This companion volume to *Archaeology as Long-term History* focuses on the symbolism of artefacts. It seeks at once to refine current theory and method relating to interpretation and show, with examples, how to conduct this sort of archaeological work. Some contributors work with the material culture of modern times or the historic period, areas in which the symbolism of mute artefacts has traditionally been thought most accessible. However, the book also contains a good number of applications in prehistory to demonstrate the feasibility of symbolic interpretation where good contextual data survive from the distant past.

In relation to wider debates within the social sciences, the volume is characterised by a concern to place abstract symbolic codes within their historical context and within the contexts of social actions. In this respect, it develops further some of the ideas presented in Dr Hodder's *Symbolic and Structural Archaeology*, an earlier volume in the *New Directions* series.

Contributors: SHEENA CRAWFORD; LIV GIBBS; IAN HODDER; ROBERT JAMESON; NICK MERRIMAN; KEITH RAY; TONY SINCLAIR; MARIE LOUISE SØRENSON; TIMOTHY TAYLOR; LINDA THERKORN; SARAH WILLIAMS.

New Directions in Archaeology

0 521 32924 8

Archeology as Long-term History

Edited by Ian Hodder

In marked contrast with the anthropological and cross-cultural approaches that have featured so prominently in the archaeological research of the last twenty-five years, this contributory volume emphasises the archaeological significance of historical method and philosophy. Drawing particularly on the work of R. G. Collingwood, the contributors show that the notion of 'history seen from within' is a viable approach that can be applied in ethnoarchaeology and in both history and prehistoric archaeology. There is a discussion of short, medium and long-term historical structures in relation to social events generating observed material culture patterning. Examination of the relationship between structure and event within historical contexts leading to new insights into the interdependence of continuity and change, and into the nature of widely recognised processes such as acculturation, diffusion and migration.

Contributors: DAVID COLLETT; ALEXANDER VON GERNET; KEVIN GREENE; KNUT HELSKOG; IAN HODDER; PAUL LANE; HENRIETTA MOORE; JACQUELINE NOWAKOWSI; AJAY PRATAP; PETER TIMMINS; ELISABETH VESTERGAARD; JAMES WHITLEY

New Directions in Archaeology

0 521 32923 X

Specialisation, Exchange and Complex Societies

Edited by Elizabeth M. Brumfiel
and Timothy Earle

This book, the first comparative study of specialised production in prehistoric societies, examines both adaptionist and political approaches to specialisation and exchange using a worldwide perspective. What forms of specialisation and exchange promote social stratification, political integration and institutional specialisation? Can increases in specialisation always be linked to improved subsistence strategies or are they more closely related to the efforts of political elites to strengthen coalitions and establish new institutions of control? Are valuables as important as subsistence goods in the development process?

These and other questions are examined in the contexts of ten prehistoric societies, ranging from the incipient complexity of Mississippian chiefdoms through to the more complex systems of West Africa, Hawaii and Bronze Age Europe, to the agrarian states of Mesopotamia, Mesoamerica, Peru and Yamato Japan.

Contributors: GINA L. BARNES; ELIZABETH M. BRUMFIE; TIMOTHY K. EARLE; KATHLEEN F. GALVIN; ANTONIO GILMAN; KRISTIAN KRISTIANSEN; JON MULLER; PRUDENCE M. RICE; MICHAEL ROWLANDS

New Directions in Archaeology

0 521 32118 2

Symbols of Excellence

Precious Materials as Expressions of Status

Grahame Clark

Pithily written, rich in anecdote and superbly illustrated with examples of ancient craftsmanship, this book by an archaeologist of world renown ranges freely over the civilisations of the last five thousand years. The theme is a fascinating one. Why is it, Professor Clark asks, that human beings value precious metals, gems and a few organic materials like ivory and pearls so highly? All are difficult to obtain and largely useless for practical purposes. Yet the prestige associated with possession down the ages is undoubted. Position, sanctity and – by extension – the social and political hierarchies of entire societies have become embodied in these materials. Though first exploited to the full in the service of early cults and rulers, their appreciation has survived social change, and personal jewellery and insignia of rank are today more common that ever before. The reasons why are authoritatively explored in this remarkable book.

'The great clarity of the author's style, the appositeness of his example and the originality of his basic approach, [are] entirely felicitious. This is a handsome book which any archaeologist could read with profit, yet its interest is certainly not restricted to the archaeological reader alone.'   Colin Renfrew, *Antiquity*

0 521 30264 1

Island Societies

Archaeological Approaches to Evolution and Transformation

Edited by Patrick Kirch

Concentrating their attention on the Pacific Islands, the contributors to this book show how the tightly focused social and economic systems of islands offer archaeologists a series of unique opportunities for tracking and explaining prehistoric change. Over the last thirty years excavations in Fiji, the Marianas, and Hawai'i have revolutionised Oceanic archaeology and, as the major problems of cultural origins and island sequences have been resolved, archaeologists have come increasingly to study social change and to integrate newly acquired data on material culture with older ethnographic and ethnohistorical materials. The fascinating results of this work, centring on the evolution of complex Oceanic chiefdoms into something very much like classic 'archaic states', are authoritatively surveyed here for the first time.

Contributors: R. C. GREEN; GEORGE J. GUMERMAN; ROBERT J. HOMMON; TERRY L. HUNT; PATRICK V. KIRCH; BARRY ROLETT; MATTHEW SPRIGGS; CHRISTOPHER M. STEVENSON.

New Directions in Archaeology

0 521 30189 0

Prehistory in the Pacific Islands

A Study of Variation in Language, Customs and Human Biology

John Terrell

How, asks John Terrell in this richly-illustrated and original book, can we best account for the remarkable diversity of the Pacific Islanders in biology, language and custom? Traditionally scholars have recognised a simple racial division between Polynesians, Micronesians, Melanesians, Australians and South-east Asians: peoples allegedly differing in physical appearance, temperament, achievements, and perhaps even intelligence. However, Professor Terrell shows that such simple divisions do not fit the known facts and are indeed little better than a crude, static snapshot of human diversity.

In a fresh and stimulating study that brings to bear a wide range of data drawn from anthropology, archaeology, geography, biogeography, human ecology and linguistics, he poses a whole series of unfolding and interlinked questions about prehistoric life in the Pacific that effectively unite the human imagination with logical and empirical methods of evaluation.

0 521 30604 3

Production and Exchange of Stone Tools

Prehistoric Obsidian in the Aegean

Robin Torrence

The aim of Robin Torrence's important new study is to develop new methods for reconstructing the processes of prehistoric exchange. Recent archaeological work has concentrated on mapping obsidian finds relative to source areas using trace-element analysis and on investigating the effects of trade on particular cultural groups. Dr Torrence, in contrast, draws extensively on ethnographic analogy to develop a new approach which uses differences in the level of efficiency for the acquisition of raw materials and the production of goods to infer the type of exchange. Regional patterns of tool manufacture, specialist craft production at central places and quarrying are analysed in detail in the context of the prehistoric Aegean and previous ideas about the importance of trade in the growth of civilisations are re-assessed.

The methodology developed by Dr Torrence will be applicable to a wide range of artefact types and her book will therefore be of value to archaeologists working in many different places and periods.

New Studies in Archaeology

0 521 25266 0

Prehistoric Adaptation in the American South-West

Rosalind L. Hunter-Anderson

This book is about post-Pleistocene adaptive change among the aboriginal cultures of the mountains and deserts of Arizona and New Mexico. Conceived essentially as a natural science alternative to the prevailing culture history paradigm, it offers both a general theoretical framework for interpreting the archaeological record of the American South-West and a persuasive evolutionary model for the shift from a hunter-gatherer economy to horticulture at the Mogollon/Anasazi interface.

Technical, architectural and settlement adaptations are examined and the rise of matrilineality, ethnic groupings and clans are modelled using ecological and ethnographic data. In the last part of the book, Dr Hunter-Anderson evaluates the 'fit' between her model and the archaeological record and argues vigorously for future research into the evolution of ethnicity in the adaptive context of regional competition.

New Studies in Archaeology

0 521 30751 1

Stone-Age Prehistory

Studies in Memory of Charles McBurney

Edited by Geoff Bailey and Paul Callow

The studies in this wide-ranging volume focus on the analysis of stone artefacts and industries and on the ways these can be used to throw light on human behaviour from the earliest times. They have a broad chronological and geographical spread – from Europe and Africa to Australia and New Guinea – and pay particular attention to the information that may be sought at different levels of investigation, from the detailed examination of individual objects to a regional or even continental perspective. Papers on two parallel lines of enquiry – prehistoric art and the physical development of the early hominids in Africa – demonstrate the wider relevance of many of the theoretical issues raised in the course of the enquiries into lithic technology.

The collection has been produced in memory of Charles McBurney, formerly Professor of Quaternary Prehistory in the University of Cambridge, and its authorship is drawn largely from his former pupils.

Contributors: P. ALLSWORTH-JONES; G. N. BAILEY; A. BILSBOROUGH; B. A. BRADLEY; P. CALLOW; J. G. D. CLARK; J. D. CLARK; J. CLEGG; A. E. CLOSE; I. DAVIDSON; H. DIBBLE; J. A. J. GOWLETT; M. HAYNES; G. Ll. ISAAC; P. A. MELLARS; L. McBRYDE; J. E. PARKINGTON; N. ROLLAND; C. G. SAMPSON; J. P. WHITE; L. P. WILKINSON.

0 521 32132 8

The Palaeolithic Settlement of Europe

Clive Gamble

A major new survey of the prehistoric hunter-gatherer societies of Europe, this book reviews the newest information and interpretations for scientific research. The palaeolithic is at an exciting point of transition. The explosion in ethno-archaeological studies has fundamentally challenged our models and interpretations amongst all classes of data and at all spatial scales of analysis. Furthermore the traditional concerns of dating and quaternary studies have also passed through their own revolutions and palaeolithic archaeology is the direct beneficiary. Dr Gamble presents in an imaginative but comprehensive framework the changing perspectives of Europe's oldest societies.

'This book . . . is a serious discussion of how to use the archaeological record as a bridge to understanding the past. It is a demonstration that patterning at the regional level, while being important and fascinating, is also a necessary empirical framework in terms of which we must approach the task of learning about the past. It both opens up archaeology to new dreams of things to be accomplished and broadly outlines some very new challenges.'

Lewis Binford

Cambridge World Archaeology

0 521 24514 1
0 521 28764 2 (paper)